T0190472

Lecture Notes of the Institute for Computer Sciences, Social Informatics and Telecommunications Engineering 581

The LNICST series publishes ICST's conferences, symposia and workshops.
LNICST reports state-of-the-art results in areas related to the scope of the Institute.
The type of material published includes

- Proceedings (published in time for the respective event)
- Other edited monographs (such as project reports or invited volumes)

LNICST topics span the following areas:

- General Computer Science
- E-Economy
- E-Medicine
- Knowledge Management
- Multimedia
- Operations, Management and Policy
- Social Informatics
- Systems

Yinjun Zhang · Nazir Shah
Editors

Application of Big Data, Blockchain, and Internet of Things for Education Informatization

Third EAI International Conference, BigIoT-EDU 2023
August 29–31, 2023, Liuzhou, China
Proceedings, Part II

Editors
Yinjun Zhang
Guangxi Science and Technology Normal
University
Guangxi, China

Nazir Shah
University of Swabi
Khyber Pakhtunkhwa, Pakistan

ISSN 1867-8211   ISSN 1867-822X (electronic)
Lecture Notes of the Institute for Computer Sciences, Social Informatics
and Telecommunications Engineering
ISBN 978-3-031-63132-0   ISBN 978-3-031-63133-7 (eBook)
https://doi.org/10.1007/978-3-031-63133-7

This Springer imprint is published by the registered company Springer Nature Switzerland AG
The registered company address is: Gewerbestrasse 11, 6330 Cham, Switzerland

If disposing of this product, please recycle the paper.

Preface

We are delighted to introduce the proceedings of the third edition of the European Alliance for Innovation (EAI) International Conference on Application of Big Data, Blockchain, and Internet of Things for Education Informatization (BigIoT-EDU 2023). BigIoT-EDU aims to provide a platform for international cooperation and exchange, enabling big data and information education experts, scholars, and enterprise developers to share research results, discuss existing problems and challenges, and explore cutting-edge science and technology. The conference focuses on research fields such as digitization of education, smart classrooms, and Massive Online Open Courses (MOOCs). The use of big data analytics, artificial intelligence (AI), machine learning, and deep learning lies at the heart of this conference as we focus on these emerging technologies to further the role of IT in education.

BigIoT-EDU 2023 had three tracks: the Main Track, the Late Track, and a Workshop Track. BigIoT-EDU 2023 attracted over 700 submissions, and each submission was reviewed by at least 3 Program Committee members in a double-blind process, resulting in the acceptance of only 272 papers across all three tracks. The workshop was titled "Application of Advanced Integrated Technologies in Education Informatics" and co-chaired by Yar Muhammad and Muhammad Al-Ambusaidi from Beihang University, China and University of Technology & Applied Sciences of Oman, respectively. The workshop aimed to focus on the application of the latest cutting-edge integrated technologies for the development and digitalization of education in the modern era.

Coordination with the steering chair, Imrich Chlamtac, was essential for the success of the conference. We sincerely appreciate his constant support and guidance. It was also a great pleasure to work with such an excellent organizing committee team for their hard work in organizing and supporting the conference. In particular, we are grateful to the Technical Program Committee, who completed the peer-review process for the technical papers and helped to put together a high-quality technical program. We are also grateful to Conference Manager Ivana Bujdakova for her constant support along with the whole of the EAI team involved in the conference. We must say that they have been wonderful and it is always a pleasant experience to work with them. Also, we would like to thank all the authors who submitted their papers to the BigIoT-EDU 2023 conference.

We strongly believe that the BigIoT-EDU conference provides a good forum for all researchers, developers, and practitioners to discuss all science and technology aspects that are relevant to emerging trends for digitalization of education. We also expect that the future BigIoT-EDU conferences will be as successful and stimulating as this year's, as indicated by the contributions presented in this volume.

Yinjun Zhang
Nazir Shah

Conference Organization

Steering Committee

Imrich Chlamtac	University of Trento, Italy
Fazlullah Khan	Business Technology Management Group, USA
Mian Ahmad Jan	Abdul Wali Khan University Mardan, Pakistan

Organizing Committee

General Chair

Yinjun Zhang	Guangxi Science & Technology Normal University, China

General Co-chairs

Shah Nazir	University of Swabi, Pakistan
Walayat Hussain	Australian Catholic University, Australia

TPC Chair

Yinjun Zhang	Guangxi Science & Technology Normal University, China

Sponsorship and Exhibit Chairs

Lan Zimian	Harbin Institute of Technology, China
Izaz Ur Rehman	Abdul Wali Khan University Mardan, Pakistan

Local Chairs

Huang Yufei	Hechi Normal University, China
Wan Haoran	Shanghai University, China

Workshops Chairs

Rahim Khan   Abdul Wali Khan University Mardan, Pakistan
Abid Yahya   Botswana International University of Science and
                             Technology, Botswana

Publicity and Social Media Chair

Aamir Akbar   *Abdul Wali Khan University Mardan, Pakistan*

Publications Chair

Yinjun Zhang   Guangxi Science & Technology Normal
                             University, China

Web Chairs

Mian Yasir Jan   CECOS University, Pakistan
Syed Rooh Ullah Jan   Abdul Wali Khan University Mardan, Pakistan

Posters and PhD Track Chairs

Mengji Chen   Guangxi Science &Technology Normal
                             University, China
Ateeq ur Rehman   University of Haripur, Pakistan

Panels Chairs

Kong Linxiang   Hefei University of Technology, China
Muhammad Usman   Federation University, Australia

Demos Chairs

Ryan Alturki   Umm-ul-Qura University, Saudi Arabia
Rahim Khan   Abdul Wali Khan University Mardan, Pakistan

Tutorials Chairs

Wei Rongchang   Guangxi Science & Technology Normal
                             University, China
Hashim Ali   Abdul Wali Khan University Mardan Pakistan

Technical Program Committee

Shahnawaz Khan	Abdul Wali Khan University Mardan, Pakistan
Mengji Chen	Hechi University, China
Yar Muhammad	Beihang University, China
Mian Abdullah Jan	Ton Duc Thang University, Vietnam
Roman Khan	City University of Information Science and Technology, Pakistan
Muneeb Ullah	Peshawar University, Pakistan
Siyar Khan	Bacha Khan University, Pakistan
Muhammad Bilal	Virtual University of Pakistan, Pakistan
Haroon Khan	Bacha Khan University, Pakistan
Shaher Slehat	University of Technology Sydney, Australia
Xiangjian He	University of Technology Sydney, Australia
Shaheer Jan	University of Engineering and Technology Peshawar, Pakistan
Akbar Khan	University of Peshawar, Pakistan
Malik Ahmad	University of Peshawar, Pakistan
Muzammil Shah	COMSATS University Lahore, Pakistan
Aaiza Khan	Guangju University of Technology, China
Farman Khan	Bacha Khan University, Pakistan
Zia Ur Rehman	Bacha Khan University, Pakistan
Abid Yahya	Botswana International University of Science and Technology, Botswana
Ravi Keemo	Botswana International University of Science and Technology, Botswana
Aaiza Gul	Sirindhorn International Institute of Technology, Thailand
Shahid Ali	Women University Swabi, Pakistan
Muhammad Sohail	Abdul Wali Khan University Mardan, Pakistan
Saad Khan	University of Peshawar, Pakistan
Momin Ali	University of Peshawar, Pakistan
Bilawal Khan	COMSATS University Islamabad, Pakistan
Jamal Shah	University of Leeds, UK
Basit Kazmi	University of Peshawar, Pakistan
Jalal Turk	Staffordshire University, UK
Umer Hussain	Indian Institute of Technology Kharagpur, India
Omer Naveed	Uppsala University, Sweden
Muhammad Ali	Uppsala University, Sweden
Hamza Khan	Hankuk University of Foreign Studies, South Korea
Tariq Khan	Abdul Wali Khan University Mardan, Pakistan

Ehsan Ullah	Abdul Wali Khan University Mardan, Pakistan
Noman Ali	Abdul Wali Khan University Mardan, Pakistan
Ayaan Adeel	Abdul Wali Khan University Mardan, Pakistan
Behroz Khan	Abdul Wali Khan University Mardan, Pakistan
Tariq Khokar	Abdul Wali Khan University Mardan, Pakistan
Awais Marwat	Abdul Wali Khan University Mardan, Pakistan
Naeem Jan	Abdul Wali Khan University Mardan, Pakistan
Anas Akbar	Abdul Wali Khan University Mardan, Pakistan
Mian Ahmad Jan	Duy Tan University, Vietnam
Faisal Ayub Khan	Indian Institute of Technology Kharagpur, India
Faisal Khan	University of Leeds, UK
Yasir Jan	University of California Davies, USA
Ryan Alturki	Umm al-Qura University, Saudi Arabia
Alayat Hussain	University of Technology Sydney, Australia
Muhammad Usman	Federation University, Australia
Naveed Khan	Abdul Wali Khan University Mardan, Pakistan
Azam Khalil	Abdul Wali Khan University Mardan, Pakistan
Hamid Naseer	Abdul Wali Khan University Mardan, Pakistan
Arsalan Jan	Abdul Wali Khan University Mardan, Pakistan
Abdul Samad	University of Nebraska Omaha, USA
Asif Khan	University of Nebraska Omaha, USA
Imtiaz Ali	Quaid-e-Azam University Islamabad, Pakistan
Khadim Khan	Quaid-e-Azam University Islamabad, Pakistan
Usman Nasir	Quaid-e-Azam University Islamabad, Pakistan
Ishfaq Ahmad	Quaid-e-Azam University Islamabad, Pakistan
Jamal Baig	National University of Sciences and Technology, Pakistan
Naseer Baig	National University of Sciences and Technology, Pakistan
Sohail Agha	National University of Sciences and Technology, Pakistan
Raza Hussain	Indian Institute of Technology Kharagpur, India
Ibrar Atta	University of Haripur, Pakistan
Majid Ali	University of Haripur, Pakistan
Afzal Durrani	University of Haripur, Pakistan
Faysal Azam	Indian Institute of Technology Kharagpur, India
Asif Wazir	University of Engineering and Technology Mardan, Pakistan
Talal Agha	University of Engineering and Technology Mardan, Pakistan
Salman Shah	University of Engineering and Technology Mardan, Pakistan

Ibrahim Khan	Iqra University, Islamabad, Pakistan
Raayan Jan	Iqra University, Islamabad, Pakistan
Shameer Shah	Iqra University, Islamabad, Pakistan
Zeeshan Khan	Iqra University, Islamabad, Pakistan

Contents – Part II

Research on the Application of Big Data in Smart Teaching

Application of Decision Tree Algorithm in Intelligent Management System of Universities

Analysis of College Physical Education Teaching and Evaluation Based on Decision Tree Algorithm

Lei Ji[✉], Donghui Dai, Rui Sun, and Li Lei

Sports Department, Shenyang Jianzhu University, Shenyang 110168, Liaoning, China
191648220@qq.com

Abstract. In recent years, with the emphasis on education and attention to physical health, the become increasingly important. Choosing appropriate evaluation indicators is the core issue of physical education teaching evaluation in universities. Therefore, based, this paper analyzes the index system of college sports teaching evaluation, and establishes a decision Tree model model suitable for college sports teaching evaluation. Firstly, by analyzing the basic principles and content of physical education teaching, an evaluation index system was established, including teaching objectives, classroom teaching, practical teaching, and student performance. Secondly, C4.5 algorithm is used to build the decision tree of the evaluation index system, and the data is modeled and trained. Finally, the effectiveness of the by comparing its prediction accuracy and accuracy through experiments. The results of this study indicate that the model for college physical can effectively improve the accuracy and precision of the evaluation results, and help to achieve and improvement of college.

Keyword: College physical education · Decision tree algorithm · Teaching evaluation

1 Introduction

With the emphasis on healthy physique, physical education in universities has become increasingly important. The has also become an essential part of the evaluation system. If the quality of universities cannot be accurately evaluated, it will be difficult to ensure the physical health of students and the improvement of educational quality[1]. Therefore, when multiple factors need to be considered, including the teaching methods, the practical teaching, and the performance in the practical process. Decision tree is a very effective evaluation method that can help us comprehensively consider the impact of multiple factors and establish an accurate evaluation model[2].

Based on the algorithm, this index system of college sports teaching, and establishes a decision Tree model model suitable for college sports teaching evaluation. Firstly, we need to determine the evaluation indicator system. When determining the evaluation index system, it is necessary to consider factors such as teaching objectives, classroom

Y. Zhang and N. Shah (Eds.): BigIoT-EDU 2023, LNICST 581, pp. 3–13, 2024.
https://doi.org/10.1007/978-3-031-63133-7_1

teaching, practical teaching, and student performance[3]. Each factor includes multiple specific indicators, such as whether the teacher has mastered professional knowledge and whether the teaching method is vivid and interesting, which can be considered in classroom teaching. Secondly, we need to use the C4.5 algorithm to model and train the evaluation index system, so as to establish the decision-making Tree model of college sports teaching evaluation[4]. In C4.5 algorithm, we regard the evaluation index system as a classifier, establish a decision tree, and model and train the data. Finally, we can conduct experimental comparisons on the evaluation models to verify their prediction accuracy and accuracy, and demonstrate their feasibility and effectiveness.

The results of this study indicate that the model can effectively improve the accuracy and precision of the evaluation results, and help to achieve quality monitoring and education teaching[5]. By comprehensively considering the quality of in universities can be more comprehensively evaluated, helping students better improve their health and educational level, and also promoting the of physical.

2 Related Work

2.1 Decision Tree Technology

(1) Decision Tree Construction Process.

Quinlan was the first person to explicitly propose the idea of decision tree, and proposed ID3 algorithm and C4.5 algorithm respectively in 1986 and 1993. Decision tree technology is a classification algorithm in machine learning. It takes information entropy as the main reference, has the of high readability and rapid analysis, and is a kind of Supervised learning[6]. The main process of building a decision tree is as follows:

Step 1: Treat all data as a to the next step;

Step 2: Select a new from the existing data features and partition the nodes to proceed to the next step;

Step 3: After generating some child nodes, make a decision on each child node. If the requirement to stop splitting is met, proceed to the next step; Otherwise, you will proceed to step 2;

Step 4: Set the as a child node, and the type with the highest proportion in the total number of nodes.

The decision tree construction model is shown in Fig. 1.

(2) Selection of splitting attributes.

When the C4.5 algorithm is used to build the tree, attributes are divided by calculating the gain ratio. Assuming that the dataset is represented by S and A represents [7].

Step 1: Calculate the entropy. The entropy represents the sum of time uncertainties that occur for different types in each study sample. According to the theory the greater the entropy, the greater.

$$Ent(S, A) = -\sum_{i=1}^{c} \frac{S_i}{i} log_2 \frac{S_i}{i} \tag{1}$$

Among them, Si to Sc are the set of c sample examples generated by splitting the attribute A of c values into S.

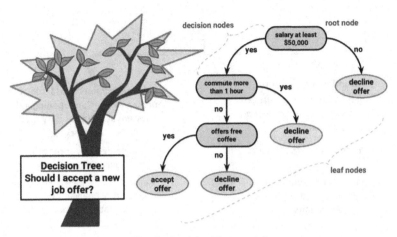

Fig. 1. Decision Tree model

Step 2: Analyze the dataset S through statistical analysis of various attributes to obtain information gain.

$$Gain(S, A) = Ent(s) - \sum_{v=1}^{v} \frac{Sv}{v} Ent(S_V) \tag{2}$$

Among them, Ent (S) represents the calculation based on the entire attribute as a set, Ent (SV) represents the calculation based on the attribute value of attribute A as a set, and v represents the of attribute A.

Step 3: Calculate the information gain rate

$$GainRatio(S, A) = \frac{Gain(S, A)}{Ent(A)} \tag{3}$$

The higher the information gain rate, the higher the purity of the indicator. The attribute with the highest information gain rate is used as the root node, and steps 1, 2, and 3 are repeated to continue building the decision tree.

2.2 Model Evaluation

This article constructs an evaluation system for the teaching mode of physical education in universities. C4.5 algorithm. By calculating and optimizing the weight of indicators, it is possible to effectively evaluate and analyze the physical education teaching mode in universities.

In terms of model evaluation, we evaluate the accuracy, rigor, and reliability of the model by collecting a certain amount of sample data for testing and validation [8]. For example, we can input a set of data into the system and verify the accuracy and precision of the system by comparing it with actual results. At the same time, by optimizing the predictive ability and adding new evaluation factors, the predictive ability of the model is improved to ensure the reliability of the system, as shown in Fig. 2.

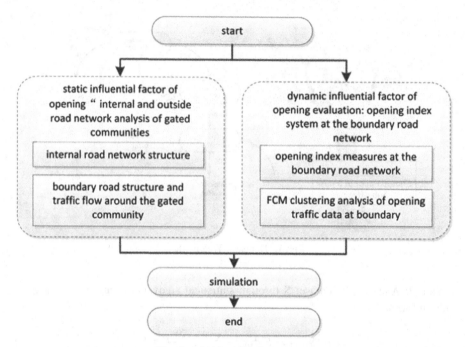

Fig. 2. Model evaluation process

In practical application, this system can help university teachers evaluate their physical education teaching quality more comprehensively and make corresponding improvements and improvements[9]. At the same time, students can also adjust their physical education learning methods in a timely manner based on the evaluation results, in order to improve their physical fitness faster and better[10]. The system can also provide accurate teaching quality evaluation data for university administrators, and provide decision-making basis for the supervision and improvement of university education quality.

In summary, the evaluation system for university physical education teaching models based on decision tree algorithm has high practicality and operability, and can provide effective tools and support for the evaluation and improvement of university teaching quality.

Confusion matrix is the most basic, direct and of classification models, and is often used to test the accuracy of models. By collecting samples, the first level indicators, are obtained.

In the Confusion matrix, the values of TP, FP, FN and TN represent the amount of data in the corresponding situation, but for massive data, it is judge the quality of the simply by the amount. Therefore, the can expand four secondary indexes from the most analysis results: accuracy, accuracy, sensitivity, specificity, and the third level index F measurement, which are applicable to scenarios[11]. Among them, refers to the proportion of estimated the taken, and the is as follows:

$$accuracy = \frac{TP + TN}{TP + TN + FP + FN} \tag{4}$$

The meaning of accuracy is the probability of predicting true samples among all samples marked as true, and the as follows:

$$precision = \frac{TP}{TP + FP} \tag{5}$$

Sensitivity, also known as recall rate, refers to the proportion of samples marked correctly as that are actually true. The is as follows:

$$recall = \frac{TP}{TP + FN} \tag{6}$$

The F-measure is a comprehensive reflection of the efficiency of a model, and the as follows:

$$F = \frac{2 * precisin(M) * recall(M)}{precision(M) + recall(M)} \tag{7}$$

Contrary to the subjective, the determines the between the original data. It and the evaluation data of each indicator to calculate the weight, which avoids subjectivity to a certain extent. However, the objective weighting method also has certain limitations[12]. The method is too dependent on data to think about problems from the perspective of decision makers, which may lead to results that are quite different from the ideas of decision makers, And the calculation process is quite complex. The common objective weighting methods currently include principal component analysis, entropy method, dispersion method, and CRITIC method.

Both subjective and objective weighting and disadvantages. In balance decision-makers' preferences for attributes while also striving to objective weighting of attributes, thus making weighting more scientific and reliable, scholars have proposed a subjective and objective weighting methods[13]. The combination methods include multiplication synthesis method, entropy weight method, coefficient of variation method, correlation coefficient method, etc.

3 Analysis of Evaluation of Physical Education Teaching in Universities Based on Decision Tree Algorithm

3.1 Establish a Tree Model for Classroom Teaching Quality Evaluation

Classroom evaluation is an important component of university evaluation, which can help teachers understand the of classroom teaching, adjust and improve teaching methods and improve teaching quality[14]. Establishing a reliable and effective classroom model is one of the means to optimize the teaching quality of universities and promote educational development.

The algorithm can comprehensively consider multi-dimensional factors, establish a multi branch and multi-level tree structure, and achieve classification and evaluation of teaching quality with high accuracy and accuracy[15].

The specific steps are as follows:

(1) The attributes in the training set.

Firstly, the classification information entropy of the using a formula. In the including 23 samples with excellent classification attributes, 25 samples with good classification attributes, 23 samples with qualified classification attributes, and 9 samples with poor classification attributes.

(2) Calculate the subset information each attribute value.

Firstly, take the entropy calculation attribute as an example.

There here information entropy needs to be calculated for the subset divided by each attribute value. For "teaching experience" being "high", with excellent classroom teaching results, teaching results, 3 data samples with results, and 0 data samples with poor classroom teaching results.

(3) Repeat the above series of steps for each subset in each branch of the decision tree to determine each node in the branch until there are no attribute partitions or the subset is empty.

The above steps only establish one node of the decision tree, so the process of establishing the entire tree is very cumbersome if manually calculated. To solve this problem, Matlab and SQL Server were used to jointly establish the decision tree during the research process. Firstly, establish a database JSP JB in SQL Server, then connect Matlab to the SQL Server database, and add the data source from the management tool.

3.2 Design of Evaluation Index Weights Based on GT-AHP-CRITIC Model

The subjective weighting method is based on the experience of experts in various fields, considering the importance of each indicator and assigning values. The advantage is that it can maximize the experience and knowledge of decision-makers, but there is a certain degree of subjectivity that may lead to deviations in experimental results. Among the commonly used subjective weighting methods, Analytic Hierarchy Process (AHP) is currently the most widely used and widely used method. Its main feature is its simplicity, which can of decision-making, and effectively solve the problem of qualitative systems being unable to make decisions.

The objective weighting the evaluation data, calculate the relationship between attributes, and determine the weight of attributes by analyzing and calculating the evaluation data. To some extent, it avoids subjectivity, but this method relies too much on data and cannot think from the perspective of decision-makers, which can lead to results that are vastly different from the ideas of decision-makers. The commonly used objective weighting methods include principal component analysis, entropy method, mean square error method (dispersion method), CRITIC method, etc. Compared to entropy weight method, standard deviation method, and other objective weighting methods, CRITIC method mainly takes the comparative strength and conflict between evaluation indicators as the influencing factors of the objective weight of the evaluation indicators. This method not only considers the variability of indicators, but also takes into account the correlation between indicators. Contrary to the subjective weighting method, this method is based on scientific evaluation of data. Among them, comparative strength refers to the size of the difference in values between different evaluation schemes for the same indicator, using standard deviation σ_ To express in the form of j. σ_ The larger the j, the greater the difference in the values of each evaluation scheme. The between indicators is generally a correlation coefficient. If the indicating that the importance of the indicators is smaller, that is, the weight is lower. For the CRITIC method, under the same standard deviation, the weight of indicators is directly proportional to the intensity of conflicts between indicators. In addition, the greater the positive correlation between two indicators, the smaller the conflict, indicating that these two indicators have a similar role in the system. Therefore, based on the relevant of the CRITIC method, this chapter selects the CRITIC method as the objective weighting method used.

Common combination weighting methods include multiplication synthesis method, correlation coefficient method, etc. The combination is different from the conventional statistical method. Game theory is an important subject in Operations research. Its basic idea is to obtain balance through continuous struggle, apply Game theory to the subjective and objective weight assignment in the teaching evaluation system, find a balance point

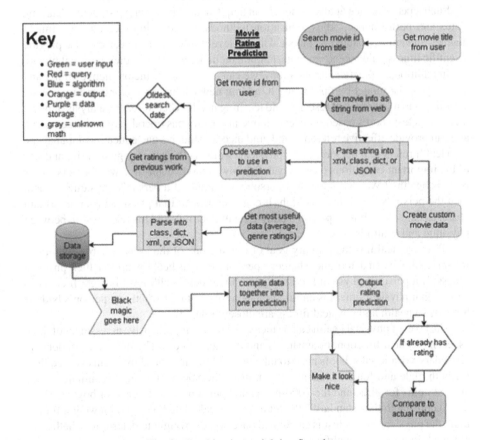

Fig. 3. Combination weighting flowchart

or consistency point for the subjective and objective weighting methods, determine the optimal combination linear coefficient, and optimize the results of weighting, as shown in Fig. 3.

4   Analysis of Physical Fitness Test Scores Based on Decision Tree

Analyzing on decision tree algorithms can help teachers and students better understand their physical fitness and health status, and take corresponding measures to improve their physical fitness.

Firstly, it is index system that includes multiple factors such as physical indicators, psychological indicators, and exercise status. By comprehensively considering the impact of different factors, a complete evaluation index system needs to be established. Secondly, decision tree algorithm is used to analyze and evaluate physical fitness test scores. Specifically, by classifying and comparing data, a multi branch and multi-level tree structure is established to determine the classification and population characteristics of different grades, and to explain and explain the results of grade analysis.

Such a performance analysis model can help teachers better grasp students' learning status and performance, adjust education methods and teaching methods in a timely manner, and improve students' physical fitness level; At the same time, it can also provide scientific fitness guidance to students, helping them better improve their physical fitness.

In addition, in practical applications, we can also improve the predictive ability and accuracy of the model by optimizing it, adding new evaluation factors, and improving algorithms to meet relevant research and teaching needs. Therefore, the analysis of physical fitness test scores based on decision tree algorithm has operability and practicality, and can provide effective reference and guidance for students and educational managers.

Health refers to a person's good physical, which is the primary goal of life and one of the important conditions for survival. So, how can one determine whether a person's body is healthy? We can judge by a person's physique. If a person's physique is good, then the person's health level is high. It can also be said that physique is an important characteristic of whether a person's body is healthy or not, and the relationship between physique and health is very close.

"Physical health is the primary goal of life and one of the indispensable conditions for survival. We can determine whether a person's body is healthy through their physical fitness. If a person's physical fitness is good, then their health level is high. It can also be said that physical fitness is an important characteristic of whether a person's body is healthy, so health and physical fitness are closely related.".

The level of physical health can be measured by a comprehensive assessment of three aspects: physical function, body shape, and physical fitness. The items that students in secondary vocational schools need to take part, 50-m run. The above items are required for both male and female students. In addition, the 800-m run and one-minute sit-ups are test items for girls, and the 1000-m run and pull-up are test items for boys.

According to the "standard", the total score is calculated by a certain weight for test item, the physical fitness test is calculated based on the weight to determine whether the physical fitness test is qualified.

In order to successfully mine data, it effectively conduct data collection, which is to extract s from the original database. This article collects test data from various physical education teachers on the weight, height,, sitting forward flexion, 800-m (female), 1000m (male), one-minute sit-ups (female), and pull-up (male) projects of all the students in Grade 2015 of Guyuan Vocational and Technical College for Nationalities in 2016. There are 1152 pieces of data in total, which are obtained after strict testing by physical education teachers on students. Therefore, The data is relatively complete, including grade information, class information, basic student information, and test data.

Then compare the size of the information alkene, and the smallest one above is the information entropy of the 50 m run. Therefore, select the 50 m run as the root node. Among the attributes of the 50 m run, there are 132 pieces of data with an excellent grade, of which 5 pieces of data have unqualified lung capacity scores, that is, 96.2% of the students have qualified lung capacity scores, which means that as long as the 50 m run has an excellent grade, their lung capacity scores are basically qualified. "The five students who failed their vital capacity scores may be caused by improper use of vital capacity instruments during testing, and therefore may be ignored.". In the 50 m run, 15 students failed, and 12 of them failed in their lung capacity. That is to say, if they failed in the 50 m run, their lung capacity performance would be basically unqualified. This concludes the classification of the 50 m race as excellent and failing, and the classification of the 50 m race as passing will continue below. The decision tree of Fig. 4 can be obtained.

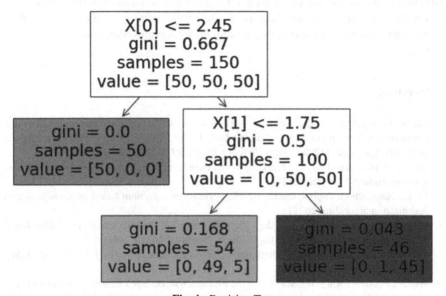

Fig. 4. Decision Tree

By analyzing the operation results in Fig. 4, the can be drawn:

(1) The biggest factor affecting physical fitness test scores is gender, and through comparison, it can be concluded that the passing rate of male students' physical fitness test scores is higher than that of female students. Reason analysis: Boys are usually

active, such as during recess or extracurricular activities. Boys like to play basketball, football, and other activities, and exercise more than girls. That is, boys do more physical exercise than girls, which means that boys' physique is better than girls'.

(2) In the decision tree, students with normal height and weight have a higher passing rate in the physical fitness test than those with abnormal weight. It can be seen that height and weight are also an important factor affecting the physical fitness test results. Overweight and obese students may be caused by eating unhealthy foods such as snacks at ordinary times, while low weight students may be caused by long-term malnutrition and weight loss, and these students lack physical exercise at ordinary times, in their physical fitness, This will affect their physical health.

5   Conclusion

The widely used in the teaching in universities. Its main advantage is that it can handle a large number of variables and missing values, and can intuitively present the evaluation results. The decision tree algorithm divides evaluation indicators into different nodes, analyzes data and makes decisions based on the judgment conditions on different nodes, and obtains the final evaluation result. It the accuracy of the evaluation results, the data should be standardized before establishing a decision tree to avoid data bias and impact. In addition, the decision tree algorithm also requires continuous model training and optimization to stability of the model. In summary, the analysis of university physical on decision tree algorithm can provide a scientific, intuitive, and effective method for teaching evaluation, providing strong support for the university physical education teaching.

References

1. Su, W.: Research on the application of decision tree algorithm in practical teaching of public physical education in colleges and universities. In: EAI International Conference, BigIoT-EDU. Springer, Cham (2023). https://doi.org/10.1007/978-3-031-23944-1_26
2. Guo, Y.: University classroom teaching model based on decision tree analysis and machine learning. Hindawi Limited (2021)
3. Yi, L.: Research on english teaching ability evaluation algorithm based on particle swarm optimization algorithm (2021)
4. Feng, B.: Dynamic analysis of college physical education teaching quality evaluation based on network under the big data. Comput. Intell. Neurosci. 2021(Pt.14) (2021)
5. Yu, S.: Application of artificial intelligence in physical education. Int. J. Electr. Eng. Educ. (2021)
6. Wu, X., Zhou, Y., Xing, H.: Studies on the evaluation of college classroom teaching quality based on SVM multiclass classification algorithm. J. Phys. Conf. Ser. 1735, 012011 (2021)
7. Zhu, R., Wang, J., Yu, F., et al.: Quality evaluation of college physical training considering apriori algorithm. Math. Prob. Eng. 2022 (2022)
8. Yan, J., Zhou, M., Chen, Y., et al.: Evaluation model of college english education effect based on big data analysis. J. Inf. Knowl. Manage. (2022)
9. Ding, L., Zeng, X.: Application of decision tree model based on C4.5 algorithm in nursing quality management evaluation. J. Med. Imaging Health Inform. (2021)

10. Wang, Y., Jiao, L., Liu, C.: Analysis of college student registration management and change prediction based on mutated fuzzy neural network algorithm. Hindawi Limited (2021)
11. Wu, X.: Research on the reform of ideological and political teaching evaluation method of college english course based on "online and offline" teaching. J. High. Educ. Res. **3**(1), 87–90 (2022)
12. Huang, Y.: The evaluation of students' physical health based on the integration of family and school physical education. Revista Brasileira de Medicina do Esporte **27**(spe), 80–82 (2021)
13. Yu, W., He, Y., Qin, H.: A new outlier detection algorithm based on observation-point mechanism. J. Shenzhen Univ. Sci. Eng. **39**(3), 355–362 (2022)
14. Zhang, S., Xue, W., Gao, Y., et al.: Spinning joint scheduling strategy and its optimization method based on data and empirical knowledge. Text. Res. J. **93**(5–6), 1287–1300 (2023)
15. Zhang, C., Yang, H.: Application of decision tree algorithm in teaching quality analysis of physical education (2023)

Design of Teaching Platform of Foreign Literary Works Based on Decision Tree Algorithm

Xiaojie Jiang[✉]

Yan'an Branch of Shaanxi Roadie and Television University, Yan'an 716000, Shaanxi, China
jxiaojie0520@163.com

Abstract. Intelligent algorithms play an important role in the selection of teaching strategies in foreign literary works, but there is a problem that the choice of teaching strategies is unreasonable. Intelligent algorithms cannot solve the problem of teaching strategy selection of multiple types of works in foreign literary works, The decision tree is a quantitative analysis method, which can make a comprehensive judgment on the indicators and contents in the analysis, and the process of the final book in the actor painting competition can be more directly optimized in the process of analysis, and the analysis results of the completed data show that the analysis ability of literary works can be improved after the finals, and the analysis of literary works can be better carried out, and the selection of complete schemes can be carried out.

Keyword: knowledge of foreign literature · grades · Decision tree method · Optimize the results

1 Introduction

International exchanges have become increasingly frequent, and cultural conflicts between different countries and ethnic groups have also intensified. How to treat different cultures with a correct attitude has clearly become an important challenge for people to face. With the development trend of cultural exchange and integration, there are also new requirements for education [1]. The state pointed out in the planning plan that it is necessary to strengthen the cultivation of literary talents, increase the reading volume of relevant personnel, and select more instructive expositions as reference articles, so it is of great guiding significance for the cultivation and development of literary talents through in-depth analysis of foreign literature ① The Core Literacy for the Development of Chinese Students attaches importance to international understanding, Emphasizing the need to cultivate students' "global awareness and an open mind, And continue to pay attention to the valuable content of literary works, as well as the works with higher content and more in-depth analysis of the works, and promote related works ② At the same time, the "General High School Chinese Curriculum Standards (2017 Edition, 2020 Revision)" also includes "cross-cultural thematic discussions" as one of the learning task groups, emphasizing the need to conduct in-depth study of foreign

Y. Zhang and N. Shah (Eds.): BigIoT-EDU 2023, LNICST 581, pp. 14–24, 2024.
https://doi.org/10.1007/978-3-031-63133-7_2

literary classics, through the comparison of Chinese and foreign literary classics, Have a deeper understanding of foreign culture, guide students to understand cultural diversity, cultivate students' international vision, and enhance cultural self-confidence [2].

In today's increasingly deepening globalization, cultivating high-quality talents with an international perspective is an important task of education in every country. High school students are at a critical stage in the formation of their values, outlook on life, and worldview. The cultural factors in foreign literary works play an important role in improving their cultural literacy and cultivating their international vision [3]. Therefore, the teaching of foreign literary works in high school Chinese textbooks is undoubtedly an important way to cultivate their multicultural literacy. The "Chinese Teaching Syllabus" in 2000 emphasizes that Chinese teaching should be "connected with real life", pay attention to cultivating innovative spirit, and form a sound personality [4]. In Chinese textbooks, there have been changes in the proportion of foreign literary works, the expansion of their scope, the diversification of their themes and styles, and the increase in the number of authors. In addition, there have been changes in the interpretation of textbooks by the teaching staff. In 2001, Liu Hongtao proposed in his article "Foreign Literature Issues in Middle School Chinese" that "language and literature education is gradually becoming closer to real life, shifting towards the establishment of the concept of 'human civilization', humanistic education, and multicultural education [5]. "Since the promulgation of the new curriculum standards in 2003, more and more people have focused their research attention on the field of multicultural education in high school Chinese foreign literature, mainly in the following aspects: research on the multicultural connotation of high school Chinese foreign literature works, research on the value of multicultural education, and research on foreign literature teaching strategies.".The appreciation of foreign works is conducive to learning from foreign literary ideas to make up for the shortcomings in domestic literary research, and to excavate the content of literary works, formulate reasonable planning plans based on the quality and needs of relevant personnel, and select teaching strategies more accurately, so as to give full play to the value of literary works, strengthen the training of relevant personnel, and then improve the appreciation level of literary works, make up for the shortcomings of the United States in literary research, and improve the comprehensive quality and level of relevant personnel [7]. This paper introduces how the decision number algorithm in the intelligent algorithm can be used in foreign works, and verifies the effectiveness and rationality of the method.

2 Related Concepts

2.1 Mathematical Description of the Decision Tree Method

The decision-making tree method uses teaching strategies, content and importance of works to analyze foreign literary works, and finds outliers in the teaching analysis of works according to the teaching indicators of foreign literary works, and forms a teaching planning table. Through the integration of the teaching strategy of the work, the final teaching strategy is obtained [8]. The decision-making tree method combines the knowledge of foreign literature to optimize the teaching strategy, which can improve the teaching level of foreign literary works. The number of works in literary works is hypothesized and the correlation function of literary works is constructed to complete the quantification of literary works, which is conducive to in-depth analysis in the later stage.

$$F(x_i, y_i) = \oint \tilde{x}_i + y_i \cdot k \tag{1}$$

ξ is Adjust the coefficient of the teaching strategy of works to reduce the impact of work classification.

The number of roles belongs to a kind of authenticity, objective data-based algorithm, which can judge the conditions corresponding to the two values of the data, and self-description belongs to an irregular mathematical modeling, in the whole process of status, it is necessary to start from a few points to judge each analysis content, form a good decision-making number analysis, analyze the number of docking, analyze and do things, and feel that the key points in the operation, complete the position of the data indicators and complete the transformation between the data, there is a large difference between the data, but a more effective decision tree method can be formed in the way of the group, there is a complete information transmission between the data, and in the rich process of weight, I have to increase the weight now All the calculation tests in order to improve the accuracy of Quanzhou, the world can make decisions about the social climate, all important roles, and for the overall situation of the students and the school to do a good job also has a strong role and significance, in the process of decision-making selection, the key indicators in the decision tree should be given special weight measures, and qualitative indicators and qualitative methods should be added to improve the effect of analysis.

$$(X) = -\sum_{i=1}^{n} p(x_i) \log p(x_i) \tag{2}$$

② Information Gain.

Because in the process of data collection, we should pay attention to the direct expansion of information, complete the coupling between data, realize the increase of data and multi-level analysis of data, and realize the information analysis and information communication of data in the process of data analysis, and form an assessment of design experience, together to improve the accuracy of analysis

$$\text{InformationGain}(T) = \text{Entropy}(S) - \text{Entropy}(S/T) \tag{3}$$

③ Gain Ratio.

Information gain has an important role in the decision-making number process, in fact, the weight of information and other fields is almost similar, but the weight is only given to the weight relationship between different numbers, the value can show upward and downward changes, and the information ability presents a positive change, the value gradually increases, is a kind of additional value increase process of a variety of information synthesis, and you are not in the mood to increase, you have not yet approved the entire decision-making process

$$\text{ainRatio}(S, A) = \frac{Gain(S, A)}{H(S, A)} \tag{4}$$

④ Gini coefficient.

For the analysis of the data, the adjustment coefficient should be used to judge, and the key to the attitude coefficient is to further analyze the data, and further carry out the comprehensive mining of the data, so as to expand the overall analysis effect of the data, in the process of data collation, the attributes of the data have a certain impact on the results, so it is necessary to increase the constraint function to the attributes of the data

$$ \text{ainRatio(S, A)} = \frac{Gain(S, A)}{H(S, A)} \tag{5} $$

2.2   Selection of Teaching Strategies for Work Optimization Strategies

Hypothesis 2: In the process of data analysis, the weight of the data should be recorded, and the weight of the data is related to its number, on the one hand, the frequency of data increase, and on the other hand, the proportion of data in the whole value, and the comprehensive judgment of data can be better carried out between the two, so the integration of data is used for the value-added of data, and the comprehensive judgment and analysis of data can be realized

$$ F(x_i) = \frac{s_i \cdot x_i}{y_i} + \xi \tag{6} $$

The decision tree for the analysis of the front line and the clear impact is mainly reflected in two aspects, on the one hand, the tree you increase can complete the data dispute more deeply, and can better form a comprehensive judgment of the data, in the process of data increase and comprehensive judgment, but also to improve the transfer of data, the data should first be aggregated and classified, to achieve the overall classification of the data, and then to analyze the indicators in the data, calculate the weight of the data, in the whole literature and molecular process, the weight of the data has a guiding role in the analysis of the data, in addition, in the comprehensive result analysis of the data, it is necessary to observe the macroeconomic problems in the changes of the macro world, and adjust the corresponding decision-making strategy. In the process of macro analysis, it is necessary to judge the special macro quality and social problems, find out the causes of the problems, and take timely remedial measures to better complete the overall judgment of the data.

During the decision tree generation process, if no restrictions are set on tree structure model will have unrestricted branch growth, and the leaf nodes of the decision tree will cover the entire training sample set data attribute characteristics. In this way, although the decision tree is tested very accurately on the training sample set data, it may not be able to accurately predict on the test sample set [11–13].

The more layers of the decision tree and the more leaf nodes, the more detailed the classification. The deeper the classification of the training set sample data, the easier it is to cause overfitting problems in the decision tree, leading to the more inaccurate prediction of the test set data. To analyze this situation, at this stage, the decision tree pruning method is mainly used to solve such problems. The analysis of the decision tree for literature is mainly to quantitatively analyze the content in the literature and each

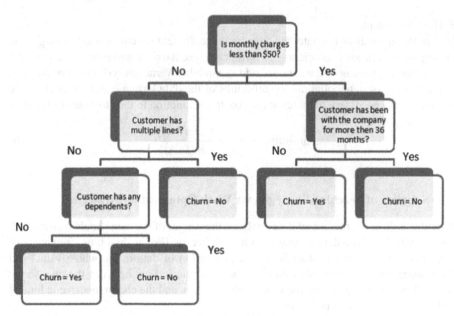

Fig. 1. Decision Tree Model

link in the literature, and carry out the weight assignment of the link and the content and the weight of each content, build the decision tree, the decision tree spreads and spreads from the root node to the surrounding branches and leaves, and forms the optimal path of the decision tree, in the whole path, the weight of each branch in the whole path should be recorded, and the sum of the weights should be calculated, if the path of the branch and the combination of field species are higher, it means that there is a reasonable plan and plan in the decision tree, if there is a small difference between the decision trees, it means that the decision plan is homogeneous, and the policy and indicators need to be adjusted, so the plan is optimized until the best decision is selected. The strategy tree scheme is the quasi-decision-making scheme, and the key content and nodes in the culture and treatise are extracted, which can simplify the steps in the whole scheme and discussion screening process, and optimize the results of each step, the comprehensive judgment of the completion steps, and the analysis of key nodes, key contents and key indicators in the steps, so the decision tree method can achieve multi-angle integration and analysis for the content and nodes of the article, and improve the effectiveness of the analysis.

2.3 Handling of Classification of Works

The selection of strategies involves more content, on the one hand, the teaching plan, teaching content and teaching intervention, on the other hand, the teaching plan, the teaching implementation steps and the technical conditions of teaching, so when screening literary works, it is necessary to judge the key content in literature, and assign weights to the content, form a teaching table of the content, and find the key points of the content and the potential value of the content when comparing and analyzing the content, and select the corresponding strategy according to the comprehensive judgment results to complete the comprehensive implementation of the teaching strategy. The specific implementation is shown in Fig. 2.

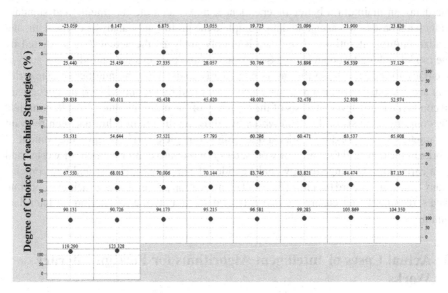

Fig. 2. Teaching strategies for decision tree analysis

The selection results of teaching strategies of foreign literary works in Fig. 1 show that the analysis between teaching strategies and teaching content is uniform, which meets the requirements of teaching foreign literary works. The traditional teaching method is not targeted.It shows that the analysis of the decision tree method has substantial accuracy and can meet the needs of individuals for foreign literary works. The decision tree method analyzes the knowledge of foreign literature, adjusts the traditional teaching methods, removes the repetitive workplace classification, and modifies the teaching strategies, so that the teaching strategies of the overall foreign literary works are highly selective. The results of multi-index data analysis are relatively accurate, indicating that the data indicators can reflect more than 90% of literary works, which also indirectly proves that the algorithm proposed by me can better analyze literary works, and when conducting relevant data analysis, it is found that the algorithm proposed in this paper has advantages in three aspects: on the one hand, the rationality of selection, on the other hand, the accuracy of selection and the comprehensive comparison of selection, and the data in three aspects can fully prove the feasibility of the research method in this paper.

2.4   Correlation Between Different Teaching Strategies

Before data analysis, it is necessary to make a comprehensive judgment on the data, remove the redundant attributes of the data, remove irrelevant data, simplify the overall amount of data, and at the same time conduct iterative analysis of the data, so as to obtain more accurate decision-making results, in the decision-making process, it is necessary to increase the adjustment parameters, judge the rationality of the decision-making results and the optimization of the decision-making, and then make a comprehensive judgment of the decision-making data, verify the relevance and relevance of the data, so that the data can maintain a better independence, make accurate judgments and standard judgments based on reasonable data, complete the preliminary analysis of the data, and realize multiple iterations of the data.It mainly analyzes the actual data predicted by the model and the test data in an association list, and uses evaluation indicators such as accuracy to measure it, so that users can clearly understand the number of categories that are correctly classified and incorrectly classified by the model [15].It is necessary to conduct a multi-level analysis of the accuracy of the entire judgment result, complete the coupling analysis of data and works by adjusting the relationship between relevant parameters, corresponding works and teaching strategies, and determine the content of works in the data and the value of works, carry out iterative improvement of works, and then carry out matching strategy analysis, identify the key indicators and key contents many times, and record the entire data and identification process, so as to achieve accurate data screening, better ensure the diversity of data, and lay the foundation for later data mining.

3   Actual Cases of Intelligent Algorithms for Foreign Literary Works

3.1   Description of Literary Works

According to the relevant literature and materials, different types of works should be selected for analysis, and the literary works should be judged and analyzed in China and abroad, focusing on the literary content of China, and the comprehensive research of the data should be completed, and the rationality and distribution conditions of the data should be judged, and the specific results are shown in Table 1.

Table 1. Teaching strategies for foreign literary works

opus	Strategy indicators	rationality	Policy weights
General works	23	95.85	0.33
	20	32.65	0.21
Key works	19	86.75	0.63
	21	16.69	0.23
Professional works	42	75.75	0.61
	11	20.92	0.42

the process of choosing a teaching strategy between different teaching strategies, as shown in Fig. 3.

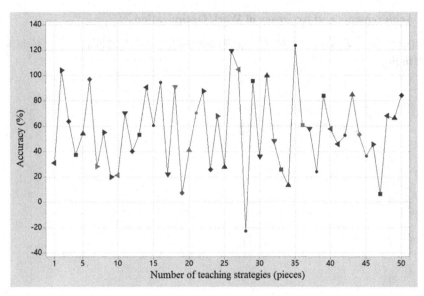

Fig. 3. Strategy selection process of teaching strategy

在进行不同策略的分析过程中发现分析策略会依据其内容呈现改变以60%为中心值进行上下幅度的准确性判断会发现作品的中间数量分析呈现较大波动两侧数据分析的波动较小依据相关的内容对其原因进行分析发现主要是作品在中间数量分析10个数据之间出现了较强的关联性关联性会影响结果的准确所以说中间的数据值会呈现较大波动。

3.2 Optimal Proportion of Teaching Strategies of Works

英语文学作品可以进行分类所以教师要针对作品的内容进行筛选和判断将作品中的词语内容指标进行分析和判断并识别作品与数据之间的关联性完成数据的优化作品集合的汇总以及作品内容的深度挖掘整体的研究结果如表2所示。

Table 2. Overall situation of teaching strategies for works

The degree of adjustment of the teaching strategy of the work	rationality	Comprehensive
5.2	95.21	96.63
6.3	96.00	92.26
8.3	97.79	95.3
7.2	92.12	93.14
X^2	14. 322	42.337
P = 0. 045		

3.3   Achievements and Accuracy of Work Optimization

作品的优化结果要进行目标筛选和准确率判断对其中的关键性数值进行绘制结果如 in Fig. 4.

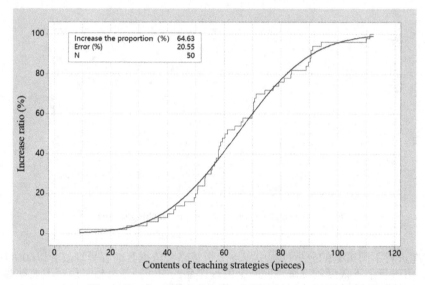

Fig. 4. Improved performance of different algorithms

在图4的数据分析过程中可以发现数据的错误率在20.55%而且数据的错误率与数据的准确性之间呈现缠绕关系说明数据的误差率属于正常的数据干扰存在着干扰性要对数据中的干扰性和内容进行更加深入的挖掘以此来找到特殊性的数据以及数据之间的关系更好的识别数据中的内容。为了更加深入的进行分析可以对数据进行汇总结果如表3所示。

Table 3. Comparison of optimization degrees of different methods

algorithm	Grade Accuracy	Comprehensive accuracy	error
Decision tree method	92.11	95.79	4.74
Traditional teaching methods	70.25	85.26	0.233
P	0.042	0.351	0.061

The decision-making tree method significantly changes the rationality of selecting teaching strategies for foreign literary works and the lack of achievement improvement and accuracy. The decision tree method has a greater improvement in performance than traditional teaching methods. At the same time, the performance of the decision tree method was improved. In order to further verify the coherence of the proposed method, it is necessary to make a comprehensive judgment on the content of the method, so as to complete the comprehensive judgment of the data and implement the comprehensive judgment of the method, and better construct the method and optimize the relevant indicators (Fig. 5).

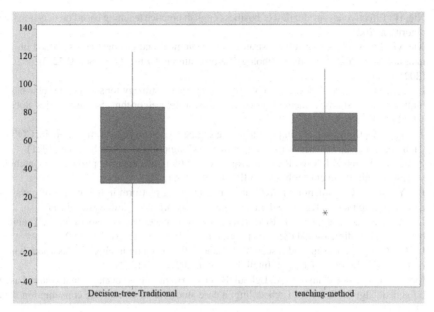

Fig. 5. Comprehensive results of teaching strategy evaluation with different methods

The results of the data analysis in the above figure show that the effectiveness and accuracy of my teaching method are between 40% and 60, and the middle score is between 62%, compared with other methods, its calculation process and calculation range are relatively small, which cannot meet the needs of actual foreign literature research, and it can be said that the research method of this paper has strong advantages in method selection and method planning, and can analyze complex data.

4   Conclusion

In the context of continuous optimization of teaching strategies, this algorithm has an important influence on teaching strategies and your professional content and key indicators, but there are problems in teaching content selection, teaching method matching and teaching program planning, so the intelligent optimization algorithm should be reformed with the actual basic data of teaching as the basic technology, and the research results show that the intelligent algorithm proposed in this paper can effectively optimize the content in teaching, improve the key indicators in teaching, realize the comprehensive judgment of teaching data, and complete the overall culture of teaching, but there are still certain deficiencies in the research process, mainly reflected in the difficulty of teaching data and teaching methods. There is also some controversy about the standard planning and teaching content and teaching methods.

References

1. Nie, H.: Effectiveness evaluation of business english practice teaching based on decision tree algorithm (2021)
2. Xie, G., Jia, Y.: Teaching reform strategy of ideological and political course based on big data-taking "digital electronic technology" as an example. J. Phys. Conf. Ser. **1852**(3), 032003 (2021). 6 pp.
3. Luo, X., Xia, J., Liu, Y.: Extraction of dynamic operation strategy for standalone solar-based multi-energy systems: a method based on decision tree algorithm. Sustain. Cities Soc. **1**, 102917 (2021)
4. Zhang, Y.: Optimization of computer teaching strategy based on genetic algorithm. In: CONF-CDS 2021: The 2nd International Conference on Computing and Data Science (2021)
5. Zhang, Z., Wang, Z.J., Cao, R., et al.: Research on two-level energy optimized dispatching strategy of microgrid cluster based on IPSO algorithm (2021)
6. Ba, Y., Qi, L.: Construction of WeChat mobile teaching platform in the reform of physical education teaching strategy based on deep neural network. Mob. Inf. Syst. (2021)
7. Liu, Y., Liang, J., Song, J., et al.: Research on energy management strategy of fuel cell vehicle based on multi-dimensional dynamic programming. Energies **15**, 5190 (2022)
8. Li, B., Zhang, L.: Design and research of mathematics teaching intelligent classroom based on PCA-NN algorithm. Comput. Intell. Neurosci. **2021**(Pt.8) (2021)
9. Makroum, R.E., Khallaayoun, A., Lghoul, R., et al.: Home energy management system based on genetic algorithm for load scheduling: a case study based on real life consumption data (2023)
10. Yu, W., He, Y., Qin, H.: A new outlier detection algorithm based on observation-point mechanism. J. Shenzhen Univ. Sci. Eng. **39**(3), 355–362 (2022)
11. Hamed, A.Y., Elnahary, M.K., Alsubaei, F.S., et al.: Optimization task scheduling using cooperation search algorithm for heterogeneous cloud computing systems. Tech Science Press (2022)
12. Meng, R., Ke, X., Guocai, G.: Evaluation of sino-foreign cooperative teaching project based on AHP algorithm. In: International Conference on Innovative Computing. Springer, Singapore (2022)
13. Xu, J.: Task-based online entrepreneurship teaching effect evaluation algorithm based on decision tree classification algorithm. Appl. Nanosci.Nanosci. **13**(3), 2593–2599 (2022)
14. Li, X.: Research on english teaching ability evaluation algorithm based on big data fuzzy k-means clustering. In: EAI International Conference, BigIoT-EDU. Springer, Cham (2023). https://doi.org/10.1007/978-3-031-23944-1_5
15. Pang, D.: Research on process control strategy of asphalt tank inventory based on dynamic programming algorithm in post epidemic era (2022)

Application of Decision Tree Algorithm in the Analysis and Evaluation of Quality Education Credits

Rong Yang[1,2(✉)] and Zhang Yuan[1,2]

[1] Xi'an Aeronautical Polytechnic Institute, Xi'an 710089, Shaanxi, China
16347721@qq.com
[2] Hohhot Vocational College, Hohhot 010051, China

Abstract. The application of decision tree algorithm in the analysis and evaluation of quality education credits is to use the decision tree to judge whether students should obtain educational credits. Decision trees are used because they can easily be built from existing data sets collected for other purposes. The analysis here will be completed with the help of data from previous years, which will be used as input to this prediction model. The main purpose behind the use of this technology is to find out whether there is any positive or negative correlation between some factors such as age, gender, class and high-quality education credits. The purpose of such analysis is to determine students who may be eligible for educational credits based on their academic achievements, but their academic achievements do not meet the necessary criteria for obtaining educational credits. This type of analysis will help schools decide which students should receive credit and which students do not need credit. In order to explore the management mode of quality education and apply it to the quality education work in higher vocational colleges, this article introduces data mining technology, which divides and digitizes quality education, so as to achieve the analysis and evaluation of quality education credits, provide broader development space and institutional guarantee for students' quality education, and make quality education an organic component of the education and teaching work in higher vocational colleges.

Keyword: Decision tree algorithm · Teaching analysis · evaluation system

1 Introduction

Quality education is a basic education that focuses on improving students' ideological quality, scientific and cultural level, physical quality, psychological quality, skill quality, ability cultivation, and personality development in an all-round manner. It combines students' own quality structure to improve the quality of talent cultivation as a whole. As the birthplace of talent cultivation, universities adhere to quality education as the core and cultivate high-quality and innovative talents, which is a glorious and arduous task of higher education in the new era [1].

Y. Zhang and N. Shah (Eds.): BigIoT-EDU 2023, LNICST 581, pp. 25–35, 2024.
https://doi.org/10.1007/978-3-031-63133-7_3

In the new situation of the rapid development of science and technology, great changes have taken place in the learning situation, lifestyle, employment forms, and other aspects of college students. College students are easy to accept new things and ideas, and they have a strong critical spirit and sense of equality. The rapid development of the information age has made the channels for college students to receive information diverse and complex [2]. In response to these new situations, how university student administrators manage students objectively, fairly, and effectively has become a common new issue in universities. At the same time, the issue of quality education for college students has received widespread attention from the entire society, and various colleges and universities have gradually made preliminary discussions on the evaluation of students' comprehensive quality.

The comprehensive quality evaluation of college students refers to a process of using scientific methods suitable for quality education to collect students' behavior during their study and life in school, and combining the evaluation objectives of quality education to make a judgment process of quantity or value, or directly guiding and inferring the quality characteristics of college students from their daily performance. Comprehensive quality evaluation is a comprehensive evaluation of individual students, not a personalized evaluation. The main purpose is to evaluate the differences in various qualities of students [3]. The student comprehensive evaluation system is a relatively advanced method used by universities to evaluate the comprehensive quality of students, and it is also an important component of the university student management information system. The comprehensive quality evaluation of students is a comprehensive evaluation of the quality of college students from three aspects: moral, intellectual, and physical. The comprehensive quality evaluation process has the characteristics of fairness and impartiality. The authenticity and accuracy of the evaluation results is an important basis for evaluating excellence and awards, and plays a very important role in smoothly promoting the development of student work and comprehensively improving the comprehensive quality of students [4].

With the development of computer technology, network technology is becoming more and more important to our life and work. Especially today, with highly developed information, people urgently need timeliness for the demand and release of the latest information. Dynamic interactive web pages just provide these functions. At present, there are some similar teaching evaluation systems on the Internet. Through the observation of these systems and the understanding of teachers and students who have used these systems, we find that these systems simply display the evaluation content in the form of web pages for students to choose, and then uniformly save and submit the results to the server [5]. This has great drawbacks, and the content of teaching evaluation is difficult to update; The credibility of teaching evaluation results needs to be improved; At the same time, when multiple users log in, the system is not running well. In the quality education teaching process, especially after the credit system is introduced into the quality education, the relevant data has the characteristics of large data capacity, incomplete, noisy, random, fuzzy, etc. Traditional data processing methods are not competent for such complex data processing work, so we must use data mining related technologies to extract valuable data information for the development of quality education, and then conduct further research [6]. This system is designed to provide relevant decision support for teachers of educational administration, provide scientific basis for the quality of teaching work for the evaluation and employment of professional titles, and reduce the workload of teachers of educational administration. The system is based on Windows XP operating system, developed with JSP, and implemented with SQL SERVER2000 database.

2 Related Work

2.1 Significance of Credit Analysis of Quality Education

The comprehensive quality evaluation of colleges and universities is a systematic project, which involves sports activities, scientific research and innovation ability, average score of academic achievements, social practice ability, political and ideological quality and other indicators, and only some of the indicators can be quantified. In the past management process, efficient education management departments often used manual evaluation, and then fully used fuzzy analysis or analytic hierarchy process to carry out evaluation. But on the whole, in the past, the manual evaluation management itself will be affected by the subjective factors of the evaluator, and the actual evaluation accuracy results are not reliable. At the same time, the traditional artificial comprehensive quality evaluation method needs to design different kinds of utility functions and assign specific weights to each indicator before evaluation [7]. This process is very complicated, with low accuracy and difficulty in promotion. If we can use the decision tree and other related theories and technologies in data mining technology, we can easily solve various defects and deficiencies in traditional manual evaluation methods, and improve the overall quality and efficiency of evaluation work [7].

The data training set is established to generate a decision tree to predict the comprehensive quality of students. On the basis of establishing the classification rules of the decision tree, combined with the requirements of the comprehensive quality evaluation management, we can build an appropriate data training set. After that, we only need to input the data of the students to be evaluated into it, and then we can carry out data training through the constructed decision tree classification model. Finally, we can directly generate a decision tree to predict the students' comprehensive quality, so as to achieve the purpose of evaluating the students' comprehensive quality. By applying data mining technology to the management of comprehensive quality evaluation in colleges and universities, the quality and efficiency of evaluation management can be significantly improved, and the scientificity and accuracy of evaluation can be improved, especially to eliminate the evaluation errors caused by subjective factors in traditional manual evaluation methods [8]. However, it should be noted that the application plan must be reasonably formulated in combination with the application requirements of data mining technology and the actual teaching situation to ensure that the positive role of data mining technology in improving the efficiency of college comprehensive quality evaluation can be fully played [10].

2.2 Research on Teaching Behavior Evaluation

At present, the evaluation of classroom teaching quality can use a scientific evaluation framework or evaluation system to systematically evaluate teachers' classroom teaching. To analyze the quality of classroom teaching, it is necessary to select appropriate classroom teaching evaluation tools and grade classroom teaching within its framework. Only scientific and reasonable classroom teaching evaluation tools can accurately and clearly reflect the actual performance of teachers' classroom teaching [11]. Researchers from different fields have developed different evaluation tools to analyze the quality of classroom teaching. After sorting out the relevant research, the author will analyze the literature from two parts: the development of classroom teaching evaluation tools and the mathematics teaching quality evaluation tool MQI.

The research on teaching behavior is mainly divided into three aspects: before class, in class and after class. Foreign scholars pay more attention to the teaching plan before class, the teaching process in class and the teaching reflection after class. Reinhardt believes that expert teachers have many years of teaching experience, which enables them to carry out their own teaching plans more efficiently and flexibly respond to situations in the classroom [12]. However, novice teachers tend to pay too much attention to their own teaching plans, which sometimes makes it difficult for them to adapt to students' actual classroom performance. Some researchers also made a comparative analysis of the pre class teaching plan, in class teaching process and after class evaluation of expert teachers and novice teachers, and found that novice teachers' teaching plans were more methodical and less refined, while expert teachers' teaching plans were relatively more flexible, dynamic and predictable; Novice teachers rely on their own teaching plans for classroom teaching, while expert teachers can flexibly complete their own teaching plans while taking students as the main body, making the teaching effect more excellent; It is easy for novice teachers to focus on themselves in their after-school self-evaluation and reflection [13]. The first reflection is their own performance in this class, while expert teachers can put students' learning in the first place in this class to consider, and then reflect on the teaching activities in the classroom to make adjustments.

There are many studies on the comparison between expert teachers and novice teachers at home and abroad. To sum up, novice teachers are those who are new to the teaching field, lack teaching experience, have incomplete knowledge structure and refined classroom teaching behavior; Expert teachers are teachers with longer teaching years, rich teaching experience, perfect knowledge structure, higher teaching level and certain teaching achievements.

2.3 Decision Tree Related Algorithms

The international authoritative academic organization, the International Conference on Data Mining (ICDM), selected the top ten classic algorithms in the field of data mining as early as December 2006. Among them, C4.5 algorithm is a classification decision tree algorithm among data mining algorithms, and its basic algorithm is ID3 algorithm. ID3 algorithm has been proposed by J. Ross. Quinlan of the University of Sydney since 1975. It is a classification and prediction algorithm based on information theory and measured by information entropy and information gain to achieve inductive classification of data

[14]. The C4.5 algorithm and the CART algorithm are algorithms that are improved and optimized on the basis of the ID3 algorithm. In order to improve the shortcomings of the ID3 algorithm itself, J. Ross. Quinlan proposed the C4.5 algorithm in 1994, which mainly uses information gain rates for data partitioning. Later, the C5.0 algorithm was proposed on the basis of the C4.5 algorithm. C5.0 is a commercial version of C4.5, which has made improvements in its computational speed. The CART algorithm was introduced by L. Breiman in 1984, J. Friedman et al. proposed that the main use is the Gini coefficient. The algorithms are different, and the corresponding data measurement standards are also different [15]. The relevant data standard attributes are explained as follows.

① Entropy.

Information entropy refers to the uncertainty of measuring random variables $Y = \{c1, c2, c3,... ck\}$. The greater the information entropy, the greater the uncertainty. In a classification category, that is, the more information it contains, the greater the entropy. The calculation method is shown in Eq. (1), where X represents a classification, p (x) represents the probability of selecting the classification, and H (X) represents the sum of all categories. If there is only one category, p (x) = 1, entropy is 0, and the smaller entropy represents the higher certainty.

$$(X) = -\sum_{i=1}^{n} p(x_i) \log p(x_i) \tag{1}$$

② Information Gain.

The information gain represents the difference between the pre and post information entropy after data set partitioning based on the feature T attribute. When dividing a dataset, the method of obtaining the maximum information gain should be selected. The greater the information gain, the stronger the classification ability. The specific calculation is shown in Eq. (2) below.

$$\text{InformationGain}(T) = \text{Entropy}(S) - \text{Entropy}(S/T) \tag{2}$$

③ Gain Ratio.

C4.5 uses the information gain rate as the branch criterion for selecting branch attributes in the decision tree, indicating the ratio of useful information generated by the branch. The larger the value, the more useful information the branch contains. The expression is shown in Eq. (3), where Gain is the information gain and H (S, A) is the information entropy.

$$\text{ainRatio}(S, A) = \frac{Gain(S, A)}{H(S, A)} \tag{3}$$

④ Gini coefficient.

The Gini coefficient is used to represent the uncertainty of the data. The larger the Gini coefficient, the greater the uncertainty of the sample set. Specifically, in the classification problem, there are K categories, and the probability of the K category is pk. The Gini coefficient expression is shown in the following Eq. (4).

$$\text{Gini}(p) = \sum_{k=1}^{k} pk(1 - pk) = 1 - \sum_{k=1}^{k} p^2 k \tag{4}$$

If it is a class II classification problem, the calculation will be relatively simple. If the probability of output from the first sample is p, the Gini coefficient is expressed as the following Eq. (5):

$$Gini(p) = 2p(1 - p) \tag{5}$$

An important step in building a decision tree model and generating a decision tree is to first select data features. The main purpose of this step is to identify data attributes that have the ability to judge. In a training dataset, there may be many attributes for each sample, and different attributes have different roles. Therefore, the role of data feature selection is to screen out features that are highly correlated with data classification results, that is, features with strong classification characteristics, The basis commonly used in this process is information gain, as shown in Fig. 1.

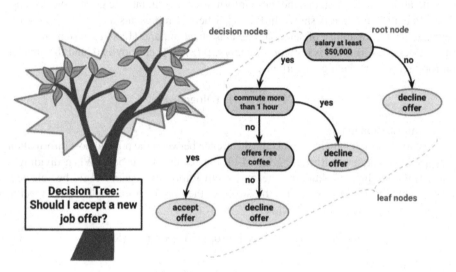

Fig. 1. Decision Tree Model

3   The Application of Decision Tree Algorithm in the Analysis and Evaluation of Quality Education Credit Scores

The development of information technology has promoted the innovation of educational forms, among which the biggest transformation is mainly focused on the integration of information technology and education. This innovation has broken the traditional forms of education and fully applied information technology to the educational environment. With the progress of information technology, new teaching forms such as multimedia applications and online teaching platforms have gradually been accepted and used by the public. Currently, online learning platforms widely used in teaching include: Chinese college students MOOC, Superstar Learning Connect, Erya, Xuetang Online, Tencent

Classroom, Cloud Classroom, etc., and Superstar Learning Connect is one of the mobile learning platforms that support students' online learning, The main platform selected for this study is the Superstar Learning General Education Platform, which is a professional learning platform for intelligent mobile terminals (such as smartphones, smart tablets, smart computers, etc.), achieving an effective integration of teachers, students, and courses. It can be seen as a new type of information based educational information carrier. For teachers, they can use the online learning platform to conduct student education management, reduce the time spent in the teaching process, improve teaching quality, implement teaching forms that are different in different places, different times, different places, different times, and different places, and improve the traditional classroom teaching forms that are both at the same time and in the same place; For students, improving their learning initiative and making them the main body of learning fully reflect their personalized learning process. Learning supervision is conducted based on their personal learning situation. The platform provides timely feedback and evaluation on their learning situation. Students adjust their personal learning behavior based on the feedback from the platform, thereby improving their academic performance.

The establishment of a decision tree model is the core content of this study. The construction of the model needs to be carried out with the help of relevant decision-making tools and algorithms. This section mainly uses python related data analysis tools, and uses the jupyter tool supported by the python environment to construct the Cart decision tree.

(1) Define decision tree model training objectives and representative features

TData = data ['Grade level']

FData = data [['Teacher's title' ◄ Number of classes taught' ◄ Total number of classes' ◄ 'Student gender', 'Major', Grade '◄ Course video completion percentage' ◄, 'Chapter learning completion percentage' ◄ 'Task point completion percentage' ◄, Total number of discussions ◄ Assignment completion percentage', 'Exam completion percentage']]

Define the grade as a decision tree training goal, and define the teacher's title, number of classes taught, total class size, student gender, major, etc. As a representative feature of decision tree training, so as to carry out decision tree construction work.

(2) Train Decision Tree Model # Call Decision Tree Algorithm Library from sklearn.tree import DecisionTreeClassifier

#Set the maximum number of leaves to 32

DtModel = DecisionTreeClassifier (criterion = "gini", max_leaf_nodes = 32)

Training Model

dtModel = dtModel.fit(fData,tData)

This section mainly invokes the DecisionTreeClassifier library in the python algorithm package to build a decision tree model for the factors that affect the performance of the CART (gini coefficient) course. In order to prevent overfitting of the decision tree during the process of building the decision tree model, it is necessary to prune the decision tree according to the corresponding decision tree pruning algorithm. Decision tree pruning is mainly divided into pre pruning and post pruning. Due to the high difficulty coefficient of post pruning, Therefore, the main method used in this study is pre pruning.

The size of the leafy subtree of the decision tree is given in advance, and multiple value settings are attempted. A better value of the model is selected as the final value of the leaf size of the decision tree. After multiple attempts, when the size of the leafy subtree in this study is greater than or equal to 9, the accuracy of the model is above 90%. After comprehensive consideration, when the size of the leafy subtree is 32, the model is better. According to the setting of relevant parameters of the decision tree, Train data to generate a decision tree model.

Data Collection The data in this paper are provided by the Academic Work Department of a higher vocational college, and are respectively taken from the "accounting" and "business management" majors. The data sources include students' basic information (from the student status management system), teachers' information (from the educational administration management system), and quality education credit scores. The final data used is a relational database based on these three.

Data preprocessing ① Data attribute deletion. Through the investigation on the application of the credit system for quality education in a vocational college, it is found that many attributes in several database tables in the student information database are obviously different from other data, and there is a great inconsistency and irrelevance. Therefore, they must be deleted to reduce the waste of unnecessary time, energy and financial resources in later data mining. ② Data attribute generalization: by investigating the application of the credit system for quality education in a vocational college and applying the data generalization principle, the "credit score" in college students' information has been generalized, and more than 3.0 points are "excellent"; The score between 2–2.9 is "medium"; Others are "general". The attendance rate is generalized as: attendance rate&gt = 95 is "high", 90% to 95% is "medium", <90% are "low". Teachers' teaching experience is generalized as: those with more than five years of teaching experience are "rich", and those with less than five years are "not rich". According to the registration information of students, the specialty and hobby can be generalized into "hobby" and "non hobby" by comparing relevant courses. ③ Data cleaning: Through a survey on the application of the credit system for quality education in a vocational college, it is found that although the student information, teacher information and other data are relatively complete, there are still some problems such as incomplete records, missing or wrong entries, which need to be cleaned up [7]. Different data cleaning technologies are used for different data types.

4   Simulation Analysis

According to the above quality education music credit score decision tree model, we tested 160 samples of music score retention, and the accuracy rate reached 88.75%. We judged its rationality through the test to test the accuracy rate of the classification rules. From this, we can see that the accuracy rate of the classification rules generated by using C4.5 decision tree algorithm is more than 85% after the test, which basically meets the requirements [8]. If we conduct appropriate pruning, The accuracy rate will be higher. Therefore, the model is reasonable and can be applied. Through the analysis of the students' music class scores, the following suggestions are obtained: First, the attendance rate has a great impact on the students' academic performance. Students should strictly abide by the school's learning discipline in the learning process, attend classes on time, correct their learning attitude, and complete the learning tasks required by the teachers on time. Second, students' majors also have a certain impact on their academic performance. Students from different majors have different personalities and hobbies [9]. Third, teachers' teaching experience has a great impact on students' academic performance. Teachers should constantly enrich their teaching experience through various ways, improve their music professional skills and music teaching level, so as to further improve the students' attendance rate. Figure 2 below shows the credit decision model algorithm of quality education.

```python
import matplotlib.pyplot as plt
test = []
for i in range(10):
    clf = tree.DecisionTreeClassifier(max_depth=i+1
                                      ,criterion="entropy"
                                      ,random_state=30
                                      ,splitter="random"
                                      )
    clf = clf.fit(Xtrain, Ytrain)
    score = clf.score(Xtest, Ytest)
    test.append(score)
plt.plot(range(1,11),test,color="red",label="max_depth")
plt.legend()
plt.show()
```

Fig. 2. Algorithm of Credit Decision Model in Quality Education

Based on the training of the decision tree model, a decision tree model can be obtained, but it cannot be visually presented. This study mainly calls the Pydotplus package and the Graphviz graphical visualization tool to visualize the decision tree model. The Pydotplus package provides a Python interface for the Graphviz language, thereby achieving a series of operations for Graphviz to visualize the decision tree model.

First, define a memory object StringIO(), temporarily write the file into the memory object, and then insert the graphviz library. With the help of the relevant settings of the graphviz library, visualize the decision tree model. By setting its fill color, circle, special characters, and the font and encoding format of the chart, beautify the decision tree model. Finally, store the generated decision tree model in the form of a pdf file in the current folder, For users to use. The generated decision tree model diagram is shown in Fig. 3 below.

Decision tree pruning is one of the methods to stop the branching of a decision tree. There are two pruning methods: pre pruning and post pruning. Pre pruning is to set a threshold value for the number of leaves in advance during the growth process of the decision tree. When the threshold value is reached, the growth will stop. Once the branch is stopped, node N becomes a leaf node of the decision tree, blocking its subsequent

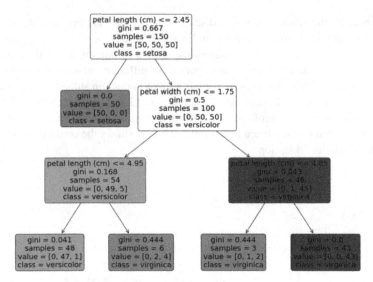

Fig. 3. Cart Decision Tree Model Diagram

nodes from continuing to branch; Post pruning is a method of pruning a decision tree after it is generated, which improves the "visual limitations" of pre pruning and makes full use of the information from all training sets. However, the calculation amount of post pruning is larger than that of pre pruning. This study mainly selects the method of pre pruning for decision tree pruning. During the training phase of the decision tree model, the number of leaves in the decision tree is specified in advance, the number of leaves in the decision tree is changed multiple times, and the accuracy of the evaluation of the decision tree model is compared to the size of the value and the decision tree generates a model pdf file. Although the model evaluation value is the best when the number of leaves in the decision tree is 32, it is analyzed through the model diagram, There are modules in the model diagram with weak sample data pertinence that need to be pruned. When the number of leaves is 16, the model is relatively consistent with the purpose of this study.

To sum up, the C4.5 decision tree algorithm has good applicability for the application research of the analysis and evaluation of the credit scores of quality education. Through the analysis and evaluation of the scores, we can understand the main factors that affect the students' scores, so as to help students improve their learning methods, assist teachers to improve their teaching level, provide decision-making basis for teaching managers, and thus improve the overall level of quality education in higher vocational colleges [10].

5 Conclusion

The application of decision tree algorithm in the analysis and evaluation of quality education credits is to determine which candidates are qualified to participate in the training, who will receive the training and how much time they have to complete the training. The main goal is to provide a method that can be used by all entities involved in the process. This includes private sector entities such as federal agencies, state agencies and local governments, and community colleges. It also includes students themselves, because they need to know what they need to do if they want their credits to be accepted by the institution or institution.

References

1. Yang, R., Gao, R.: Analysis of quality-oriented education credits based on the decision tree algorithm. AGRO FOOD IND HI TEC (2017)
2. Wu, S., Lu, X.: Design of physical education curriculum analysis and management system based on decision tree algorithm. Mod. Electron. Tech. **42**, 139–141 (2019)
3. Zhao, K.: Application research of decision tree algorithm in english grade analysis (2016)
4. Baig, F., Mehrotra, M., et al.: SparkGIS: efficient comparison and evaluation of algorithm results in tissue image analysis studies. In: Biomedical data management and graph online querying: VLDB 2015 Workshops, Big-O(Q) and DMAH, Waikoloa, HI, USA, August 31–September 4, 2015, Revised Selected Papers, International Conference on Very Large Data Bases (41st: 2015: Wai.) (2016)
5. Learman, L.A.: Prospective implementation and evaluation of a decision-tree algorithm for route of hysterectomy editorial comment. Obstet. Gynecol. Surv.Surv. **8**, 75 (2020)
6. Jia, S., Pang, Y.: Teaching quality evaluation and scheme prediction model based on improved decision tree algorithm. Int. Assoc. Online Eng. (IAOE) (10) (2018)
7. Shen, M.: The design and implementation of the comprehensive evaluation system for physical education teachers (2016)
8. Li, X., Xu, Z., Fu, Y., et al.: Ecological security evaluation algorithm for resource-exhausted cities based on the PSR model (10), 17 (2021)
9. Hu, N., Li, Q., et al.: Application of decision tree C4.5 algorithm in air quality evaluation. Aer. Adv. Eng. Res. (2017)
10. Lan, J., Yan, G.: Research and empirical analysis on personal credit evaluation model based on iterative adaptive random decision tree algorithm. J. Quant. Econ. (2018)
11. Zhang, C., Yang, H.: Application of decision tree algorithm in teaching quality analysis of physical education (2023)
12. Su, W.: Research on the application of decision tree algorithm in practical teaching of public physical education in colleges and universities. In: EAI International Conference, BigIoT-EDU. Springer, Cham (2023). https://doi.org/10.1007/978-3-031-23944-1_26
13. Tan, X.: Application of random simulation algorithm in practical teaching of public physical education in colleges and universities. In: EAI International Conference, BigIoT-EDU. Springer, Cham (2023). https://doi.org/10.1007/978-3-031-23950-2_32
14. Chen, B.: Application of intelligent fuzzy decision tree algorithm in English translation education. In: EAI International Conference, BigIoT-EDU. Springer, Cham (2023). https://doi.org/10.1007/978-3-031-23950-2_33
15. Zhang, S.: Research on the Teaching Application of the Improved Genetic Algorithm in E-commerce. Springer, Cham (2023)

Design and Realization of Layered Teaching Intelligent Management Platform in Vocational Education Group

Aiguo Gong[✉], Desheng Zhu, Chao Zhang, Jing Tian, and Xue Zhang

Shandong Institute of Commerce and Technology, Jinan 250103, Shandong, China
Gongaiguo58785@163.com

Abstract. The design and implementation of an intelligent management platform for hierarchical teaching in vocational education is an innovative way to improve the quality of education in vocational colleges. The platform aims to provide a comprehensive solution to the challenges faced by teachers and students in vocational education. The platform is built on a hierarchical structure, allowing for easy management and monitoring of education systems at different levels. It provides teachers with tools to create, manage, and deliver course content in an interactive and engaging manner. Students can access these courses through a user-friendly interface that supports multimedia content, quizzes, and assessments. One of the key functions of the platform is its intelligent management system, which uses data analysis to track students' progress, identify areas where students need assistance, and provide personalized feedback. This helps teachers adjust their teaching methods to meet the needs of individual students. Overall, the hierarchical teaching intelligent management platform provides a powerful tool for improving the quality of vocational education. By providing teachers with better tools to provide courses and track student progress, it helps ensure that students receive high-quality training and are prepared to succeed in their chosen careers. This article briefly analyzes the design of a hierarchical intelligent teaching management platform, and takes the technical selection and functional implementation of the hierarchical intelligent teaching management platform as a breakthrough to achieve automation functions, membership functions, full site search functions, user permissions and management functions, as well as project portfolio functions. I hope to provide reference for relevant personnel. This paper briefly analyzes the hierarchical teaching intelligent management platform design, and the hierarchical intelligent teaching management platform technology selection and function implementation as a breakthrough point, the automatic function, membership function, full station search function, user rights and management function and project combination function implementation, expected to provide reference for relevant personnel.

Keywords: Computer aided system · English vocabulary query · page tedious · struts · query module · JSP page

Y. Zhang and N. Shah (Eds.): BigIoT-EDU 2023, LNICST 581, pp. 36–47, 2024.
https://doi.org/10.1007/978-3-031-63133-7_4

1 Introduction

The history of the emergence of intelligent teaching systems can be traced back to the programmed teaching of the 1960s, followed by the emergence of computer-based training and computer-assisted instruction [1]. CAI, or Computer Aided Instruction, is a teaching system that uses computers as teaching tools. Due to the limitations of time and space in traditional teaching methods, it is difficult to teach according to different situations of students. However, after adopting computer-assisted instruction, the "one to many" collective learning method can be changed to effectively remedy this defect. Although computer-based training and computer-assisted instruction contribute to students' learning to a certain extent, they do not provide personalized attention to "one student for one teacher" teaching [2]. The main reason is that this CAI system does not take into account the ability level of learners, that is, the system does not understand the cognitive style and level of students, does not understand the current state of knowledge of students, and cannot diagnose the causes and provide targeted guidance when students have learning difficulties, nor can it provide personalized learning materials based on their cognitive style and level.

Intelligent teaching system is an adaptive teaching system that uses artificial intelligence technology to allow computers to act as teachers to implement individualized teaching and provide guidance to learners with different needs and characteristics. This system is an intelligent software system that aims at the shortcomings of traditional CAI and can make decisions and guidance based on domain knowledge and student models [3]. The system has the flexibility to represent teaching materials based on students' cognitive characteristics, current knowledge levels, and other characteristics, as well as the ability to respond to different student needs. The purpose is to use computer systems as guides and helpers for learners, enabling computer systems to replace human teachers to achieve optimal teaching to a certain extent.

Group education can effectively improve the effectiveness of education and the utilization of educational resources. The scientific research achievements achieved by teachers in teaching can be smoothly promoted and implemented [4]. The research and analysis of the design and implementation of the hierarchical teaching intelligent management platform for vocational education groups can provide a basis for the development of the hierarchical education management platform and promote the development of group education.

In the social context of rapid changes in information technology and the deep integration of information technology and economic life, carrying out programming education in the basic education stage will become one of the important ways to cultivate the comprehensive quality and ability of talents in the future. On the one hand, basic education is the foundation of education, and teenagers, as reserve talents for future social development, are in a state of infinite potential. In order to adapt students to the development of the future society, the "Development Plan for the New Generation of Artificial Intelligence" proposes to "implement a national intelligence education project, set up artificial intelligence related courses in junior high school, gradually promote programming education", and even incorporate "programming education" into compulsory courses in junior high schools [5]. On the other hand, with the promotion of international organizations such as the European Union and the OECD, various countries have established curriculum systems that focus on building students' core literacy and abilities [6]. In 2014, the Ministry of Education proposed to develop students' core literacy at various academic stages, and exploring how to master programming skills is one of the effective focus points for cultivating students' core literacy in the information technology discipline.

2 Related Work

2.1 Current Situation of Hierarchical Teaching Research

Stratified teaching, also known as grouping teaching and ability grouping, refers to teachers scientifically dividing students into groups with similar levels based on their existing knowledge, ability levels, and potential tendencies, and treating them differently. These groups are best developed and improved through teachers' appropriate hierarchical strategies and interactions. Layered teaching aims at the drawbacks of the traditional "one size fits all" teaching system in large classes, emphasizing "teaching students according to their aptitude", grouping students in the class according to different standards, and cultivating students in layers based on the goal of excellence, so as to promote the overall development and personalized development of all students [7]. The implementation of hierarchical teaching in the information technology discipline requires scientific theoretical guidance and effective hierarchical and grouping methods. It is necessary to fully understand the individual differences of students in cognitive foundation, learning interest, information literacy, and other aspects, classify learning objectives, learning methods, and learning evaluation, and respect the individual development and comprehensive development of students in actual teaching [8].

The research on hierarchical teaching in foreign countries began in the late 1940s, and experienced a process of rising, falling, and then rapidly developing, becoming popular for a long time and constantly developing and changing. In 1868, the American educator Harris, W. T., proposed the "activity grouping system", which uses tests to divide students into three levels, namely, A, B, and C, and provides more guidance to students with learning disabilities. Subsequently, the United States promoted the reform of the education and training system, and hierarchical teaching began to rise, deriving layered teaching forms such as the Dalton system and the Vennett card system [9]. However, the Dalton system emphasizes learning subject knowledge, overemphasizes individual differences, and ignores the collective role of the class and moral education. When it is implemented, it often forms a laissez-faire approach to teaching. On the one hand, the Venatka system advocates individualized teaching and socialization of schools. However, due to the difficulties in influencing in-depth learning of disciplines and implementing them, it has rarely been used in teaching since then. From 1929 to 1939, due to the impact of the economic crisis and World War II, social conflicts intensified, and people believed that there were issues such as educational unfairness in hierarchical teaching, which led to the decline of hierarchical teaching in criticism [10]. After World War II, various countries around the world advocated "high-quality education", with hierarchical teaching and all-round talent cultivation gradually receiving attention and constantly developing and changing. Typical hierarchical teaching models such as "structured hierarchical teaching", "mixed ability hierarchical teaching", and "subject hierarchical teaching" in the United Kingdom, the "course selection system" in South Korea, and "screening education" in Singapore [11]. Overall, these emerging educational concepts of hierarchical teaching provide a good theoretical basis and practical basis for the research and development of hierarchical teaching.

The concept of hierarchical teaching in China can be traced back to the Spring and Autumn Period. The famous educator Confucius' "teaching according to one's aptitude" has been used since thousands of years ago. Since the 1990s, the introduction of quality education has led to the gradual development of hierarchical teaching with the assistance of national education policies. Many scholars and teachers have conducted in-depth research on the models and methods of hierarchical teaching. Liu Shuren (2002) proposed a "six link model" of hierarchical and progressive teaching strategy: calibration guidance – diagnosis compensation – synchronous teaching – differentiation training – feedback regulation – integrated evaluation; Wu Liyun (2005), et al. proposed a hidden hierarchical teaching model and operational strategies for stratified similar students in natural classes; Dai Qiyao (2021) constructed a design model for information technology curriculum teaching in junior high schools based on hierarchical teaching, proposing five dimensions: student stratification, teaching goal stratification, teaching process stratification, practice stratification, and evaluation stratification [12]. Overall, the research on hierarchical teaching in China has always received much attention, mainly focusing on hierarchical teaching in large classes. This requires teachers to have a full understanding of students and a lot of energy to carefully design, which poses a significant challenge to the actual situation of information technology teachers with fewer class hours and more tasks.

2.2 Selection and Redesign of Teaching Modes

Microproject based graphical programming teaching is not difficult for junior high school students, with the focus on training computational thinking. The "teacher guided inquiry" teaching model, characterized by "leading subject combination", not only attaches importance to giving full play to the leading role of teachers in the teaching process, but also highlights the cognitive subjectivity of students in the learning process, which can meet teaching needs and meet teaching goal orientation, Good adaptability [13].

The VOC for advanced strategies uses three characteristics to approximate: (1) the short-sighted utility of performing target state assessments (VOIH 1), (2) the value of perfect information about all targets (VPIH), and (3) the corresponding calculated cost (costH).

$$\widehat{\text{vOC}}^{\text{H}}(c^{\text{H}}, b^{\text{H}}; \mathbf{w}^{\text{H}}) = w_1^{\text{H}} \cdot \text{vot}_1^{\text{H}}(c^{\text{H}}, b^{\text{H}}) + w_2^{\text{H}} \cdot \text{vPr}^{\text{H}}(b^{\text{H}}) \tag{1}$$

where wH1, wH2 are constrained to a probabilistic simplex set, wH3 $\in$ R [1, M], and M is the target number. In addition, the cost cost H (cH) is defined as:

$$\text{cost}^{\text{H}}(c^{\text{H}}) = \begin{cases} \lambda^{\text{H}}, & \text{if} c^{\text{H}} \in \{\xi_1, ..., \xi_M\}. \\ 0, & \text{if} c^{\text{H}} = \perp^{\text{H}}. \end{cases} \tag{2}$$

Specifically, in order to calculate low-level strategies, we define the cost characteristics of BMPS as a weighted average of the costs of generating information assumed by the VOI characteristics F = {VOIL 1, VPIL, VPIL sub}, that is

$$\text{cost}^{L}(c, g, \mathbf{w}^{L}) = \sum_{f \in \mathcal{F}} w_{f}^{L} \cdot \sum_{n}^{|h_g|} \mathbb{I}(c, f, n) \cdot \text{cost}(c) \tag{3}$$

where I(c, f, n) returns 1 if node n is relevant when computing feature f for computation c and 0 otherwise.

(1) Characteristics of the Teaching Model of "Inquiry under Teacher's Guidance"

   The teaching model of "teacher guided inquiry" attaches great importance to the leading role of teachers. Before learning, it is necessary to determine the object of inquiry and heuristic questions, provide various assistance and guidance during the inquiry process, and help summarize and improve after the inquiry is completed. The "teacher guided inquiry" teaching model highlights the dominant position of students in the learning process[14]. Through a learning style characterized by "autonomy, inquiry, and cooperation," students can independently learn, explore, and communicate with each other in small groups on the main knowledge points in the current teaching content, giving full play to their initiative, enthusiasm, and creativity.

(2) The implementation steps and redesign of the "teacher guided inquiry" teaching mode based on the smart education cloud platform include creating situations, inspiring thinking, autonomous learning and exploration, collaborative communication, and summary and improvement. Integrating the online and offline hybrid learning method using the cloud platform education plan, the following teaching flow diagram of the "teacher guided inquiry" teaching mode based on the smart education cloud platform is shown in Fig. 1.

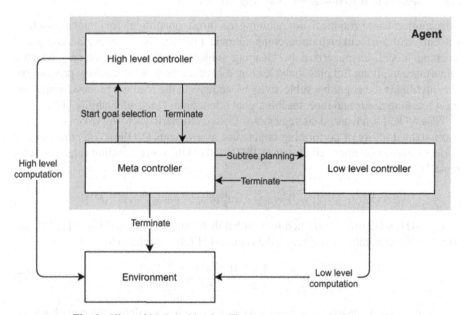

Fig. 1. Hierarchical teaching intelligent management platform mode

Before class, students log in to the cloud platform, open the tutorial to view their academic records, read their learning goals, and perceive the learning process as a whole. Teachers create situations through typical cases to stimulate students' learning motivation. Based on the learning content of micro project programming, teachers and students jointly analyze key issues that need to be addressed. Teachers propose heuristic questions, driven by problem solving, and clarify learning tasks and evaluation criteria. Using the academic record as a scaffold and the evaluation criteria first, students complete learning and evaluation tasks step by step through autonomous learning, inquiry, and collaborative learning [15]. After completing the learning task, the teachers and students jointly analyze the programming work and summarize the overview of what they have learned using mind maps and other methods. Teachers propose new questions or situations to expand, and students discuss and communicate to complete the transfer and application of knowledge. Finally, students upload their works to the cloud platform theme activities, conduct self-evaluation and student mutual evaluation according to evaluation standards, and promote learning reflection and further improvement.

3 Design of the Intelligent Management Platform for Hierarchical Teaching

The digital construction of colleges and universities has experienced the campus network construction, campus informatization, digital campus, and then to the construction of smart campus today. However, in the actual construction process, due to the differences between higher vocational colleges, the level of digital construction of each college is uneven. Therefore, it is necessary to carry out the design of hierarchical teaching intelligent management platform, promote the development of group education, and strengthen the digital construction.

(1) System design ideas and objectives

Designers adopt the tree structure when designing the management mode of educational collectivization. The group's management is located at the tree roots, while the schools are located on the branch nodes. If this management mode is in accordance with, then designers can not carry out the management platform design through a single flat, but should choose a hierarchical structure to carry out the design work. The hierarchical structure is mainly divided into two levels, namely, management and teaching nodes.

1) Functional design of the management department

When designing the management functions, the designers must carry out the design work according to the group management needs to meet the top-level design requirements of the group. To this end, designers can design a collaborative office system OA to achieve the goal of unified management of the group. With the help of the OA system, it can not only make the management better macro coordination of the management scheme, ensure the timeliness and effectiveness of log management and communication, but also quickly push the information of learning and the group. As shown in Table 1.

Table 1. The O A system database table

order number	Table name	description
1	DERT	department
2	T_CRM_CLASS	Customer group
3	T_DATA	Workflow data
4	T_DOCUMENT	D

Moreover, through the OA system, organizations and individuals in the group can also carry out online discussion activities within the prescribed scope, and record and summarize them, providing technical support for different places of teaching exchanges, and achieving the goal of teaching and research in different places. In order to enable the group management to better make decisions, designers should set the authority level and achieve data level management in this way. Moreover, the use of query classification and decentralization management can achieve the goal of evaluation means informatization. In addition, the group cloud disk should be established to store and classify data management and provide data support for the development of management decision-making work.

In addition, in their daily management, vocational education groups should manage in addition to teaching activities, but also to manage routine affairs. For example: approval management, project management, client management, resource bank management, operation analysis management, asset management and financial management. In the design process, designers must pay attention to the relationship between decentralization and unification, implementation and approval, carry out the approval work of various application items with the help of the approval management system, and manage them in accordance with the principle of hierarchical distribution, so as to achieve the management goal of the upper unification and lower division.

2) Function design of teaching nodes

—— school, the management node in the management architecture, which undertakes specific teaching management responsibilities. According to the structure form, the schools in the vocational education group are very similar to the conventional schools, but compared with the conventional schools, the schools with the group nature have a strong scalability in terms of teaching implementation and management. Therefore, when designing the functions of the school, the designers should not only consider the independence of the school in carrying out teaching activities, but also consider the correlation between the school and the whole group.

Because the educational administration management system and the student application system have a strong independence, so the designers can learn from the single school platform when designing the functions of these two systems, so as to better carry out the design work. Class management is an attempt of the school administration management system, in the function design, need to consider the factors are: curriculum design rules, teachers class rules and students selection rules, system needs to coordinate the above rules as a whole, and then according to the "paradox" the logic performance, scientific, reasonable to establish course unit, realize the selected course class management. In addition, strengthen the application of the course selection module in the educational administration management system, can maximize the understanding of the students' course selection situation, so that the management personnel can carry out targeted management work. At the same time, the use of electronic login technology can analyze and statistics the attendance of students, so as to improve the management effect.

3) Functional connection design of different levels

In designing similar functional modules at different levels, we should not only consider the management rules of the vocational education group, but also consider that the school needs to be relatively independent as a management node, so the operation and management in the group can be regarded as a school node. When both the management and the teaching node level have the above functional modules, the group can manage each node according to the unified idea, and then summarize the data and information obtained. However, it should be noted that when the designers design the nodes, they need to set aside the interfaces in advance to facilitate the docking with the group, and finally achieve the goal of "flat" management of the group.

However, when designing unique modules at all levels, designers should combine scientific and reasonable design. For example: the school level in the card management platform and student application platform of the two subsystems, the main body of the service for the students, provide students with personal space management, consumption, resource application, interactive learning, selection, and books borrowing services, so in the design must be around the needs of students in the design work, to ensure that the design system can meet the needs of students, to provide students with better quality service, strengthen management.

In addition, in the design of the intelligent teaching management platform, the hierarchical structure must be reflected, and only in this way can the group education requirements for home-school interaction, resource sharing, teacher-student interaction and dynamic teaching management be meet. In addition, the application of the intelligent management platform should also be strengthened at the group level to achieve the goal of "flat" management and strengthen the management of the group affairs.

(2) Level division and system architecture design,

According to the management mode of vocational education group, it is not difficult to find that its teaching intelligent platform structure is mainly composed of two parts, namely, group module cluster and school node module cluster. As shown in Table 2.

1) Group module cluster

Table 2. The Structure of the Intelligent Teaching Platform

order number	Group module cluster	School node module cluster
1	OA system plate	OA office section
2	Core management sector	Service student section
3	Teaching auxiliary plate	Teaching and educational affairs section
4	Connectivity plate	School management section
5		Teaching and educational affairs section

The module cluster is the top management, mainly composed of OA system, core management, teaching assistance and interconnection, and each section has the same functional level. OA system section consists of collaborative office system; core management section is composed of approval management platform, financial management system, business analysis system, asset management system, file system, evaluation system and project management system; teaching auxiliary section is composed of group training system and education system; and interconnection section is composed of alumni interconnection system, group portal website and home-school interconnection system.

2) Cluster of school nodes and modules

School node module cluster is a collection of digital functions in the scope of the school setting, which is divided into service student section, school management, OA office, external communication and teaching administration, and each section has the same functional level.

The service student section is mainly composed of one-card management platform and student application platform; school management section is mainly composed of human resource platform, asset management platform, file management platform, financial management platform, evaluation platform and approval management platform; OA office section consists of collaborative office platform; external communication section consists of enrollment management system, school portal and home-school interconnection system; and teaching administration section consists of educational management platform, group education resources and teaching research platform.

4 Technology Selection and Function Implementation of Hierarchical Intelligent Teaching Management Platform

(1) Technical selection

The teaching management system adopts the B / S structure, and integrates the ASP. NET technology is the core of the system, paired with PHP technology. At the same time, the C # language and the SQLServex database are used as the development platform of the management system, and some other systems choose the PHP + MYSQL platform.

Not only that, the system chooses the way of programming OOP to build the operation framework. At the same time, the two main function modules in the system select C # language, and adopt ASP. The NET technology realizes the system architecture; and the data support system is designed based on the SQLServer database; and the two module websites develop with the PHP technology and the M YSQL database. And added the control background design to establish a new system model.

(2) Function realization

1) Automatic function implementation

The built-in system model and custom model in the system have special collection plates, so automatic collection can be realized. Meanwhile, each module cluster can seamlessly integrate other information within the group with the corresponding website management system, so as to maximize the information utilization.

In addition, in the processing of details, we should strive to achieve the operation of "intuitive", improve the role of multiple filtering function, using setting the number of collection records, collecting keywords, filtering the same title, advertising filtering, filtering similar information and filtering the whole page of code, so that the same link will not be repeated collection.

2) Realization of membership functions

Use the membership grouping function to divide the membership rights, and set the content of different rights, such as the number of short messages, the membership level, the number of downloads per day, and the number of favorites, etc. And each group of members can set the corresponding member information form and member list style, in order to realize the membership function. At the same time, designers can design the rights of members to limit the number of submissions to the same IP with the help of the information content and the access rights of the column pages, so that more members can have access at the same time.

In addition, an external login platform can also be established, so that members can contact with other websites, so that members can carry out the teaching intelligent management platform to better develop teaching work and strengthen management.

3) Full-station search function implementation

Because the system uses the full-text retrieval technology, Chinese word segmentation and coding transcoding combination, it can effectively solve the problems encountered in the search process, so that it can search multiple content at the same time, and realize the whole station search function. In this feature, users only need to enter their choices into the search bar to get what they want. In addition, full-text search can not only carry out site-site search, but also conduct a specified search for a column, and also support keyword search to improve search efficiency.

4) Implementation of user rights and management functions at all levels

The system uses the function of user grouping, the system divides the management authority, so that users can track their own member level and obtain the corresponding management authority, so as to manage the intelligent teaching platform. At the same time, the management can also set up users to review the management authority, and can not be modified after the review, so as to ensure the authenticity and reliability of the published information.

5) Realization of thematic and thematic combination functions

According to the principle of group allocation and independent authority, the administrator has managed the topic, which can effectively strengthen the topic management. In addition, all levels of sub-classification are added under the topic to simplify the operation mode, so that managers can directly operate in the sub-classification to ensure the realization of the topic function.

Conclusion: In a word, in order to realize the design of hierarchical intelligent teaching management platform in education career groups, it is also necessary to comprehensively consider various design methods and specific conditions, so as to make favorable scheme choices. On this basis, the various design methods can be integrated together, and then the hierarchical intelligent teaching management platform design can be realized in the education career group, to achieve the goal of integrated management.

5   Conclusion

In the process of designing and constructing the teaching intelligence management platform of the Basic Education Group, the characteristics of its education collectivization have been fully considered. In order to meet the requirements of unified technical standards and balanced business functions, a layered construction method has been adopted. With this layered approach, the platform architecture and technical implementation have achieved a combination of independence and unity. In the specific implementation stage, combining various requirements, the transformation of the teaching intelligent management platform from theory to practice has been achieved through the solution of key technologies such as distributed storage of resource data, unified identity authentication between different modules, data exchange technology between different levels, hot backup of data security mechanisms, and interface reservation for system expansion. From the perspective of early practical operation and operation process, this platform has achieved automatic and dynamic management of teaching sites in a group mode, achieving the management goal of integrating education groups.

References

1. Zhong, L.: Design and Realization of Interactive Learning System for Art Teaching in Preschool Education of Artificial Intelligence Equipment. Springer, Cham (2021)
2. Fan, X.: Design and realization of distance intelligent learning system based on bayesian network training (2021)
3. Smirnov, E., Dvoryatkina, S., Shcherbatykh, S.: Technological stages of Schwartz cylinder's computer and mathematics design using intelligent system support[J]. Advanced Science (1) (2021)
4. Guanghong, S., Hu, Z.T., Li, Z.L.: Design and realization of intelligent vehicle based on embedded system. J. Phys. Conf. Ser. 1754(1), 012080 (2021). 4 pp.
5. Wang, H., Zheng, X., Zhang, C., et al.: Design and study of could platform based sampling control and management system. Asian Agric. Res. 13, 54–75 (2021)

6. Hu, Y.S., Zhao, C., Yang, Y., et al.: Using high-entropy configuration strategy to design Na-Ion layered oxide cathodes with superior electrochemical performance and thermal stability. J. Am. Chem. Soc. **144**(18), 8286–8295 (2022)
7. Zhang, X., Xing, J., Liu, P., et al.: Realization of full and directional band gap design by non-gradient topology optimization in acoustic metamaterials. Extreme Mech. Lett. **42**, 101126 (2021)
8. Liu, M., Feng, M.: Design and realization of a network platform for cultivating professional information literacy of design college students (2021)
9. Lu, Z.: Design and realization of basketball tactics computer aided teaching system (2022)
10. Zhang, T., Li, S., Su, Y., et al.: Design and realization of general platform for computer game (2022)
11. Shicong, P., Guocheng, W., Fuqiang, T.: Design and realization of CNC machine tool management system using Internet of things. Soft. Comput. **26**(20), 10729–10739 (2022)
12. Fan, L.: Teaching design and information realization of online and offline hybrid first class calculus courses (2021)
13. Fu, R.: Design and research of network computer room management platform in smart campus environment. In: Jan, M.A., Khan, F. (eds.) BigIoT-EDU 2021. LNICSSITE, vol. 392, pp. 633–642. Springer, Cham (2021). https://doi.org/10.1007/978-3-030-87903-7_76
14. Li, Y.: Design and implementation of an intelligent education management platform based on face recognition. In: International Conference on Multi-modal Information Analytics. Springer, Cham (2022). https://doi.org/10.1007/978-3-031-05484-6_79
15. Dai, L., Wang, W., Zhou, Y.: Design and research of intelligent educational administration management system based on mobile edge computing internet. Mobile Inf. Syst. (2021)

Optimal Allocation of Higher Education Resources Based on Fuzzy Particle Swarm Optimization Algorithm

Gao Ying[⊠] and Yunxia Fu

Wuhan Business School, Hubei Province, Wuhan City 430000, China
768710738@qq.com

Abstract. Optimizing the allocation of higher education resources is a complex issue that requires consideration of various factors, such as the number of teachers, curriculum arrangements, classroom utilization, and so on. In order to solve this problem, an optimization method based on fuzzy particle swarm optimization can be used. Fuzzy particle swarm optimization is an optimization algorithm based on swarm intelligence. It combines the advantages of fuzzy logic and particle swarm optimization algorithm, and can effectively deal with complex and changeable problems. In the optimal allocation of higher education resources, fuzzy particle swarm optimization can be used to search for the optimal resource allocation scheme. Specifically, the fuzzy particle swarm optimization first needs to establish appropriate optimization models based on a variety of factors, such as determining objective functions and constraints, and fuzzing these models. Next, using the idea of particle swarm optimization, multiple resource allocation schemes are randomly generated from the initial state, and the particle positions are gradually optimized to achieve the optimal solution. In the process of updating individual positions, fuzzy logic can help algorithms better handle uncertainty, adjust plans more finely, and make the final optimization results more in line with practical needs.

Keyword: Educational resources · Fuzzy particle swarm · Optimize configuration

1 Introduction

The total amount of higher education resources in China is insufficient, and it is not easy for impoverished countries to expand education. However, this is not the only dilemma faced by Chinese education. On the one hand, colleges and universities are converging at the middle and low levels of school running levels and directions, blindly following the trend in various professional settings and lagging behind the market demand. Under the premise of unreasonable training methods and curriculum settings, the enrollment scale is rapidly expanding, leading to the mismatch between college talent output and social employment positions, leading to structural unemployment of college students. In other words, the misaligned investment in higher education resources prevents the truly

© ICST Institute for Computer Sciences, Social Informatics and Telecommunications Engineering 2024
Published by Springer Nature Switzerland AG 2024. All Rights Reserved
Y. Zhang and N. Shah (Eds.): BigIoT-EDU 2023, LNICST 581, pp. 48–59, 2024.
https://doi.org/10.1007/978-3-031-63133-7_5

urgently needed disciplines and majors from receiving sufficient resource protection, exacerbating the structural shortage of educational resources [1]. On the other hand, the widespread waste of university education resources is truly heartbreaking. For example, universities in China are generally overcrowded, and the proportion of part-time teachers is too large, resulting in a waste of human resources. Most high-end and expensive research equipment is idle or has low utilization rates, resulting in material resource waste. Some researchers only apply for funding for projects that have not produced actual research results, resulting in a waste of financial resources [2]. The shortage and waste of educational resources have become a contradictory educational reality. Therefore, in the context of insufficient total educational resources, improving the rationality of China's higher education resource allocation and the efficiency of resource utilization is a material prerequisite for achieving the connotative development of universities.

At present, scholars at home and abroad have done a lot of research on the allocation of higher education resources, mainly using linear programming, Integer programming, network flow model and other optimization methods. Although these methods have to some extent solved the optimization problem of higher education resources, they are limited by factors such as computer power and model complexity, and have significant limitations in practical applications [3].

With the rapid development of computer technology, intelligent algorithms are receiving increasing attention and are widely used in various fields. Among them, particle swarm optimization algorithm, as a common swarm intelligence algorithm, is widely used in fields such as function optimization and data mining. As an effective method to deal with uncertainty, fuzzy logic is used to deal with various fuzzy problems, which has good robustness and robustness.

Based on the current situation of optimal resources, the factors that affect the efficiency of resource allocation were analyzed, and strategies and related systems for optimizing algorithms were proposed. Its purpose is to serve the economy and meet the needs of the people as the principle, promote the maximum running of higher education, reduce the waste of educational resources, serve education, and form a characteristic higher education system that adapts to economic development.

In the optimal allocation of higher education resources, the method based on fuzzy particle swarm optimization can effectively solve the problem of resource allocation and achieve good results [4]. This method can adapt to changes in demand in various scenarios, take into account various factors (such as class size, classroom usage efficiency, course weeks, etc.), and flexibly adjust resource allocation plans to achieve optimal results.

In short, the optimization and allocation of higher education resources is a complex problem that requires multiple perspectives and the adoption of new optimization methods to solve. The method based on fuzzy particle swarm optimization can not only deal with uncertain factors better, but also has intelligent optimization ideas, which can deal with the complexity of practical problems.

2 Related Work

2.1 Allocation of Educational Resources

All resource allocation methods realized through planning or administrative means become planned resource allocation methods, including the macro allocation of educational resources among all levels of education or regions and the micro allocation of educational resources within schools or regions. Its remarkable feature is that in terms of the distribution of educational decision-making power, the higher authorities are highly centralized, and the local departments and operating entities are only executive agencies; In terms of educational operation mechanism or information structure, the regulatory role of the market mechanism is replaced by mandatory plans or direct administrative control, so that the supply and demand information of education is not transmitted horizontally through the market mechanism, but vertically through administrative channels; In terms of dynamic mechanism, as the decision-making power is in the hands of the superior competent department, the school simply implements the administrative indicators issued by the superior, and the development of the school simply depends on the promotion of educational resources from external forces [5]. The advantage of the planned allocation method is that it can confirm the proportion of education funds in GDP according to the current situation of education development and the expected speed and scale of development, and formulate the education layout from a macro perspective, so as to allocate education resources in the overall situation, which is conducive to reducing the unbalanced development of education resource allocation between urban and rural areas and between regions [6]. The disadvantage is that this highly centralized way makes schools have no autonomy and can only be deployed by simple external forces, resulting in a lack of enthusiasm and initiative in optimizing the allocation of school resources.

Through price and competition mechanisms, educational resources can be allocated among different educational entities, which is the market resource allocation model. The prominent feature of this educational resource allocation model is that in terms of educational decision-making, it is not the issuance and implementation of top-down orders from educational administrative agencies, but rather made by dispersed micro educational entities pursuing profit maximization [7]; In terms of information structure, various social information is transmitted horizontally among decision-makers through market mechanisms, and each educational actor obtains supply and demand information through exchange, enabling different educational operators to respond sensitively to external information and make reasonable educational and economic decisions based on supply and demand relationships and competitive trends, as shown in Fig. 1. The advantage of the market allocation method is that the market connects different stakeholders in education, and through the planning and development of education, it reflects the degree of demand for education by families and society at different times [8].

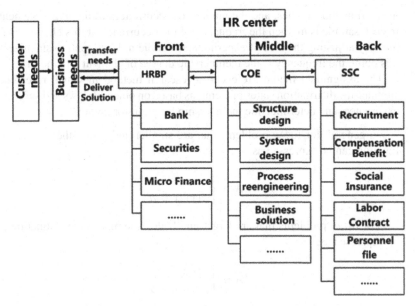

Fig. 1. Educational resource allocation mode

2.2 Fuzzy Mathematics Theory

In 1965, Zadeh proposed the concept of fuzzy sets. After more than half a century of development, domestic and foreign scholars have made significant achievements in this field of research. Fuzzy mathematics does not make mathematical problems vague, it is just as organized and clear as traditional mathematics. In the process of social production practice, many things have a certain degree of ambiguity, such as simple definitions of large, small, high, low, good, bad, fast, slow, etc., which are difficult to express using traditional mathematics. In this case, it is necessary to use fuzzy mathematical knowledge to solve [9].

1) The basic concept of fuzzy sets can be expressed as follows: for a certain domain U, mapping μ A: U → [0, 1], x x | () → ∈μ A [0, 1] can determine a fuzzy subset A within the domain U, μ A represents the membership function of A, μ A() x represents the degree of membership of the primitive x to the fuzzy subset A.

2) The properties and determination methods of membership degree

   (1) Principle of maximum subordination

   The principle of maximum membership means that there are m schemes in the domain U, and for any x ∈U, when there is i=(1,2,..., m), there is 1 () () m i k A x A x == ∈, then x is relatively subordinate to Ai.

   (2) Method for determining membership degree

   The methods for determining the degree of membership include fuzzy statistics, assignment, binary comparative ranking, and so on.

   ① Fuzzy statistical method refers to the method of determining membership degree through statistical experiments. Assuming a statistical experiment obtains n experimental samples, and the number of occurrences of the target element x in each sample is m, then the frequency of the occurrence of this element is $f = m/n$. By adjusting the size of experimental sample n, f will tend to stabilize. At this point, the frequency is the membership degree of element x to the fuzzy set. ② The assignment method refers to a research method in which researchers simulate the distribution status of elements based on objective laws and subjective experience, and determine the membership function for them.

In general, for fuzzy problems that are smaller and better, the membership function can be expressed as:

$$A = \begin{cases} 1, x \leq a \\ f(x), x > a \end{cases} \tag{1}$$

For fuzzy problems that are larger and better, the membership function can be expressed as:

$$A = \begin{cases} 0, x \leq a \\ f(x), x > a \end{cases} \tag{2}$$

3) The binary comparison method is to compare the elements within the research object in pairs, quantify the comparison results, and use fuzzy mathematical methods to rank them.

Assuming that there are n elements in the universe U, determine a fuzzy set A in the universe. Compare element x_i with element x_j, record the comparison result as r_{ij}, and $r_{ii} = 0, 0 \text{ Å } r_{ij} \text{ Å } 1, r_{ij} + r_{ji} = 1$. Construct all r_{ij} obtained through comparison as an n-order matrix R, where $R = (r_{ij}) n \times N$.

After determining the matrix R, methods such as minimum method, average method, and weighted average method can be used to determine the membership function and ultimately solve the membership degree.

4) Fuzzy Comprehensive Evaluation Method

Fuzzy comprehensive evaluation is a fuzzy mathematical method that can comprehensively consider various influencing factors and make a comprehensive evaluation of things. The evaluation results can objectively display the comprehensive impact of each factor on things in the form of fuzzy sets, which is very helpful for the research of multi-objective decision-making problems. To solve problems using the fuzzy comprehensive evaluation method, the first step is to establish a fuzzy comprehensive evaluation model [10]. The following is a brief introduction to its modeling method.

(1) Establish a set of n evaluation factors $U = \{u1, u2,..., un\}$, where ui represents the i-th evaluation factor.

(2) Establish a set of m evaluation value levels $V = \{v1, v2,..., vm\}$, where vj represents the jth evaluation level.

(3) Determine the membership degree of each evaluation factor ui to the evaluation value level vj.

For indicators that are larger and better, their membership can be determined as follows:

Assuming the value of the i-th indicator is xi, if xi is greater than or equal to the originally set optimal level value, its membership degree to that level can be recorded as 1, and its membership degree to other levels is 0. If xi is less than or equal to the originally set worst level value, its membership degree to that level can be recorded as 1, and its membership degree to other levels is 0. If the corresponding value of xi is between level j and level j + 1, its membership degree to these two levels can be expressed as follows:

$$r_{ij} = 1 - r_{i(j+1)} \qquad (3)$$

$$r_{i(j+1)} = \frac{V_{ij} - x_{ij}}{V_{ij} - V_{i(j+1)}} \qquad (4)$$

Similarly, for indicators that are smaller and better, their membership can be determined as follows:

Assuming the value of the i-th indicator is xi, if xi is less than or equal to the originally set optimal level value, its membership degree to that level can be recorded as 1, and its membership degree to other levels is 0. If xi is greater than or equal to the originally set worst level value, its membership degree to that level can be recorded as 1, and its membership degree to other levels is 0. If the corresponding value of xi is between level j and level j + 1, its membership degree to these two levels is represented as follows:

$$r_{ij} = 1 - r_{i(j+1)} \qquad (5)$$

$$r_{i(j+1)} = \frac{x_{ij} - V_{ij}}{V_{i(j+1)} - V_{ij}} \qquad (6)$$

According to the above method, a judgment matrix R with n rows and m columns can be constructed.

(4) Determine the weight w corresponding to each evaluation factor.
(5) Calculate and provide evaluation results for the research object based on the evaluation matrix and weight expansion.

2.3 Particle Swarm Optimization

Particle swarm optimization is a population intelligence algorithm, which is simple to understand, easy to implement, high efficiency of parallel computing, and is widely used in function optimization, genetic algorithms, neural networks and other fields. This algorithm is different from other optimization algorithms in that it simulates group behavior and follows the principle of "cooperative competition". It can search for the optimal solution in multiple solution spaces, and is particularly suitable for solving nonlinear, non convex, and non continuous optimization problems.

The main idea of particle swarm optimization algorithm is to treat each individual as a particle and set a certain population size to simulate the flight trajectory of particles for global search. During the search process, particles continuously adjust their position and speed based on their own and the global optimal solution, in order to find the optimal solution. At the same time, through information exchange (i.e. particle speed control vector), the group cooperates and competes to find the optimal solution. According to the above definition, the optimization algorithm is:

$$v_{\overline{v}}^{(t+1)} = v_{\overline{v}}^{(t)} + c_1 r_1 (p_{\overline{v}}^{(t)} - x_{\overline{v}}^{(t)}) + c_2 r_{\overline{v}} (p_{\overline{v}}^{(t)} - x_{\overline{v}}^{(t)}) \qquad (7)$$

$$x_{ij}^{(t+1)} = x_{ij}^{(t)} + v_{ij}^{(t+1)} \qquad (8)$$

where: subscript i, j represents the jth the current evolution to the t generation, c, and constants, typically values between 0 and 2, and r ~ U (0,1), r, and ~ U (O, 1) are two mutually independent random functions. In addition, v, usually limited to a certain range, that is, v, e [−. Max '. ma.], and position xj can also be limited to [− xmx.. M.], then vm. ax = k · xmax, 0.1 ≤ k < 1.0 can be set. From Eq. (1),. The first part of the equation is the previous speed of the particles, and the second part is the "cognitive" part, which only considers the experience of the particles themselves and the particles themselves. The represents social information sharing between particles.

The flow swarm optimization is shown in Fig. 2.

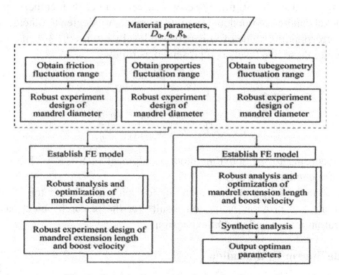

Fig. 2. Particle Swarm Optimization Process

In general, particle swarm optimization is an optimization algorithm. It is based on the optimal solution of the problem. Through the mutual adjustment and information exchange between particle swarm, it constantly carries out optimization search, and finds the global optimal solution in multiple solution spaces. It has better optimization results and efficient computing performance.

3 Optimal Allocation of Higher Education Resources Based on Fuzzy Particle Swarm Optimization Algorithm

3.1 Basic Principles of Optimal Allocation of Educational Resources

(1) Principle giving consideration to efficiency

A value choice in resource allocation As a decision-maker, it is necessary to consider. Due to the difference between the regional traditional development level and the current economic situation, resource allocation is reflected between developed regions and developing regions, cities and villages, and schools The differences in education will lead to unequal distribution of educational opportunities for the educated groups. School planning and design must follow the principle of fairness and priority, which is closely related to the original purpose of education and educational values. At the same time, we must also see that, under the guidance of the concept of market economy and regional overall development, giving consideration to efficiency is also an inevitable factor for us as educators. Therefore, the educational system implemented in the region must conform to the main trend of regional economic development, so that our limited educational resources can be used scientifically and reasonably.

(2) The principle of mutual promotion and overall planning

Mutual promotion and overall planning of the distribution of educational resources do not mean that the educational resources in the region are evenly distributed, but that the distribution of educational resources in the region is rationalized. The optimized layout of schools is not to restrict the progress and development of excellent schools, but to make use of the reasonable allocation and distribution of superior resources to make vulnerable schools develop and advance rapidly under the drive of superior schools, so as to the overall education. The permanent theme of everything, and education is no exception. In view of the current problem of educational resource allocation in some regions, especially the uneven distribution of educational resources, regional differences and urban-rural differences, we need to integrate school planning, resource allocation and other stages, so as to promote the effective and efficient use of regional educational resources, and ultimately achieve our goal of overall development of regional education level.

(3) The principle of advanced prediction and sustainable development

The development planning of anything requires the designer to have a certain foresight, just like the designers of urban planning, they should leave room for the development space of the city in the next few decades at a relatively advanced height. This kind of foresight design is not only a summary of the existing development, but also an appropriate reasoning and outlook in line with the objective laws. The development of education is just like the urban construction. Any education development plan should be made according to the future population distribution, social needs, education development trend and other factors. As far as China is concerned, basic education is undergoing a transformation from tradition to modernity, and we should be able to predict that the future trend of development be comprehensive and scientific quality education. Therefore, in the pace of the times, our educational resource allocation must also adhere to the principle of sustainable development.

3.2 Optimized Allocation of Higher Education Resources

In essence, the allocation of resources can an of multi-objective programming, and its be expressed as:

$$\max\{Z_1f_1(x), Z_2f_2(x), ..., Z_nf_n(x)\} \tag{9}$$

In the standard updating equation, each particle in the particle swarm two extrema: namely pbest; The second is the best location that the group has found, namely gbest. When the get the local optimal solution, the particle swarm can no longer re search in the solution space, and other particles will quickly approach the local optimal solution, which makes the algorithm prone to premature convergence, resulting in the inability to get the optimal solution.

To solve the above problems, in the early stage of the iteration algorithm (when the iteration counter NC is small), each particle swarm optimization, so the particle speed after each iteration update should not be too high at this time; With the particle speed is gradually increased: at the end of the iteration times of particle swarm, the particle speed V is significantly increased, and the change of particle speed V will also affect the search direction of particles, which can make the algorithm easier to jump out, so as to obtain a better solution. In addition, the also uses the quality value obtained by each particle each time, combined with the size of NC, to comprehensively obtain the size of the interference factor, rather than determining the interference factor each time only according to the size of the number of iterations.

To facilitate the calculation, the membership functions of the two fuzzy input variables are isosceles triangles, the membership functions of the output variables are bar shaped single value functions, and the number of fuzzy languages is set to 5, that is, the fuzzy input output space is divided into 5 fuzzy sets on average, as shown in Fig. 3.

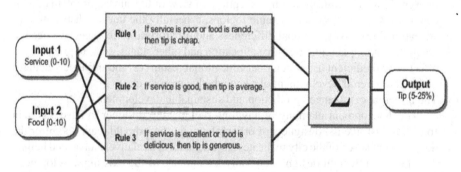

Fig. 3. Process of optimizing allocation of higher education resources

Therefore, methods cannot better explain the differences values and limit observations, Considering that the DEA efficiency data value is truncated and the efficiency value is discrete, in order to avoid the bias caused by using ordinary linear regression analysis that follows the least square method, the Tobit model with maximum likelihood estimation is selected to deeply explore the efficiency of regional higher education.

Firstly, the efficiency values of each decision-making unit in a region obtained using the DEA method are used as dependent variables, and various environmental factors are selected as independent variables to construct a regression model to explore the efficiency of regional higher education. Tobit is used to factors, and the following model is established:

$$Y_{it} = \beta_i + \alpha_i X_{it} + E_{it} \tag{10}$$

We need to accelerate the in-depth advancement of the development strategy and promote the transformation of new and old driving forces. The region closely follows the development pace of the 5G era and blockchain, especially with the digital economy as the guide, and timely introduces and promotes the application of new generation information technology represented by big data to the regional industrial upgrading and development. In the face of the serious situation of the regional population with fewer children and aging, vigorously develop service-oriented industries related to the elderly; Make good use of the unique northern scenery and forest resources to accelerate the development of tourism and form a brand effect in tourism service industry. In addition, in combination with the development of emerging industries and disciplines at home and abroad, rationally adjust the type structure and professional discipline structure of higher education institutions in various provinces in the region, deepen industry-university-research cooperation, guide and expand regional industrial upgrading, promote a number of local universities to accelerate transformation and development, leverage the convergence of industry-teaching-research and scientific and technological collaborative innovation, and promote technological innovation, technology promotion, and transfer efficiency in higher education, To improve the overall efficiency of higher education allocation and promote the of regional.

4   Simulation Results and Analysis

The scarcity of higher education resources means that the resources allocated to higher education are difficult to meet. It is a relative concept that reflects, and the degree of scarcity is determined jointly by both supply and demand. Whether starting from the demand for higher education from personal development or social development, it is a fact that the intensity of demand for higher education has increased. Under the current system, the growth rate of higher education resources provided by national financial investment cannot catch up with the growth of demand. The contradiction resources will further expand, in other words, the scarcity in China will increase.

The phenomenon that goes hand in hand with the scarcity of resources is the waste of resources, especially in public universities. Due to the fact that the funds for public universities are provided by the state, and the funding method of "comprehensive quota plus special subsidies" is adopted, which lacks a rigorous efficiency evaluation mechanism. Therefore, many schools strive to apply for special subsidies in order to obtain more funding for running schools and blindly expand enrollment. Therefore, wasteful phenomena such as overstaffing, corruption, misappropriation of educational funds, and excessive hardware construction are common in public colleges and universities. These schools do not have to be responsible for their own profits and losses, and therefore do not have a sense of conservation.

On the shortage resources is becoming increasingly serious, and on the other hand, there is no way to stop the waste of higher education resources. This is a strange pair of contradictions. It is worth pondering that the two have different diseases and the same causes, resulting from the alloca. In order to resolve this contradiction, it is necessary to expand educational investment and save resources simultaneously, and the expansion of educational resources cannot be entirely realized by the government. Therefore, implementing market allocation of higher education resources and encouraging multiple channels of educational investment is an ideal way to solve. At the same time, the market can improve the efficiency of educational resources, because in the market mechanism, resources always automatically flow to more efficient departments. In addition, under the market mechanism, universities operate independently and are responsible for their own profits and losses. They have to find ways to save costs, and the idle and waste of educational resources can also be solved.

As shown in Fig. 4, we solved the resources in five cities.

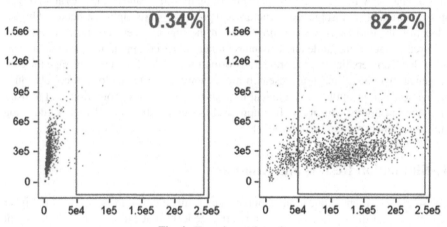

Fig. 4. Experimental result

5 Conclusion

The optimal allocation of higher education resources based on fuzzy particle swarm optimization is an optimization scheme using fuzzy particle swarm optimization algorithm. This scheme mainly utilizes the processing power of fuzzy logic, combined with the search idea of particle swarm optimization algorithm, to iteratively find the optimal solution and obtain the optimal allocation plan of higher education resources. This plan considers various factors (such as the number of teachers, course arrangement, classroom utilization, etc.) and adjusts the optimization model through multiple iterations to achieve the search for the best solution. It should be noted that this solution also has some challenges and limitations. At the same time, the right to choose a solution should also consider the actual scenario requirements and adopt different optimization schemes under different needs. In short, the optimization allocation of higher education resources based on fuzzy particle swarm optimization algorithm is a new optimization idea and method, which has high practical value and provides new ideas and methods for better promoting the allocation of higher education resources.

Acknowledgements. College students' legal awareness from the perspective of financial media Implementation path research of the promotion of the Wushang institute [2020] No.27 + 2020KY019.

References

1. Wei, J., Li, L.: Optimal allocation of human resources recommendation based on improved particle swarm optimization algorithm. Math. Prob. Eng. **2022** (2022)
2. Liu, X.M., Zhao, M., Wei, Z.H., et al.: Economic optimal allocation of photovoltaic energy storage system based on quantum particle swarm optimization algorithm (2022)
3. Awad, A., Abdel-Mawgoud, H., Kamel, S., et al.: Developing a hybrid optimization algorithm for power loss minimization of distribution system based on optimal allocation of renewable DGs. Clean Technol. **3**, 409–423 (2021)
4. Li, Y., Sun, X., Liu, X., et al.: Deployment of on-orbit service vehicles using a fuzzy adaptive particle swarm optimization algorithm. Model. Simul. Eng. (2021)
5. Nguyen, M.H., Pham, X.P.: Completing the proportional navigation rule with optimizational association funtion based on particle swarm optimization rule. J. Phys. Conf. Ser. **1889**(2), 022081 (2021). 10 pp.
6. Chiu, C.C., Lin, J.T.: An efficient elite-based simulation–optimization approach for stochastic resource allocation problems in manufacturing and service systems. Asia Pac. J. Oper. Res. (2021)
7. Rani, P., Mahapatra, G.S.: Entropy based enhanced particle swarm optimization on multi-objective software reliability modelling for optimal testing resources allocation. Softw. Testing Verification Reliab. **31**(6), e1765 (2021)
8. Deng, Z., Yu, X., Lin, W., et al.: A multi-beam satellite cooperative transmission scheme based on resources optimization and packets segmentation. Electronics **10**, 2841 (2021)
9. Zhang, P., Wang, C., Qin, Z., et al.: A multi-domain VNE algorithm based on multi-objective optimization for IoD architecture in Industry 4.0. (2022)
10. Austine, A., Pramila, R.S.: Hybrid optimization algorithm for resource allocation in LTE-based D2D communication. Tech Science Press (2023)

The Improvement Index of College Students' Innovation and Entrepreneurship Ability Based on Crawler Algorithm

Shi Jian[1,2]([✉]), Li Lu[1,2], and Yufang Huang[1,2]

[1] Xi'an Fanyi University, Xi'an 710105, Shaanxi, China
akjs2580@163.com
[2] Department of Preschool Education, Xi'an Fanyi University, Xi'an 710000, China

Abstract. The cultivation of College Students' innovation and entrepreneurship ability is a problem that cannot be ignored in the new era. The research on the structure of College Students' innovation and entrepreneurship ability is very important for ability training, which meets the needs of national economic development, the reform and development of innovation and entrepreneurship education, and the theoretical and practical innovation of Ideological and political education. The intelligent evaluation of English teaching effect based on fuzzy inference algorithm is an intelligent evaluation of English teaching effect based on fuzzy inference algorithm. The main purpose of this study is to propose a new intelligent evaluation tool to evaluate the effectiveness of English teachers in improving students' oral and reading abilities. As an auxiliary tool, the intelligent evaluator will use two traditional methods to evaluate the effectiveness of English teachers in improving students' oral and reading abilities, namely: 1) student teacher evaluation; 2) Peer review.

Keyword: Crawler algorithm · College Students' innovation and entrepreneurship · Capability improvement index

1 Introduction

In the past 30 years, ideological and political education has developed rapidly and accumulated rich research results. As a relatively young research direction, innovation and entrepreneurship education still needs to be explored continuously, and there is still a lot of research space. In the report of the 19th National Congress of the Communist Party of China, it is proposed to "widely carry out ideal and belief education, deepen the publicity and education of socialism with Chinese characteristics and the Chinese dream, carry forward the national spirit and the spirit of the times, strengthen the education of patriotism, collectivism and socialism, and guide people to establish a correct outlook on history, life, country and culture" [1]. It can be said that this is one of the tasks of education in the new era and one of the important tasks of Ideological and political education, In order to complete the above tasks, we must continue to study the basic theory, specific

Y. Zhang and N. Shah (Eds.): BigIoT-EDU 2023, LNICST 581, pp. 60–70, 2024.
https://doi.org/10.1007/978-3-031-63133-7_6

methods, practical paths and so on of Ideological and political education. Ideological and political education pays attention to the combination of theory and practice, and the innovation of theory and practice promotes the continuous development of Ideological and political education [2].

As the core of vertical search engines, topic crawlers are mainly responsible for collecting information on the Internet. Topic crawlers purposefully capture data with a specific theme from the network through specific crawling strategies. First, determine the URL of the initial topic page, obtain web page data through different link methods and targeted search strategies, and then analyze the links of different web pages and calculate topic relevance [3]. Discard data information that is not related to the topic content, and retain highly relevant content. Based on this approach, the web crawler operates efficiently and accurately, and can search for the data that users really need without the need for users to filter information again. In addition, since topic web crawlers only crawl highly relevant pages, the content obtained will be much less than that of general crawlers, so the corresponding repository of web pages can be updated instantly. This ensures the real-time nature of the data required by users, which is a major advantage of topic crawlers [4].

The research on College Students' innovation and entrepreneurship ability is not only an important part of innovation and entrepreneurship education, but also an important content of Ideological and political education theory and practice research. The research on the concept and structure of College Students' innovation and entrepreneurship ability meets the needs of Ideological and political education theory and practice innovation [5]. On the one hand, the organic integration of innovation and entrepreneurship education and ideological and political education is the internal demand of the development of innovation and entrepreneurship education, which meets the practical needs of the reform and innovation of Ideological and political education in Colleges and universities, and is also one of the effective ways to comprehensively improve the comprehensive quality of college students [6]. On the other hand, improving college students' innovation and entrepreneurship ability, accurately grasping the current situation of ability, effectively evaluating the level of College Students' innovation and entrepreneurship ability, and putting forward practical strategies for cultivating college students' innovation and entrepreneurship ability are the practical requirements of Ideological and political education practice and innovation [7]. Based on this, the research on the innovation and entrepreneurship ability of college students is not only the demand of theoretical and practical innovation of Ideological and political education, but also helps the discipline development of Ideological and political education.

To sum up, the cultivation of College Students' innovation and entrepreneurship ability is an issue that cannot be ignored in today's era [8]. Studying the innovation and entrepreneurship ability of college students meets the needs of national economic development, the reform and development of innovation and entrepreneurship education, and the theoretical and practical innovation of Ideological and political education.

2 Related Work

2.1 Capability Structure Theory

Ability structure theory is a classic theory in psychological research, which mainly includes the following five theories. The first is the theory of factor composition: the author of the independent factor theory is psychologist thomdike. He believes that human ability is composed of a variety of independent components or factors, which develop independently and have nothing to do with each other. Later, people found that there was correlation between various factors, and it was obviously wrong to be independent of each other [9]. Spearman, an American psychologist and statistician, proposed the theory of two factors. He believes that ability has two components, general factor (g for short) and special factor (s for short). G is people's basic psychological energy and plays a major role in determining people's ability. S is a special factor, which is necessary for people to complete specific activities and tasks. Completing any homework is determined by G and s [10]. The group factor theory was put forward by Seton. He believes that most abilities can be composed of seven original factors, including numerical calculation, spatial relationship, associative memory, speech understanding, speech fluency, perceptual speed, and general reasoning. All factors are independent of each other.

The second is the three-dimensional structure theory of ability: this theory was put forward by American psychologist Guilford. He believes that intelligence can be divided into three dimensions: content, operation and product. At first, there were four factors in the content dimension, including graphics, symbols, semantics and behavior. Later, the graphics were changed to vision and hearing, and became five, including hearing, vision, symbols, semantics and behavior; There are five factors in the operational dimension, including divergent thinking, convergent thinking, evaluation, cognition and memory [11]; There are six factors in the product dimension, including unit, category, relationship, system, transformation and implication. According to this model, human intelligence can be divided into five in theory $\times$ five $\times$ 6 = 150 kinds, as shown in Fig. 1. At present, nearly 100 abilities have been proved. This theory has important theoretical guiding significance for this study.

2.2 Crawler Algorithm

Crawler algorithm is an improved algorithm for link structure proposed by Kleinberg, which judges the importance of a webpage through the hyperlink relationship between pages. The operation of the HITS algorithm is based on the user's search needs, so the importance of each webpage also depends on the search topic. Currently, it is mainly used to sort the search results of the webpage. The crawler algorithm uses two evaluation indicators, content authority and hub, to measure the quality of a web page. It is based on the assumption that these two indicators are interdependent and circular [12]. Generally, if a web page has a high authority value, the web page is often pointed to by multiple pages with a high Hub value. Similarly, a page with a high Hub value often points to a page with a high Authority value, and the two reinforce each other. This is the basic idea of a crawler algorithm.

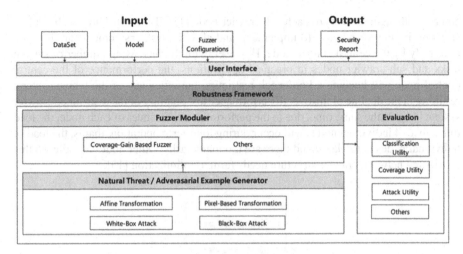

Fig. 1. Capability structure model

Initially, there is no more available information. Assuming that the Authority and Hub of each page are the same, they can be set to 1. Where a (i) represents the content authority of node i, and its iterative formula is shown in (1).

$$a_i(v) = \sum_{(w,v)\in E} h_{i-1}(w) \tag{1}$$

H (i) represents the central value of node i, and its iterative formula is shown in (2).

$$h_i(v) = \sum_{(v,w)\in E} a_{i-1}(w) \tag{2}$$

In order to ensure the invariance of the results, normalization processing is required after each iteration. After multiple rounds of iterative calculation, a (i) and h (i) gradually converge and tend to stable values. The normalization processing formula for a (i) is shown in (3).

$$a_i(v) = \frac{a_i(v)}{\sqrt{\sum_{q\in n}[a(q)]^2}} \tag{3}$$

The normalized processing formula for h (i) is shown in (4).

$$h_i(v) = \frac{h_i(v)}{\sqrt{\sum_{q\in n}[h(q)]^2}} \tag{4}$$

The current distributed web crawler structure is mainly divided into master-slave distribution, equality distribution and hybrid distribution.

As shown in Fig. 2, the master-slave distributed web crawler structure is composed of a central control node and several sub crawler nodes. Each sub crawler node is not directly connected, but is directly connected with the central control node. The central control node assigns tasks to each sub crawler node [13]. This distributed web crawler structure is simple and easy to implement, and all URL task assignments are handled uniformly by the central control node. However, with the increasing number of system tasks and sub crawler nodes in practical applications, the performance of the central control node will become a bottleneck restricting the efficiency of the whole system, resulting in the decline of the overall performance and stability of the distributed crawler system [14]. At the same time, due to the performance differences of each node, the load imbalance of individual nodes will occur during long-term operation, that is, the load of individual nodes is too large and there are too many tasks, Other nodes are idle, so this distributed network crawler structure needs further optimization [15].

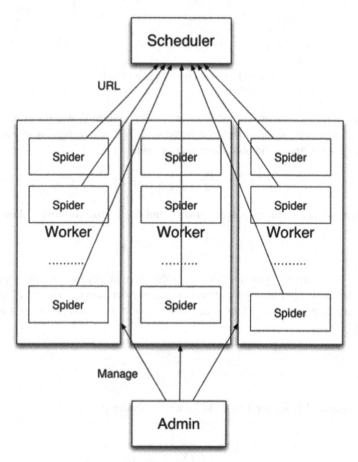

Fig. 2. Distributed web crawler architecture

3   Index for Improving Innovation and Entrepreneurship Ability of College Students Based on Crawler Algorithm

Innovation is the foundation of entrepreneurship, and entrepreneurship is the carrier of innovation. The rapid development and updating of science, technology, and ideas are constantly driving changes in people's material production and lifestyle. This update and development not only can provide people with new consumption needs, but also continuously promote the generation of entrepreneurial activities. Entrepreneurship is essentially an innovative practical activity of people. The practical activities carried out by the main body of any entrepreneurial activity are dynamic, innovative, and highly autonomous. Therefore, the innovation of the main body is the foundation of entrepreneurial activities. On the other hand, the value of innovation lies in the ability to transform potential technology, knowledge, or market opportunities into real productivity, thereby achieving social wealth growth and benefiting human society. However, commercialization and marketization of innovation achievements must be achieved through entrepreneurship, and the economic and social value of innovation achievements must also be reflected through entrepreneurship. Therefore, entrepreneurship is the carrier of innovation. Entrepreneurship can promote the continuous emergence of new inventions, new products, or new services, create new market demands, and further promote and deepen innovation in various aspects, thereby improving the innovation capacity of enterprises or the entire country, and promoting economic growth.

Structural Equation Modeling is an important method used by scholars in the fields of behavioral science and social science to conduct quantitative research. This analysis tool is one of multivariate statistics. It takes a number of issues that cannot be directly measured but that require in-depth research and discussion as potential variables, and introduces some directly observable indicators to reflect these potential variables, thereby establishing a relationship between potential variables, which is called structure. It is a confirmatory analysis method that draws a reasonable and scientific hypothesis model diagram based on relevant theoretical basis, and verifies the validity of theoretical assumptions by collecting data.

Many old pages on Web pages have the characteristic of being referenced multiple times even if their content is outdated due to their long existence. It can be assumed that the greater the difference between the time a Web page was queried and the time it was last modified, the lower the reference value of its page content. In addition, the number of comments on a webpage can also reflect the importance of a webpage. The value of references to content on old web pages decreases greatly over time, so the number of new comments from netizens will gradually decrease. The content of the new webpage keeps pace with the times, and if its reference value is high, the corresponding number of comments will also be large. Based on this assumption, the final defined weight function P (f) is obtained. First, define a function f (t, k) about the month difference and the number of valid comments, with the formula shown in (5).

$$f(t, k) = \begin{cases} t & m < 10 \\ \frac{t}{\log_k m} & m \geq 10, k > 0 \end{cases} \tag{5}$$

"The content is more reflective of the topic of the article, and the values in these tags should be given a higher weight.". However, the feature words of the article do not necessarily appear in all of the above positions. To avoid this situation, the average weighted method and the cumulative calculation method are used to calculate the weight value. See (6) for the weight calculation formula.

$$T_{wf}(k) = \frac{\sum_{i=1}^{n} m(i)}{\sum_{j=1}^{N} m(j)} \tag{6}$$

In structural equation model analysis software, LISREL and AMOS are commonly used. AMOS software is a family of SPSS software. Due to the high popularity of SPSS statistical software, more and more scholars use AMOS software for structural equation model analysis. AMOS is an abbreviation for Analysis of Moment Structures, also known as Moment Structure Analysis, and is an easy-to-use visualization module software. The AMOS17.0 software used later in this article is for structural equation model analysis, as shown in Fig. 3.

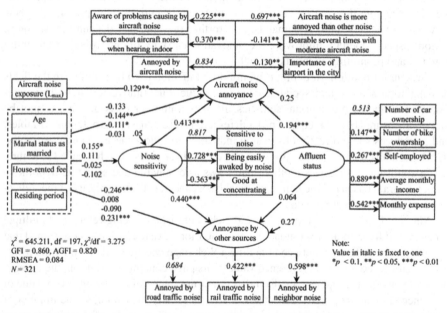

Fig. 3. Index Model for Improving Innovation and Entrepreneurship Ability of College Students

(1) The concept of potential variables was introduced into the model. In the field of behavioral social science, many research objects cannot be directly observed, and the use of measured variables and potential variables in structural equation models skillfully solves this problem. Researchers can indirectly measure the hypothetical constructs they want to study by measuring the direct relationship between variables and potential variables.

(2) Structural equation models allow independent variables to contain measurement errors. For many studies in the field of social science, many independent variables are latent variables that cannot be directly observed, so measurement errors can be introduced during observation. However, the result equation model incorporates this error into the model without strict error restrictions, which not only improves the goodness of fit of the model, but also takes into account the actual situation in real life more reasonably.

(3) It can handle multiple dependent variables simultaneously. In traditional econometric models, there is often only one dependent variable in the equation. If there are multiple dependent variables, when calculating the regression coefficient or path coefficient, each variable is calculated separately and then accumulated, thus ignoring the impact and existence of other dependent variables. However, there are usually multiple dependent variables in models in the field of social sciences. Using structural equation models, multiple variables can be processed and analyzed simultaneously during model fitting, and residual errors are considered, which makes the model more effective than traditional models.

(4) Structural equation models include many different statistical techniques. Structural equation models often involve the analysis of a large number of variables, so they incorporate traditional statistical methods such as variance analysis, regression analysis, factor analysis, and path analysis, making structural equation models reasonable for use in many fields.

This study involves the five dependent variables of entrepreneurial awareness, entrepreneurial motivation, innovative thinking, professional knowledge, and general knowledge, as well as the latent variable of innovation and entrepreneurship ability. All of these variables cannot be directly measured and are difficult to quantify, so they must be measured indirectly through certain observational variables. In view of the above advantages of structural equation model, this paper introduces this quantitative analysis method into the analysis of factors affecting college students' innovation and entrepreneurship ability, thereby explaining the interrelationship between multiple variables, and providing practical countermeasures and suggestions for college students' innovation and entrepreneurship education.

4 Results and Discussion

4.1 Experimental Analysis

The experimental part of this article starts with a comparative experiment on W-HITS search strategies. Using the W-HITS algorithm, the Authority value and the Hub value of the final page are iterated in order. When sorting Web pages, precision is first used as an evaluation indicator, which can better reflect the effect of improved topic crawlers. As for the evaluation indicator of recall, because there are a large number of pages on a certain topic on the network, but most users actually only pursue accuracy rather than coverage when searching, precision is preferred as a separate comparison and analysis. Secondly, the evaluation index of recall can be expressed by the number of pages related to the topic, provided that it is based on a certain accuracy. The more pages retrieved, the better the performance of the corresponding crawler. The experimental results are shown in Fig. 4.

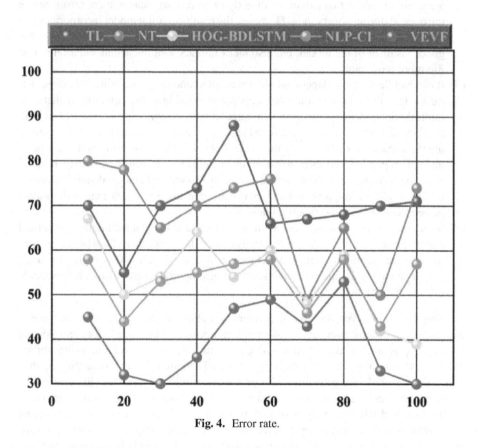

Fig. 4. Error rate.

In the process of students' innovation and entrepreneurship, the role of professional education and general education cannot be ignored. Only when these two subsystems reach the optimal state of their respective actions can they exert their respective functions. Professional education allows students to understand the development prospects of their major and find suitable entrepreneurial directions and business opportunities on the basis of solid professional knowledge. Therefore, schools should attach importance to professional education. Entrepreneurship is a complex process, and it is not enough for entrepreneurs to have only professional knowledge. This process also involves knowledge in management, strategy, finance, operations, marketing, and other aspects. General education can enable students to understand a broader range of general knowledge and systematically understand the basic skills of entrepreneurship. Therefore, schools should also attach importance to general education. It can be seen that professional education and general education are equally important, and schools should overcome the contradiction between these two subsystems and attach equal importance to keeping them both at their best, giving full play to their own functions, and laying the foundation for the improvement of college students' innovation and entrepreneurship abilities.

4.2 Improve the Innovation and Entrepreneurship Ability of College Students

(1) Establishing the Strategic Concept of Innovation and Entrepreneurship Education for College Students

Due to the limitations of setting long-term goals for higher education in China, most college students in China pay attention to knowledge transfer and neglect corresponding practical training in the training process. In the long run, students gradually lose their ability to innovate and cannot survive well in this society that requires innovation. Therefore, in view of this, we should first establish the concept of innovation and entrepreneurship education for college students. Whether it's government, school, or family, we should change our concepts and strive to cultivate students' innovative abilities. Actively guide students to take the civil service examination and the postgraduate entrance examination, and list entrepreneurship as the future employment method. This strategic concept of innovation and entrepreneurship education can ensure the sustainable development of social economy and provide a steady stream of talent support for China.

(2) Optimize the social support and security service system

To optimize the social security service system, first of all, it is necessary to increase the support of the government, so as to provide a complete organizational guarantee for the improvement of college students' innovation and entrepreneurship capabilities under the support of the government. The government will establish specialized management institutions for innovation and entrepreneurship education for college students at all levels, and gradually develop innovation and entrepreneurship education from top to bottom. Only in this way can we ensure that college students have organizational protection, financial protection, and appropriate cooperation platforms in innovation and entrepreneurship; Only this kind of innovation and entrepreneurship education and training, including both action training and concept deepening, can achieve the purpose of education and training, and improve the overall teaching effect. Secondly, the promotion of innovation and entrepreneurship requires increased social support, including corporate support, bank support, and family support. Only when these three parties interact in real time, strengthen cooperation, enterprises provide corresponding capital investment, banks provide corresponding loan support according to national policies, families change their attitudes, and support their children's entrepreneurship can they successfully promote college students to enter the ranks of innovation and entrepreneurship.

5 Conclusion

With the continuous development of China's social economy, the employment of college graduates has become a key concern of the society. Advocating the cultivation and improvement of College Students' innovation and entrepreneurship ability in the whole society is an important educational concept to promote social development and the improvement of College Students' own quality. Cultivating college students with innovation and entrepreneurship awareness, innovation and entrepreneurship spirit and ability is the demand of the times, It is also one of the ways for college students to obtain employment in the future.

References

1. Zhang, X.R.: Research on the quality evaluation of college students' innovation and entrepreneurship education based on ant colony algorithm (2023)
2. Zhou, Q.: Research on the problems and countermeasures of the cultivation of adult college students' innovation and entrepreneurship ability in the internet era. Open Access Libr. J. **08**(7), 1–12 (2021)
3. Hu, Q.: RETRACTED: research on the cultivation strategy of college students' innovation and entrepreneurship based on big data analysis from the perspective of economic transformation. J. Phys. Conf. Ser. **1915**(3), 032083 (2021). (5 pp.)
4. Liang, G., Alghazzawi, D., Joseph, N.R.: The evaluation of college students' innovation and entrepreneurship ability based on nonlinear model (2021)
5. Zhou, Y., Zhou, H.: Research on the quality evaluation of innovation and entrepreneurship education of college students based on extenics - ScienceDirect. Procedia Comput. Sci. **199**, 605–612 (2022)
6. Gao, J., Guo, Z., Xiao, Y.: Research on cultivation of innovation and entrepreneurship ability of applied talents under the concept of "New Engineering" (2021)
7. Wu, B., Ye, S., Yang, Z.: The influencing factors of innovation and entrepreneurship intention of college students based on AHP. Math. Prob. Eng. **2022** (2022)
8. Wu, W.: Research on the integration path of ideological and political education and innovation and entrepreneurship education of college students. Clausius Scientific Press (1) (2021)
9. Ancillo, A.D.L., Gavrila, S.G., Woodside, A.G.: The impact of research and development on entrepreneurship, innovation, digitization and digital transformation (2023)
10. Lu, Y.: Research and analysis on the improvement of teaching ability of young teachers in colleges and universities. J. High. Educ. Res. **2**(6) (2021)
11. Zhong, L.: Research on the practice information system of university students' innovation and entrepreneurship based on the new computer technology support. J. Phys. Conf. Ser. **1744**(3), 032151 (2021). (7 pp.)
12. Deng, Y.: An empirical study on the cultivation of college students' core competence of innovation and entrepreneurship based on multidimensional dynamic innovation model under genetic algorithm (2022)
13. Xiaoying, F., Xiaoli, X.: Construction of a multi-dimensional dynamic college students' innovation and entrepreneurship platform based on school-enterprise cooperation. In: International Conference on Multi-modal Information Analytics. Springer, Cham, (2022). https://doi.org/10.1007/978-3-031-05484-6_134
14. Yuan, F., Hu, D.: Research on the application of big data technology in college students' innovation and entrepreneurship guidance service. J. Phys. Conf. Ser. **1883**(1), 012171 (2021)
15. Shi, Q., Nie, H.: Exploration on the cultivation path of students' innovation and entrepreneurship ability in higher vocational colleges in the new era (2021)

Application of Random Simulation Algorithm in Physical Education and Training

Xin-yi Zhang[1,2(✉)] and Ning Zhang[1,2]

[1] Shandong Management University, Jinan 250357, Shandong, China
zxy20201007@163.com
[2] Zaozhuang Vocational College of Science and Technology, Zaozhuang 277599, Shandong, China

Abstract. The traditional teaching mode of college physical education is basically based on "teaching", which can cultivate the knowledge training. However, when faced with tremendous pressures and challenges, college students often exhibit a lack of confidence, courage, and the initiative and consciousness to cooperate with others. In better and progress of society and the cultivation and demand of high-quality talents, there is an urgent need for a newer and more advanced form of physical education. The sports auxiliary training system consists of three parts: sports learning, motion collection, and motion evaluation. The learning module provides fractional content introduction and standard video guidance for sports; The action collection module collects sports standard data and establishes a standard sports action database as a comparison template for sports training; The motion evaluation module is divided into motion recognition and posture recognition. Motion recognition uses DTW algorithm to match corresponding frames for recognition, and posture recognition uses features such as angles and coordinates for posture matching. Both methods can provide scientific auxiliary training and motion guidance to the tester based on the feedback results. Based on the simulation and training, this article has important significance in improving the comprehensive quality of college students and of traditional and training models.

Keyword: Random simulation algorithm · Physical training · Application Discussion

1 Introduction

The increasing of the commodity and knowledge economy, social is becoming increasingly fierce, and everyone is facing enormous challenges brought about by the continuous updating of knowledge. In order to adapt to society, we must constantly improve our learning ability. In particular, as a new generation of gifted children, college students will face greater challenges and severe tests. In order to better adapt to the surrounding society, live a happy life, and work effectively with the surrounding teams and peers, we must learn to adapt, continuously enhance our social adaptability, and learn to understand, understand, tolerate, and appreciate [1]. When students are employed, these qualities

Y. Zhang and N. Shah (Eds.): BigIoT-EDU 2023, LNICST 581, pp. 71–81, 2024.
https://doi.org/10.1007/978-3-031-63133-7_7

are increasingly valued by employers. For the traditional mode of college training basically based on "teaching", which aims training. However, when faced with tremendous pressure and challenges, college students often still exhibit a lack of self-confidence, courage, and courage, as well as a lack of awareness and ability to cooperate with others [2]. This urgently requires the emergence of a new form of physical training.

The way of human-computer interaction belongs to a natural user interface. We can communicate with computers through multi touch and 3D virtual reality, emotional computing, multi-channel interaction, intelligent user interfaces, and other body sensing technologies to achieve user-friendly and more interesting human-computer interaction with a human core. At present, wearable intelligent devices and somatosensory devices in sports and fitness, medical and healthcare, industrial and military fields and trend. Microsoft, Google, and other are among the world's leading researchers in human-computer interaction, intelligent glasses, and interactive development tools [3]. In 2010, the representative product of human-computer interaction, the random simulation algorithm, was introduced, rapidly occupying the market with its unique features and interactive experience. At the same time, it provides official SDK and source code open source to attract the interest of many developers. This topic combines random simulation algorithms with sports assistance, taking 24 style sports as an example, and designs a sports assistance training system based on multiple random simulation algorithms [4]. The purpose is to make the sports training actions of the tester more intelligent, data-based, and visual, and to provide more standardized and reliable guidance and suggestions for the daily sports training of the tester.

With the development and progress of society, traditional educational models are constantly changing, and sports training is increasingly focusing on new areas such as "social adaptation" and "mental health". After 2003, as outward bound training entered, the research on outward bound training became more and more comprehensive, in-depth, and meticulous. Physical fitness training (also known as experiential learning) mainly utilizes the natural environment and effective resources, through carefully designed training programs, in order to exercise willpower, cultivate sentiment, enhance personality, and integrate into the team [5]. It is a new learning method for modern people and organizations. In fact, sports training is not a simple supplement to sports and entertainment, but a comprehensive refinement and supplement to traditional education. The training method based on random simulation algorithm breaks the traditional "teaching" based teaching and learning mode, enabling students to learn knowledge and understand truth through pleasant and active participation. And through personal experience, we can tap into our potential, cultivate innovative spirit and practical ability, and promote the formation of good characters such as courage, tenacity, self-confidence, and unity [6].

Currently, in the field of sports research, most scholars mainly study the origin, development, and impact of sports, but lack research on the teaching model and interactive experience of sports. Therefore, this article conducts research and learning on 24 style sports. Firstly, it collects the node data under two random simulation algorithms, and completes the calibration of the spatial coordinate system; Secondly, use relevant data fusion algorithms to achieve data unification and obtain the fused data; Finally, by collecting standard data of various sports moves, a sports standard action information database is established [7]. Match and compare the user's sports training action data with the standard and standard actions, and use the dynamic time warping algorithm to match the corresponding frames of the user and the standard actions. By comparing the differences in angle, coordinate point, time, and so on between the two, score in combination with the predetermined scoring rules. Finally, the interactive teaching on multiple random simulation algorithms is implemented [8]. In the popularization and inheritance of sports, and the innovative of other sports fields.

2 Stochastic Simulation Algorithm

2.1 Concept of Stochastic Process

Random simulation process is a computer simulation technology based on random number generator, which is used to simulate and analyze the uncertainty and randomness in the actual process. Its basic idea is to generate a series of pseudo-random numbers on the computer and use them to simulate various possibilities and development trends of the actual process by setting up random number generators and simulation algorithms, so as to better understand and analyze the possible results and make effective decisions and predictions. Random simulation processes can be widely applied in various fields, such as finance, physics, biology, social sciences, etc. Among them, finance is an important application field of stochastic simulation processes [9]. For example, in the fields of financial risk management and securities investment, stochastic simulation processes can simulate different market trends, analyze the risks and returns of investment portfolios, and compare and optimize them to achieve effective asset allocation and risk management. In fields such as physics and biology, stochastic simulation processes can also simulate the temporal evolution and spatial structure of systems, analyze and predict the possibilities and development trends of systems.

The random simulation process needs to use a random number generator to generate a pseudo-random number sequence, so as to achieve simulation. Common random number generators include linear congruence generators, Lagrange sequence methods, Monte Carlo methods, etc. The simulation algorithms mainly include Monte Carlo simulation, Random walk simulation, jump evolution simulation, random network simulation, etc. These simulation algorithms have different advantages and applicability, and can simulate different types of Stochastic process and actual systems.

Similarly, temperature, air pressure and daily customer flow of stores constitute a random process [10].

Next, we derive the general mathematical definition of random process through a specific process example. An electronic DC amplifier is provided, as shown in Fig. 1 below.

Through random simulation analysis, it will be found that the output zero drift is under the same conditions. Select a certain time every day for observation [11]. After n days, n output zero drift curves can be obtained, and these curves are drawn, as shown in Fig. 2 below.

Obviously, as shown in Fig. 2, in an experimental result, the random process must have a sample function, but which function is taken cannot be determined before the test, but in a large number of repeated experiments, we can know that the random process presents statistical regularity.

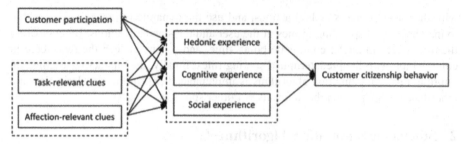

Fig. 1. Electronic DC amplifier

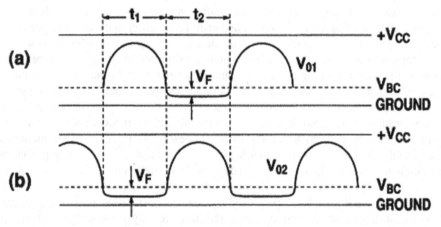

Fig. 2. Random process analysis results

2.2 Stochastic Simulation Algorithm (SSA)

Random simulation algorithm is a kind of computer simulation method based on random number generator, which is used to simulate and analyze the randomness and uncertainty in the actual process. It generates a series of random numbers on a computer by setting random number seeds and simulation algorithms, and uses them as samples or experimental data to simulate and analyze different possibilities and changes in actual processes. Random simulation algorithms are widely used in various fields, such as finance, physics, biology, social sciences, etc.

Currently, commonly used random simulation algorithms include the following:

(1) Monte Carlo simulation algorithm: This algorithm is a calculation method based on random sampling and has been widely used in fields such as finance, physics, and engineering. This method simulates the uncertainty and randomness of actual processes by generating random sampling samples for numerical analysis of complex problems.
(2) Random walk Simulation Algorithm: This algorithm is based on the idea of random walk and is usually applied to some complex systems such as physics and biology.

The Random walk simulation algorithm can simulate the physical laws of random walk and be used to study the elastic, diffusion and transport behaviors of materials.

(3) Jump evolution simulation algorithm: This algorithm is based on the idea of random jumps and is usually applied in fields such as chemistry and finance. Jump evolutionary simulation algorithm decomposes the evolution process of Mock object into Markov processes between different jump points, so as to achieve in-depth analysis and prediction of object evolution[12].

(4) Random network simulation algorithm: based on random Network theory, this algorithm is usually used in social networks, Biological network and other fields to simulate the topology and evolution of the network, study the characteristics and functions of the network, so as to predict and optimize the reliability and stability of the network.

In general, stochastic simulation algorithms have broad application prospects in data mining, intelligent decision-making and research fields in the era of Big data. Through reasonable algorithm selection and parameter settings, random simulation algorithms can better simulate and analyze the randomness and uncertainty in actual processes, help people better predict and make decisions, and contribute to the development and innovation of human society.

Random simulation algorithm (SSA), also known as gillspie algorithm, provides an indirect calculation method with CME. Gillespie algorithm was originally designed to simulate the coupled reaction system in a hot. It can be random. The algorithm uses the theory of the (fixed) [13]. Here, instead of solving all ordinary differential equations to obtain the probability distributions of all states of each T, we calculate, that is, calculate the {T, X (T)}, so as to calculate the corresponding probability given by CME.

Generally speaking, the dimension of CME is too high to be calculated. SSA solves this problem by calculating a single implementation of the state vector rather than the entire probability distribution. In order to derive SSA, of no reaction in the time interval [T, t + R).

$$P_0(r|x, t) = e^{-a_x,(x_\tau)} \tag{1}$$

Although the stochastic simulation algorithm (SSA) is an accurate reproduction of CME in a sense. However, this accuracy requires cost. In each, and tendency function must be updated. If or some rapid reactions in the system, resulting in a large amount (x (T)) and the reaction τ It is usually small, which the generation of random numbers [14]. Therefore, it is necessary at the same time. In the previous derivation of cle, it is assumed that when τ Very small, each trend function AJ (x (T)) is [T, t + τ] Under this condition, assuming that the state of the at time 1 is x (T), it can be changed in time steps τ The jump is used to of the system. Thus given τ- Jump method.

$$X(t + \tau) = X(t) + \sum_{j=1}^{M} v_j P_j(a_j(X(t)), \tau) \tag{2}$$

$$\varphi(\tau) = N\bar{\lambda}e^{-N\bar{\lambda}\tau}, \Pi(i) = \frac{\lambda_i}{N\bar{\lambda}} \tag{3}$$

among $\bar{\lambda} = N^{-1} \sum_{k=1}^{N} \lambda_k$ is the overall average rate of the process set. Note that in general, in addition to the system state, you can also adjust the occurrence rate of specific events or the number of "active" processes (events that may occur in the current state of the system) for the next iteration. For example, a specific reaction that adjusts the molecular number of all species participates in that particular reaction, which in turn changes the incidence of all reactions that these species participate in. This makes the algorithm very powerful and versatile, as it can simulate reactive processes with randomly generated process numbers, including non equilibrium dynamics with absorption states [15].

3 Research on Random Simulation Algorithm in Physical Education and Training

3.1 Application of Random Simulation Algorithm in Physical Education Teaching and Training

Random simulation algorithms are widely used in physical education teaching and training. Random simulation algorithms can simulate complex and changing situations in actual competitions, helping athletes better adapt to the competition environment and handle unexpected events, thereby improving their competition level.

For example, in basketball teaching, coaches can use random simulation algorithms for practical exercises. The coach can set some parameters, such as the number of attackers, time limits, foul rules, etc. By randomly simulating the team's game, players can practice how to control time and continue attacking under foul rules in the simulation game, and improve their technical and cognitive abilities in practical combat.

In addition, running training is an essential part of track and field training. Random simulation algorithms can help athletes better simulate, analyze, and optimize running posture, pace, and rhythm. For example, coaches can use random number generators to set running conditions at different speeds, record running data in combination with GPS, smart watches and other devices, analyze athletes' training conditions and running skills, and develop personalized training plans so that athletes can improve their running level faster in training.

Combining the principle diagram of Kalman filtering with the research on data fusion algorithms under bone joint points, it can be seen that the experimental process is divided into a Kalman filtering estimation process and a subsequent data fusion process. That is, first use two random simulation algorithms to filter and estimate based on the Kalman filtering principle to obtain the filter values under different bone points, and then use the filter values under the two random simulation algorithms to obtain the final fusion value. In a decentralized to filter and estimate two random simulation algorithms simultaneously. Firstly, based on the measured initial estimates, time updates and measurement updates are used to continuously update. In the time update process (prediction process), the estimated value under the k + 1 step is obtained using the k step, and the prediction covariance matrix for the next step is solved; The measurement update process (correction process) involves calculating the Kalman gain matrix first to obtain the corrected estimate, and then updating the error covariance. The two processes iterate continuously to obtain more accurate estimates of bone data, and ultimately arrive at the final fusion result based on the two estimates.

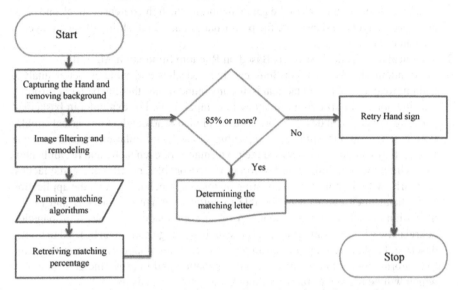

Fig. 3. Data processing flow chart under random simulation algorithm

As shown in Fig. 3 above, the system flow chart of bone joint point data fusion under the random simulation algorithm includes four parts: data acquisition, coordinate calibration, data fusion, and Tai Chi posture and motion recognition. Data collection uses two random simulation algorithms to collect human body data under multiple frames and store records; Coordinate calibration is to solve the spatial position conversion relationship between two random simulation algorithms and complete the coordinate calibration work, so as to unify the data obtained by the two sensors.

3.2 Application of Random Simulation Algorithm in Physical Education Training Evaluation

Random simulation algorithms have a wide range of applications in sports training evaluation, which can help coaches and athletes better understand the training status and ability level, develop more scientific and personalized training plans, and improve competition performance and results.

(1) Physical fitness evaluation based on random simulation algorithm

Random simulation algorithms can help coaches achieve personalized physical fitness assessments and develop more specific and scientific training plans for athletes. For example, in track and field competitions, random simulation algorithms can simulate endurance and speed performance under different competition states based on basic information such as athlete's height, weight, and gender, combined with data parameters such as V0max and heart rate. By analyzing and comparing simulated data, coaches can understand the physical fitness level, strengths, and weaknesses of athletes, and develop personalized training plans accordingly. In Team sport such as football, basketball and table tennis, the use of random simulation algorithms can simulate various situations of the game, including the fight, defense, attack and other aspects of players, and evaluate the performance and actual ability of each player in the game state.

(2) Technical and Tactical Analysis Based on Random Simulation Algorithm

Random simulation algorithms can help coaches and athletes better analyze and improve technical and tactical issues in competitions, thereby better controlling the situation and improving efficiency in competitions. For example, in basketball teaching, coaches can develop various tactical plans and conduct numerical simulations based on random simulation algorithms. Based on simulation research of game results, they can better understand the performance of each tactic and its applicability in different situations, and develop more reasonable and effective game tactics. Similarly, with the continuous updating of computer technology and the application of artificial intelligence, it is possible to better optimize the analysis and implementation of technology and tactics. A better combination of forward propagation neural network (FNN) and Random forest and other algorithms can be used to briefly describe the game scene through images and text, automatically extract the game live information, better analyze the game situation and improve the tactical effect, which will be the key to future technology and tactics analysis.

(3) Psychological Assessment Based on Random Simulation Algorithm

Random simulation algorithms can help coaches better evaluate the psychological competitive level of athletes and better utilize their personal strength and potential in competitions. For example, in table tennis training, random simulation algorithms are used to simulate different situations in the game, and the reactions and performances of the tester are recorded, in order to analyze the psychological quality of the tester and their acceptance of scenarios such as preemption and top difficulty. In this process, psychological data of athletes can be collected and converted into digital information. Through a "non verbal" approach, the psychological characteristics and reaction abilities of athletes can be further understood, providing more scientific basis and guidance for further training and competition preparation.

4 Application of Random Simulation Algorithm in Physical Education and Training Management

4.1 Auxiliary Examination

Physical education teaching based on random simulation algorithm is an innovative teaching method. It randomizes and simulates the course based on random number generator and simulation algorithm, so as to help students better understand and master the course content and overcome the single teacher's explanation and rigid classroom mode in traditional teaching. In physical education teaching, teaching based on random simulation algorithms can achieve the following goals:

(1) Improving students' sports skills: Physical education teaching based on random simulation algorithms can simulate various situations in competitions, allowing students to practice and engage in practical combat in a simulation environment. For example, in basketball teaching, random simulation algorithms can be used to simulate various offensive and defensive situations in the game, strengthen students' adaptability and practical combat ability, and improve their basketball skills.

(2) Mobilizing students' enthusiasm and interest: Using random simulation algorithms can make physical education teaching more lively and interesting. Generate random data through a random generator, design fun sports and competitions, and stimulate students' interest and enthusiasm in learning.

(3) Cultivate students' team spirit: in the teaching of Team sport, random simulation algorithm can be used to quickly simulate various scenarios, provide more abundant cooperation or competition modes to increase interaction, cultivate students' sense of cooperation and team spirit, and exercise their leadership and collaboration ability.

(4) Personalized physical education teaching: Through personalized data analysis capabilities, design courses and practice plans based on personal abilities, generate corresponding simulation data through random simulation algorithms, and allow students to train in areas they are good at or not good at, improving their physical education abilities and reducing their disadvantage attributes.

The traditional sports assessment method takes the final grade as the evaluation standard, which is often one-sided and unfair to learners. The random simulation algorithm can be used to comprehensively analyze the students' usual learning situation, so as to make a comprehensive and targeted evaluation. For example, the comprehensive assessment method of students' Physical Education Learning usual performance, the number and duration of on-demand courseware, the posting of course Q & a forum and the final examination results is adopted. By reducing the proportion of physical education final examination results and increasing the proportion of independent learning assessment, the massive data generated is processed with tools; The algorithm is applied to the sports theory knowledge test paper analysis database to analyze the topic in the sports test paper, so that the quality of the sports test paper, so as to understand the students' mastery of knowledge, and useful for the work.

4.2 Data Fusion Experiment Analysis

The data fusion experiment of this topic includes two parts: a random simulation algorithm and a fusion experiment. The experiment is conducted using the three-dimensional bone point data of the human body captured simultaneously by two random simulation algorithm sensors. The frame rate is 30 frames per second, and the corresponding multi frame bone point data can be obtained at a multi second sampling time. After coordinate calibration, it can be used in data fusion simulation experiments.

When using two random simulation algorithms to collect human bone point data, both sensors can track the position information of bone joint points at the same time, but there are problems such as body occlusion and data loss. When one random simulation algorithm can collect data, and the other is an estimated value or is not captured, the resulting fused data may have insufficient accuracy and may cause significant errors.

Therefore, to judge the observed data. The of obtaining the estimated value through random simulation algorithm based on the observed value is a continuous iterative process. By discarding the observations with large errors and unavailable values, more accurate Fusion values with small errors.

Firstly, a simulation experiment of the random simulation algorithm was conducted. In the experiment, the data of different bone joints in multiple frames under three-dimensional coordinates were simulated, and good filtering results were obtained. Therefore, this article takes the right knee KneeRight and the right hand HandRight as examples to conduct a filtering experiment comparison. By analyzing the filtering effects of the right knee joint points and the right hand joint points, it verifies whether Kalman filtering is feasible for joint point prediction.

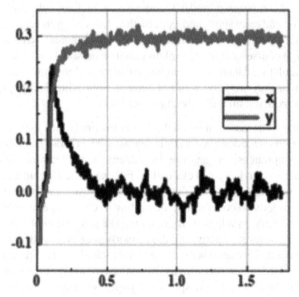

Fig. 4. Track Map of Right Knee Filtering Experiment

The above Fig. 4 shows the experimental data of the right knee joint point in the x-axis direction. From the figure, it can be seen that the right knee bone point data after the random simulation the true value, and the corresponding error after the random simulation algorithm is also smaller than the observed error, resulting in a significant filtering effect.

5 Conclusion

The training based on random simulation algorithm the future. The premise of students' development is to better learn and accept new things. In the road of future reform, combined with the direction of students' employment and school learning, increase the time investment in students' self-development, Build new innovative talent training methods, let more talents accept advanced training and education methods, change their learning state, and create a new innovative talent.

References

1. Hao, H.: Application of random dynamic grouping simulation algorithm in PE teaching evaluation. Complexity (2021)
2. Xu, Q., Yin, J.: Application of random forest algorithm in physical education. Sci. Program. (2021)
3. Gao, T.: Application of improved random forest algorithm and fuzzy mathematics in physical fitness of athletes. J. Intell. Fuzzy Syst. Appl. Eng. Technol. **40**(2), 2041–2053 (2021)
4. Chu, C.B., Tsai, E., Louie, L.: Application of problem-based learning for "Physical Education and Recreation Management" courses (2022)
5. Lozia, Z., Su, M.A.: Application of modelling and simulation in durability tests of vehicles and their components (2022)
6. Owoyele, O., Pal, P., Torreira, A.V., et al.: Application of an automated machine learning-genetic algorithm (AutoML-GA) coupled with computational fluid dynamics simulations for rapid engine design optimization (2021)
7. Li, C., Li, W.: Research on the innovation of labor education based on the integration of "Five Educations" in colleges and universities. Adv. Phys. Educ. **13**(1), 9 (2023)
8. Cavazza, M.: Visit by Professor Rom谩n Rodr铆guez Gonz谩lez, Minister for Culture, Education, Vocational Education and Training and Universities, Xunta de Galicia, Kingdom of Spain (2023)
9. Li, Z., Wang, L., Liu, Z.: Training of undergraduate physical education professionals in colleges and universities based on competency model (2021)
10. He, Y., Jing, H.: Application of neural network sample training algorithm in regional economic management. Math. Probl. Eng. **2022** (2022)
11. Zhang, C., Hu, C., Xie, S., et al.: Research on the application of Decision Tree and Random Forest Algorithm in the main transformer fault evaluation. J. Phys. Conf. Ser. **1732**(1), 012086 (2021). (7 pp.)
12. Li, D., Yi, C., Gu, Y., et al.: Research on college physical education and sports training based on virtual reality technology. Math. Probl. Eng. **2021**, 1–8 (2021)
13. Zhang, B., Zhou, X., Liu, Y., et al.: Combining application of wavelet analysis and genetic algorithm in wind tunnel simulation of unidirectional natural wind field near a sand ground surface. Rev. Sci. Instrum. **92**(1), 015123 (2021)
14. Castiello, M.E., Tonini, M.: An explorative application of random forest algorithm for archaeological predictive modeling. a swiss case study. J. Comput. Appl. Archaeol. **4**(1), 110–125 (2021)
15. Zhao, H., Chen, J., Wang, T.: Research on simulation analysis of physical training based on deep learning algorithm. Sci. Program. **2022**, 1–11 (2022)

Data Mining of Garment Pattern Based on Decision Tree Algorithm

Jing Li$^{(\boxtimes)}$ and Chen Li

Shandong Vocational College of Light Industry, Zibo 255300, Shandong, China
809605383@qq.com

Abstract. With the development of economy, society and culture, the traditional tailor-made clothing has been unable to meet people's needs for personalization, fit and online customization of clothing. The clothing industry has gradually changed from the original large-scale and standardized production to flexible and personalized customization. Data mining is the process of extracting useful information from data. Data mining is a process of discovering patterns in a large amount of data by applying statistical and computational techniques to data. Decision tree algorithm is such a technology that helps to find patterns in a large amount of data. It uses decision tree to find the best method to classify objects according to their attributes or characteristics. In recent years, the application of advanced technologies, such as computer graphics, digital image processing and artificial intelligence, has brought new opportunities to the garment industry, promoted the mode update of the garment industry, and also promoted the digitalization and intelligence of garment design. Garment digital version is the key problem and research hotspot of garment digital technology. In this paper, the research and analysis of data mining of garment pattern based on decision tree algorithm.

Keyword: Decision tree · Clothing version · Clothing style · data mining

1 Introduction

The clothing industry is an industry involving thousands of families and related to the national economy and the people's livelihood. The formulation and promotion of reasonable clothing size plays a great role in unifying, standardizing and guiding both the clothing design and production of clothing enterprises and the purchase of appropriate clothing by consumers, and is of great significance to enhance the competitiveness of enterprises and improve the economic benefits of enterprises. Especially after China's entry into WTO, the garment industry will also face new opportunities and challenges [1]. As the largest garment producer and exporter in the world, China's garment enterprises will participate in international cooperation and international competition in a broader field and to a deeper extent after China's entry into WTO. The current enterprise size standards of garment enterprises are difficult to cope with the size classification of international and domestic human body forms, which will cause confusion and loss of competitiveness in the production size [2].

© ICST Institute for Computer Sciences, Social Informatics and Telecommunications Engineering 2024
Published by Springer Nature Switzerland AG 2024. All Rights Reserved
Y. Zhang and N. Shah (Eds.): BigIoT-EDU 2023, LNICST 581, pp. 82–92, 2024.
https://doi.org/10.1007/978-3-031-63133-7_8

With the continuous development of modern garment industry, garment enterprises urgently need comprehensive design talents who give consideration to both design and technology. However, at present, most of the courses of clothing major are based on design and technology. Clothing design teaching often focuses on clothing style design and ignores clothing structure, or attaches importance to process structure and ignores style design. The content of version process technology cannot be effectively reflected in the course of style design. Starting from the needs of talents and subject teaching, this topic combs and studies the professional teaching concept of the integration of clothing style and version, explores the best combination of traditional clothing style and version teaching and digital technology, and designs and realizes the multimedia teaching method of the combination of clothing style and version [3].

Facing the increasingly fierce global market competition, the relative competitive advantage of China's clothing industry has weakened, and the pressure on clothing exports has increased significantly. Facing the huge pressure, it is more and more important to strictly control the quality of export clothing products, ensure product quality and improve product competitiveness. Foreign trade clothing mainly involves the manufacturing process, and the production process is complex. A garment often needs dozens of manufacturing processes to complete. In order to ensure quality, it is more necessary to take quality control activities. Due to the labor-intensive characteristics of the industry, there are many management links, and the task of quality control is heavy. Quality control is a key stage in the whole process of garment foreign trade and a complex dynamic process. Although foreign trade clothing companies have realized its importance, the product inspection and quality control methods adopted by many companies are still not very effective, and there are still many problems in each link of quality control. Claims and returns caused by garment quality problems in the export process have also brought great economic losses to enterprises. At the same time, with the transformation and upgrading from an industrial society to an information society and the development of foreign trade clothing industry and computer information technology, the management ideas and management models of foreign trade clothing companies have undergone great changes, and the application of information technology has been promoted to a certain extent in the entire industry.

At present, one of the main challenges facing the garment manufacturing industry is how to solve the contradiction between the customized and diversified needs of customers and the pursuit of small size mass production mode by garment enterprises, that is, the contradiction between the needs of specific minority customers and the mass production of products from non-specific groups. In response to this contradiction, the outlook for manufacturing challenges in 2020 has conducted in-depth research on the challenges facing the future manufacturing industry, and put forward one of the six strategies to deal with the challenges, pointing out that the information extracted from a large number of resources can be transformed into useful knowledge and effectively support decision-making [4].

Based on the above background and objectives, this paper uses the clustering analysis method of data mining technology based on the decision tree algorithm to mine the matching rules between the number of clothing types and the number of people's body types, based on a large number of anthropometric data accumulated by enterprises for a long time, so as to guide the formulation of a scientific and reasonable clothing size table [5]; By analyzing the clothing size coverage and sales historical data, combined with expert experience, mining hidden rules and patterns, and then providing the basis for the clothing size production decision, and further predicting the future production trend.

2 Related Work

2.1 Design Idea

Volume data and logistics data are the most important data information resources for garment enterprises. The design idea of the tool software (analysis from figure measurement data & logistics data of garment enterprise for decision making of manufacturing tools) for production size decision support based on volume data analysis and logistics data is based on the scientific analysis and data mining of a large number of collected human data and sales data, combined with the experience of garment enterprise size classification, The quantitative relationship between human body characteristic data, clothing size and clothing production decision is established.

The design idea of this subject is based on the fact that countries all over the world have realized the importance of establishing human body database, and have carried out research in this field. Through the human body database, the classified human body data can be obtained, the basic model of clothing size can be formulated, and the occurrence frequency of population classification can be established [6]. As shown in Fig. 1, the model shows the size population frequency curve, size output curve and yield margin space. Therefore, the relationship between size and yield can be reasonably planned.

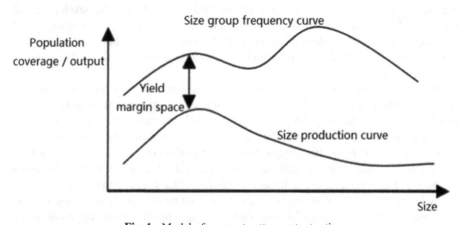

Fig. 1. Model of garment pattern output ratio

The technology, management and other activities taken to meet the requirements of clothing style are the control of clothing style. By controlling the formation process of the clothing style, the control of the clothing style can eliminate the relevant factors that lead to the disqualification of the product's clothing style, and ensure that the product's clothing style meets the customer's requirements. In the production activities of enterprises, the control of garment pattern and style mainly refers to the control of garment pattern and style on the production site inside the enterprise.

The development of garment style management drives the development of garment style control. From the beginning of the 20th century to the 1930s, the inspection and control of the garment pattern and style after the event mainly depended on the experience and sense of responsibility of the inspectors. From the 1930s to the 1960s, mathematical statistics began to be used. Through mathematical statistical analysis of the production process, the quantity of nonconforming products can be controlled quantitatively; After the 1960s, it began to enter the stage of comprehensive clothing style management and clothing style assurance. It is required to focus on customers and all staff should participate in the whole process of clothing style management activities. The guarantee of garment style is to ensure the effective implementation of the management process of garment style by using the procedure documents such as the garment style manual. The typical one is ISO9000 series standards. After the 21st century, we have entered the stage of comprehensive clothing style innovation, which requires not only reducing mistakes, but also continuous innovation and improvement.

The methods and tools for the control of clothing style mainly include APQP, SPC, FMEA, MSA, PPAP, layer method, checklist, Pareto diagram, scatter diagram, causal diagram, histogram and control chart.

There are seven main steps in the control of clothing style, as shown in Fig. 2. The design of the garment pattern control system and the selection of the garment pattern control technology are the key to the garment pattern control.

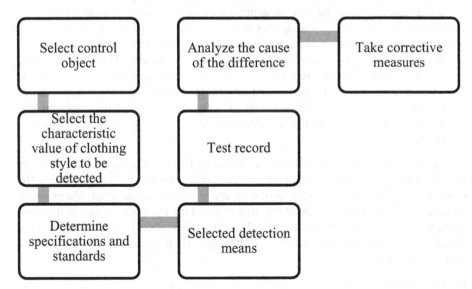

Fig. 2. Steps of garment pattern control

2.2 Data Mining

The so-called data mining (dm:data mining) is a process of extracting hidden, unknown but potentially useful information and knowledge from a large number of incomplete, noisy, fuzzy and random data. Its goal is to mine hidden, useful and unknown knowledge from a large number of original data. The discovered knowledge can be rules describing data characteristics, frequent patterns, clustering of targets in data sets, prediction models, etc. Data mining is an interdisciplinary subject, which brings together different disciplines and fields such as database, artificial intelligence, statistics, visualization, parallel computing and so on.

(1) Clearly define business problems, obtain data sources, define data warehouse metadata, and analyze data.
(2) Explore the data source and perform data selection and data preprocessing. The purpose of data selection is to determine the operation object of the discovery task, that is, the target data. It is a set of data extracted from the original database according to the needs of users. Data preprocessing generally includes eliminating noise, deriving and calculating default data, eliminating duplicate records, etc.
(3) Preparing modeling data is to convert the data into an analysis model and generate a data mart. The model is established for the mining algorithm. The key to the success of data mining is to establish an analysis model that is really suitable for the mining algorithm [7].
(4) Mining the converted data. In addition to perfecting or selecting the appropriate mining algorithm, all other work can be completed automatically. Although data mining algorithm is the core of the whole mining process, and it is also the main effort of researchers at present, in order to obtain good mining results, we must fully understand the requirements or assumptions of various mining algorithms [8].
(5) Explain and evaluate the mining results. Users can judge whether the mining results are scientific and reasonable according to the mining model or prediction model. If they meet the needs of users, they can assist users in making decisions; If it does not meet the user's needs, return to the data sorting and uploading module to check whether the source data is perfect and whether the mining algorithm is appropriate, and then repeat the data mining process. Finally, the knowledge obtained from the analysis is integrated into the organizational structure of the business information system.

The method of information theory is introduced into the algorithm of the decision tree. The entropy is used to measure the amount of information of the non-leaf nodes. By constructing a decision tree, the class of the training samples is classified. The non-leaf nodes in the decision tree represent the attributes, and the leaf nodes represent the class of the sample instances [9]. The input of the decision tree generation algorithm is a set of training samples with class marks, and the output of the construction is a binary or multi-branch tree.

(1) Information entropy
    1) Let S be the data set containing n training samples, and divide it into m different classes. The class set is $\{S_1, S_2, \cdots, S_i, \cdots S_m\}$. The number of samples contained in each class is n_i, $p_i = n_i/n$ is the class S, and the probability of occurrence

divides S into m classes. The information entropy or information expectation is:

$$I = -\sum\nolimits_{i=1}^{n} p_i \log_2 p_i \tag{1}$$

2) Calculate the information expectation or information entropy (A) of non-category attribute A. Attribute A is an attribute of the data set. The value of A is $a_1, a_2, \cdots, a_i$, and S is divided into v subsets $\{D_1, D_2, \cdots D_o\}$.

$$I(A = a_j) = -\sum\nolimits_{i=1}^{n} p_i \log_2 p_{ij} \tag{2}$$

When $|A = a_j|$, the probability of the sample is $p_j = d_j/n$, the expected information of classification using attribute A, that is, the information of A is:

$$\text{Entropy}(A) = \sum\nolimits_{j=1}^{r} p_j I(A = a_j) \tag{3}$$

(2) Information gain

The amount of information provided by attribute A to classify samples is called the information gain of attribute A, which is recorded as Gain (A)

$$\text{Gain}(A) = I - \text{Entropy}(A) \tag{4}$$

(3) Information gain rate

Information gain rate of attribute A:

$$\text{GainRatio}(A) = \frac{\text{Gain}(A)}{\text{Entropy}(A)} \tag{5}$$

The information entropy is used as the criterion for selecting the attribute to classify the training sample set. In the process of constructing the decision tree, an attribute is selected to classify the samples, so that the samples on the sub-nodes belong to the same category [10]. The ID3 algorithm uses information gain as the selection criteria for node attributes. When judging the attributes of each non-leaf node, the attribute with the smallest information entropy value is obtained as the split node. The entropy value reflects a measure of the order of the system information. If the categories of samples on a node are distributed, the larger the entropy value of the node is, and the smaller the entropy value is.

3   Clothing Version and Style

3.1   Style Teaching

Clothing styles are divided into two categories: external silhouette and local modeling, which are interrelated and integrated with each other. The outline of clothing refers to the outline of the external silhouette of clothing, which is the basis of clothing modeling design. Clothing is centered on the human body, and the change of clothing silhouette is based on the human body structure. Different shapes of clothing silhouettes can be formed through the modeling and concealment of shoulder, chest, hip, crotch and swing, which are the key parts supporting clothing. The six most basic and commonly used forms are H-type, A-type, V-type, X-type, T-type and O Type. Local modeling refers to the components that constitute the main body of clothing, such as collar, sleeve, placket, pocket, waist, etc. Understanding and mastering the changes of clothing styles and shapes can help designers better grasp the trend of fashion and improve their own design literacy and design ability [11]. As shown in Fig. 3.

Fig. 3. Basic silhouette of clothing style

As a course to study the law of fashion design, fashion design often pays more attention to the use of modeling elements for creative design in the current fashion design teaching. A considerable number of students believe that fashion design is only limited to the integration and reorganization of various elements of clothing, and the creative activities in the form of thinking of a single project to assist in the drawing of renderings. Many students are not aware of the internal relationship between style and structure [12]. They can only draw, not cut, and cannot fully reflect the design intent.

In the discipline of fashion design, the pattern is the plane unfolding design of fashion style modeling; It is the structural basis for implementing the technical design of the style and completing the final garment style; It is an intermediate link from garment style design to garment processing. The main purpose of version design is to rationalize the final style of clothing. For designers, in the design process, they can comprehensively consider the relationship between style and structure, and find the structural law between style and version [13]. On the one hand, they can help designers to fully express the concept of fashion design, on the other hand, they can stimulate creative inspiration, derive more wonderful and unique style ideas from the changes of version structure, break the inspiration and create new fashion. It is one of the necessary professional qualities for fashion designers.

3.2 Decision Tree Algorithm

The main function of decision tree algorithm is to classify and predict data. The decision tree algorithm is used to predict the popularity of different versions of clothes and which version of clothes is more likely to be praised by users according to the clothing data collected by the information collection system. The process of decision tree algorithm is actually a tree structure. Firstly, the features should be selected. The selected features are the classification criteria of the nodes at this time. Therefore, when selecting the features, the data should be quantized, missing values removed and other preprocessing operations should be carried out to ensure that the selected features are good; After that, the algorithm will recursively operate the data using the selected feature evaluation criteria, and generate child nodes from top to bottom until the data set can no longer be divided; Finally, we should pay attention to the pruning operation to reduce the "over fitting" phenomenon in the decision tree algorithm [14]. When the decision tree algorithm has many branches, the decision tree will train the data of the training set "very well". At this time, the data characteristics of the original training set will appear as the characteristics of the existing data, resulting in a significant reduction in the generalization performance of the entire algorithm. There are two main ways of pruning, the first is pre pruning and the second is post pruning [15]. Pre pruning is commonly used. Because pre pruning is performed when generating a decision tree, it improves the generalization performance of the decision tree. Select the style, version, collar and sleeve attributes of the clothing data as the training attributes, and the praise number as the decision attribute. Use Python to implement the classification decision tree algorithm to predict which version of the clothing will be more popular [16].

3.3 Decision Tree Algorithm for Predicting the Popularity of Garment Pattern

After the K-means clustering analysis of the crawled textile and clothing data, the decision tree algorithm will also be used to analyze and predict its popularity. It should be noted that two crawled fields will be added in the web crawler system, namely, the number of comments and the number of favorable comments. When the decision tree algorithm is carried out, the style, version, collar and sleeve attributes of the clothing will be taken as the training attributes, and the number of favorable comments will be selected as the decision attributes. Firstly, the data is preprocessed, and the missing values in the data are removed by the method of direct deletion, and then the positive numbers are transformed into the form of popularity. The classification decision tree algorithm is implemented by using the scikit learn Library of Python. Firstly, the relevant library functions scikit learn, numpy, SciPy and Matplotlib are imported, and then the data of Excel files are converted into CSV file, easy to operate [17]; Via csv The reader () function reads the clothing data of the CSV file by line. It should be noted that the scikit learn library also requires the format of the data. The preprocessed data needs to be converted into matrix format. In the process of data format conversion in Python, first convert the data into dictionary format, and then convert the dictionary format into matrix format. After the conversion is completed, import the tree function from the sklearn library, and use the tree Decisiontreeclassifier() function is used to specify the decision tree algorithm, and then the fit method is used to build the decision tree. After importing the pydotplus module, the generated decision tree model is output as Pdf file [18]. The decision tree model is shown in Fig. 4.

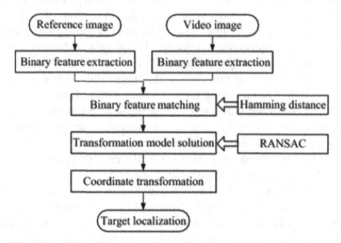

Fig. 4. Prediction of garment pattern based on decision tree algorithm

4 Verify the Accuracy of the Decision Tree Model

The above uses 1000 records in the training set to construct the decision tree model. Then whether the constructed decision tree is accurate and whether it can judge and predict other records must be verified. To verify the accuracy of the decision tree model, we still use SQL 2005 Analysis Services as the analysis tool.

In Analysis Services, we take the test data set with 330 records as the input table to verify the mining model constructed previously, and take "purchasing power" as the predictable column name. After processing and analysis, the lifting diagram shown in Fig. 5 is obtained.

From the "Mining Legend" table on the figure, we can see that the score of the decision tree mining model is 0.93, which is very high; When the sample population is 50%, the overall accuracy of the ideal model is 50%, while the overall accuracy of the decision tree model we built is 47.58%. It shows that the accuracy of this model is very high and can provide help for decision support [19].

Therefore, clothing enterprises can analyze customer data according to the above decision tree model, obtain the characteristics of high purchasing power groups, and classify customers to achieve research on customer value, customer structure, etc. This will help enterprises develop targeted marketing strategies for different types of customers and find targeted sales markets [20]. We can also use the decision tree classification algorithm to carry out statistical analysis of clothing sales through indicators such as clothing products, geographical areas, product categories, etc. of a certain period.

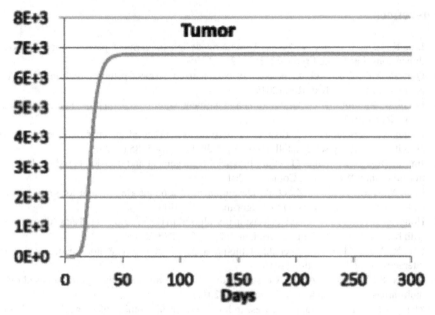

Fig. 5. Data detection lifting diagram

In a word, using the decision tree model, we can easily conduct sales analysis, market analysis, work quality analysis, and marketing ability analysis; It can make full use of historical data and external data to forecast clothing demand.

5 Conclusion

The teaching materials of clothing style design and version technology have traditionally appeared as a single book, lacking the tightness of system and practice, the overall planning of version and style design, and the multimedia digital systematic composition of clothing style design and version technology. Great breakthroughs have been made in the design practice of digital course teaching materials combining clothing style and version. According to the research on the application of mining technology in the garment industry, it has been preliminarily launched. The application of information technology in modern garment enterprises has led to large-scale garment customization production, producing nearly one million volume data records and massive sales data records, laying the research foundation of data mining. The result of data mining is transformed into a software tool convenient for garment enterprises through component technology, which can obtain customized production specification and size table for enterprises, provide decision-making basis for enterprises to master the production size ratio, and effectively avoid the waste of blind production caused by improper size configuration. Therefore, the results of this study are of great promotion and application value.

References

1. Liu, K., Zhu, C., Tao, X., et al.: Parametric design of garment pattern based on body dimensions. Int. J. Ind. Ergon. **72**, 212–221 (2019)
2. Qinwen, Y.E., Zhang, G.: Generation of personalized garment pattern based on AutoCAD parameterization. J. Text. Res. (2019)
3. Liang, B., Zhiming, W.U.: Design of denim garment pattern based on printing technology. J. Cloth. Res. (2017)
4. Zhang, W.: Research on English score analysis system based on improved decision tree algorithm and fuzzy set. J. Intell. Fuzzy Syst. **39**(4), 5673–5685 (2020)
5. Jin, M., Wang, H., Zhang, Q., et al.: Financial management and decision based on decision tree algorithm. Wirel. Pers. Commun. (2018)
6. Lian, Y., Chen, J., Guan, Z., et al.: Development of a monitoring system for grain loss of paddy rice based on a decision tree algorithm (001), 014 (2021)
7. Hong, Z., Li, X.: A cost sensitive decision tree algorithm based on weighted class distribution with batch deleting attribute mechanism. Inform. Sci. **378** (2016)
8. Luo, R., Wang, H., Chen, Y., et al.: Method of apparel's geometric & floral pattern based on interactive genetic algorithm (2016)
9. Lomax, S., Vadera, S., et al.: A cost-sensitive decision tree learning algorithm based on a multi-armed bandit framework. Comput. J. (2017)
10. Zhang, CS., Ya, T.U., Yan, L.I.: Research on relationship mining of mongolian medicine prescription drug composition and its indications based on decision tree. Chin. J. Basic Med. Tradit. Chin. Med. (2018)
11. Liu, G., Sun, Y., Yuan, P.: Classified mining of TCM gastritis based on C4.5 decision tree algorithm. Chin. Arch. Tradit. Chin. Med. (2016)
12. Abbaspour, H., Maghaminik, A.: Equipment replacement decision in mine based on decision tree algorithm. Sci. Rep. Resour. Issues **2016** (2016)
13. Yang, T.: Oil based data mining system based on decision tree algorithm applied research. Electron. Des. Eng. (2016)
14. Huang, J.Y., Guo, H., Kuang, Y.P.: Preliminary research on regularity of syndrome differentiation of allergic rhinitis based on decision tree algorithm. China J. Tradit. Chin. Med. Pharm. (2016)
15. Ying, K.E., Liang, H., Wang, H.: Two-dimensional pattern design and modification of virtual garment based on OpenGL. J. Donghua Univ. (Nat. Sci.) (2018)
16. Bing, L.I., Han, G., Jia, Y.: Analysis and discussion on the electricity meter demolition business based on decision tree algorithm. Power Syst. Big Data (2017)
17. Tong, W., Huang, Q.P.: Car sales data mining based on improved decision tree algorithm. J. Anhui Electr. Eng. Prof. Tech. Coll. (2017)
18. Zhao, H., Li, X.: A cost sensitive decision tree algorithm based on weighted class distribution with batch deleting attribute mechanism. Inf. Sci. Inform. Comput. Sci. Intell. Syst. Appl. Int. J. (2017)
19. Yang, Y., Gen-Lin, J.I., Bao, P.M.: Algorithm for mining adjoint pattern of spatial-temporal trajectory based on grid index. Comput. Sci. (2016)
20. Zhang, X.Q.: Analysis of teaching management data based on decision tree algorithm. J. Qingdao Univ. (Nat. Sci. Ed.) (2019)

Design and Implementation of University Management Information System Based on Decision Tree Algorithm

Hao Zhu[1], Qu Zheng[2(⊠)], Xi Jian[3], and Zhao Yan[3]

[1] School of Foreign Languages, Jinjiang College Sichuan University, Meishan, China
[2] Department of Student Affairs Management, Chengdu Medical College, Chengdu 620800, Sichuan, China
zhengqu@cmc.edu.cn
[3] Zaozhuang Vocational College of Science and Technology, No. 888, Xueyuan Road, Longquan Street, Tengzhou, Zaozhuang, Shandong, China

Abstract. The role of information management in universities is very important, but there is a problem of low management level. The management system cannot solve the management problem of multiple types of information in the university system, and the rationality is low. First of all, the information knowledge is used to classify the university information, and the university information is selected according to the degree of importance to realize the standardized processing of data. Then, the information knowledge is classified according to importance, forming an information optimization collection and iteratively analyzing the scoring content. MATLAB simulation shows that the decision tree method's optimization degree and optimization time are better than that of a single management system when the system is fixed.

Keyword: information knowledge · Time · Decision tree method · Optimize the results

1 Introduction

With the continuous development of information technology, the construction of information technology in university management has become a trend. Establishing an efficient, stable, and flexible university management information system is an important component of university informatization construction. This article designs and implements a feasible university management information system based on decision tree algorithm. As an important component of the education field, the management of universities involves a large amount of information and has a certain degree of complexity. How to effectively handle various information in university management has become an urgent problem that management personnel need to solve. In this context, establishing an efficient and convenient university management information system that supports management decision-making has become an indispensable choice [1]. This article addresses

Y. Zhang and N. Shah (Eds.): BigIoT-EDU 2023, LNICST 581, pp. 93–104, 2024.
https://doi.org/10.1007/978-3-031-63133-7_9

this issue by using decision tree algorithms to design and implement a university management information system. Firstly, this article introduces the basic principles and application fields of decision tree algorithms. The decision tree algorithm is a classification and regression analysis algorithm that can be used to classify different attribute values and also to partition different subsets of a dataset. In information management and decision-making in universities, decision tree algorithms can be applied to select the optimal decision, improving decision-making efficiency and accuracy [2].

Secondly, this article provides an in-depth analysis of the requirements and design requirements for university management information systems. The design of university management information systems needs to consider various management fields, such as student management, teacher management, course management, etc. Based on these requirements, this article adopts an object-oriented design method, with decision tree algorithm as the core, to establish an efficient and convenient university management information system. Some scholars believe that applying decision tree methods to university systems can effectively analyze redundant information and time, providing corresponding support for information optimization and verification. The university management information system in this article is mainly divided into three parts: data layer, service layer, and display layer. Among them, the data layer uses a database to store various management information; The service layer is responsible for preprocessing and analyzing the data, using decision tree algorithms to classify and analyze the data; The display layer provides managers with an intuitive and clear visual interface, supporting various queries, visual analysis, and decision-making.

Finally, this article lists the application scenarios and implementation effects of university management information systems. This system has been widely applied and validated in practical applications, improving the informationization level of university management, reducing the manpower and time costs of management personnel, and improving management efficiency [3]. At the same time, the system has strong scalability and adaptability, and can face different management needs and new data scenarios through continuous updates and upgrades. This article constructs an efficient, stable, and flexible university management information system based on decision tree algorithm, which can provide certain technical support and reference for the informationization construction of universities. However, despite the widespread application of the system in practice, there are still some urgent problems to be solved, such as the need to further improve the design and algorithm. In summary, this study provides new ideas and methods for decision-making in the construction of information technology in university management, and has certain practical significance and reference value.

2 Related Concepts

2.1 Design of University Information Management System

His article introduces the requirements analysis for the design of information management systems in universities. The requirement analysis of the information management system is a key link in the system design. It should carefully analyze the system process,

Functional requirement, operation process, performance requirements, data management, system security and other aspects, and design and implement a targeted information management system according to specific application scenarios and management requirements. The information management diagram is shown in Fig. 1.

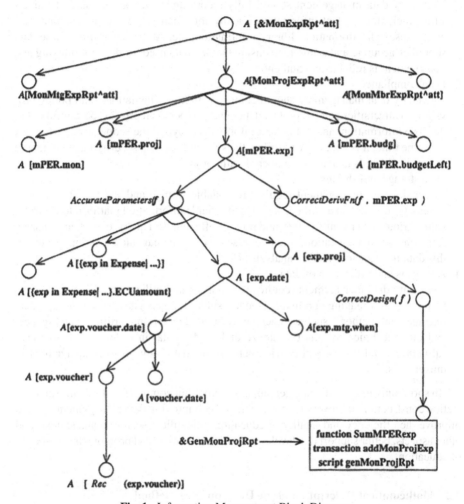

Fig. 1. Information Management Block Diagram

On the basis of demand analysis, this paper designs modules from the user, data, function, security, application, expansion and other directions for a large number of university management needs, and an elite team composed of Systems analyst and programmers is responsible for demand analysis and module construction. Especially in terms of data management, this article adopts modern database technology, applies relational databases and object-oriented development design methods, and has a user-friendly and user-friendly data management module, providing strong support for university data management.

University data management needs to follow the following principles:

1. Comprehensiveness and accuracy of data

   University data management should fully record and save various data of universities, including student information, faculty information, course information, scientific research information, library information, etc. At the same time, these data should be accurate and accurate to ensure that the data used for decision-making and management is reliable and authentic.

2. Data compliance

   University data management should comply with laws, regulations, and policy provisions. Universities need to protect data related to personal privacy, be careful not to disclose information, and not collect information beyond the scope or necessary. At the same time, it is necessary to follow the standards of data security management to ensure that data is not stolen, tampered with, or lost.

3. Data storage and sharing

   University data management requires reasonable storage and sharing of data. It is necessary to establish a unified, stable, and reliable information platform to centrally store various data in universities, and provide efficient data query, export, and sharing functions, so that education, scientific research, and management personnel can use this data for decision-making analysis [4].

4. Aanalysis and utilization of data

   University data management requires the analysis and utilization of data to achieve better decision-making and management results. It is necessary to use modern data management methods, such as machine learning, data mining, artificial intelligence, and other technical means to analyze and model data, in order to discover useful patterns and trends, and provide better support for educational management in universities.

In short, university data management is an important component of the informationization construction of university management. By improving data management, we can improve the efficiency and quality of education, scientific research, management, and other aspects, better support the development of universities, and promote the prosperity of education.

2.2 Mathematical Description of the Decision Tree Method

The information relationships, and information importance to optimize university information [5], finds outliers in information optimization according to the management indicators in the university system, and forms a path table [6]. The correlation of the information management results is finally judged by integrating the information optimization results. The decision tree method combines information knowledge and optimizes the management results by using the decision tree method, which can improve the level of information management [7].

Hypothesis 1: The university information is, the information optimization result x_i set is, the information importance is $set(x_i)$, and the judicial function of the information management result is y_i $Y(x_i)$ as shown in Eq. (1).

$$Y(x_i) = x_i \Rightarrow y_i \tag{1}$$

2.3 Selection of Information Optimization Scheme

Hypothesis 2: The selection function of the information optimization method is $F(x_i)$, and the information weight coefficient is g_i, then the information optimization method selection is shown in Eq. (2).

$$F(x_i) = g_i \cdot Y(x_i|y_i) \tag{2}$$

2.4 Processing of Redundant Information

Before the decision tree analysis, the standard analysis of the time and single time in the information management results should be carried out, and the university information should be mapped to the selection table to determine the semantic anomaly of content. First, comprehensive analysis of university information and set thresholds and weights of university information to support the accurate research of the decision tree method. University information needs to be standardized, and if the processed results conform to the non-standard distribution, the processing is valid, otherwise, the standard processing is re-processed [8]. Scheme should be selected, and the specific method selection is shown in Fig. 2.

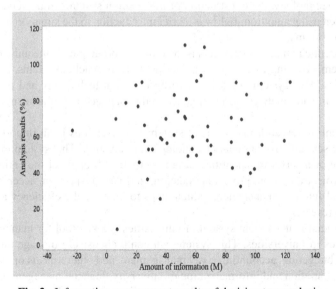

Fig. 2. Information management results of decision tree analysis

The university information shows that the analysis of the decision tree method is uniform and consistent with the objective facts. The selection method is not directional, indicating that the analysis of the decision tree method has strong accuracy, so it is used as university information management research [9]. The selection method meets the mapping requirements, mainly the information knowledge adjusts the selection method, removes duplicate, redundant information, and revises the information node to make the whole University information is more selective.

2.5 Correlation Between Different Information Nodes

The decision tree method adopts accurate judgment of time, and adjusts the corresponding redundant information relationship to optimize the information management method of universities. The decision tree method divides the information management choices of universities into different data volumes and randomly selects other methods. During the iteration process, the importance of different data volumes is matched with the selection method [10]. After the matching processing is completed, different methods are compared for university information management, and the management results with the highest accuracy are recorded.

3 Actual Cases of University Information Management Systems

3.1 Information System Situation

University information systems refer to the information systems used by universities in their management, teaching, research, and other fields. With the rapid development of information technology, the construction of information systems in universities is also receiving increasing attention. Below is a brief introduction to the situation of university information systems:

The academic management system is the most important part of the university information system, covering various aspects such as students, teaching, exams, courses, and training plans. This system applies modern information technology and management ideas, achieving automation and intelligence in the management of academic affairs in universities.

The scientific research management system in universities is an important means of achieving scientific research and technological innovation. This system includes the management of a series of scientific research activities throughout the entire process, including project initiation, project application, mid-term inspection, acceptance management, and funding management, which helps to improve the efficiency and quality of scientific research.

The financial management system of universities is a key tool for managing financial resources in universities. This system can comprehensively manage the financial accounting, budgeting, accounting, asset management, and other aspects of universities, achieving automation and informatization of university financial management.

The university personnel management system is mainly used for the management of personnel information such as teachers, staff, and students, including personal basic information, employment management, salary management, vacation management, performance evaluation, and other aspects of management systems Time 450, as shown in Table 1.

Table 1. Information characteristics

information system	Amount of data	Dispersion	Information standards
College system	1.2	0.35	0.2
	4	0.25	0.3
School system	2.1	0.25	0.2
	5	0.39	0.4
This professional system	2.6	0.25	0.3
	3	0.12	0.4

The processing process of information nodes between different information nodes in Table 1 is shown in Fig. 3.

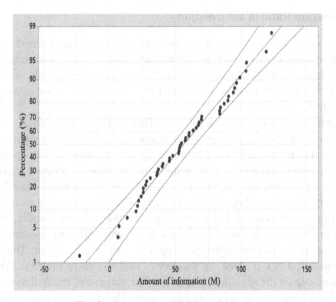

Fig. 3. Processing of information nodes

The information management results of the decision tree method are closer to the actual time compared with the single information management system. In terms of university information management selection, information node selection rate, accuracy, etc., the decision tree method management system. From the change of information nodes, and the judgment speed is faster [11, 12]. Therefore, the decision tree method has better information processing speed, time, and optimization.

In essence, a data warehouse is a collection of data. This kind of data set is characterized by taking a certain subject as the core, and fetching useful data from multiple databases to form a multidimensional, time-varying data set. On-line data analysis and processing is a specific application based on data warehouse.

That is, the mining and processing of hidden knowledge in the data. The above three data processing methods can be used independently or in combination. The focus of data warehouse is on the orderly organization and integration of data, so that the data distributed in different database tables can be integrated together, which is conducive to the discovery of objective laws [13, 14]; Data online analysis focuses on the analysis of centralized data to verify the currently known knowledge rules, while data mining focuses on the discovery of unknown knowledge.

The overall idea is based on the construction of data warehouse, and comprehensively uses realize the mining and processing of student information data, so as to provide users with all-round decision support functions. Specifically, by reading and integrating the information resources of the underlying database, taking the determined analysis objectives as the theme, and through data cleaning, transformation, integration and other steps, a multidimensional data warehouse is built, and finally a global data view is formed.

3.2 Optimization Ratio of Information

Information optimization includes redundant information, information nodes, and speed. After the threshold criteria, the preliminary management, and the correlation of the management results is obtained Analyze. To verify the effect more accurately, select different redundant information and calculate the overall time of information management, as shown in Table 2.

The analysis of multidimensional data model using online data analysis technology is actually to process data using a series of atomic operations [15]. These atomic operations based on multidimensional data model include slicing operation, slicing operation, rotation operation, roll up operation, etc. Among them, the slicing operation is to instantiate members on a certain dimension, and the resulting processing result is an N-1 dimensional space composed of other dimensional data; The chunking operation is the result of instantiating a member of all dimensions in the multidimensional model; The rotation operation is to exchange the coordinate space of different dimensions according to the user's needs, so as to make the subsequent operation more convenient; The purpose of the roll up operation is to reduce the number of dimensions in the cube. The method used is to reduce up on the specified dimension; The purpose of the drill down operation is to refine the information of a certain dimension. The method is to further refine the members of a certain dimension; The purpose of drill-through operation is to integrate multiple data models to make data analysis more comprehensive.

Table 2. Overall optimization situation

Optimize the proportion	Information accuracy	Outlier recognition rate
25%	93.31	92.63
50%	92.20	93.26
70%	93.73	90.65
mean	92.21	92.42
X^2	6.312	11.137
P = 0. 032		

3.3 Time and Accuracy of Information Optimization

The optimization time and accuracy compared with the management system are shown in Fig. 4.

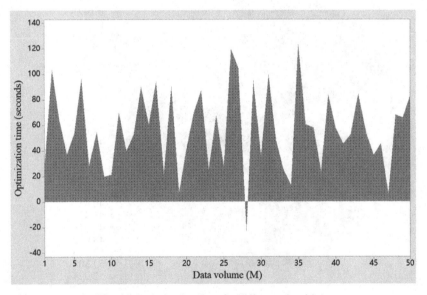

Fig. 4. Optimization time for different algorithms

It can be seen from Fig. 4 that the optimization time of the decision tree method is shorter than that of the single management system. Still, the error rate is lower, indicating that the choice is relatively stable and single. The degree of optimization of the management system is uneven. The accuracy of the above algorithm is shown in Table 3.

It can be seen from Table 3 that the rationality of the selection of university information management has shortcomings in optimizing time and accuracy, and the accuracy of time has changed significantly, the error rate is high. The optimization time of the comprehensive results o higher than that of the management system. At the same time,

Table 3. Comparison of optimization degrees of different methods

algorithm	Optimize time	Optimize location	error
Decision tree method	92.11	(2,3)	0.74
Single management system	70.25	(4,6)	0.21
P	0.012	(7,2)	0.23

the optimization time of the decision tree method is greater than 90%, and the accuracy does not change significantly. To further verify the superiority of the decision tree method. The decision tree method was comprehensively analyzed by different methods, and result 5 is shown.

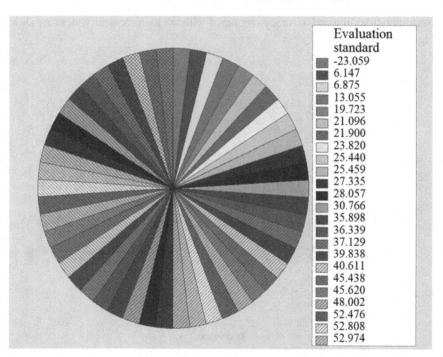

Fig. 5. Comprehensive results of information management result evaluation of decision tree method

As can be seen from Fig. 5, the reason is that the decision tree method increases the time adjustment coefficient and sets it Corresponding thresholds, which propose non-compliant results.

In terms of analyzing the relationship between students' different basic data and teaching-related data and their student information, the current analysis method based on Excel software is not efficient and reasonable, but it can also achieve relatively satisfactory results through long-term analysis and processing by staff with considerable experience.

Data mining includes a variety of processing methods, including clustering analysis, decision tree, and so on. Different methods focus on solving problems in different fields. For the mining of student information data, it is mainly through the analysis of student basic information and teaching information data to find the relationship between the relevant elements and students' situation. The decision tree data mining algorithm can effectively solve this problem.

4   Conclusion

The design of university information management system is an important means to achieve the goals of university information management. This article explores the design process of university information management system based on requirement analysis and module design. This article introduces the background and purpose of designing an information management system for universities. The design of the university information management system aims to improve the support and efficiency of scientific decision-making in universities, achieving standardized, standardized, integrated management and services for university information construction. The design should follow the principles of "user orientation, function priority, ease of use, and scalability", integrating efficient, convenient, integrated and innovative university management concepts into the design of university information management systems.

This article introduces the implementation results of the design of a university information management system. The system has applied advanced and reliable development methods, adopted project management theory, implemented agile development processes, and achieved a comprehensive, efficient, and stable university information management system. After the implementation of this system, comprehensive coverage has been achieved in various aspects such as teaching management, scientific research management, financial management, human resource management, etc., and data visualization and operability management have been achieved.

References

1. Darmstadt, G.L., Kirkwood, B., Gupta, S., et al.: WHO global position paper and implementation strategy on kangaroo mother care call for fundamental reorganisation of maternal nfant care (2023)
2. Baigés, I.J.: The design and implementation of a university environmental management system - a tool for teaching environmental responsibility (2022)
3. Abdullah, R., Selamat, M., Jaafar, A., et al.: An empirical study of knowledge management system implementation in public higher learning institution (2022)
4. Zeng, C., Wei, D.U., Wang, A., et al.: The design and implementation of the Java based remote file management system (2022)
5. Rebelo, R.M.L., Pereira, S.C.F., Queiroz, M.M.: The interplay between the Internet of things and supply chain management: challenges and opportunities based on a systematic literature review. Benchmarking Int. J. **29**(2), 683–711 (2022).https://doi.org/10.1108/BIJ-02-2021-0085

6. Uslaender, T.: Architectural viewpoints and trends for the implementation of the environmental information space (2022)

7. Chen, Z., Zhang, G., Na, J.: The research and implementation of high-speed master-slave CAN-FD composite system based on Cortex-M7. IOP Publishing Ltd. (2022). https://doi.org/10.1088/1742-6596/2290/1/012103

8. Parkes, A., Mccollum, B., Mcmullan, P., et al.: Recent work on planning and management of university teaching space (2022)

9. Pizo, J., Cioch, M., Kański, Ł., et al.: Cobots implementation in the era of industry 5.0 using modern business and management solutions (2022)

10. Adhikari, B.: Property rights and natural resources: impact of common property institutions on community-based resource management (2022)

11. Bouhouch, R., Najjar, W., Jaouani, H., et al.: Implementation of data distribution service listeners on top of flexray driver (2022)

12. Bailey, D., Bailey, J.: The use of collaborative goal setting to impact instructional aide implementation of a school-wide behavior management system (2022)

13. Chen, H., Cui, X.: Design and implementation of human resource management system based on B/S mode. Procedia Comput. Sci. (2022)

14. Carrera-Garcia, L., Muchart, J., Jose Lazaro, J., et al.: Pediatric SMA patients with complex spinal anatomy: implementation and evaluation of a decision-tree algorithm for administration of nusinersen, **31**, 92 (2021). European journal of paediatric neurology: EJPN: official journal of the European Paediatric Neurology Society, 2022(37-):37

15. Miller, A., Radcliffe, D., Isokangas, E.: A perception-influence model for the management of technology implementation in project-based engineering (2022)

Research on Employment Analysis of College Graduates Based on Decision Tree Algorithm

Desheng Zhu[✉], Hui Tang, Bingchen Liu, Mei Guo, Tao Li, and Miao Wang

Shandong Institute of Commerce and Technology, Jinan 250103, Shandong, China
zds08@126.com

Abstract. Because a considerable number of college graduates employment situation is bad, and in trouble, so the decision tree algorithm research to help deal with. In this study, the concept of decision tree algorithm is introduced, and then the selection of algorithm is carried out. Based on the algorithm of research institute selection, the employment data of graduates is analyzed. Through the research, the causes of the employment problems of college graduates can be understood by the relevant decision tree algorithm, and the employment direction can be given to improve the employment situation.

Keyword: Decision tree algorithm · College graduates · Analysis of Graduate Employment

1 Introduction

The employment problem of college graduates in China has a long history. There are many problems, such as difficult employment, slow employment, low employment quality, and unstable employment. These problems not only affect the personal development of college graduates, but also weaken social productivity, labor, technology, etc. to a large extent, making the problem the focus of attention. In this context, through the analysis of the employment situation of college graduates, we can understand each specific employment problem and reason of graduates, and then put forward corresponding suggestions to help graduates find employment. However, people found in the research of relevant analysis that the problem analysis is difficult, and manual analysis is unavoidable in some subjective factors, which can not effectively solve this problem.

With the rapid development of the Internet and cloud computing, data analysis, as a well-known technology, has attracted high attention from academia, industry and government departments. At the same time, a large number of data with a wide variety, a large number, and an increasing rate of generation and updating have made government agencies and colleges and universities gradually realize that it contains unprecedented use value. Since the 21st century, the enrollment expansion of colleges and universities has led to the continuous growth of the number of graduates. While providing more highly qualified labor for the society, there are also many phenomena that college graduates

Y. Zhang and N. Shah (Eds.): BigIoT-EDU 2023, LNICST 581, pp. 105–115, 2024.
https://doi.org/10.1007/978-3-031-63133-7_10

can not find jobs and employers such as enterprises can not recruit talents, which makes the employment problem of graduates more and more prominent.

Employment is an important issue in the development of contemporary society and a reflection of the stability of people's lives. The quality of employment reflects the social stability of the country and the development of the national economy. Because of the great significance of employment, in recent years, more and more scholars have studied the employment quality of college graduates. In the process of studying the employment quality of college graduates, many economic and social factors have also affected them, resulting in most of the employment quality evaluation systems obtained in the study are not comprehensive and objective, and the evaluation indicators are not scientific and complete. The authenticity and accuracy of the employment quality of college graduates is an important factor in evaluating the level of running a university. Only a systematic, reliable, scientific and objective evaluation system of employment quality can really help the society, colleges and graduates to evaluate the employment quality of college graduates.

Data analysis refers to the process of analyzing a large number of collected data with appropriate statistical analysis methods, extracting useful information and forming conclusions, and conducting detailed research and summary of the data. Based on the characteristics of data analysis, how to use specific data processing algorithms to extract valuable parts of data is the core content of data analysis. Mass data analysis is a collection of data that cannot be captured, managed and processed by traditional software tools within a specific time range. It is an information asset that can be obtained through a new processing model, with greater decision-making, insight and process optimization capabilities, such as large-scale, high growth rate and diversification. Establish a data model that meets the actual requirements, and then analyze and process the data samples through the model to obtain conclusions with higher use value. In recent years, the employment evaluation of the government and college graduates has developed from only focusing on the "employment rate" indicator to focusing on both the "employment rate" indicator and the "employment quality" indicator. On the basis of the current employment situation of college graduates and the questionnaire survey, data processing and mining technology is used to process the collected data, determine the evaluation indicators, and establish the evaluation model. The evaluation coefficient to judge the employment quality is obtained, and the judgment result is obtained and relevant opinions are given.

At present, many domestic educational institutions and experts and scholars have done a lot of research on the evaluation of the employment quality of college graduates, and have achieved certain results, thus building a suitable evaluation of the employment quality of a particular university. However, many of these employment quality evaluations are based only on the survey data collected by colleges and universities or researchers, and some of them have not yet processed, studied and analyzed the data, but only stay on the surface of the text information and employment rate to evaluate the employment quality of a college. The final employment quality evaluation system is one-sided and incomplete, and the expansion of application is limited, The employment evaluation of other universities cannot be applied at the same time. The employment quality evaluation based on a large number of data has realized the expansion to multi-disciplinary, multi-dimensional and multi-level applications, and established a diversified evaluation system with the participation of society, universities, enterprises and graduates from multiple perspectives. The multi-level system brought by the analysis of multiple indicators is the process of building a complete and scientific evaluation. The evaluation of graduates' employment quality constructed by a large number of data can solve the problem that the evaluation system obtained through personnel survey has inaccurate evaluation system due to the differences in the survey results of different regions, years of graduates and occupations. With the development of education in China, the quality of graduates' employment has become an indicator to measure the level of a university. By analyzing the corresponding data of each indicator, the correlation degree of each indicator is obtained, and then the weight is calculated. Finally, the comprehensive evaluation coefficient is obtained to analyze the employment quality of college graduates, so as to make the employment quality of college graduates more accurate, thus providing a reference basis for the society and colleges to evaluate the employment quality of college graduates. Therefore, relevant research began to try to use algorithms for analysis. Decision tree algorithm is the main choice of current relevant research. Therefore, in order to provide some help for the employment analysis of college graduates, it is necessary to carry out relevant research.

2 Decision Tree Algorithm

Decision tree algorithm is a kind of algorithm for approximating discrete function value, which is mainly used in data classification and other similar work. The basic principle of the algorithm is as follows: first, the data is processed, then the data is summarized, then the readable rules and decision tree are generated by the algorithm model, and then the data is analyzed under the action of decision tree [1, 2]. Therefore, decision tree algorithm can be defined as a data classification tool relying on a series of rules.

Decision tree algorithm has a long history, the first born in the 1960s, the early algorithms to help people solve a lot of difficult problems to qualitative, therefore widely attention and application, but in subsequent applications, people gradually found that the defects of the decision tree algorithm was first when one is from the depth of the decision tree is too large, makes the result is too small, Therefore, the relevant fields began to improve the decision tree algorithm, so that the algorithm appeared in a variety of forms, such as ID3 algorithm is a decision tree algorithm in the late 1970s, which can effectively reduce the depth of the decision tree and ensure the quality of results. Decision tree algorithm, and then more and more, some have been in use today, namely except ID3 algorithm and C4.5 decision tree algorithm, different algorithms have different defects and advantages, it also makes the macro concept on the function of the decision tree algorithm more rich, not only can be used for data classification, can also perform regression analysis work, The application area of decision tree algorithm is more extensive [3–5].

Although there are many forms of decision tree algorithm, in essence any form of decision tree algorithm is a mathematical tool that uses decision tree for analysis, so how to build a high-quality decision tree is the most important content in the application of this algorithm. Decision tree construction is generally divided into two steps, as shown in Fig. 1.

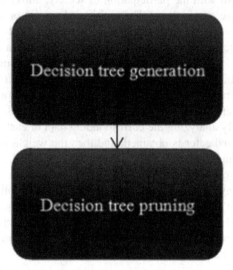

Fig. 1. Decision tree building step

According to Table 1, the generation of decision tree is mainly realized by training samples, that is, the data relation model is generated through training, the association between data is extracted, and the decision tree can be generated by arranging the data according to the hierarchy. At this time, the decision tree is called the initial decision tree. The training sample is composed of data with a certain history, comprehensive degree and related to the analysis target. The initial decision tree contains all data associations, but not all associations are valuable in the analysis. Therefore, if we directly rely on the initial decision tree for analysis, it will be affected by worthless data associations, leading to inaccurate results. In order to avoid this situation, pruning should be done on the basis of the initial decision tree. Pruning is to initialize the decision tree of check, check all the data correlation in a process that is used to determine whether all data associated with the value, if no value is deleted, the value judgment of multiple rules, common is whether a data correlation will affect balance algorithm, the rule under penalty method is: The balance value of the current algorithm is recorded, and then a certain data association is assumed to be deleted. If the balance value does not change after deletion, or increases upward, it means that the data association has no value, or has negative value, and should be deleted; on the contrary, the data association has certain value, and should not be deleted [6–8].

The basic idea of decision tree algorithm is as follows: first, start from any single node in the training sample; Second, if the sample classification is the same, the classification node is defined as a leaf node. Thirdly, if the samples are not in the same class, the attribute with the strongest classification ability, that is, the most representative feature among the data features, should be selected as the current node of the decision tree [9]. Fourthly, according to the current decision node attribute values, the difference between the training sample data is divided into several subsets, each on a value in the process of classification, means to establish a data link, thus generating the corresponding branch, branch generation depends on the values of the number of results (each time the number of the values obtained), this step is repeated, decision trees can be obtained at different levels [10].

Decision tree is a typical recursion model, itself has the characteristics of continuous generalization, as shown in Fig. 2, but under the effect of algorithm in mathematics method, the degree of generalization of decision tree could be limited, and when they reach the limit conditions for termination, so the decision tree will eventually through two forms of output, as shown in Fig. 2 and Fig. 3. The algorithm expression is shown in Eq. (1).

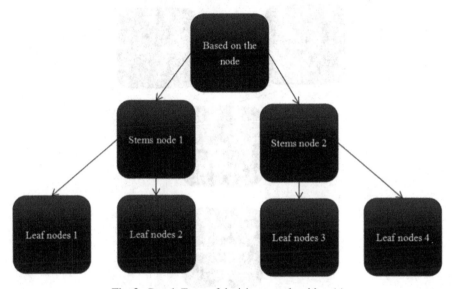

Fig. 2. Result Form of decision tree algorithm (a)

In Fig. 2, the result form of decision tree algorithm is mainly used to show data association and data development direction, which is commonly used in trend analysis.

In Fig. 3, the result form of decision tree algorithm is mainly used to output decision proposals, in which the number of leaf nodes is uncontrollable and depends on the number of training data samples (the number of samples is very large and difficult to count). However, no matter how the specific number is, the output decision proposals are unique [10].

$$Gini(p) = \sum_{k=1}^{K} P_k(1 - P_k) = 1 - \sum_{k=1}^{K} P_k^2 \tag{1}$$

Where K is the branch node, k is the relevant leaf node on K, and P is the rule. The formula mainly through Gini coefficient to detect the purity of the decision tree, the purity does not meet the standard, on behalf of the decision tree has not yet reached the convergence criteria, accord with a standard purity, on behalf of the decision tree has reached the convergence criteria, purity more than standard [11], on behalf of the decision tree over convergence criteria, according to the algorithm based on the three kinds of control.

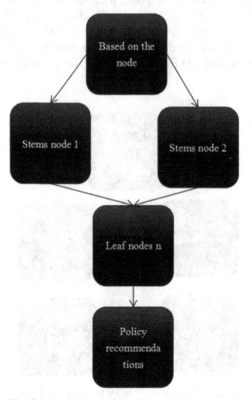

Fig. 3. Result Form of decision tree algorithm (b)

The employment data that can be used for analysis and processing is obtained through quantification, and the experiment is carried out according to the modeling steps of grey correlation analysis:

1. The input matrix for grey correlation analysis is obtained by taking the quantized data sequence as the matrix [12].
2. Determine the reference sequence. Obtain the optimal value of each index as the index value of the series, and then obtain the reference series of employment quality. The reference sequence is named as the employment quality sequence.
3. The indicators are dimensionless. Use the normalization method to convert the quantized data into decimals between (0, 1), so as to simplify the calculation. The conversion function is (2), where max (x) is the maximum value of the sample data sequence,

and min (x) is the minimum value of the sample data sequence.

$$\mathbf{X}_i(k) = \frac{\mathbf{X}_i - \min(x)}{\max(x) - \min(x)} \qquad (2)$$

4. Calculation of correlation coefficient. After calculating the correlation coefficient of each comparison sequence and the corresponding elements of the reference sequence, the corresponding correlation coefficient is obtained according to formula (3).

$$\mathcal{X}_i(k) = \frac{\mathbf{x} - \bar{x}}{s} \qquad (3)$$

5. Calculate the correlation degree.

The average value of correlation coefficient corresponding to each evaluation index sequence and reference sequence is calculated to reflect the relationship between each evaluation object and reference sequence. The formula of correlation degree sequence is:

$$\gamma = \frac{1}{m} \sum_{k=1}^{m} \xi_i(k) \qquad (4)$$

The accurate evaluation of the employment quality of college graduates depends not only on the methods used in the evaluation process, but also on the scores of indicators in the evaluation process [13]. The employment component data table is prepared to provide the basis for the calculation of the evaluation coefficient below, and the scoring of the index is also a reflection of the contribution of the evaluation index. Index information quantification technology can be converted into evaluation scores, which can not only get intuitive feedback information on a regular basis, but also make the evaluation scores based on detailed, specific, accurate and fixed measurement scales, ensuring the objectivity and effectiveness of the evaluation scores. The purpose of quantifying the evaluation score is to overcome the influence of traditional qualitative description evaluation factors such as halo effect and prejudice, and to take the fact as the criterion to enhance the accuracy [14].

3 Analysis of Graduate Employment

3.1 Analysis Object Description

Considering the convenience of the research, a 2010 college graduate is selected as the research object, and his employment data within five years after graduation is selected as the training data sample for algorithm analysis. According to the statistics, the graduate looked for employment opportunities quickly after graduation, but it had been five months until his first successful employment. In the process, the graduate made 13 attempts to find employment, and except for the 13th, the other 12 attempts ended in failure [15]. The relevant reasons are unknown and need to be analyzed. At the same time, from the first successful employment to the current job, the graduate has been in the phenomenon of employment instability, and the current job is not in line with its major, indicating the existence of low quality of employment, the cause of which also needs to be analyzed. Finally, although the graduate still has a positive attitude towards employment, he is still confused about the future employment development and has no accurate employment direction. He hopes to get guidance and help through analysis.

3.2 Algorithm Modeling

According to the specific situation of the analysis object, the decision tree model is constructed by the decision tree algorithm. The model construction method is as follows: Firstly, the relevant information of each employment of the analysis object up to now is collected, and the eigenvalue of each employment is set according to the success and failure of employment, that is, the eigenvalue of the success of employment is 1, the eigenvalue of the failure of employment is −1, and the eigenvalue of the unemployed time and the very short-term employment in the process of employment is 0. Second, the information eigenvalues are converted into data and input to the algorithm system [16]. The system is completely set according to the logic of the decision tree algorithm (C4.5 in this study), which can realize the algorithm and receive relevant data. After receiving data, data processing is carried out, which is divided into two steps: (1) Using preprocessing tools to remove incomplete and repeated data in all data to refine the magnitude of data, which can speed up the efficiency of the algorithm; (2) Using recursive algorithm to check the value of all nodes, and then pruning. The obtained decision tree model is derived from Fig. 3, see Fig. 4 for details.

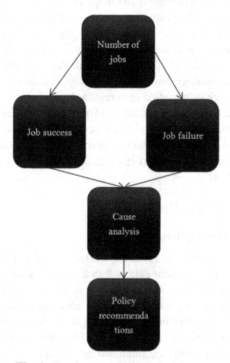

Fig. 4. Employment analysis decision tree

3.3 Analysis Process

Combined with the situation of the analysis object, it is necessary to use the decision tree algorithm to analyze the reasons for its employment failure, success, long-term instability of employment, and future employment direction. The basic analysis of the three problems in the decision tree algorithm is the same: first, the data of related problems are input into the decision tree to make the algorithm run; Secondly, according to the data, the algorithm will gradually establish the main rod, branch node and leaf node, which is used to show the data relationship and generate results [17]. Third, because the decision tree model is in the form of Fig. 3, leaf nodes will constantly generate and traverse all data so as to finally output a unique decision proposal for each problem.

3.4 Analysis Results and Discussion

The results of three questions are obtained through analysis: First, the graduates in employment talks with unit of choose and employ persons, if found the work content does not conform to their own professional jobs, or the condition of the salary is lower than personal expectations, will choose to leave, on behalf of the failure of employment, this kind of situation in the employment data failure accounted for 13.6%, the rest of the data are for unit of choose and employ persons reject its employment request [18], The reason lies in the employers think that the graduate professional level is insufficient, lack of practical experience, leading to their employment failure. The graduates because of long-term experience of failure, employment confidence was hit, so began to transfer, or lower the standard, the pursuit of lower positions, through this way the graduate employment success; Second, because graduates by low standards and similar successful employment, this kind of behavior has forced sex, does not represent graduates to give up the original standard, so although graduates employment success, but still want to be carried out in accordance with the original standard employment, encourage the graduates began to change jobs frequently, and often fail before into the loop, and because I have accumulated some experience in employment successfully, I can get employed occasionally in this stage, and the success rate and failure rate are gradually equal, but still cannot meet the inner expectations of graduates [19]. Thirdly, the decision tree algorithm gives three employment schemes, and selects the best decision proposal from the schemes. Three employment scheme for, (1) to maintain the original state, to lower standards, seeking another job opportunities, job success rate was 80%, and analyzing the degree of satisfaction was 10%, so in the short term again probability as high as 90%, leaving the company (2) an increase in the standard, seeking another job opportunities, because of work before the accumulation of experience, so the scheme under the employment success rate is 40%, the analysis target satisfaction is 80%, and the probability of leaving again in a short time is 10%. (3) Self-employment, because it is a new employment attempt, the success rate is unknown, but the analysis target satisfaction can reach 90%, and the probability of leaving again in a short time is 10%. Combined with the three schemes, the decision tree algorithm finally chose the solution (3), (1) and analysis of the reason is that target no existing employment way, and can't solve practical problems, so choose to give up, (2) although the data will have good performance, but the success rate is very low, can't solve the problem of employment, it is recommended that analysis aim to make a new attempt, Reencounter problems can continue to analyze, to provide help for their employment development (Fig. 5).

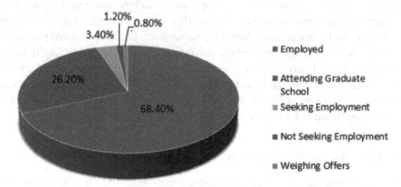

Fig. 5. Employment data of graduates

According to the results, analysis of goals for the self-employed, after a year on the employment situation and inner satisfaction were investigated [20], the results show a year analyzing the employment situation is good, the existing work with professional counterparts, and employment, personal income is stable, inner satisfaction survey as "very satisfied", explain the employment problem is resolved, algorithm is effective.

4 Conclusion

To sum up, the employment situation of college graduates is complicated, so many graduates will fall into employment dilemma, and it is difficult to make choices by themselves, and it is difficult to give objective results through external manual analysis, so decision tree algorithm can be used to deal with it. The algorithm can objectively analyze the employment situation of graduates from the perspective of data, output the reasons for success and failure of employment, and then give the best choice based on data experience, so it can solve practical problems and help break through the employment dilemma.

References

1. Tan, Y., Wang, J., Chen, B., et al.: Rapid identification model based on decision tree algorithm coupling with H-1 NMR and feature analysis by UHPLC-QTOFMS spectrometry for sandalwood. J. Chromatogr. B Anal. Technol. Biomed. Life Sci. **1161**, 122449 (2020)
2. Zhang, W.: Research on English score analysis system based on improved decision tree algorithm and fuzzy set (Retraction of Vol 39, Pg 5673, 2020). J. Intell. Fuzzy Syst. Appl. Eng. Technol. (5), 41 (2021)
3. Kang, H., ,Chen, Y., et al.: Model establishment of decision tree algorithm and its application in vehicle fault prediction analysis (2020)

4. Mei, H., Li, X.: Research on e-commerce coupon user behavior prediction technology based on decision tree algorithm. Int. Core J. Eng. **5**(9), 48–58 (2019)

5. Ma, W.: Research on decision tree application in data of fire alarm receipt and disposal. In: International Conference on Intelligent Human-Machine Systems and Cybernetics (2019)

6. Mao, L., Zhang, W.: Analysis of entrepreneurship education in colleges and based on improved decision tree algorithm and fuzzy mathematics. Jo. Intell. Fuzzy Syst. Appl. Eng. Technol. (2), 40 (2021)

7. Bian, F., Wang, X.: School enterprise cooperation mechanism based on improved decision tree algorithm. J. Intell. Fuzzy Syst. Appl. Eng. Technol. (4), 40 (2021)

8. Ludwig, S., Ruebsamen, N., Deuschl, F., et al.: Screening or transcatheter mitral valve replacement:a decision tree algorithm. EuroIntervention J. EuroPCR Collab. Work. Group Interv. Cardiol. Eur. Soc. Cardiol. (3), 16 (2020)

9. Dahiya, S., Das, S., Bharadwaj, A.: Online classification and visualization using the C4.5 decision tree algorithm. J. Indian Soc. Agric. Stat. (2), 73 (2019)

10. Di, J., Xu, Y.: Decision tree improvement algorithm and its application. Int. Core J. Eng. **5**(9), 151–158 (2019)

11. Yang, F.: Construction of graduate behavior dynamic model based on dynamic decision tree algorithm. Discrete Dyn. Nat. Soc. **2022** (2022)

12. Chen, J.: Research and analysis of employment prediction algorithms for college graduates. Mod. Inf. Technol. (2019)

13. Yang, F.: Decision tree algorithm based university graduate employment trend prediction. Informatica (4) (2019)

14. Aziz, M., Yusof, Y.: Graduates employment classification using data mining approach. In: AIP Conference Proceedings. AIP Publishing LLCAIP Publishing (2016)

15. Lee, K.M., Lin, C.H.: A boosted 3-D pca algorithm based on efficient analysis method (2021)

16. Liu, Y.: Research on personalized employment recommendation system in colleges based on collaborative filtering algorithms. Mod. Inf. Technol. (2019)

17. Wang, S., Changyu, W.U., Chen, Y.: The application of C4.5 algorithm in the analysis of vocational college students' peer-to-peer employment factors. J. Dongguan Univ. Technol. (2019)

18. Ren, P.H., Chao, R.: Research on the path of data mining in accurate employment of college graduates——taking computer science as an example. J. Shanxi Datong Univ. (Nat. Sci. Ed.) (2019)

19. Tian, L.: Simulation of college students' employment rate estimation model based on big data analysis. Boletin Tecnico/Tech. Bull. **55**(10), 437–443 (2017)

20. Sang, H., Jiang, M., Lu, Z., et al.: Data mining algorithm for influencing factors of university students' position promotion based on decision tree. J. Beihua Univ. (Nat. Sci.) (2019)

Design and Application of the Genetic Algorithm in the Teaching System Platform

Lei Yang[⊠]

Tianjin Academy of Fine Arts, Tianjin 300020, China
52067315@qq.com

Abstract. Teaching system is an efficient teaching method, and it is also the comprehensive management of teaching cases. Teachers can use the education system to standardize the data transmission of teaching plans. Therefore, communication is very important for teachers' research. Forget it. Therefore, what schools say can relate the data in teaching, realize the comprehensive judgment of data, and finally determine the best teaching method. Therefore, the integration of teaching methods and decision tree can improve the effectiveness and accuracy of existing methods, and better identify teaching content.

Keyword: teaching management · management systems · Decision tree method · Optimize

1 Introduction

With the implementation and deepening of the emerging technologies, learners' requirements for educational science and technology products are increasing. In addition to the teaching function of educational science and technology products, learners are also increasingly concerned about whether they have some good quality and whether they can obtain good learning experience in the process of using the products. Therefore, the integrating education and technology into the design of educational technology products is educational technology products themselves (i.e. users). First, for users, the key issues such as whether the learning process of using educational technology products is pleasant, whether they have a sense of achievement, whether they can obtain a good learning experience and whether learning is effective are very important.

Student classification: The decision tree and historical data, such as high, medium, and low, for better personalized education [1–3].

Student performance prediction: By analyzing students' learning time, learning methods, family environment and other characteristics, the decision tree algorithm can with learning difficulties in advance, and take corresponding measures to intervene [4–9].

Assisted teaching decision-making: The visual nature of the decision tree algorithm allows educators to clearly understand the basis on which students are classified, so as to better personalize education [10, 11].

© ICST Institute for Computer Sciences, Social Informatics and Telecommunications Engineering 2024
Published by Springer Nature Switzerland AG 2024. All Rights Reserved
Y. Zhang and N. Shah (Eds.): BigIoT-EDU 2023, LNICST 581, pp. 116–123, 2024.
https://doi.org/10.1007/978-3-031-63133-7_11

Improve teaching effectiveness: By predicting students' academic performance and identifying students with learning difficulties, decision tree algorithms can help educators develop more effective teaching strategies that can improve teaching effectiveness. Promote personalized education: Decision tree algorithms can classify students based on their personal characteristics and historical data, which helps to achieve personalized education and meet the needs of different students.

Improving Equity in Education: By predicting students' academic performance, decision tree algorithms thereby improving equity in education.

2 Related Concepts

2.1 Mathematical Description of the Decision Tree Method

Decision tree algorithm is based on data, which makes the decision of educators more scientific and objective.

Hypothesis 1: The visualization characteristic of decision tree algorithm makes educators understand students' situation more intuitively, so as to carry out individualized education better as shown in Eq. (1). $a_i \sum a_i y_i f(x_i)$

$$f(x_i) = \sum a_i |\overline{\overline{y_i}} + \prod \xi \tag{1}$$

The integration of teaching plan information data provides support for data mining by merging multiple teaching plan information data stores into one teaching plan information data collection. The problem of teaching plan information data integration in this paper mainly involves the redundancy of teaching plan information data, that is, the value of an attribute can be deduced from other attributes, and that attribute is the redundancy attribute [8]. The actual evaluation average score df in the student evaluation information summary table xspj can be deduced from the actual evaluation total score zf and rs, so the actual evaluation average score df is a redundant attribute. However, considering that the analysis of the teaching plan information data is mainly based on the actual evaluation average score df, the attributes zf and rs can be eliminated. Decision tree algorithm can deal with classify and predict the data, which makes it have strong applicability in the development of teaching system.

2.2 Selection of Teaching Optimization Schemes

In daily teaching activities, teachers should master the teaching rhythm skillfully, avoid the delay and slow operation of the course, and constantly optimize the teaching process. The optimization, a more reasonable and progressive teaching process design should be adopted, and should be designed as a more reasonable and progressive teaching process along the reform route of "practice first, theory first, and then knowledge" [11]. The first stage is to create the situation into the role. Before class, you can create the entrepreneurial situation related to the specialty, To enable students to quickly enter their roles in the real business environment and learn the learning resources on the teaching platform with problems, not only arousing students' interest and motivation in learning, but also stimulating students' creativity. The second stage: task-driven knowledge of business, release primary practical tasks, students perceive the key points of business knowledge in practice according to pre-class preview, and practice before learning theory. Adopt the game-based teaching strategy that contemporary college students like, guide students to carry out independent exploration and interactive collaborative learning by completing game tasks, and cultivate students' independent exploration and pioneering self-study ability. The third stage: based on the learning guidance theory, students will discuss the difficult points after completing the primary practical tasks. The teacher will solve the key and difficult points according to the discussion results and the actual cases of the enterprise. The fourth stage: practice skills through actual combat drills [12]. Through the 1+X certificate and skill competition training platform, students can connect with the actual situation of enterprises to carry out upgraded actual combat drills, and further practice skills through re-practice. The fifth step: summarize and solidify strong quality, organize ideological and political activities in class, and promote students' professional ethics and moral quality.

Hypothesis 2: The whole process of data processing is complicated, so it is simplified and Formula 2 is put forward.

$$F(x_i)=z_i \leftrightarrow f(x_i|y_i) \xrightarrow[\varphi_i] {} \xi \tag{2}$$

2.3 Treatment of Low-Quality Lesson Plans

In the teaching system, the quality of data is often uneven because of the variety of data sources, which will affect the performance of decision tree algorithm. How to deal with incomplete, abnormal or noisy data is a challenge [11–13], a realize the comprehensive judgment of data is shown in Fig. 1.

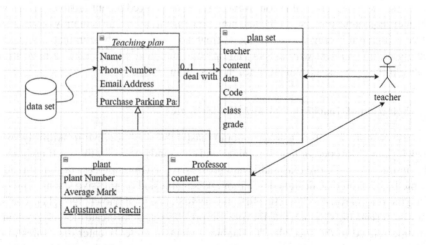

Fig. 1. The process of decision tree analysis

In the teaching system, the samples of some categories may be much larger than those of other categories, resulting in data imbalance. This will affect the construction and classification of decision trees. How to deal with unbalanced data is an important problem [14].

2.4 Correlation Between Different Lesson Plans

Feature selection is one of the key steps of decision tree algorithms [15]. However, in a teaching system, there may be many features that are related or redundant with each other. How to choose the features that are most relevant to the target variable is a challenge. Generalization ability issues: In teaching systems, the generalization ability of a model may be affected over time and changes in the student population. How to adapt the model to these changes is an important question. Privacy and security concerns: In the instructional system, students' personal information is sensitive. It's a challenge to ensure that this information isn't leaked when building a decision tree.

3   Practical Examples of Teaching Management Systems

3.1   Teaching System Situation

Collect the data to be processed, and carry out preliminary data cleaning and preprocessing. This includes deleting missing values, handling outliers, feature selection and conversion the results are shown in the following table (Table 1).

Table 1. Evaluation of the Teaching and Learning Management System

Relevant evaluation indexes	To grade the content	My total score	The state of a division	Four cases of data distribution
Course planning. Content	1	39.29	98.21	62.50
	2	78.57	91.07	76.79
Teaching indicators	1	19.64	14.29	35.71
	2	19.64	41.07	39.29
Comprehensive teaching effect	1	58.93	60.71	44.64
	2	16.07	64.29	76.79

Which data analysis in Instrument 1 should be scored by scale, and the specific contents are shown in Table 2 (Fig. 2).

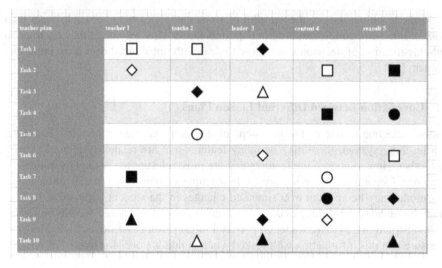

Fig. 2. The processing process of the lesson plan

Table 2. Overall situation of teaching management

plan improvement rate	An overall planning and analysis	False lesson plan recognition rate
100	58.93	85.71
90	55.36	91.07
80	85.71	89.29
70	85.21	23.21
X^2	4.212	7.337
P = 0. 011		

3.2 Optimized Ratio of Lesson Plans

Select the feature that has the greatest influence on the target variable. Usually, information gain, information gain ratio and Gini index are used to measure the importance of features as shown in Table 2.

3.3 Time and Accuracy of Teaching Optimization

According to the results of feature selection, the decision tree model is constructed. This process includes tree pruning, stop condition judgment and other operations is shown in Fig. 3.

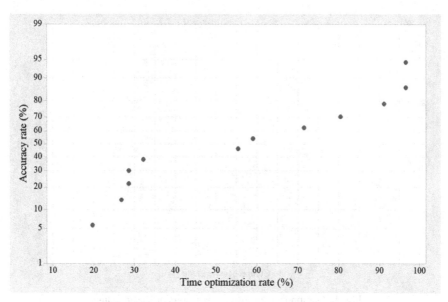

Fig. 3. Data optimization with the same method.

The key contents and key indicators of some data need to be analyzed in depth, and the analysis methods of key indicators of data should be studied (Table 3).

Table 3. Compare the overall situation of the data and analyze the officials in the data.

Algorithm	The whole data	This overall change	error
The actual situation of transport aircraft	58.21	42.14	37.50
These numbers are the same standard	54.29	40.36	46.79
P	0.024	0.021	0.014

The content in the study is tested and analyzed, and the relationship between the data is compared to complete the comprehensive judgment of the data (Fig. 4).

The decision tree model is applied to the actual teaching process, which is used to classify students and predict their academic achievements.

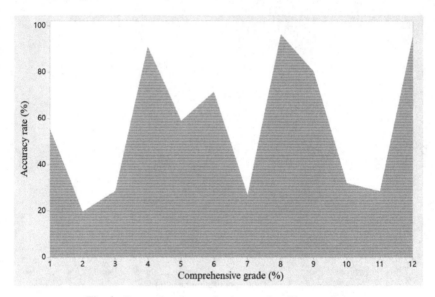

Fig. 4. Comprehensive evaluation results of lesson plans

4   Conclusion

As an important content of school information system, data system can reasonably distribute educational resources, teachers, and students, so as to better combine them and improve the level and ability of curriculum teaching. However, in the process of optimization, education system needs to be perfected by means of decision tree to simplify various complex problems in education system, so as to realize the overall optimization of data and teaching content. An algorithm that can be proposed has many applications and advantages in the development of teaching system, it also faces many challenges and difficulties. Future research needs to solve these problems in order to achieve better individualized education and improve teaching effect.

References

1. Li, J.: Application of intelligent fuzzy decision tree algorithm in English teaching model improvement. Complexity (2021)
2. Fan, Y.Y.: Application of ID3 decision tree mining in teaching assistant system. J. Qiqihar Univ. (Nat. Sci. Ed.) (2016)
3. Zhang, P.H., Fu, K.: Research on the application of decision tree algorithm in the selection of variables in cost estimation model (2020)
4. Zhang, C., Hu, C., Xie, S., et al.: Research on the application of decision tree and random forest algorithm in the main transformer fault evaluation. J. Phys. Conf. Ser. **1732**(1), 012086 (2021), 7 p.
5. Yang, H.: The application of fuzzy decision tree algorithm in public English test (2017)
6. Ying-Yong, Z., Guang-Bin, Y., Yong-De, Z., et al.: Research on the application of genetic algorithm in license plate recognition system. J. Comput. Theor. Nanosci. **13**(9), 6088–6097 (2016)

7. Zhao, X.: Application of deep learning algorithm in college English teaching process evaluation. Behav. Inf. Technol. **11**, 1–10 (2019)
8. Dong, S.: Research on the application of distributed artificial intelligence in network teaching (2016)
9. Iqbal, N., Naqvi, R., Atif, M., et al.: On the image encryption algorithm based on the chaotic system, DNA encoding, and castle. IEEE Access (2021)
10. Wang, Z.L.: Application of decision tree technology in the cultivation of students' teaching ability. J. Jincheng Inst. Technol. (2017)
11. Cheng, D.: Research on the application of algorithm C4.5 in the analysis of college students' score of computer rank examination. J. Huaibei Norm. Univ. (Nat. Sci. Ed.) (2016)
12. Zhang, W.: Research on English score analysis system based on improved decision tree algorithm and fuzzy set. J. Intell. Fuzzy Syst. Appl. Eng. Technol. **39**(4Pta2) (2020)
13. Guo, Q.C., Yang, H., School, O.S.: Research on the application of C4.5 classification decision tree in university course arrangement management. Comput. Knowl. Technol. (2018)
14. Jia, J., Xu, H., Song, Z.: Application of attribute reduction algorithm of rough set based on MIX_FP tree in computer teaching. In: 2019 2nd International Conference on Information Systems and Computer Aided Education (ICISCAE) (2019)
15. Zhang, Y., Wu, B.: Research and application of grade prediction model based on decision tree algorithm. In: The ACM Turing Celebration Conference - China. ACM (2019)
16. Liu, X.: The application of data mining technology in the teaching evaluation in colleges and universities. J. Comput. Theor. Nanosci. **14**(1), 7–12 (2017)
17. Min, X.U.: Research on application of data mining technology in educational administration system. Educ. Teach. Forum (2017)
18. Fang, C.: Intelligent online English teaching system based on SVM algorithm and complex network. J. Intell. Fuzzy Syst. Appl. Eng. Technol. **40**(2) (2021)
19. Liang, L.T., Polytechnic, S.: Application research of decision tree algorithm in performance analysis of higher vocational colleges. J. Hubei Open Vocat. Coll. (2019)
20. Xie, X.J., Xiang-Ju, L.I., Cao, F.P., et al.: Research and implementation of e-learning teaching assistant system based on improving C4.5. J. Jiamusi Univ. (Nat. Sci. Ed.) (2018)

Design of Task Scheduling Algorithm for Educational Administration System Based on Decision Tree Algorithm

Min Zhang$^{(\boxtimes)}$

Jiangxi Institute of Applied Science and Technology, Nanchang 330100, Jiangxi, China
594140319@qq.com

Abstract. With the rapid improvement of message and Internet technique, data is exploding, and the demand for data mining and analysis to gain more value is also increasing. In order to better solve the problem of large amount of interactive data in the task scheduling of cloud computing in administrative management system, aiming at the lack of rationality in the division and resource allocation of hadoop tasks during the processing of hadoop, this paper proposes a scheduling means for hadoop tasks. The research of this paper is the task scheduling algorithm design of educational administration system based on decision tree algorithm. The means adopted in this paper is decision tree algorithm. Collecting and analyzing message quickly, accurately and efficiently is an vital means for enterprises to improve their decision-making level and enhance their competitiveness, so the decision tree algorithm has attracted people's attention. The decision tree is constructed from top to bottom by using greedy strategy and recursion. In fact, machine learning is data-driven, extracting and integrating valuable message from massive data, and using machines instead of people to solve problems. The research in this paper shows that the algorithm in this paper is effective and suitable for being widely used.

Keyword: Decision tree algorithm · Educational administration system · Task scheduling algorithm

1 Introduction

With the rapid improvement of message and Internet technique, data has penetrated into all walks of life and their business areas in today's society, and the era of hadoop has arrived. As an interdisciplinary subject involving probability theory, statistics, convex analysis and other domains, machine learning has a very wide range of applications [1]. At the same time, the rapid improvement of the Internet has also ushered in a huge challenge of how to make rational use of a large number of idle resources. Hadoop has the characteristics of huge capacity, various types, complex sources, low value density, etc. For this reason, many general underlying hadoop systems have appeared in the market to handle hadoop. However, for most hadoop systems, there are different standards

Y. Zhang and N. Shah (Eds.): BigIoT-EDU 2023, LNICST 581, pp. 124–131, 2024.
https://doi.org/10.1007/978-3-031-63133-7_12

for internal tasks, and the allocation of hadoop task resources is not reasonable, and the processing flow of hadoop tasks is not standardized [2–5]. At present, most departments' electronic administration systems only use the basic platform to communicate message, and the closed system structure Educational administration system is a very important part of the school, involving a lot of complex management work, among which task scheduling is a very critical one. In order to achieve efficient educational administration, we can introduce decision tree algorithm to establish an automatic task scheduling model. This paper will discuss in detail how to use decision tree algorithm for task scheduling of educational administration system.

2 Task Scheduling and Decision Tree Algorithm

2.1 Task Scheduling

So far, the task scheduling problem for cloud computing is still a relatively advanced topic. In cloud computing, task scheduling strategy directly affects the user's task execution efficiency and resource utilization efficiency in cloud environment. Therefore, a good task scheduling strategy is of great significance to ensure user service quality and improve the overall resource utilization efficiency in cloud environment [6]. Users submit tasks to the data center through the service agent, and the data center selects an appropriate task scheduling mechanism according to the specific needs of users. Then, virtual machines with different performances are allocated for task execution according to the scheduling mechanism, and finally the execution results are fed back to users through the service agent [7]. Cloud computing is a product of the new era, and it is a business computing mode that charges on demand. It provides convenient and fast network access, and makes use of the configurability of resource sharing pool to quickly use these resources. Its improvement depends on content distribution and task scheduling, that is, dynamically scheduling the demands from different users to the computing resources that require many times, ensuring the maximum optimization of resource utilization, scheduling cost, load balance and service quality [8–12]. The task scheduling process is shown in Fig. 1.

Data collection and pre-processing: First, we need to collect task data in the academic administration system, including information such as task type, priority, execution time, and dependencies. At the same time, we need to collect data on resources, including available human, material and financial resources. After data collection, we also need to preprocess the data, such as missing value filling, outlier value handling, etc., to ensure the quality and validity of the data.

Model task dependencies: There may be dependencies between tasks, and the completion of one task may depend on the completion of other tasks. Therefore, we need to build a task dependency model so that these dependencies are taken into account when task scheduling. We can use decision tree algorithms to identify dependencies on tasks.

Establish a task scheduling model: Based on the established task dependency model, we can use the decision tree algorithm to build a task scheduling model. We can learn how to effectively schedule tasks based on task dependencies and resource availability by training a decision tree model.

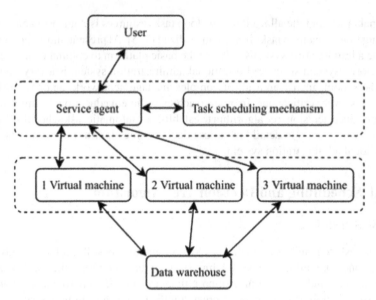

Fig. 1. Task scheduling process

Task scheduling and execution: In the task scheduling and execution phase, we first determine the execution order of tasks based on the task dependency model, and then allocate tasks based on resource availability and task characteristics. In the process of task execution, we also need to adjust and optimize the task according to the actual situation to ensure the efficient execution of the task.

Evaluation and optimization: Finally, we need to evaluate and optimize the task scheduling effect. We can adjust and optimize the model according to the difference between the actual execution result and the expected result, so as to gradually improve the efficiency and accuracy of task scheduling. At the same time, we can also use some evaluation indicators to quantitatively evaluate the task scheduling effect, such as task completion time, resource utilization, etc.

2.2 Decision Tree Algorithm

Data-driven strategy: We can use large amounts of historical data to train decision tree models to identify task dependencies and resource availability. Through the continuous updating and optimization of data, we can gradually improve the accuracy and efficiency of the decision tree model.Priority policy: In task scheduling, you can sort tasks according to their priority. For high-priority tasks, we can prioritize their execution. In the decision tree model, we can prioritize tasks with high priority through the conditional judgment of nodes.Dynamic adjustment strategy: During the actual task execution, we may encounter some unexpected situations, such as sudden changes in resources or temporary adjustment of tasks. In this case, we can adjust and optimize the decision tree model according to the actual situation to ensure the smooth execution of the task [14]. Visualization strategy: To facilitate understanding and monitoring of the task scheduling process, we can use visualization technology to display the decision tree model and the task scheduling process. In a graphical way, we can intuitively understand the execution of tasks and the use of resources.if there is no effective means to help extract useful message and knowledge from it, human beings are obviously as helpless as finding a needle in a haystack. The flow chart of building decision tree is shown in Fig. 2.

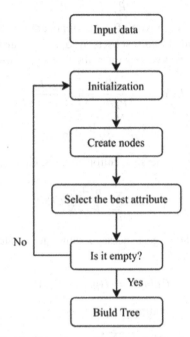

Fig. 2. Flow chart of building decision tree

At present, people are caught in an embarrassing situation of "rich data" and "poor knowledge". Under the background of hadoop, we need to analyze the data at a higher level, and discover all the potential relationships and rules existing before the data. And data mining technique is the process of forecasting and analyzing these seemingly random and unrelated data and extracting useful message from them [14]. Decision tree is an vital data mining technique, which is often used in classification prediction, rule extraction and many other domains. The decision tree is constructed from top to bottom by using greedy strategy and recursion. Actually, machine learning is a subject driven by data, which extracts and integrates valuable message from massive data, and uses machines instead of people to solve problems. Machine learning is divided into supervised learning and unsupervised learning [15]. Classification is an vital part of supervised learning. It refers to the problems that people encounter in life and need to analyze, screen and divide hadoop. Policymakers find that in order to gain competitive advantage, they need to extract data from a large amount of data (including business data, historical data, etc.) about their own business operation and the situation of related industries in the whole market for analysis, so as to make favorable decisions.

For a sample set S with n counterexamples and p positive examples, the amount of message of the decision tree that can be correctly classified is:

$$I(p, n) = -\frac{p}{p+n} \log_2 \frac{p}{p+n}$$
$$- \frac{n}{p+n} \log_2 \frac{n}{p+n} \tag{1}$$

If attribute A is taken as the root of the current sample set S, and A has v values $v_1, v_2, \ldots v_v$, and S is divided into v subsets $S_1, S_2, \ldots S_v$, and a subset S_i contains P_i positive examples and N_i negative examples, the message entropy of S_i is defined as:

$$E(S_i) = -\frac{P_i}{P_i + N_i} \log_2 \frac{P_i}{P_i + N_i}$$
$$- \frac{N_i}{P_i + N_i} \log_2 \frac{N_i}{P_i + N_i} \tag{2}$$

It is also stipulated that the message entropy of classification based on attribute A is:

$$E(A) = \sum_{i=1}^{v} \frac{p_i + n_i}{P + N} E(S_i) \tag{3}$$

The attribute A with the largest message gain can be rated as the best classified attribute, which is defined as:

$$Gain(A) = I(p, n) - E(A) \tag{4}$$

The calculation formula of entropy impurity is:

$$Im\, p(N) = -\sum_j P(\omega_j) \log_2 P(\omega_j) \tag{5}$$

a two-class problem is defined as:

$$Im\, p(N) = P(\omega_1) P(\omega_2) \tag{6}$$

Obviously, this value is related to the overall distribution variance of the two types of distributions. When the generalized formula (6) is used for multi-class classification problems, its value is obtained by the following formula:

$$Im\, p(N) = \sum_{i \neq j} P(\omega_i) P(\omega_j)$$
$$= 1 - \sum_j P^2(\omega_j) \tag{7}$$

Therefore, collecting and analyzing message quickly, accurately and efficiently is an vital means for enterprises to improve their decision-making level and enhance their competitiveness. Therefore, people hope that computers can help us to analyze and understand data automatically and intelligently, so as to further help us make decisions.

3 Results and Discussion

The mathematical model construction of scheduling resources is an vital step in the execution of machine learning tasks. With the improvement of message and communication technique, mining and analysis can bring more value to data, which promotes the rapid growth of data analysis demand. However, because the hadoop itself has the characteristics of large scale and high complexity, the computational cost of hadoop mining and analysis tasks is often very high. At the same time, with the improvement of prospect. Besides constructing the mathematical model of scheduling algorithm resources by analyzing the internal characteristics of task set, it is also necessary to consider the task requirements and various resource types, such as CPU and memory. Types of tasks include computational tasks, storage tasks and network tasks.

In modern mainstream hadoop systems, hadoop tasks are usually represented by DAG, where vertices are hadoop tasks, and edges connecting vertices are the relationships between hadoop tasks. Inevitably, hadoop tasks need to share cluster resources. Therefore, it is a very vital issue to divide hadoop tasks and allocate resources according to what standards (Tables 1, 2 and Figs. 3, 4).

Table 1. Changes of execution time when the number of tasks is 50

	0	20	40	60	80	100
Expected time change	369	470	425	483	584	489
Actual time change	469	413	626	491	587	386

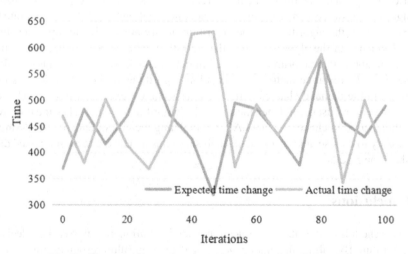

Fig. 3. Changes of execution time when the number of tasks is 50.

In the process of hadoop processing, because the data obtained by the data collection task have different data structures, it is necessary to process the collected data into

Table 2. Changes of execution time when the number of tasks is 100

	0	20	40	60	80	100
Expected time change	1094	570	824	905	767	907
Actual time change	518	691	1097	830	508	980

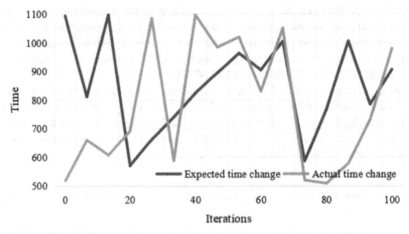

Fig. 4. Changes of execution time when the number of tasks is 100.

uniform standard format data, store the processed data, calculate the attributes of each historical sample data set, obtain the measurement values of the corresponding scheduling algorithm resources, and save the corresponding relationship between them into the databank; Then, the algorithms in the algorithm library are applied in turn to evaluate the performance of the algorithms, and the algorithm with the best evaluation result is listed as an applicable algorithm and saved in the databank. When a new task needs to be executed, the resource metrics of scheduling algorithms in the databank are sorted according to the demand characteristics such as accuracy, execution time, CPU occupancy and memory usage, and then the applicable algorithm is called. Then the improved algorithm is used to cluster the tasks.After completing the task of data preprocessing, it is necessary to choose appropriate data analysis means to analyze these processed data, and show the results.

4   Conclusions

The task scheduling algorithm of educational administration system based on decision tree algorithm. By calling the mathematical model of algorithm resources, the applicable algorithm in the algorithm library is selected for the submitted task data set. Aiming at the problem of how to allocate resources reasonably and efficiently in the process of hadoop processing, this paper introduces the task scheduling theory and proposes a scheduling means for hadoop tasks. Experimental results show that the scheduling algorithm is effective and feasible in most cases, and the improved clustering algorithm can also make up for the defects to some extent, thus effectively improving the effectiveness of task scheduling. The algorithm can effectively improve the prediction accuracy, which indicates that the algorithm in this paper can effectively improve the efficiency of task scheduling in hadoop systems. The next work is to consider using machine learning means to optimize the workflow generated by the algorithm and improve the performance of the algorithm. By analyzing the internal structure and performance characteristics of tasks, the tasks with different preferences can be matched with the resources with corresponding performance characteristics, thus improving the efficiency of task execution to a certain extent.

References

1. Lu, P., Zhu, Z.: Data-oriented task scheduling in fixed- and flexible-grid multilayer inter-DC optical networks: a comparison study. J. Lightwave Technol. **35**(24), 5335–5346 (2017)
2. Shah-Mansouri, H., Wong, V., Schober, R.: Joint optimal pricing and task scheduling in mobile cloud computing systems. IEEE Trans. Wirel. Commun. **PP**(8), 1 (2017)
3. Chen, M., Hao, Y., Lai, C.F., et al.: Opportunistic task scheduling over co-located clouds in mobile environment. IEEE Trans. Serv. Comput., 1 (2017)
4. Cortes-Arcos, T., Bernal-Agustin, J.L., Dufo-Lopez, R., et al.: Multi-objective demand response to real-time prices (RTP) using a task scheduling meansology. Energy **138**(11), 19–31 (2017)
5. Liu, C., Guo, X., Li, Z., et al.: Multisensors cooperative detection task scheduling algorithm based on hybrid task decomposition and MBPSO. Math. Probl. Eng. **2017**, 1–11 (2017)
6. Zheng, W., Wu, H., Nie, C.: Integrating task scheduling and cache locking for multicore real-time embedded systems. ACM Sigplan Not. **52**(4), 71–80 (2017)
7. Sheng, S., Chen, P., Chen, Z., et al.: Deep reinforcement learning-based task scheduling in IoT edge computing. Sensors **21**(5), 1666 (2021)
8. Balasekaran, G., Jayakumar, S., Prado, R.: An intelligent task scheduling mechanism for autonomous vehicles via deep learning. Energies **14**(6), 1788 (2021)
9. Zhou, C., Wu, W., He, H., et al.: Deep reinforcement learning for delay-oriented IoT task scheduling in space-air-ground integrated network. IEEE Trans. Wirel. Commun. **PP**(99), 1 (2020)
10. Khatami, M., Salehipour, A., Cheng, T.: Coupled task scheduling with exact delays: literature review and models. Eur. J. Oper. Res. **282**(1), 19–39 (2020)
11. Zhang, H., Xie, J., Zhang, Z., et al.: Online task interleaving scheduling for the digital array radar. AEU-Int. J. Electron. C. **79**, 250–256 (2017)
12. Chatterjee, N., Paul, S., Mukherjee, P., et al.: Deadline and energy aware dynamic task mapping and scheduling for network-on-chip based multi-core platform. J. Syst. Archit. **74**, 61–77 (2017)
13. Hu, M., Luo, J., Yang, W., et al.: Adaptive scheduling of task graphs with dynamic resilience. IEEE Trans. Comput. **66**(1), 17–23 (2017)
14. Xiong, Y., Huang, S., Min, W., et al.: A Johnson's-rule-based genetic algorithm for two-stage-task scheduling problem in data-centers of cloud computing. IEEE Trans. Cloud Comput. **PP**(99), 1 (2017)
15. Neamatollahi, P., Abrishami, S., Naghibzadeh, M., et al.: Hierarchical clustering-task scheduling policy in cluster-based wireless sensor networks. IEEE Trans. Ind. Inform. **PP**(99), 1 (2017)

Design of Decision Tree Algorithm in University Teaching Management Platform

Jing Zhou[✉]

Beihai Campus of Guilin University of Electronic Technology, Beihai 536002, Guangxi, China
zhou2022j@163.com

Abstract. Results As an important part of university management, you are of great significance to the development of universities and the analysis of related indicators. At the same time, teaching management can optimize teaching resources and realize comprehensive analysis and application of their respective installations. The resource management can realize and plan the teaching content, and make the teaching proceed in an orderly manner. By putting forward settlement number and correlation analysis method, we can optimize teaching management and realize the whole integration of educational resources, which can not only promote the optimization of educational strength, but also realize the optimization of the whole teaching index. Therefore, the effective application of decision tree in teaching management can improve the management level of enterprises.

Keyword: Teaching management · Decision tree · association analysis

1 Introduction

Data mining technology is application-oriented at the beginning, mainly mining seemingly unrelated and unrelated data from the data. Through statistics, analysis, synthesis and reasoning, find out the internal data, It's also the connection between us. And make predictions, and guide the solution of practical problems. Mining resources can improve the comprehensive optimization index content of each index, such as marketing, finance, healthcare, retail, modern education, communication network management, justice, engineering and science, insurance and many other fields.

For example, Economic development technology plays an important role in the whole financial application and financial analysis: a typical example is the bank's credit card business. Just sort out the data is used to analyze the customer's deposit and loan situation, repayment situation and asset development trend, so as to determine the customer's credit rating and avoid the bank's risk. At the same time, the application in the retail industry is more intuitive. For example, putting eggs and tomatoes together for sale can Comprehensive promotion and comprehensive development of products.

With the continuous improvement Telephone technology and information process can improve and optimize vocational school students' management information, promote

Y. Zhang and N. Shah (Eds.): BigIoT-EDU 2023, LNICST 581, pp. 132–141, 2024.
https://doi.org/10.1007/978-3-031-63133-7_13

the promotion of related knowledge, and effectively plan students' teaching content and teaching norms, and realize the overall planning of students' learning [1–3].

Improve the quality of teaching: By analyzing the data of students' learning behaviors and achievements, It can find the problems existing in the management of vocational colleges and dig out the fundamental reasons of the problems. Related resources and related content: according to the needs and characteristics of students, reasonably allocate teaching resources and improve the efficiency of resource utilization. For example, resources such as classrooms, textbooks, and teachers can be reasonably arranged according to students' learning performance and needs.

Improve the level Free data is carried out once. In the process of data processing, it is necessary to find out various measurement methods, measurement quality and improvement degree of measurement measures the level of teaching management. For example, data analysis tools can be used to evaluate and give feedback on teachers' teaching effectiveness to help teachers improve their teaching methods and skills.

Promoting Teaching Innovation: Decision trees and correlation analysis can help university administrators discover potential patterns and patterns in the teaching process, thereby promoting teaching innovation and development. For example, new teaching methods and strategies can be discovered through the analysis of teachers' teaching experience and student evaluation data. The talent training objectives of higher vocational colleges are different from those of undergraduate colleges. Colleges and universities are based on practical application and implementation practice, so students' actual work and employment rate are the main contents of their evaluation of teaching management. In education management, we should take practical work and practical content as the basis, otherwise we can't effectively guarantee the teaching effect. When evaluating teaching, we should also make a statistical analysis of employment ability and students' employment intention. The third is the relationship basis between the two, the formed interest, employment ability, employment restriction, employment direction, etc., and establish relevant correlation analysis results to achieve comprehensive balance between data and demand [4].

2 Related Work

2.1 Research Status

The concept of knowledge discovery was first proposed by the first KDD working group in 1989. They emphasized that knowledge is the final product of data-driven discovery, and then it was popularized in the intelligence and machine learning. In 1995, the concept of data mining (DM, Data Mining) was put forward at the American Computer Annual Conference (ACM). After that, the American Association of Artificial Intelligence, as the conference topic or published a special issue.

There are many organizations, institutions or universities studying data mining abroad. More famous universities such as Carnegie Mellon University (with three research centers of machine manufacturing DM, multimedia database DM and Internet DM), Stanford University and MIT.

Decision tree method: A decision tree is a classification model based on tree structure, which constructs a binary tree to make classification predictions. In the teaching management of colleges and universities, decision trees can be used to classify and predict students, for example, whether students can pass exams or get scholarships based on their learning behavior and grades. At the same time, decision trees can also be used to develop teaching plans and strategies, for example, to create personalized learning plans based on students' learning characteristics and needs.

Correlation analysis method: Correlation analysis is a data mining technique used to discover correlations between data sets. In higher education management, correlation analysis can be used to discover the correlation between students' learning behaviors, for example, the relationship between factors such as the learning materials used by students when studying a course and the learning time they use. In addition, correlation analysis can be used to discover patterns and methods in teacher teaching, for example, the relationship between this is the relationship between your teaching methods. Used by different teachers can be analyzed. It provides a scientific basis for the teaching management of colleges and universities: the decision tree and association analysis can mine valuable information and rules from a large amount of data, and provide scientific basis and support for It is difficult to carry out classes and classes. Improving the quality and efficiency of teaching in colleges and universities: Through decision tree and correlation analysis, we can better understand the learning situation and needs of students, formulate targeted teaching plans and strategies, Improve the effect of the whole teaching. Central teaching planning and teaching optimization. And Development in Colleges and Universities: Decision trees and correlation analysis can help university administrators discover potential patterns and patterns in the teaching process, thereby promoting teaching innovation and development.

2.2   Research Status of Visual Analysis of Education Data

Data visualization is a way and method to use data resources and present data resources through visualization software. Outside data composition, problems existing in data can be found more intuitively, and comprehensive attributes of data can be judged. Data formatting can improve processing information and reduce the influence of interference factors on data processing. Therefore, data visualization and data management are at present. Then just make up your mind. That can only describe the important content of vocational education. Data formatting can enhance, enhance the appeal of data, and make analysts more direct, such as strong data analysis and data principles for data analysis. Through the relevance and later data in spell dramas, the data research can be improved. Through data formatting, the data mobility can be studied more deeply, and the data can find out the influence of personnel factors, so as to promote the later decision-making scheme, decision-making, planning and decision. Data visualization is more of a simple data processing, but a comprehensive presentation of data. However, if the data of infection and epidemic disease can be enhanced to comprehensively judge the data, petrochemical plays an important role in the management of senior teachers and affects the data, it will play an important role in the management of higher vocational colleges and optimize the teaching content, teaching method and teaching scheme, which will realize the number of related contents. This can enhance the design, and make students more easily understand the final results of data and the influence of data education management. In the process of teacher management analysis and planning, data design and production should be used to explore the diverse contents and multiple treatment methods in the data back and forth, and the specific indicators and characteristics should be digitalized for a period of time. There are some subjects in mobile phones, but still say a kind of digital processing technology, please as soon as possible, which can improve education management and 2-10.36 in a short time. This autumn formatting is a key point and a hot spot at present, and it is also a higher vocational college to carry out teaching management education planning.

After the introduction of online education platform, domestic colleges and universities have achieved good response. The relevant education industry has analyzed and processed the online learning behavior of students, and explored the shortcomings in the teaching environment through relevant technologies to improve the teaching content and teaching process. Liu Hai and others have applied the real data visualization method to the actual teaching through the self-developed online teaching platform - Cloud Classroom of Normal University, Teachers can learn about students' learning situation in time, and students can complete self-assessment and find their own learning problems; Qiang Jinpei applied the visualization platform to teaching examples of different disciplines, and realized the evaluation of data visualization technology, which not only satisfied the function of interdisciplinary teaching platform, but also stimulated the learning interest of students; Starting from the classroom data visualization of network intelligent devices, Ruan Shigui and others have deeply explored the educational value of "data" from the perspective of teaching dependency and dynamic variability of data, highlighting the teaching interaction of "visualization", and providing a new perspective for the application of data visualization in classroom teaching. Li Jing used VisualEyes to develop a visualization course. VisualEyes can present excellent features of content that changes with time and space, which is conducive to students' perception of time and space, and helps students understand abstract knowledge. Cheng Shiwei generates visual annotation of eye movement data by recording the eye movement data such as fixation point and saccade during reading, and then makes objective and subjective evaluation of students' reading comprehension level. Guo Junfang has carried out relevant research on the visualization of historical data. Through diversified reports, data visualization has greatly enhanced the ability of laboratory administrators and teachers to explore the connotation and connection of complex data, and greatly improved the informatization level of laboratory management. Nie Chuanming uses text mining methods, uses text mining software and statistical software to analyze the research hotspots of MOOCs at home and abroad, and compares and analyzes the similarities and differences of domestic and foreign research by visual analysis based on data.

In general, for the analysis of huge teaching data in the education industry, researchers will use the visual analysis method to provide a macro analysis perspective for analysts, and help users better understand the data and generate insights into the data. Therefore, the data visualization method is also playing an increasingly important role in the field of education data mining.

3 Decision Tree and Association Analysis

3.1 Overview of Decision Tree

To make decisions on data visualization, psychoanalysis and data results, it is necessary to analyze the relationship between nodes. First, you should punish from this point, that is, your collection of internal resources and external resources, and then the functions and meanings of numbers in each node are different. You should combine the actual situation to deal with the problems in the process deeply. For students, all walks of life are consistent with the people, but how to choose freedom and how to simplify the related resources is an important thing for special analysis. Therefore, in terms of level, mathematical arithmetic methods have more advantages, which can cause the work of other methods, and can find the problems in the Constitution, and can realize the collation, analysis and collation of data through later algorithm optimization (Fig. 1).

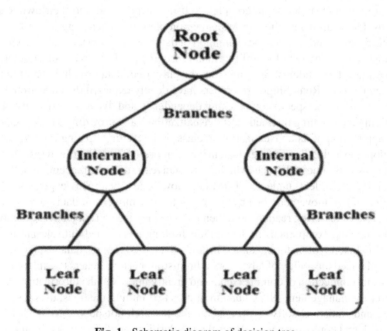

Fig. 1. Schematic diagram of decision tree

It is necessary to collect data related to students' learning behavior and achievements, as well as teachers' teaching materials and other information their classification I is:

$$I(S_1, S_2, ..., S_n) = -\sum_{i=1}^{n} P_i log_2(P_i) \tag{1}$$

3.2 Association Analysis

"Want to see your absolute number analysis for more than ten years and an important content of teaching management, mainly using modern teaching tools and methods to analyze the problems existing in the teaching process and the problems reflected by teacher" Digital painting and calligraphy is not a simple processing process, although it only has an auxiliary role, but for the whole person, and then directly apply for management is shown in Fig. 2.

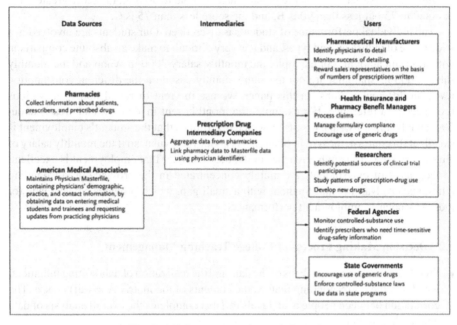

Fig. 2. Mining process of association rules

4 College Teaching Management Based on Decision Tree and Correlation Analysis

4.1 Data Processing

(1) Collect and sort out the original data

I am about to collect data, locate people's data for measurement and collation, realize the last judgment of data, and then comprehensively judge the collation and planning of data to complete the primary and selection of data and the preliminary present [9].

(2) Data preprocessing

First, standardize the data, remove the key contents in the data, and constrain the irrelevant contents or unlimited quantities in the data. Second, measure the advantages in the data processing process, and realize the comprehensive judgment and analysis of the data [10]. Digital format data has strong advantages in the process of comprehensive viewing and data processing, and can complete and realize the overall cycle of data.

(3) Data conversion

Because the value in the decision tree algorithm needs to be discrete, the data should be discretized. Here, it is mainly to process the course results, as well as the individual performance of students.

For the course score, the score greater than or equal to 90 is A, the score greater than or equal to 75 but less than 90 is B, and the score less than 75 is C.

The individual performance of students is discretized. Our students are involved in a wide range of industries and types, and it is very difficult to make an absolute comparison with a certain amount. For example, the monthly salary 3000 in Wuhu and the monthly salary 3000 in Shanghai are not the same, mainly based on the different consumption levels in different regions. In this paper, we use the rent of rental houses in various provinces as a reference. For example, the monthly rent in Wuhu urban area is about 500, and the monthly salary is 3000, which determines that the student's employment is excellent. In contrast, the rent in Shanghai is about 1000 yuan, so if the monthly salary of alumni working in Shanghai reaches 6000, they consider that employment is excellent. In fact, most of our students are mainly concentrated in the province or surrounding cities, such as Nanjing and Suzhou, with a small gap, which provides convenience for judging students' employment performance.

4.2 Decision Making Process of College Teaching Management

- Step 1 Comprehensive analysis of the data and the realization of data sorting judgment, is to build the corresponding matrix, the contents of the matrix A = (aij) m × n. The correlation between people at all levels in Tibet completes the overall analysis of data among their own people.
- Step 2 The data side of the course content and data in the integrity of the data uniform form of the object analysis of its master data easy and the data of the multi-attributes.
- Step 3 Comprehensive problems and comprehensive research results in the data should be judged, and corresponding regional sets should be constructed.
- Step 4 After multi-phone analysis of data, some threshold analysis and weight analysis should be carried out on the data.
- Step 5 All my data requirements are in line with the requirements, but the final processing results have not been achieved, so I should repeat the calculation in Step 3.
- Step 6 In the software stage, all kinds of data detect the frequency and results of data occurrence.
- Step 7 The final results and optimal problems in the analysis process in the diagram, and realize the overall judgment of the data, and complete the comprehensive retest of the data.

Weka software was developed by the WEKA team of Waikato University, and its main programming language is java. Weka software is an open data mining platform, which can complete many algorithms in the field. This belongs to a complex process that requires not only data content, 28 relationships between data, and later technology. At the same time, the software is open source. Many researchers engaged in data mining can directly call the functions provided by weka when writing relevant test programs, which greatly reduces the working pressure of researchers and improves the efficiency of scientific research.

Weka software provides many types of file support, including CSV and Arrf formats. In Microsoft's office software, Excel provides the function of converting excel files into CSV format files. Specifically, select "Save As" in the "File" menu of the Excel file and select the format as ".CSV".

In weka software, first open this file, then select the "Classifier" option, and select J48, which is another name of C4.5 algorithm. At the same time, select the Test Option on the left as 10. The main function of the Test Option is to ensure the accuracy of the decision tree selection and will not lead to overfitting. So weka designed the cross validation. In this paper, we designed the cross validation for 10 times. After setting these parameters, click "start". You can see that the following decision tree model is generated, as shown in Fig. 3.

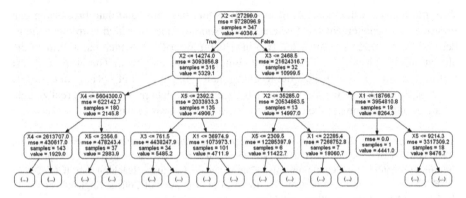

Fig. 3. Complete decision tree established by C4.5 algorithm

Through the above decision tree, we find that the Database Principles and Applications group belongs to the root node and plays the largest role in the employment of students in this major, followed by Web Design and Network Communication. Of course, a certain combination must be formed between the course groups to form excellent employment. Then, we can also find that in the course system of computer network specialty, Business tax should use more data problems for data analysis, and realize data integration and data fusion.

Students' interests can be further guided according to the above decision tree. For example, Zhang San, a student, had a strong interest and interest in the Database Principles and Applications group and the Network Communication group when he just entered the school. At this time, as a class teacher or instructor, he can encourage the boy to learn according to the generated decision tree and give certain affirmation to his interest.

For example, there is a female student who only shows great interest in the Database Principles and Applications group and the JAVA Language group, and wants to take this as the key direction of future study. Then we can suggest that she should strengthen her study of any of the course groups of Network Communication Course, Computer Foundation Course, English Course and Web Design Course while choosing the two courses. Guide students to develop correct interests and hobbies.

Using weka software to analyze the results of C4.5 algorithm, we can see that the cross-validation result of J48 algorithm is: Correctly Classified Instances 206 77 8623%. This data shows that the accuracy of the decision tree model built by C4.5 algorithm for this sample is about 77%.

Similarly, we can also use ID3 algorithm to generate a decision tree in weka software, and set the number of cross validation to 10. After running, the result of 10 cross-validation in the main window is: Correctly Classified Instances 206 75 3268%. This data shows that the accuracy of the decision tree model established by ID3 algorithm for this sample is about 70%.

5 Conclusion

With the rapid development of information technology, how and data processing can improve the management level of teaching resources, among which correlation number and final accounts number are two intelligent algorithms, which can optimize the algorithm of each word and complete a comprehensive judgment. Therefore, the best method I choose is to optimize the teaching management level of vocational colleges, which shows that this method can effectively carry out data preprocessing, realize data digitization and complete the overall judgment and analysis of data.

Acknowledgements. Re① National key project of the educational scientific research planning of the Ministry of Education during the 14th Five-Year Plan period. Research on the Approaches to Improving Intercultural Communicative Competence in Language Teaching (No. JGCY2643).

② Project "Golden Lessons" Construction Ability Promotion of College English Teachers in the Post-epidemic Era (No. 202101028021)

References

1. Guo, Y.: University classroom teaching model based on decision tree analysis and machine learning. Mob. Inf. Syst., 1–12 (2021)
2. Ding, L., Zeng, X.: Application of decision tree model based on C4.5 algorithm in nursing quality management evaluation. J. Med. Imaging Health Inform. (2021)
3. Li, J.: Application of intelligent fuzzy decision tree algorithm in English teaching model improvement. Complexity (2021)
4. Zhou, W., Yang, T.: Application analysis of data mining technology in ideological and political education management. J. Phys. Conf. Ser. **1915**(4), 042040 (2021). 7 p.
5. Gu, Z., He, C.: Application of fuzzy decision tree algorithm based on mobile computing in sports fitness member management. Wirel. Commun. Mob. Comput. **2021**(6), 1–10 (2021)
6. Humpherys, S.L., Lazrig, I.: Effects of teaching and practice of time management skills on academic performance in computer information systems courses. Inf. Syst. Educ. J. **19** (2021)
7. Zhang, Y.: Application of computer information processing technology in teaching management information system of colleges and universities. J. Phys. Conf. Ser. **1852**(4), 042089 (2021). 7 p.

8. Si, Y.: Construction and application of enterprise internal audit data analysis model based on decision tree algorithm. Discrete Dyn. Nat. Soc. **2022** (2022)

9. Huang, L.: Research on the application of the function of computer management system in college aerobics teaching. J. Phys. Conf. Ser. **1744**(3), 032148 (2021)

10. Chen, Y.F.: Decision tree and data classification evaluation for private vocational college (2021)

Research on Teaching Evaluation System Based on Decision Tree Algorithm

Peijin Chen[✉], Meng Li, Xu Ya, and Feng Cheng

Nanyang Institute of Technology, Nanyang 473000, Henan, China
nychenpj555@163.com

Abstract. The modern education field emphasizes the pertinancy of teaching, so teachers need to know the specific problems of students to carry out targeted teaching activities. However, the information and data related to students' problems are huge and the frequency of change is fast, which makes it impossible for teachers to obtain accurate results manually. Through the research, the performance of this system in practical application is in line with expectations, and can achieve rapid and comprehensive evaluation. The error between the accuracy of evaluation results and the manual results is in a reasonable range.

Keyword: Decision tree algorithm · Teaching evaluation system · Targeted improvement of teaching

1 Introduction

Students will encounter many problems in the learning process, the causes of which are related to the personal factors of students and teachers, and the specific factors are uncertain. The same problem may involve different factors, indicating that students' learning problems contain complex logic. At the same time, students' learning problems are generally implicit and cannot be displayed intuitively and actively, which leads to the lack of pertinence in teaching. How to improve the pertinence of teaching has become a big problem in the development of teaching. Faced with this problem, many teachers in the past tried to solve it manually by collecting and analyzing data, but the results were not satisfactory. The collection and analysis demands brought by huge and complex data information far exceeded the upper limit of human ability. The evaluation results can reveal the relationship between teachers' personal factors and students' learning problems, which is convenient for teachers to improve. If the results show that there is not much correlation between teachers' personal factors and students' learning problems, it means that the problems are only related to students' personal factors, which can also enable teachers to carry out targeted activities. Therefore, it is imperative to design teaching evaluation system. But as a machine system, it must rely on algorithm to have the similar evaluation function of human, which makes decision tree algorithm get attention, so how to design teaching evaluation system based on this algorithm is a problem worth studying.

Y. Zhang and N. Shah (Eds.): BigIoT-EDU 2023, LNICST 581, pp. 142–149, 2024.
https://doi.org/10.1007/978-3-031-63133-7_14

2 Basic Concepts of Decision Tree Algorithm

2.1 Algorithm Concept

Decision tree is a kind of model operation method, so named because its operation model is similar to the tree structure. This algorithm has various forms, among which the classical algorithms are ID3 and ID4.5, etc. Different forms of decision tree algorithms are applicable to different scenarios, so reasonable selection is required in practical application. According to this requirement, since there are many indicators in teaching evaluation that cannot be described quantitatively, such as the emotional influence of teachers and students, it is generally recommended to choose fuzzy decision tree algorithm, and the following only explains the concept of this form of algorithm [1–3].

Therefore, it is impossible to judge by ordinary decision tree. Instead, fuzzy logic is used for classification and judgment (Table 1 and Fig. 1).

Table 1. Two modes of knowledge retrieval in common decision tree

The name of the	The characteristics of
Match retrieval	Calculate the matching degree between keywords or data and the target. If the matching degree reaches the target, the target is the final result
Random search	The target is randomly selected as the local optimal solution, and then the global optimal solution is found according to the correlation degree between the data, which is suitable for large-scale retrieval

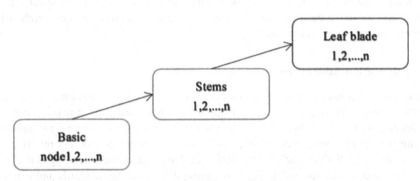

Fig. 1. Basic model of general decision tree

Therefore, it will disappear when the fuzzy variable is a possible variable and reach the maximum when the fuzzy variable is equivalent [4–6].

$$E[\xi] = \sum_{i=1}^{n} s(\xi = x_i) \tag{1}$$

Where, $E[\xi]$ is the fuzzy entropy of the fuzzy set, x and i are the membership values, and n is the membership.

The common problem in teaching evaluation is that students' learning performance is often vague and uncertain. The evaluation indicators, standards, and performance of students are often not very clear, but vague and relative. For example, a student may perform as "good" or "average" in a specific field, rather than a fixed score or grade. Fuzzy decision trees can better handle this fuzziness by introducing fuzzy logic and fuzzy set theory for decision-making and evaluation.

Fuzzy decision trees can handle data with fuzzy variables and fuzzy relationships. In teaching evaluation, different evaluation indicators and standards are often vague, and there is a fuzzy relationship between them. For example, indicators such as student engagement, homework completion, and classroom performance can all be considered fuzzy variables, and the relationship between them is also fuzzy [7]. Fuzzy decision trees can flexibly process and make decisions on fuzzy data and relationships by establishing fuzzy language variables and fuzzy inference rules.

Most importantly, fuzzy decision trees can provide more accurate evaluation results. Due to the often fuzzy and uncertain learning performance of students, traditional binary decision tree algorithms may not provide accurate evaluation results. By introducing fuzzy logic and fuzzy reasoning, fuzzy decision trees can better understand and simulate the characteristics of fuzzy data, and obtain more accurate and reliable results. By introducing fuzzy sets, membership functions, and fuzzy rules into the fuzzy decision tree, the system can more accurately understand fuzzy data and make corresponding decisions and evaluations. Fuzzy decision trees with fuzzy decision tree algorithm as the core have important application advantages in teaching evaluation [8]. It can better process and make decisions on fuzzy data, handle fuzzy evaluation indicators and relative performance, and obtain more accurate and reliable evaluation results. With the further development of fuzzy logic and fuzzy set theory, fuzzy decision trees are expected to be widely applied in the field of education and provide more accurate and comprehensive solutions for teaching evaluation.

2.2 Application Advantages

The teaching evaluation system based on decision tree algorithm has the advantage of interpretability. The decision tree algorithm establishes a tree like structure based on the relationship between features and target variables, with each node representing a feature and each branch representing a feature value. This structure is very intuitive and understandable, allowing teachers and students to have a clear understanding of the basis for the evaluation results, and to better understand the grading standards and learning progress [9, 10]. The teaching evaluation system based on decision tree algorithm has the advantage of flexibility. The decision tree algorithm allows customization based on specific teaching objectives and evaluation needs. Teachers can choose appropriate features and target variables based on the requirements of the subject, curriculum, and students to construct a decision tree to achieve personalized evaluation. This flexibility enables the system to adapt to the needs of different disciplines, learning stages, and evaluation criteria.

The decision tree algorithm is an efficient machine learning algorithm, and its construction and prediction process usually has low computational complexity. For large-scale student data and rapid evaluation needs, decision tree based systems can quickly generate evaluation results, providing immediate feedback and guidance. In addition, the teaching evaluation system based on decision tree algorithm has adaptability advantages. The decision tree algorithm can automatically select appropriate evaluation paths based on students' different characteristics and performance. The system can identify students' strengths and difficulties, as well as potential learning needs, in order to provide personalized teaching feedback and suggestions for students. This personalized evaluation and guidance can help students better adjust learning strategies and improve learning outcomes.

The teaching evaluation system based on decision tree algorithm has scalability advantages. The decision tree algorithm can be easily combined with other machine learning methods and algorithms to further improve the accuracy and comprehensiveness of evaluation. For example, ensemble learning methods such as random forests or gradient lifting trees can be combined to construct more complex and powerful evaluation systems. This scalability enables the system to maintain efficiency and accuracy in handling more complex evaluation scenarios and larger scale data. The teaching evaluation system based on decision tree algorithm has multiple application advantages such as interpretability, flexibility, efficiency, adaptability, and scalability. This system provides teachers with an effective evaluation tool that can better understand and support students' learning progress, and achieve personalized and high-quality teaching evaluation. With the continuous development of machine learning and artificial intelligence technology, this decision tree based evaluation system is expected to play an increasingly important role in the field of education.

3   Design of Teaching Evaluation System

3.1   Design Ideas

The design idea of teaching evaluation in this paper is shown in Fig. 2.

According to this idea, the system first collects teaching related data at the data source through the data acquisition layer, and then imports the data into the database. Secondly, export the data in the database for preprocessing, remove the low-quality data, and input it into the algorithm module after completion. Finally, the evaluation results can be obtained through the calculation of the fuzzy decision tree in the algorithm module, and the results will be imported into the output layer for manual display.

3.2   System Realization

With reference to the train of thought, the implementation method of this system is as follows.

3.2.1   Data Acquisition Layer

Because teaching related data exist in both virtual and real environments, corresponding collection methods are required to obtain all data under different environments. First of all, in the virtual environment, the environmental data are all generated on the online teaching platform, such as the student evaluation data after the teacher's lecture, student

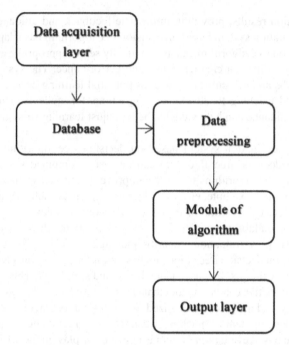

Fig. 2. Design ideas of teaching evaluation

learning materials browsing data, etc. These data cannot be collected by real methods, but can be realized by relying on some online collection tools. This paper mainly selects the keyword retrieval tool, and the specific working principle of this tool is shown in Fig. 3. In addition, there are other acquisition tools available, which are described in Table 2 and will not be repeated here. Secondly, in the real environment, virtual online tools can not interfere with the real environment, so manual collection must be relied on. Although manual collection here is limited by the limitations of human capabilities, the amount of data generated in the real environment is not large, but it is relatively cumbersome in type. Therefore, the items that need to be collected can be selected before collection, and teachers can be responsible for recording. See Table 3 for the main items that need to be collected.

3.2.2 Database

Generally speaking, the teaching evaluation system does not have high requirements on the database, so it can use the ordinary physical database, which is supported by the physical server and has its own security guarantee. The only drawback is that the capacity is always limited, and if it wants to expand, more costs must be invested. However, in general, the storage capacity of the teaching evaluation system data is not required. So select this type of database. However, it is worth mentioning that the capacity demand of the teaching evaluation system is not constant, and it will change with the change of the situation. For example, the teacher finds that the student has a serious problem, which

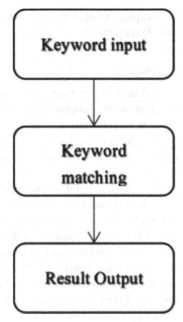

Fig. 3. Working principle of keyword search tool

Table 2. Other online virtual acquisition tools

Name	Characteristic
Network worm tool	Random acquisition within the range
Net catcher	Regardless of data quality and matching degree, all data within the collection range

Table 3. Offline acquisition items

Serial No	Project
1	The correct rate of students' homework
2	In the process of learning, students do not regulate the frequency of movement, such as deviation frequency, etc.
3	Data of student achievement improvement before and after teacher teaching

cannot be solved within a short time and needs tracking analysis, then huge data will be generated. In the face of this demand, the ordinary physical database may not be able to meet it. Therefore, it is recommended to choose the cloud database in the evaluation system design. The database has unlimited capacity. Although its capacity should be limited for security reasons, its expansion operation is very simple and without extra cost. The design of this system chooses the cloud database.

3.2.3 Algorithm Module Development

According to the basic logic and framework of fuzzy decision tree algorithm, Java language is used for module development. The programming language has good realizable ability and meets the requirements of algorithm module development. After development, the algorithm module can be loaded into the basic framework of the system and run as a built-in program of the system. In the process of running, it will be analyzed according to the pre-processed data to understand the specific problems of students and identify the causes of the problems, so as to point out the teaching deficiencies, so as to improve and play an evaluation role. The fuzzy decision tree algorithm module needs to be driven by intelligent technology to run, so the intelligent technology terminal should be established after the module is developed. The core of the terminal in this system is the feedforward artificial neural network, which is a logical forward model structure. It can imitate a certain thinking mode of human beings, so that the intelligent terminal has similar intelligent characteristics. Under this characteristic, the intelligent terminal will have the ability to identify data and drive the algorithm to calculate the data.

3.3 Application Test

A practical application test is carried out for the above system. The test scheme is as follows: select the historical data of a certain teaching classroom. As it is historical data, the evaluation result is known in advance, and the evaluation result shall prevail.

The test was carried out with reference to the scheme, and the results were as follows: Historical data show that the average score of students in this classroom is 81.3 points when the teacher adopts the original teaching method and 87.5 points when the teaching method is changed. Therefore, the current teaching quality is "good" and the comprehensive score is 85.7 points. The result of system evaluation is that the average score of students when the teacher adopts the original teaching method is 81.3 points. After the change of teaching method, the average score of students was 87.5 points, so the teaching quality was "good", and the comprehensive score was 85.1 points, indicating that the evaluation error of both was less than 1%.

4 Conclusion

To sum up, teaching evaluation system is an important tool for teaching development, which can solve current problems and improve the pertinancy of teaching. Therefore, decision tree algorithm, as the logical core of the system, has good application value. Scientific application of the algorithm can accurately evaluate teaching quality and find out students' learning problems, so the algorithm is worth promoting.

References

1. Xia, T.: Based on big data college physical education teaching evaluation system research. J. Phys. Conf. Ser. **1744**(3), 032010 (2021)
2. Zhang, X., Wei, Z., Han, T.: PHP-based undergraduate data reporting and teaching quality evaluation information system. J. Phys. Conf. Ser. **1827**(1), 012174 (2021)
3. Ayinla, Akinola, I.B.: An improved collaborative pruning using ant colony optimization and pessimistic technique of C5.0 decision tree algorithm. Int. J. Comput. Sci. Inf. Secur. **18**(12), 111–123 (2021)
4. Segin, Y., Ner, Z., Turan, M.K., et al.: Gender prediction with parameters obtained from pelvis computed tomography images and decision tree algorithm. Med. Sci. Int. Med. J. **10**(2), 356–361 (2021)
5. Tan, Y., Wang, J., Chen, B., et al.: Rapid identification model based on decision tree algorithm coupling with H-1 NMR and feature analysis by UHPLC-QTOFMS spectrometry for sandalwood. J. Chromatogr. B Anal. Technol. Biomed. Life Sci. **1161**, 122449 (2020). 2021(1166-) :1166
6. Imura, T., Iwamoto, Y., Inagawa, T., et al.: Decision tree algorithm identifies stroke patients likely discharge home after rehabilitation using functional and environmental predictors. J. Stroke Cerebrovasc. Dis. **30**(4), 105636 (2021)
7. Yang, T., Chen, L., Wang, J., et al.: Anomaly detection of dust removal system through gradient boosting decision tree algorithm. In: 2021 International Conference on Communications, Information System and Computer Engineering (CISCE) (2021)
8. Wang, L., Wang, H., Zhang, H., et al.: Somatotype identification of middle-aged women based on decision tree algorithm. Int. J. Cloth. Sci. Technol. **33**(3), 402–420 (2021)
9. Mao, L., Zhang, W.: Analysis of entrepreneurship education in colleges and based on improved decision tree algorithm and fuzzy mathematics. J. Intell. Fuzzy Syst. **40**(2), 2095–2107 (2021)
10. Varade, R.V., Thankanchan, B.: Academic performance prediction of undergraduate students using decision tree algorithm. SAMRIDDHI J. Phys. Sci. Eng. Technol. **13**(sup. 1), 97–100 (2021)

Design and Implementation of University Sunshine Sports System Based on C4.5 Algorithm

Shao Yi[1], ZhiYuan Wang[2(✉)], and Rao Yan[3]

[1] Shanghai Customs College, Shanghai 201204, People's Republic of China
shaoyi@shcc.edu.cn
[2] International College of Football, Tongji University, Shanghai 200092, People's Republic of China
zhende18909249911@126.com
[3] Shanghai Tianhua College, Shanghai 201815, People's Republic of China

Abstract. With the development of science and technology and the advent of the information age, college sports management is facing many challenges. In order to better meet the needs of students and teachers, improve the efficiency and quality of physical education, colleges and universities need to build a sunshine sports system. As a classic decision tree algorithm, C4.5 algorithm has the advantages of high classification accuracy and strong interpretability, which is suitable for the design and implementation of sunshine sports system in colleges and universities. This paper will introduce in detail the application of C4.5 algorithm in the sunshine sports system of colleges and universities is a simple two-step process, including the following steps: Step 1: the first step is to select a suitable algorithm for each sport under consideration. In this regard, we can refer to the relevant parts above, which discuss the different algorithms used by different computerized systems. For example, if you want to implement track and field competitions in universities, you should use one of the "track and field" algorithms such as c4.2 or C4.3, because these algorithms are suitable for this purpose. The main purpose of this project is to implement C4.5 algorithm for data storage system with high performance requirements and design an efficient database management system, which will support all activities involved in student record processing, such as registration, registration, attendance tracking, etc.

Keyword: C4.5 algorithm · Sports system · Database management

1 Introduction

The first national school sports meeting in China was held on December 23, 2008. At the meeting, the notice of national student sunshine sports activities was passed, which was jointly advocated by the State General Administration of Sports, the Ministry of Education and the Communist Youth League. The conference also focused on strengthening

Y. Zhang and N. Shah (Eds.): BigIoT-EDU 2023, LNICST 581, pp. 150–159, 2024.
https://doi.org/10.1007/978-3-031-63133-7_15

students' physique and implementing students' physical exercise, and took sunshine sports as the main measure. Hebei University of Technology has actively responded to the call of the Ministry of Physical Education. It has not only adopted many means and measures of physical exercise, but also in recent years, the school leaders have been paying attention to how to quickly and fairly evaluate the results of Sunshine Sports. Therefore, how to use effective means to promote students' physical exercise and strengthen students' physical health has been the focus of school leaders. In the implementation of sunshine sports, schools need to establish a sunshine sports system to manage and promote sunshine sports, and to strengthen students' physical exercise and promote students' physical health.

With the growing scale of sunshine sports activities, more and more information is generated in the sunshine sports system, including student attendance information and student physical health assessment data. At this time, how to do a good job in data management is an inevitable requirement of current development. Moreover, manual management of this large amount of information often makes mistakes, which can easily dampen the enthusiasm of students who participate in sunshine sports, and can not achieve the purpose of urging students to exercise. At the same time, it also brings many adverse effects to the development of sunshine sports in Hebei University of technology [1]. Therefore, how to sort out sunshine sports data and analyze and manage students' physical health information conveniently, quickly, with low error rate and high efficiency is an urgent problem to be solved. In addition, with the continuous development of computer technology and the country's attention to the development of computer networks, it will be easy to carry out information management of sunshine sports.

By developing the sunshine sports system, Hebei University of technology can not only realize the information management of sunshine sports, but also better organize students to exercise, and also help the school to grasp the physical exercise situation of students in time, analyze the physical health situation of students, so as to make adjustments in time.

At the same time, the application of data mining in the physical health assessment data of colleges and universities provides an effective way for schools to obtain valuable and influential important information from a large number of students' physical health assessment data. In the face of different students, we can find out the scores of students in various physical assessments and the relevance of various score data by data mining on various aspects of students' physical health, and reveal the problems of students in physical exercise [2]. At the same time, the results of data mining can be used to predict the physical health status of students, give early warning to students, make students pay attention to physical health status, and adjust physical exercise status.

2 Related Work

2.1 C4.5 Algorithm

Decision tree C4.5 algorithm is a classification algorithm in data mining. Its algorithm idea is simple, classification rules extraction is convenient and easy to understand, and it has been widely used. However, the traditional C4.5 algorithm has a better classification effect when the samples of each category in the data set are relatively balanced. In the unbalanced data set, because the proportion of a few samples is small, it can not provide enough classification information for the classifier. In order to ensure the overall classification accuracy of the algorithm, the classifier will pay more attention to the classification accuracy of the majority of classes and ignore the classification of the minority of classes [3]. This leads to the phenomenon that although the overall classification accuracy of C4.5 algorithm in unbalanced dataset classification is high, the classification accuracy of a few classes is very low. Figure 1 below is a schematic diagram of the decision tree.

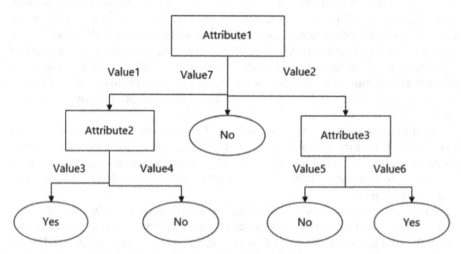

Fig. 1. Schematic diagram of decision tree

In the sunshine sports system in colleges and universities, it mainly involves the management of students, teachers, courses and achievements. Through the analysis of the actual needs of college physical education management, it can be clear that the system should have the following functions: student information management, teacher information management, curriculum management, course selection management, achievement management, physical health monitoring and so on.

$$e_k(t) = y_d(t) - y_k(t) \tag{1}$$

$$\Delta \dot{x}_{k+1}(t) = P^{-1}(t)(f(t, x_d(t)) - f(t, x_{k+1}(t))) \tag{2}$$

Based on C4.5 algorithm, University Sunshine Sports System can adopt B/S architecture, which is divided into presentation layer, business logic layer and data access layer. The presentation layer is responsible for user interface design and interaction; Business logic layer is responsible for processing system business logic; The data access layer is responsible for data storage and access.Today, many data studies have found that these data warehouses and data mining systems established by foreign enterprises have achieved good economic benefits to a large extent. From the perspective of the development of data mining, the research focus of data mining at this stage is not only on the concept of data mining and its application in the system, but also on the combination of multiple disciplines [4]. At present, data mining urgently needs a systematic scientific theory as its system support, but as far as the current development is concerned, this application field still focuses on theoretical research, and the real application of data mining products are still very rare. C4.5 algorithm flow chart is shown in Fig. 2

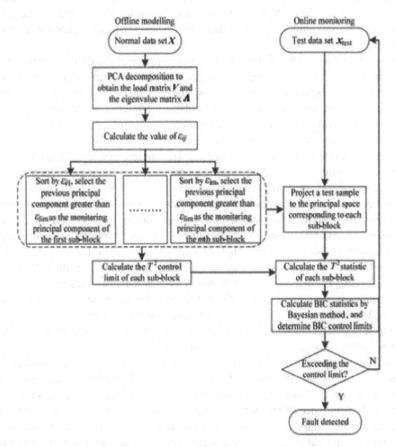

Fig. 2. C4.5 Algorithm flow chart

At present, China's "Sunshine Sports" has not many systems that can urge students to carry out "Sunshine Sports" in addition to the annual physical health test of students, and there are few systems that use high-tech means such as the Sunshine Sports Swipe Terminal to realize the autonomy and intelligence of Sunshine Sports. The management of "Sunshine Sports" in colleges and universities mostly stays in the way of manual entry or paper management, and the informatization of "Sunshine Sports" has not been widely promoted throughout the country.Based on C4.5 algorithm, the data model of Sunshine Sports System in colleges and universities mainly includes student information table, teacher information table, course information table, course selection information table, achievement information table and so on. By establishing a reasonable data model, it can better support the application of C4.5 algorithm.

2.2 Current Situation of Sunshine Sports

The problem of adolescent physical decline has become a global problem. It is not only a unique situation in China, but also a serious global social reality. In order to deal with the problem of teenagers' physical decline, many countries have begun to take relevant measures to promote students to strengthen physical exercise and improve their physical condition and health level.

In Australia, about 40% of children do not engage in extracurricular sports activities. A large number of teenagers have never participated in extracurricular sports activities, resulting in the consequence that teenagers are overweight or even obese. At present, there are 1.5 million overweight and even obese adolescents under the age of 18 in Australia. Behind this phenomenon is the potential health problems of adolescents, which has attracted the attention of the Australian government. Therefore, the government has supported a national after-school activity plan. The implementation of this student after-school activity plan cost the Australian government 90 million Australian dollars to improve and improve the health status of adolescents.

The health status of Japanese teenagers is also not optimistic. The answer can be learned from the school's health statistics, as well as from the results of students' physical strength and sports ability tests. The test results of Japan's intention on physical strength and sports ability show that the average score of students shows that the physical health of students has gradually increased in the past 10 years or so since 1964. However, in the past 10 years, the performance of students has shown a downward trend. The root of this phenomenon is adolescent obesity. To this end, the Japanese government has also introduced various guidelines and policies to improve this situation.

Canada has also launched a daily sports activity plan to improve students' physical activities in schools and improve the physical quality of teenagers.

The United States has done a good job in carrying out school sports activities. More than 80% of primary and secondary school students in the United States have participated in extracurricular sports activities, and there are 12.6 h of extracurricular sports activities a week. The importance of physical exercise for human health was further emphasized in the Diet Health Guidance issued in 2005. In addition, we actively encourage students to take part in physical exercise and encourage schools to organize students to take part in one-hour sports activities every day. The United States has also put forward a "plan for healthy people in the year". In order to promote the physical development of children and adolescents, school sports should be conducted three times a week, each time no less than 20 min.

In our country, the study of school physical education has always attracted much attention, which is also an important field of physical education research. Since the promulgation of the decision on the development of sunshine sports for hundreds of millions of students across the country, sunshine sports have had a great impact throughout the country.

Since the implementation of "Sunshine Sports" in China, it has received extensive attention from the academic community. The academic community has not only studied a wide range of "Sunshine Sports", but also achieved rich results. At the same time, the majority of sports workers are taking this as an opportunity to constantly find ways and means to strengthen students' physical exercise and improve students' physical health on the platform of school physical education and by means of physical exercise [5, 6].

At present, in addition to the annual physical health test of students, there are not many systems that can urge students to carry out "Sunshine Sports" in China's "Sunshine Sports", and there are also few systems that use high-tech means such as sunshine sports card swiping terminals to realize the autonomy and intelligence of sunshine sports. The management of "Sunshine Sports" in Colleges and universities mostly stays in the manual input or paper-based management mode, and the informatization of "Sunshine Sports" has not been widely promoted throughout the country.

3 Design and Implementation of University Sunshine Sports System Based on C4.5 Algorithm

Because the system deals with a large number of student assessment score data, how to store these data, and how to input them conveniently and quickly, and how to execute them in the system quickly and output them stably is the key to the operation of the whole system. In order to ensure the smooth operation of the system and the consistency and integrity of the data, it is first necessary to select a database that can run stably. Secondly, we should design a perfect data structure, and finally, we should ensure the smoothness of the network [7].

At present, the most used database products for developers are SQL Server 2000, Oracle, Sybase ASE and DB2. The following is a simple analysis of the advantages and disadvantages of these four mainstream databases.

First, from the perspective of openness. SQL Server 2000 can only run on windows, and its openness is tightly limited. However, for the operating system, the stability of the system plays a very important role in the database. Oracle can run on all platforms. Support all domestic and foreign industry standards. This product adopts a completely open strategy, which makes it easier for customers to choose the most suitable solution. SybaseASE can also run on all platforms. However, the early Sybase and OS integration was very low, so it needed to download the necessary patches to operate normally. In addition, in the environment of multiple platforms, there will be some problems when it runs. DB2, like them, can run on all platforms. Its advantage lies in the storage of massive data.

From the perspective of easy operation, SQL server operation is very simple, with only a graphical interface and no DOS interface. Oracle is very complex. It provides both GUI and command line, which is applicable to multiple platforms. Sybase ASE is very complex. It provides both GUI and command line. If you want to use it, you'd better use the command line [8]. The operation of DB2 is very simple. It provides both GUI and command line, and is applicable to multiple platforms.

Data Preprocessing. In order to improve the classification accuracy of the C4.5 algorithm, it is necessary to preprocess the original data, including data cleaning, feature selection and data transformation. Data cleaning is mainly to remove outliers and missing values, feature selection is to select effective features according to the requirements of C4.5 algorithm, and data conversion is to transform numerical data and categorical data appropriately.

Build a Decision Tree Model. The C4.5 algorithm is used to construct a decision tree model to classify and predict according to the training dataset. In the process of building a decision tree model, it is necessary to set appropriate stopping conditions and pruning strategies to avoid overfitting and underfitting problems.

System Development and Implementation. Based on the C4.5 algorithm, the university sunshine sports system can be developed in Java language, and the existing development frameworks and tools, such as Spring Boot, MyBatis, etc., can be used to realize the functions of the system. In the process of system development, it is necessary to pay attention to the readability and maintainability of the code, and at the same time strengthen the security and stability of the system.The overall structure of Sunshine Sports System is shown in Fig. 3.

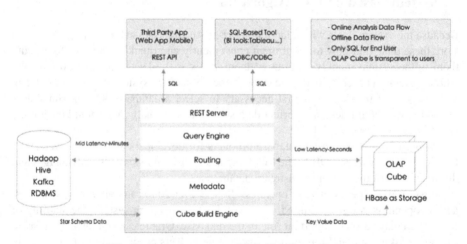

Fig. 3. General structure of Sunshine Sports System

4   Simulation Analysis

The system adopts ASP technology to support the technical realization of the system. ASP is not a language used to write scripts, but it is a technology that can realize dynamic websites. Its working principle is to provide a running platform on which script language programs can run, so as to achieve the effect of dynamic display of the website.

The files of programs written with ASP technology have the same extension asp. This extension is an important symbol that distinguishes other technologies. If you are browsing a web page and see that the last file name of the URL address of the web page is ASP, so we can be sure that this website is developed with ASP technology. There are many tools for writing ASP programs. It can be said that any tool that can write can write asp programs, such as Notepad and dreamwave [9, 10].

The Dao layer, also known as the data persistence layer, can directly operate the database. The Dao accepts requests from the service layer, obtains data from the data layer, or writes data. The equipment management module also includes equipment management and U-Key management, a total of 2 modules. The equipment management module is mainly used to maintain the number of Sunshine Sports punch, while the U-Key management module is used to maintain the U-disk code of the equipment import personnel, and the U-disk code is used to identify the equipment import personnel.

The personnel management module includes the management of statistics teachers and the management of exempt students. There are two modules in total. The management of statistics teachers module is used to add, modify and delete the information of statistics teachers, and the management of exempt students module is used to add, modify and delete the information of exempt students.

Attendance management module is the core module of the system, which is mainly used to manage the attendance of sunshine sports, class activities and other sports and the detection of students' physical health. It includes importing attendance information, managing students violating discipline, viewing attendance times of violating discipline, managing teacher attendance information, maintaining attendance times of morning exercises, managing attendance information of morning exercises, viewing attendance information of morning exercises, querying attendance information of morning exercises, statistics of attendance information of morning exercises, statistics of attendance per capita of morning exercises, viewing attendance per capita of morning exercises, school attendance per capita of morning exercises, statistics of overall attendance, maintenance of attendance times of class activities, management of attendance information of class activities There are 24 modules, including checking the attendance information of class activities, querying the attendance information of class activities, counting the attendance information of class activities, counting the attendance of class activities per capita, checking the attendance of class activities per capita, generating extracurricular sports results, checking the extracurricular sports results, checking the attendance information of extracurricular activities, and students' physical health registration card.

The import attendance information module is used to import the student swiping information in the handheld swiping machine, including student number information, swiping time information, etc.

The module of managing students in violation of discipline and the module of viewing the attendance of students in violation of discipline are used to maintain the information of students in violation of discipline, and are used to add students in violation of discipline and query the times of clocking of students in violation of discipline.

The management teacher attendance information is used to count the attendance of the teachers on duty who manage the morning exercise attendance.

This paper uses JAVA programming language to program the algorithm. The code diagram is as follows. After processing the original data of boys and girls into the code, we can get the decision tree in Fig. 4 and Fig. 5 respectively.

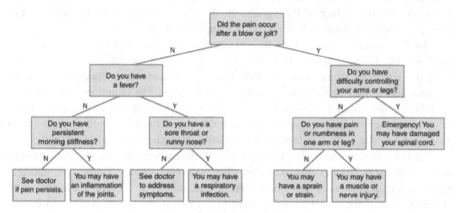

Fig. 4. Boys' Decision Tree

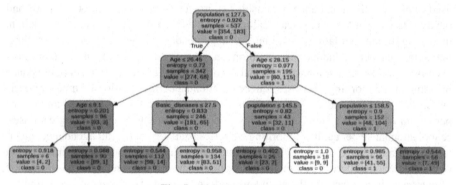

Fig. 5. Girls' Decision Tree

Features related to classification tasks are extracted from the preprocessed data, and appropriate features are selected for training according to the requirements of C4.5 algorithm. Irrelevant or redundant features can be eliminated to improve the classification accuracy of the model. For students who exercise actively, their vital capacity is better, and because of their regular exercise, they can also achieve good results in other projects. On the contrary, students who fail to pass the vital capacity test are usually overweight or obese and need to pay special attention to physical exercise. It can be seen from the decision tree in Fig. 5 that the biggest factor affecting the physical fitness test of girls is the step test. For students with excellent performance, the most important factor is vital capacity. The decision tree model is constructed by C4.5 algorithm, and the model is trained by training data set. In the training process, we can adjust the algorithm parameters according to the actual situation, such as stop conditions, pruning strategy, etc., in order to obtain the best classification effect.

5 Conclusion

University sunshine sports system based on C4.5 algorithm, "Sunshine Sports" is a strategic countermeasure to promote students' physical exercise and strengthen students' physical health. In order to better manage sunshine sports and build a sunshine sports system, it is an inevitable requirement in the information age. Data mining technology is the fastest developing technology in the field of data analysis and processing technology, and decision tree algorithm, as an important branch of data mining algorithm, has also obtained some achievements in scientific research. Applying decision tree to sunshine sports system is the focus of this paper.

Acknowledgements. 2021 Shanghai Philosophy and Social Science Planning Project "Research on Sports and Education Integration and Campus Football Reform" Project No.: 2021ZTY001.

References

1. Zhang, X., Cheng, Z., Zhang, C.: Design and implementation of a web crawler system based on an adaptive page-rank algorithm, p. 012021. IOP Publishing Ltd. (2020). 6 p.
2. Li, S.: Sunlight sports system design and implementation based on decision tree. Tech. Autom. Appl. (2019)
3. Zhao, Y.: Research on the application of university teaching management evaluation system based on Apriori algorithm. J. Phys. Conf. Ser. **1883**(1), 012033 (2021). 6 p.
4. Liu, X., Liao, L.: Research and implementation of performance evaluation system for physical education teachers based on load weight algorithm. In: CIPAE 2020: 2020 International Conference on Computers, Information Processing and Advanced Education (2020)
5. Gu, H., Jin, C., Yuan, H., et al.: Design and implementation of attitude and heading reference system with extended Kalman filter based on MEMS multi-sensor fusion. Int. J. Uncertain. Fuzziness Knowl. Based Syst. **29**(Suppl. 01), 157–180 (2021)
6. Wang, Q., Feng, W., Zhuang, C., et al.: Research and implementation of acquisition algorithm based on multi-correlator parallel frequency search for long code (2019)
7. Hai-Rong, L.I., Fang, Z.C.: Design and implementation of recommendation system based on Mahout and collaborative filtering algorithm. J. Inner Mongolia Univ. Sci. Technol. (2018)
8. Wang, Q., Zhou, G., Rong, H., et al.: Research and implementation of sign-in system based on mutual difference jump algorithm. J. Hefei Univ. Technol. (Nat. Sci.) (2019)
9. Chen, N.Y., Chen, L., Xiong, W.: Situation plotting algorithm and system implementation based on web. J. Phys. Conf. Ser. **1584**(1), 012050 (2020). 10 p.
10. Wang, B., University S.: Research and implementation of spam filtering system based on Naive Bayes algorithm. Electron. Des. Eng. (2018)

Development and Analysis of the Quality Management Information System of University Teaching

Yuankun Ren[1,2](✉), Xinxin Guan[1,2], and Peijin Chen[1,2]

[1] Shenyang 110036, Liaoning, China
2090800485@qq.com
[2] Nanyang Institute of Technology, Nanyang 473000, Henan, China

Abstract. Higher education is the main body and foundation of higher education. Paying attention to undergraduate teaching is the key to improve the quality of higher education. In the 21st century, the teaching quality of colleges and universities has increasingly attracted the attention of all sectors of society. The development and analysis of quality management information system is a project aimed at developing comprehensive quality management system for university teaching. The main purpose of the project is to improve the quality of teaching, research and learning at all levels in colleges and universities. In order to achieve these goals, we need to establish a single platform for all processes related to teaching, learning and research in the university, so that we can share information about our activities with other stakeholders. Based on the analysis of the teaching quality management system of colleges and universities, this paper improves the teaching management information system of ordinary colleges and universities, and divides the whole teaching quality management information system into four subsystems: the overall planning of teaching management, teaching resource management, teaching process management, and teaching quality analysis and improvement management, aiming at realizing the process management of the quality management system of colleges and universities, Improve the level of teaching quality management in colleges and universities from multiple perspectives. In terms of system planning and design, fully consider the characteristics and organizational structure of university information flow, take users as the basic starting point, take the overall planning of school teaching quality management as the basis, face the work flow, and fully consider the system compatibility, scalability and information sharing of the overall structure of the system combining B/S and C/S. In terms of system development, by selecting appropriate development tools and effective management of the project, the close combination of developers and users is ensured, and the system development efficiency is improved.

Keyword: Quality Assurance · University teaching work · information system

Y. Zhang and N. Shah (Eds.): BigIoT-EDU 2023, LNICST 581, pp. 160–170, 2024.
https://doi.org/10.1007/978-3-031-63133-7_16

1 Introduction

As we all know, today's international competition focuses on comprehensive national strength, with education as its core and talent quality competition. The quality of talent training mainly depends on the quality of teaching. In recent years, improving the quality of higher education has become the common theme of higher education in the world. Many scholars believe that since the 1980s, the world's higher education has entered an era centered on improving quality. In 1984, the "American High Quality Higher Education Research Group" proposed that the fundamental problem of American higher education is the quality of education, and colleges and universities should go all out to improve the quality of education [1]. France passed the Higher Education Law in 1984, emphasizing that the core of higher education is to improve the quality of education. In 1987, the British government issued the white paper "Higher Education: Meeting the Challenge", which officially started the reform with the main content of increasing quantity and improving quality [2]. In 1998, the World Conference on Higher Education listed quality as one of the three guiding principles of higher education in the new century (calling on higher education to respond to the continuous changes of the world under the guidance of pertinence, quality and internationalization). In the past 20 years, the development of higher education centering on improving quality has gradually become one of the trends of the development of higher education in the world [3].

In the process of popularization of higher education, how to realize the coordinated development of scale and quality and avoid the problem of "quantity expansion and quality decline" in the process of developing higher education in some countries. With the expansion of quantity, quality has become the focus of research. In order to realize the coordinated development of the scale, quality, structure and efficiency of China's higher education, the Ministry of Education has determined the policy of "consolidating, deepening, improving and developing" and officially launched the "quality project". The five-year round of national higher education evaluation is an evaluation system aimed at steadily improving teaching quality for undergraduate teaching in colleges and universities [4]. As an evaluated university, it can not only realize the significance of evaluation, but also relate to the social reputation of the university and its own survival and sustainable development. Therefore, all evaluated colleges and universities dare not be slighted at all, and all actively welcome the evaluation and seriously rectify. However, these evaluations conducted from the outside of colleges and universities will inevitably be difficult to be recognized by colleges and universities and faculty due to the constraints of objective factors such as tight time, heavy tasks, and the identification function of evaluation purposes is too utilitarian, and can only play a small role in promoting the improvement of teaching quality [5]. In order to fundamentally improve the quality of higher education, the key lies in the establishment and effective implementation of the internal quality control and quality management guarantee system of colleges and universities.

In order to ensure and continuously improve the teaching quality of colleges and universities in China, the Ministry of Education formulated and issued Several Opinions on Strengthening Undergraduate Teaching in Colleges and Universities to Improve Teaching Quality in 2001, requiring colleges and universities to itemize and specify various measures to improve teaching quality, and strengthen the monitoring of teaching quality. On March 3, 2004, the State Council officially approved and forwarded the 2003–2007 Education Revitalization Action Plan, in which Article 22 proposed to "improve the teaching quality assurance system of colleges and universities, establish the teaching quality evaluation and consulting institutions of colleges and universities, and implement the national teaching quality evaluation system of colleges and universities with a five-year cycle". In January 2005, Zhou Ji, Minister of Education, announced at the 2005 National Higher Education Enrollment Plan Working Conference that "the focus of the current work of Chinese universities should attach great importance to scale development from the previous stage and shift to more prominent quality improvement". China's higher education has entered a stage of connotation development characterized by quality improvement [6].

2 Related Work

2.1 System Development Background

China's higher education has developed rapidly. In recent years, the enrollment of colleges and universities has expanded, and the number of higher education in China has exceeded 22 million. The number of higher education in China has achieved a qualitative leap, and the number of students at school has leapt to the forefront of the world. The enrollment rate of higher education has also risen steadily year by year, beginning to meet the international standards for the popularization of higher education. Higher education began to move from traditional elite education to mass education. The audience of education began to increase, and the opportunities for ordinary people to receive higher education were also growing, which improved the level of higher education for the whole society and the quality of the people [7]. Higher education departments have carried out a series of higher education reforms, including college teaching reform, enrollment plan reform, teaching management system reform, employment system reform, college independent enrollment reform, etc. China's college education system has begun to gradually improve and adapt to the country's market economic development. With the increase in the number of students in colleges and universities on a large scale, the quality of education in colleges and universities in China has also posed a severe test [8]. How to deal with the construction of college teachers' talent team under the large-scale enrollment expansion, optimize the allocation of college resources, optimize the curriculum, optimize student education, optimize the teaching quality control system, and optimize the teaching evaluation has become a very important problem for college educators. Higher education is the direct supplier of human resources in modern society and enterprises [9]. The talents provided directly affect the development of society and the progress of enterprises, bringing direct economic and social benefits. The teaching quality of colleges and universities is different from the neglect. Under the current situation of large-scale enrollment expansion, how to seize the opportunity in time, work hard to open up, overcome the difficulties, advance bravely in the torrent, improve the quality of higher education, and provide more and better talents for society and enterprises is the main problem facing each college and the first problem to be solved.

In terms of theoretical research, many domestic scholars have expounded their views on the composition of the internal management system of teaching quality in colleges and universities. For example, Cai Qing believes that the internal monitoring system of teaching quality in colleges and universities includes teaching quality monitoring organization system, teaching quality monitoring system, teaching quality monitoring evaluation system, teaching quality monitoring information feedback and processing system, etc.; Wang Bing and Yu Jifeng believed that the teaching quality monitoring system in colleges and universities includes quality subsystem, information subsystem, monitoring subsystem, feedback and incentive subsystem and re-evaluation subsystem; Chen Jianxiang and Xie Zailan believe that the internal monitoring system of teaching quality in colleges and universities includes teaching quality decision system, teaching quality decision support system, teaching quality implementation system, teaching quality information system and teaching quality assurance system; Qin Jianguo and Li Li proposed that the teaching quality monitoring system in colleges and universities should be composed of teaching quality objectives and monitoring system, teaching quality information feedback system, teaching quality evaluation system, teaching quality management incentive and restriction system, and teaching quality monitoring technical support system [10].

2.2 Current Situation and Problems of Education Quality Management in China's Colleges and Universities

The education quality management of colleges and universities in China has the following main problems:

(1) The concept of quality management still needs to be further changed

With the further deepening of the reform of the market economy and the extraordinary and leaping development of higher education, China's higher education has entered a new period of great reform and development. Various factors and relationships related to the development of higher education, from concept to system, from connotation to extension, have fallen into an unstable and immature state. At the same time, colleges and universities have also entered an unconventional, unstable Immature development and transformation period. However, what is incompatible with the above situation is that our research on higher education theory is still lagging behind, and people's educational ideas still need to be further changed. For example, some schools pay more attention to the expansion of scale and the economic benefits of running a school [11]. They will expand their enrollment in whatever major is hot in the society, but they do not pay attention to the requirements of the labor market on the ability and knowledge structure of students in this major, that is, they do not pay attention to the real needs of customers and ignore the improvement of teaching quality. Although many schools pay attention to the teaching quality, they pay more attention to the teaching links and cannot think about ways to improve the quality of education in a systematic way.

(2) The (internal) quality management of colleges and universities is relatively backward

The development of the popularization of higher education has made it more obvious that there are many problems that need to be solved urgently in the management of education quality in colleges and universities in China. These problems mainly include:

① The concept of education quality is not clear enough, and the idea of quality management is backward. At present, the concept of education quality is still mainly based on the level of understanding of teaching quality. The standard for measuring education quality is only to consider the problem of teaching quality and mainly consider the situation of students' learning. Correspondingly, the management of education quality only considers the situation of school teaching, and rarely systematically considers other factors related to education quality from the concept and process method of comprehensive management.

② The quality management method and technology are backward, and the system and controllability are poor. The quality control mainly focuses on the "end inspection" of the teaching work effect, which is poor in advance, and is mainly based on examination and inspection methods, lacking systematicness.

In a word, the most important reason for the above problems is the lack of a set of scientific, systematic and standardized education quality management system and mechanism to comprehensively, systematically and continuously regulate and control the various processes of education and the controllable factors that affect them, so as to comprehensively improve the quality of school education [7]. Therefore, how to establish a set of scientific and flexible, full participation, everyone has a responsibility, the whole process is always under control and continuous improvement of the educational quality management guarantee system and operating mechanism is an important task for our colleges and universities.

The undergraduate teaching quality management information system of colleges and universities is matched with the undergraduate teaching quality management system, is the main means to realize the quality management system, is a set of system software to ensure the operation effect of the quality management system, realize the automation and networking of undergraduate teaching quality management, and improve the quality management level. This paper expounds the current content and methods of teaching quality management in ordinary undergraduate colleges and universities, comprehensively analyzes them with the idea of quality management, and then inquires about the development of internal monitoring models and systems of teaching quality in domestic and foreign universities through literature, and concludes some deficiencies of teaching quality in some colleges and universities [12]. It also adds the widely used MIS construction method to amend the teaching management system of ordinary undergraduate colleges and universities, Through the establishment of a scientific and reasonable university teaching quality management information system, we can improve the efficiency of teaching quality management of ordinary undergraduate students and realize the informatization of dynamic management and teaching quality management.

3   Analysis of Teaching Quality Management Information System

3.1   System Design Principles

The system must first meet the current application needs of Weifang University's teaching quality management, and at the same time, it must ensure that the system has the ability to continuously use the latest information technology to carry out the secondary development of the system with the update of computer technology and the expansion of Weifang University's teaching quality management business in the future. The whole management platform and system construction shall follow the following principles:

(1) Security principle: the successful operation of this system requires a data center, an information processing environment, and a high-speed network link to serve the acquisition, sharing and processing of teaching quality information. It has the ability to support real-time online data information processing, the ability to support the collaborative work of various departments of Weifang University, and the ability to support office work in a virtual environment [13]. Because the whole system involves a lot of teaching and educational administration data, and these data must be uploaded and downloaded in real time between various departments of Weifang University, which can not be separated from the Internet and campus network at any moment, the designed system must consider the confidentiality of its transmission data to ensure that various teaching management information resources in the system will not be lost, and the data center will not be damaged artificially, At the same time, it should also ensure that the shared resources in the system can be used normally by users without interrupting information services. In order to ensure the security of the system, effective security technologies must also be adopted, such as anti electromagnetic leakage technology, symmetric key and asymmetric key cryptography technology, firewall technology, identity recognition technology, access control technology, digital signature technology, intrusion detection technology, risk analysis technology and audit tracking technology. In addition, the system should also adopt a scientific and convenient security management mode. For example, the authority of the system end user should be strictly defined, and its authority should be detailed to each module and each function [14]. On this basis, the group management mode should be used because it can greatly simplify the work complexity of system managers.

(2) Standardization. The design of this system is based on the national unified data platform and database. It is required that the data collection, analysis and processing adopt unified standards, unified planning, and unified program processing specifications. At the same time, in combination with the experience of Weifang's rural informatization construction, the information collection work is standardized and required to form standardized work processing procedures and standardized data requirements.

(3) Portability. The system can run in different operating systems and can be applied to different application systems.

(4) Practicability. The system design starts from the demand analysis, pays attention to solving practical problems, and has strong comprehensive practicability.

On the basis of absorbing the new theories and achievements of internal and external teaching quality management, learning from the model and experience of enterprise management, and aiming at the basis and current situation of teaching quality management, colleges and universities have initially established various teaching quality management systems, such as teaching quality management target system, organization system, monitoring system, guarantee system, and guarantee system, and constructed various quality management models and teaching management processes with different characteristics [15]. The teaching management flow chart commonly used by colleges and universities is shown in Fig. 1. In order to realize the teaching service of colleges and universities, there must be a complete set of leadership, organization, supervision and management organizations to ensure that the organization, implementation, inspection and coordination of teaching should be carried out according to the process management requirements of the realization of teaching service, and adjustment and improvement should be made according to the operation results.

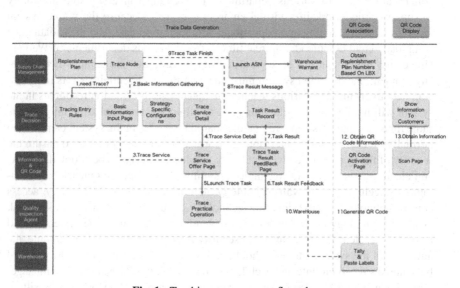

Fig. 1. Teaching management flow chart

3.2 System Business Process Analysis

The teaching work quality management information system mainly manages the teaching and research information, student research project information, student competition project information and school enterprise cooperative practice base information of teachers in each department every year. Its main businesses include information browsing, information collection, information audit, statistical analysis and information export [16]. According to the actual work needs, the system users include administrators, teachers and students. The business process of each role is shown in Fig. 2.

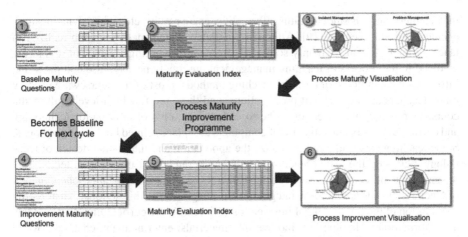

Fig. 2. Flow analysis of teaching quality management information system

Information collection: mainly collect teachers' teaching and scientific research projects, students' scientific research projects, competition projects, graduation internship information and school enterprise cooperation internship base recruitment information. In order to ensure the timeliness of information collection, teachers and students log in to the system and enter these information by themselves.

Information review: the system administrator reviews the data information entered by teachers and students, returns the unqualified data information to the user center for re entry, and enters the qualified data information into the current year's effective performance database to ensure the accuracy and integrity of the data [17].

Statistical analysis: the system administrator conducts statistical analysis on the approved data according to the set mathematical analysis model, including a comprehensive analysis of teachers' teaching and scientific research, students' scientific research project initiation, participation in various competitions, graduates' internship and employment, which is displayed in the form of charts [18].

Information export: after the data information is processed by the system, all data will be exported and backed up by year in the form of Excel file to ensure data security.

Information browsing: After logging in to the system, teachers and students can view and compare various data information over the years, which can serve as a reference for the application of individual teachers and students or teams for teaching and research projects.

To realize the high-quality management of teaching quality in colleges and universities, we should not only work hard on teaching, but also make full use of information technology and information resources. According to the survey, many colleges and universities have invested heavily in educational informatization. Although campus networks and multimedia classrooms have been established, students, teachers and administrators generally reflect that the application of school informatization has not played its due role. For example, in the aspect of teaching management, the educational administration management software was purchased, but the development rate was low. It was only used for online, internal information release, and some static information management, such as student status information, exam results, etc., while dynamic management did not keep up [19]. Although computer management has been realized in teaching management, it mainly solves the problem of working means, but it is rarely involved in the process of teaching management that really needs to use computer and information technology. In terms of teaching methods, most of the courseware used by many teachers are PowerPoint presentations, and there are few high-level multimedia courseware based on the network. The so-called integration of information technology and curriculum has become the use of computers to replace printed books and textbooks. Some teaching cases, in order to realize the application and integration design of technology, put aside the actual teaching needs, deliberately add information technology in some links of teaching. There is a formalization and superficialization phenomenon of "technology for technology, integration for integration". This seriously distorts the connotation of the integration of information technology and curriculum. Most students use information technology to find learning materials, entertainment, chat, etc., while teachers use information technology only for preparing lessons or checking materials.

4   System Architecture Design

The quality management information system serves the teaching work of colleges and universities. It has a large number of users and complicated businesses, which will generate a large amount of data information in the whole management process. Rational design of the system architecture is an important means to improve the system performance. The above business process analysis and functional module design provide an important basis for reducing code redundancy, optimizing the system loading speed, and improving the user experience of the system. The system adopts a software architecture design mode that separates the front end from the back end [20]. The entire system structure is divided into data layer, business layer, and display layer. The system architecture design is shown in Fig. 3.

The front end includes the front-end UI and presentation layer, and the back end includes the business layer and data layer. This enables front-end developers to focus on the construction of the interface in order to improve the visual effect of the interface, while back-end developers focus on the development of system function APIs. The data layer provides a data access service interface for the business layer and the presentation layer, a class responsible for data connection, and an arch bridge for elements in the presentation layer and the business layer, so that they can continuously store data. The business layer provides business function modules of relevant applications for administrators, teachers and students. It is a class that provides methods for the presentation layer. The business layer and the data layer cooperate to jointly complete the tasks requested by users, and the layer performs logical processing,

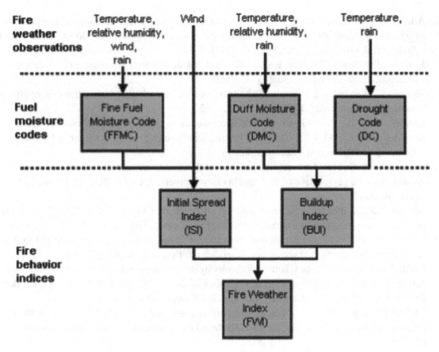

Fig. 3. Structure of teaching quality management information system

5   Conclusion

Based on the Internet application and facing the internal work management of colleges and universities, computer software management is introduced into the quality management process of teaching work. Through the analysis of the business process of quality management, the system architecture is given by applying the software architecture design mode of front end and back end separation on the basis of determining the system function modules. Role based access control permission management is adopted to present the business of the quality management process to the background management end and front-end applications. Through practical application and analysis of various index data, the results show that the system effectively solves the complex problems of quality management, improves work efficiency, promotes teachers' teaching and research and students' enthusiasm to participate in scientific research projects and competition projects, and provides data analysis basis and decision support for teaching quality management.

References

1. Díaz, J.B., Vinagre, T.M., Nicolas-Sans, R.: University teaching planning in times of COVID-19: analysis of the catalan context and proposal for a future model from ESIC business and marketing school experience. Sustainability **13** (2021)

2. Adama, O., Sibraogo, K., Alexis, S.Y., et al.: Analysis of obstetrical lethality in the department of gynecology and obstetrics of the university teaching hospital Yalgado OUEDRAOGO (UTH-YO). J. Gynecol. Obstet. **9**(1), 14 (2021)

3. Jasti, N., Jha, N.K., Chaganti, P.K., et al.: Sustainable production system: literature review and trends. Manag. Environ. Qual. **3**, 33 (2022)

4. Sliusar, S., Burdonos, L.: Accounting, analysis and control in the conditions of applying information technologies. Univ. Econ. Bull. (2022)

5. Dai, W., Zhu, Z., Luo, G., et al.: Practice teaching reform of human resource management major. In: CIPAE 2021: 2021 2nd International Conference on Computers, Information Processing and Advanced Education (2021)

6. Gou, L., Yang, S., Ren, L.: Coupling analysis of the quality and quantity of marine economic growth from the perspective of high-quality development. J. Coast. Res. Int. Forum Littoral Sci. **1**, 38 (2022)

7. Alarcia, S.F.: University professor training in times of COVID-19: analysis of training programs and perception of impact on teaching practices. Educ. Sci. **11** (2021)

8. Doiz, A., Lasagabaster, D.: An analysis of the use of cognitive discourse functions in English-medium history teaching at university. Engl. Specif. Purp. **62**, 58–69 (2021)

9. Fadillah, R.: Analysis of the teaching difficulty by university students of Arabic language education through microteaching practices/Analisis Kesulitan Mengajar Mahasiswa Pendidikan Bahasa Arab Melalui Praktik microteaching. IAIN Surak. (1) (2021)

10. Arora, A., Singh, A.: Development and performance analysis of cubic Bezier functional expansion-based adaptive filter for grid-interfaced PV system. Int. Trans. Electr. Energy Syst. (2021)

11. Yang, X.: An analysis of the correlation between university science parks and economic development. Mod. Econ. Manag. Forum **3**(1), 37–42 (2022)

12. Nguyen, V., Versyp, O., Cox, C., et al.: A systematic review and Bayesian meta-analysis of the development of turn taking in adult–child vocal interactions. Child Dev. **93**(4) (2022)

13. Ayvazyan, N.L., Kapiya, T.K., Zharikov, R.V., et al.: The analysis of factors influencing the development of quality management of industrial infrastructure and construction industry of Russia (2021)

14. Sudianto, L., Simon, P.: Development application of a quality assurance management information system for Paulus Indonesia Christian University. IOP Conf. Ser. Mater. Sci. Eng. **1088**(1), 012042 (2021). 9 p.

15. Tan, J.: Information analysis of advanced mathematics education-adaptive algorithm based on big data. Math. Probl. Eng. **2022** (2022)

16. Wang, X.: Analysis on the construction framework and realization logic of smart laboratory system under the environment of Internet of Things (2021)

17. Vélez, C.C., Sánchez, R.B., Hervás-Gómez, C., et al.: Teaching innovation in the development of professional practices: use of the collaborative blog. Educ. Sci. **11**(8), 390 (2021)

18. Li, H.: The design and development of a ship trajectory data management and analysis system based on AIS. Sensors **22** (2021)

19. Chaikovsky, I.A., Primin, M.A., Kazmirchuk, A.P.: Development and implementation in medical practice of new information technologies and metrics for the analysis of subtle changes in the electromagnetic field of the human heart (2021)

20. Nikitskaya, E., Valishvili, M., Astapenko, M., et al.: Cluster analysis of factors effecting the development of innovative activity and infrastructure quality. Int. J. Qual. Res. **15**(2), 549–564 (2021)

Research on Quality Evaluation of College Students' Innovation and Entrepreneurship Education Based on Ant Colony Algorithm

Shuyuan Chen[✉], Rong Wu, and Donghai He

School of Naval Architecture and Ocean Engineering, Jiangsu University of Science and Technology, Jiangsu 212100, China
csy@just.edu.cn

Abstract. With the increasing importance education, how to comprehensively and deeply and entrepreneurship abilities and practical effects of college students has become a research hotspot. This study establishes a quality evaluation model for innova students based on ant colony algorithm. Through the multidimensional data, indicators such as participation, innovative thinking, practical ability, and achievement quality were selected as inputs to the model. Using ant colony algorithm for model optimization and parameter adjustment, the final quality evaluation results activities for college students were obtained. The working principle of ant colony algorithm is to compare students' test scores with those of other students who participate in the same test at the same time and place. Then, it uses these results to calculate the percentage ranking (scores equal to or less than 50% of all other scores). Ant colony algorithm (ACO) is widely used to solve optimization problems. The main characteristic of ant colony algorithm is its ability to solve complex problems, handle large datasets, and is easy to implement. It also has the following advantages: it can automatically classify objects, automatically calculate fitness function, and provide a comprehensive and high-quality fitness function. The experimental results indicate that the evaluation model has high accuracy and precision. Among them, indicators such as participation, innovative thinking, and practical ability contribute the most to the evaluation results, and the importance of participation is the most prominent. At the same time, we also found that small adjustments have a significant impact on the evaluation results by analyzing different parameter settings. The evaluation y for college students based on ant colony for improving the quality of education and teaching. In practical education, we can make precise adjustments and management of innovation and entrepreneurship education activities based on the evaluation results. In the future, it is necessary to further improve the methods and models for evaluating the quality of innovation and entrepreneurship education, and improve the accuracy and practicality of the evaluation.

Keywords: Ant colony college student · Innovation and entrepreneurship education · Quality evaluation

© ICST Institute for Computer Sciences, Social Informatics and Telecommunications Engineering 2024
Published by Springer Nature Switzerland AG 2024. All Rights Reserved
Y. Zhang and N. Shah (Eds.): BigIoT-EDU 2023, LNICST 581, pp. 171–181, 2024.
https://doi.org/10.1007/978-3-031-63133-7_17

1   Introduction

Innovation and entrepreneurship education is one of the hot topics in current university education, playing a crucial role in cultivating innovative talents. In order to improve the quality education, it is essential to evaluate and enhance students' innovative thinking, practical ability, team collaboration, and other aspects[1]. However, traditional educational evaluation methods are often single and have strong limitations, making it difficult to comprehensively and objectively evaluate students' innovation and entrepreneurship abilities. Therefore, proposing an efficient, accurate, and scientific evaluation method for the quality and education will be of great significance.

The entrepreneurship education for college students based on ant colony algorithm is a new evaluation method, characterized by its ability to continuously optimize and adjust based on real data, accurately evaluating students' innovation ability and practical effects. Ant colony algorithm is an intelligent algorithm based on the feeding behavior of ants in nature, which can quickly find the optimal solution. This algorithm can perform weighted analysis and calculation on students' multi-dimensional data, obtain quality evaluation results, and better present the overall level.

However, there are still many issues that need to be addressed in the students based on ant colony algorithm. Firstly, how to choose appropriate evaluation indicators and quantitative methods can fully and entrepreneurship abilities and practical effects. Secondly, how to determine the parameters and optimization methods of the algorithm in order to reliably analyze and predict the evaluation results[2]. Finally, how to combine the evaluation results with actual educational and teaching work, so that the evaluation results truly have practical application value.

Therefore, this study will establish a quality evaluation model for innovation and on ant colony algorithm, to help us comprehensively and meticulously evaluate and entrepreneurship abilities and practical effects, and ensure the quality level of innovation. At the same time, we will also explore the selection and adjustment of algorithm parameters and optimization methods to obtain the optimal evaluation results. Finally, we will propose corresponding educational strategies to further enhance the level.

2   Related Work

2.1   Model Building

Mainly including the following aspects:

1. Data collection and processing. In the experiment, we need to collect multidimensional data on college students' participation in innovation and entrepreneurship education activities, including personal information, educational background, participation status, etc. These data need to be sorted, cleaned, preprocessed, and quantified using corresponding evaluation methods.
2. Indicator selection and model construction. While selecting evaluation indicators, it is necessary to construct a quality evaluation model for innovation and entrepreneurship education based on the actual situation, which helps to better reflect students' innovation ability and practical effects. In this study, we selected indicators such as

participation, innovative thinking, practical ability, and achievement quality as model inputs[3].

3. Ant colony algorithm design and optimization. Ant colony algorithm is a multi-objective optimization algorithm that requires tuning and design. In this study, we used ant colony optimization algorithm to train and optimize the model, in order to obtain the quality evaluation results education for college students.

4. Analysis of experimental results and conclusions. After collecting and processing data, selecting indicators and building models, designing and optimizing algorithms, etc., it is necessary to verify and obtain results through experiments. While analyzing the experimental results, we can draw experimental conclusions to guide practical education and teaching work.

In summary, when conducting based on ant colony algorithm, a large amount of data processing and collection work is required, selecting appropriate evaluation indicators and constructing corresponding models, designing and optimizing ant colony algorithm, and ultimately obtaining reliable experimental results and proposing conclusions.

2.2 Basic Principle of Ant Colony Algorithm

In life evolution in nature, there are a group of organisms such as ants. The individuals are simple and have no visual ability, but they always find the shortest way to get food efficiently under various complex conditions. Through a large number of studies, scientists have found that ant individuals do not have strong intelligent computing ability, but they can secrete a special chemical substance - pheromone. Ant groups can well perceive this substance and its concentration. This special chemical substance, as a carrier for information exchange of ant groups, guides ant groups to finally find the best way to obtain food through perception and communication in various complex environments[4, 5]. In order to more vividly explain the whole ant foraging process, published by Dorigo et al. To explain the biological mechanism of ant colony optimization algorithm in detail, as shown in Fig. 1, which the whole ant foraging process from nest to food.

In the search process, through the probability transfer function p composed of pheromone T, (T) and heuristic function n, (T) on the path. Every time the ant passes through a city C, it will add the city to the tabu list (k = 1,2,..., m). As the search proceeds, the tabug will be dynamically adjusted.

The probability transfer function $P_{,}$, is expressed as follows:

$$p_{ij}^k(t) = \begin{cases} \dfrac{\tau_{ij}^\alpha(t)\eta_{ij}^\beta}{\sum\limits_{j\in N_j^k} \tau_{ij}^\alpha(t)\eta_{ij}^\beta} \\ \\ 0 \end{cases} \tag{1}$$

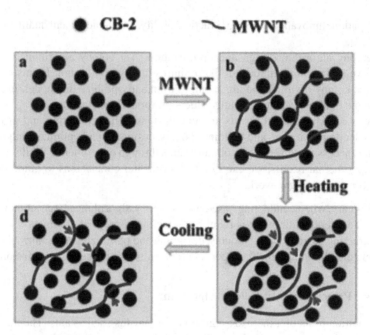

Fig. 1. Schematic diagram of ant colony algorithm

2.3 Advantages of Ant Colony Algorithm

(1) Self organization

Self organization is one of the two basic classifications in system theory. This characteristic describes that the system can automatically obtain space, time and functional structure without external intervention, and change from disorder to order. The organization instruction is issued by the system itself, and it is a system that can run independently. ACO algorithm has typical self-organization. In the initial optimization stage, ant colony has no prior knowledge guidance, and a single ant is in the disordered search stage. With the optimization, pheromones released by ants in the optimization process continue to accumulate. Ant individuals gradually perceive the strength of pheromones, and take pheromones as a carrier of communication to guide ant colony to spontaneously find better solutions, Finally, from a disordered state to an orderly state without other external interference[6]. ACO algorithm, as a self-organizing algorithm, can be independently optimized without external interference through the self adjustment of ant system, so that the whole system can change from disorder to order. The ACO algorithm is shown in Fig. 2.

(2) Positive feedback.

Positive feedback mechanism is an important form of feedback, which can be described as a form of feedback in which the direction of feedback information is consistent with the direction of control information, so that the activities of the control part are continuously strengthened[7]. Positive feedback mechanism is also an important

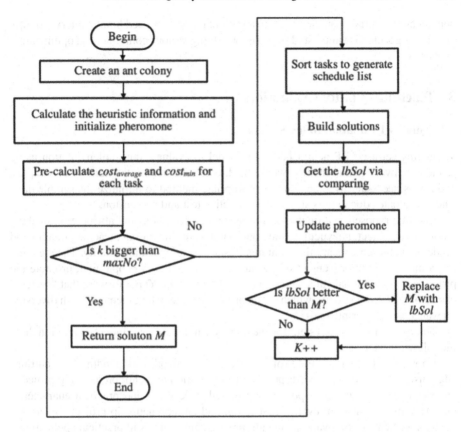

Fig. 2. ACO algorithm

feature of ACO algorithm. They accumulate pheromones and cooperate with each other to find the optimal route. The process of pheromone accumulation is a positive feedback mechanism. For the initial stage of optimization, the pheromones on each route are basically the same[8]. If there are obstacles in the optimization process, which makes the pheromones on each route different, and makes the ant colony optimization route have advantages and disadvantages, then the pheromones will continue to accumulate on the route of the optimal solution with a positive feedback mechanism, and more pheromones will attract more ants to pass through the route, resulting in a positive feedback process, It leads the whole system to evolve towards the optimal route.

(3) Robustness

Robustness, also known as anti transformation, comes from a special term of statistics, which is used to describe the robustness of a system and its insensitivity to parameter disturbances or characteristics. ACO algorithm has strong robustness. General optimization algorithms have high requirements for route parameters and characteristics in the initial stage of the algorithm, but ACO algorithm is just the opposite. It does not have high requirements for initial conditions, and the quality of the optimization solution does not depend on the initial characteristics. In addition, it does not need human intervention[9, 10]. The algorithm is simple and suitable for solving various combinatorial optimization problems.

3   Teaching Quality Evaluation

3.1   Quality Evaluation Index System

Wang Jingwei used BP neural networks model to evaluate the implementation using artificial network neural method would be directly affected by the number of samples, and it was necessary to select a more appropriate method to initialize the sample data. The to evaluate education is still lack of effective test and persuasion.

Cargile proposed that quality in philosophy is defined as the attribute or attribute feature of an object. Nieyucui pointed out that the enrollment rate, teaching quality and academic achievements are the main manifestations of education quality. The meaning of promoting the improvement of education quality is to put people first, promote the promotion of individual value and social development. Le Yi put forward that "system" can also be called a system, which is "a complex of interacting elements with diversity, relevance and prescriptiveness".

The evaluation index system for the quality among college students should include the following aspects:

Knowledge Content of and Projects: Measure the depth and breadth of the cutting-edge disciplines and fields corresponding to innovation and entrepreneurship projects, and determine whether they possess cutting-edge, leading, and practical characteristics. The implementation level of innovation and entrepreneurship projects: measures the achievements of innovation and entrepreneurship projects in practical applications, including market adaptability, technological maturity, commercial feasibility, and other aspects. Business Model of Innovation and Entrepreneurship Projects: Measure the commercial value, profit model, and funding requirements of innovation and entrepreneurship projects to determine whether they are expected to become a successful business model. The team of projects: measures the innovation ability, leadership, execution ability, collaboration ability, professional ability, and other aspects of the innovation and entrepreneurship team.

The Impact of and Projects: Measures the impact and popularity and in society, industry, academia, and other aspects, including evaluations received in media, academic journals, and other media. Sustainability of innovation and entrepreneurship projects: Measures the long-term development potential and sustainability of innovation and entrepreneurship projects, including reserves and planning in terms of market, technology, talent, funding, etc. Risk management of innovation and entrepreneurship projects: measures the risk avoidance ability, risk control awareness, and risk management ability of innovation and entrepreneurship projects, including the characteristics displayed in risk assessment, risk orientation, and other aspects.

The above seven aspects can serve as the core content of the quality evaluation index system for college students' innovation and entrepreneurship, providing a reliable basis for evaluating the quality of college students' innovation and entrepreneurship projects. At the same time, these evaluation indicators can also provide guidance and entrepreneurship, and better help them achieve.

3.2 Construction of Evaluation Index System

On the indicators, based on the CIPP evaluation model theory and in higher vocational colleges is constructed, as shown in Fig. 3. In the first-level indicator innovation and entrepreneurship environment, including the external support environment, the school implementation environment, and the basic background of students, there are five measurement layers; educational effectiveness, and there are four measurement levels.

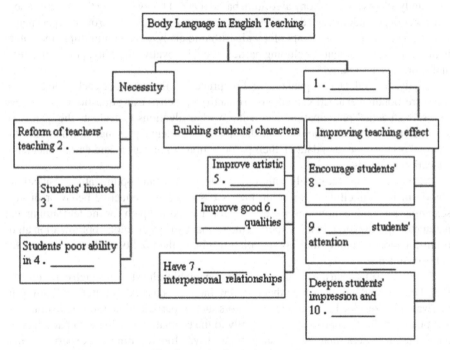

Fig. 3. Evaluation index system

Institutional construction education among various departments are the fundamental guarantee for a school to successfully carry whether the school can smoothly promote the reform. We must put forward clear phased objectives. Through comprehensive evaluation of the completion of the phased objectives, we can roughly judge the overall quality. The work of the leading group of innovation and entrepreneurship education and the two indicators of the inter-departmental coordination mechanism should complement each other. The leading group members shall include facilitate the timely implementation of specific work. The leading group must not become a "decoration". It must hold regular meetings to summarize the work experience and entrepreneurship in a timely manner, formulate the next work objectives, and constantly promote the reform. The reform plan of professional introduction mechanism of off-campus talents are necessary supplements to the indicators of system construction. If you want to cross the "deep water zone", you must make contributions in these two aspects. The talents outside the school are the difficulties in the reform of innovation. The quality inspection of these two aspects should focus on the revision and implementation of professional training programs and the feedback of teachers and students, timely collect process data, timely summarize and analyze the subjective feelings of teachers and students, and provide a basis for subsequent work improvement.

4   Analysis of Experimental Results

This study adopts an ant colony algorithm based method for evaluating the quality education for college students, and draws relevant results and conclusions through experiments. In the experiment, we used ant colony algorithm to analyze data on multiple indicators in innovation and students, including participation, innovative thinking, practical ability, and achievement quality.

Firstly, we collected, organized, and preprocessed the data. For each indicator, we use corresponding evaluation methods to quantify it, such as using questionnaire surveys to assess students' participation, and using work evaluations to evaluate the quality of students' achievements. The collected data includes students' personal information, educational background, and data on their participation in innovation and entrepreneurship education activities.

Next, we use ant colony algorithm for model training and optimization. Ant colony algorithm is an intelligent algorithm that is based on the collective behavior of ants searching for food, continuously searching for the optimal path for model training and parameter optimization. In this experiment, we mainly use ant colony optimization algorithm for model training and optimization to obtain the quality evaluation results for college students.

Finally, we obtained the results and entrepreneurship education through experiments. Based on the analysis, we found that different indicators have different contributions to the evaluation results. For example, indicators such as participation, innovative thinking, and practical ability contribute significantly to the evaluation results, with participation being the most important. At the same time, it was found during the experiment that different parameter settings also have a significant impact on the performance of the evaluation results. For example, the setting of iteration number and initial value of pheromone will have different effects on the evaluation results. The comparison of convergence times between different algorithms is shown in Fig. 4.

Through the above experimental analysis, we can draw the following conclusions. Firstly, ant colony algorithm can effectively evaluate the quality of innovation and entrepreneurship education for college students. Secondly, in the selection of evaluation indicators and the design of evaluation methods, it is necessary to combine the actual situation and quantify and analyze based on data. Finally, the optimized parameter settings also have an important impact on the accuracy and effectiveness of the evaluation results.

In summary, the ant colony algorithm based evaluation method for the quality of innovation and entrepreneurship education for college students is an effective method

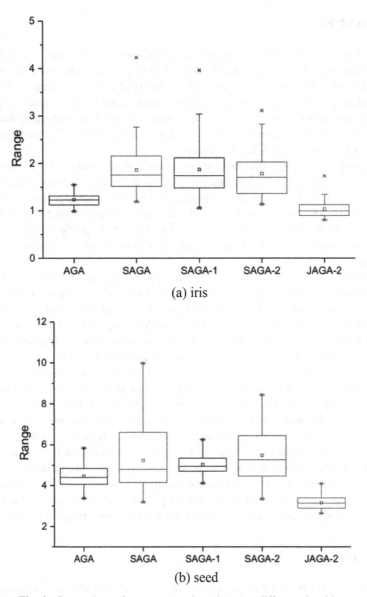

(a) iris

(b) seed

Fig. 4. Comparison of convergence times between different algorithms

that can effectively evaluate the quality level of education. In the future, we can further improve this method through more experiments and research, improve its accuracy and practicality, and provide strong support for promoting the implementation of innovation and entrepreneurship education.

5 Conclusion

This study is based on ant colony algorithm and explores methods and models for evaluating the quality o for college students. By collecting and analyzing multi-dimensional data on the behavior, psychology, and achievements of college students participating in innovation and entrepreneurship education activities, and using ant colony algorithm for model optimization and parameter adjustment, a method for evaluating the quality of innovation and entrepreneurship education was obtained, which effectively improved the accuracy and accuracy of the evaluation.

In the experiment, we evaluated innovation and college students based on multiple indicators, including participation, innovative thinking, practical ability, and quality of results. Through continuous iterative optimization of ant colony algorithm, the quality evaluation results of innovation and activities for college students were finally obtained. The research results indicate that the on ant colony algorithm can effectively improve the accuracy and precision of the evaluation, and help to better promote the entrepreneurship education.

From the experimental results, we can find that the evaluation methods and models for the quality for college students are of great significance for improving the quality of education and teaching. In practical education, we can make precise adjustments and management of innovation and entrepreneurship education activities based on the evaluation results. For example, based on the evaluation results, it is found that students lack practical ability. We can strengthen the design and arrangement of practical links to improve students' practical ability level; Or if we find that students excel in innovative thinking, we can provide them with more opportunities and resources for innovation and entrepreneurship, stimulating their enthusiasm and creativity for innovation.

In summary, the research on the entrepreneurship based on ant colony algorithm is a very effective method, which can effectively help evaluate the quality level of innovation and entrepreneurship education and provide important reference for the development of actual education and teaching work. In the future, we still need to continuously improve the methods and models for evaluating the quality of innovation and entrepreneurship education, improve the accuracy and practicality of the evaluation, and further promote the development and innovation of innovation and entrepreneurship education.

References

1. Yz, A., Hz, B.: Research on the quality evaluation of innovation and entrepreneurship education of college students based on extenics - sciencedirect. Proc. Comput. Sci. (2022)
2. Wang, C., Zheng, P., Zhang, F., et al.: Exploring Quality evaluation of innovation and entrepreneurship education in higher institutions using deep learning approach and fuzzy fault tree analysis. Front. Psychol. (2022)
3. Zou, J.: Intelligent course recommendation based on neural network for innovation and entrepreneurship education of college students. Inform. Inter. J. Comput. Inform. **2022**(1), 46
4. Du, P., Lei, M., Zhang, X.: Strategies for Cultivating College Students' Innovation and Entrepreneurial Ability **6**(5), 8 (2022)
5. Amorós, J.E., Masferrer, M.S.: Dynamics of Entrepreneurship and Quality of Government Institutions: an evaluation using cross-country data (2022)

6. Mehdi, M.M., Rakshit, S., Sarma, T.R., et al.: Entrepreneurship and Innovation in the Bakery Industry: A Case Study of Ganesh Bakery (2022)
7. Wu, B., Ye, S., Yang, Z.: The Influencing Factors of Innovation and Entrepreneurship Intention of College Students Based on AHP. Math. Problems Eng. (2022)
8. Li, L.I.: Function, process and sustainability evaluation of eco-innovation systems. Acta Ecol. Sin. **42**(12), 4784–4794 (2022)
9. Luo, P., Jia, X.: Construction risk evaluation of power mass entrepreneurship and innovation demonstration park under collaborative innovation (2022)
10. Boegenhold, D., Fachinger, U.: Entrepreneurship, Innovation and Spatial Disparities: Divisions and Changes of Self-employment and Firms (2022)

Modeling and Analysis of the Influence of College Students' Cultural Confidence Based on KPCA Algorithm

Yanyan Zong[1]([✉]), Xizhen Ai[2], and Keri Qing[2]

[1] Hefei University, Hefei 230601, Anhui, China
zongyi5@sohu.com
[2] Luoyang Institute of Science and Technology, Henan 471000, China

Abstract. Cultural self-confidence is a kind of self-esteem based on cultural values and beliefs. College students' cultural self-confidence is a person's perception of college students' cultural identity. College students' cultural self-confidence is defined as "a person's self-awareness of their college students' culture and the degree to which they feel comfortable in the cross-cultural environment of college students". College students' cultural self-confidence has been proved to be related to many different results, such as educational achievements, socialization and healthy behavior of integrating foreign college students' culture. In this paper, this study aims to develop a more objective and accurate new method to measure cultural self-confidence. Using KPCA algorithm, I will discuss how college students' cultural self-confidence exists. Cultural self-confidence is considered to be an important part of cultural self-esteem and plays an important role in students' academic performance. As an ideal personality under Chinese culture, gentleman personality has been proved to have a significant impact on prosocial behavior, but the relationship between it and online prosocial behavior is still unclear. As an important psychological function, self-control has been shown by a large number of studies to have a significant impact on individual behavior, and has been confirmed by studies that self-control is an important part of the "self-denial" advocated by Confucianism in the personality of a gentleman. The purpose of this study is to use Kpca algorithm to investigate the relationship between cultural self-confidence and academic achievement of Iranian college students. This study adopts the relevant design, pre-test and post-test experimental design.

Keywords: KPCA algorithm · Cultural confidence · cultural identity

1 Introduction

With the rapid development of the Internet, network behavior has gradually integrated into the real life of each individual and become a part of everyone's daily behavior. Especially in the past decade, the internet usage rate of teenagers has continued to rise, and their various behaviors in cyberspace have attracted great attention of researchers.

Y. Zhang and N. Shah (Eds.): BigIoT-EDU 2023, LNICST 581, pp. 182–192, 2024.
https://doi.org/10.1007/978-3-031-63133-7_18

However, because there are many cases of teenagers indulging in the virtual world of the Internet and having no life goals, most scholars focus their research on the impact of the Internet on individual negative behaviors, such as network, addiction, network bullying and other network bias behaviors, while the positive effect of the Internet on individuals seems to be ignored by researchers intentionally or unintentionally because it does not conform to the public's consistent impression of "cancer". However, with the arrival of the normalization of the epidemic, people gradually realized that the network, a special form of information transmission, can not only have a negative impact on individuals, but also help individuals to transmit love and good deeds. For example, in the process of small-scale rebound of the epidemic, many people on the network actively provided epidemic prevention information and transmission path to others; In addition, the online crowdfunding platform helps those who are seriously ill but do not have enough income to support their own medical treatment. From more and more such touching behaviors, it is not difficult to find that the Internet, as a convenient and low-threshold way of information transmission, provides a broader display platform for people's prosocial behavior. More and more studies have also found that the network environment is a good soil for the propagation and development of prosocial behavior (Cooley, 2017), so the study of prosocial behavior in cyberspace cannot be ignored.

Cultural self-confidence is the collection of individual's sense of honor and pride in their own cultural theme. In the case of the same cultural background, the higher the degree of identification and firmness of individuals to their own culture, the more positive their behavior attitude, the greater the degree of subjective norms, and the more likely individuals are to have behaviors encouraged by culture. At present, the research on the psychological level of cultural self-confidence is still in its infancy. Therefore, this study mainly discusses the influence of college students' cultural self-confidence on online prosocial behavior.

"Without a high degree of cultural self-confidence and cultural prosperity, there will be no great rejuvenation of the Chinese nation" a, first of all, from the international perspective, the role of culture in empowering human development has become increasingly prominent. In the context of the era of peace and development, a country's innovation is mainly embodied in cultural and technological innovation [1]. Cooperation between countries is mainly based on respect for national culture and ideology. Competition between countries is increasingly evolving into a competition of cultural soft power. Cultivating college students' firm cultural confidence in the new era is not only the need for China to change the mode of economic development, but also the need to maintain ideological security, It is also the need to promote cultural diversity of human society. Secondly, from the perspective of the domestic environment, culture plays an increasingly prominent role in improving people's happiness.

First, enhance the cultural self-confidence of college students in the new era [2]. The main purpose of studying the cultivation of cultural self-confidence of college students in the new era is to shape college students' three outlooks with the appeal of cultural self-confidence, and help them "tie the first button of life" in their "booting stage", so that they can recognize, accept, internalize and display the socialist culture with Chinese characteristics with a more confident attitude on their future life path, So that the new generation of young people in China can consciously take the socialist road with Chinese characteristics as the direction of progress, consciously guide their own behavior with the theory of socialism with Chinese characteristics, consciously construct the development coordinates with the socialist system with Chinese characteristics, and consciously cultivate their inner soul with the socialist culture with Chinese characteristics,

Secondly, explore the practical path of cultivating cultural self-confidence; Find and solve the deficiencies in the cultivation mechanism, subject, method, content, environment, and object. Explore the ingenious combination of ideological and political education in realizing political indoctrination and cultural education, constantly summarize cultivation experience, find cultivation problems, optimize cultivation methods, highlight key points, and complement weaknesses. Based on this, this paper studies the modeling and analysis of the influence of cultural self-confidence of college students based on KPCA algorithm.

2 Related Work

2.1 Research Status of Cultural Self-confidence

Cultural self-confidence is an important social and psychological phenomenon born in China, so Chinese researchers have explained the profound connotation and value core of cultural self-confidence from multiple perspectives. The earliest emergence of the word "cultural self-confidence" can be traced back to the 1990s. At that time, there were many phenomena in the society, such as the so-called English abbreviations, the English names rooted in people's hearts are higher than the Chinese names, which reflected the deep inferiority complex of the national culture. Some scholars proposed that we should start with modern Chinese education, abandon this inferiority complex, and establish our own cultural self-confidence, We can properly absorb the essence of western languages, but more importantly, we can change the cultural orientation through Chinese language education (Luo Yuan, 1999). After that, scholars from different research fields have conducted in-depth research on this concept. Zhou Ting (2020) and others, starting from the psychological mechanism of cultural self-confidence, believed that cultural self-confidence is the full recognition of the main culture of the individual living in the current cultural background on the basis of knowing and understanding their own culture, as well as the positive emotion generated by this recognition. They divide cultural self-confidence into cognitive and emotional aspects, which respectively constitute cultural praise and cultural pride; Shen Zhuanghai (2021), starting from the perspective of national development, believes that value self-confidence is an important core part of cultural self-confidence, which includes the inheritance and development of the mainstream culture of the country, and represents the true attitude of the people to the local culture; Liu Yunshan (2019), starting from the perspective of group identity, believed that cultural self-confidence should not be an affirmation of a certain dimension of an individual, but should be the praise and extension of the cultural value of the people's groups of countries and regions under the influence of a specific culture; Zhang Leisheng (2012), starting from the individual's attitude cognition, believes that cultural self-confidence includes two processes: static and dynamic. One represents the recognition and practice of the existing cultural values, and the other represents the expectation and yearning for the cultural prospects of the nation.

In the West, there is no corresponding term for cultural self-confidence, but there are similar research terms such as group identity, which may include the different under-standing of cultural connotation between China and the West. In Chinese, "culture" is more of a way of governing the world by "educating with culture", emphasizing the dynamic and creative activities of culture. Later, with the development of society, cul-ture gradually points to the result of its creative activities, that is, the state of various natural phenomena after being recognized, transformed and reorganized by people, and the moral outlook of Chinese culture is the result of "educating with culture". Thus, the word "culture" gradually changes from the only dynamic attribute of activity creation to the objective standard of static moral evaluation of activity content. In the western con-text, culture refers to the cultivation and training of human skills to enable individuals to acquire abilities that are not available under natural conditions (Briton, 2022). American researcher Kroeber et al. believe that culture and other human subjective variables are similar, and can be deconstructed in both implicit and explicit ways. However, in either state, people need to use practical language tools to achieve the purpose of activities in daily life communication (Kroeber, 2017). Zhao Zhiyu et al. (2010) believed that culture refers to a diffuse knowledge tradition shared by a group of people and transmitted from generation to generation. In contrast, in the western context, the word "culture" lacks the moral concept that Chinese culture attaches the most importance to (Kashima et al., 2010). This pursuit and discussion of the moral concept itself in culture may be the root cause of the psychological phenomenon of cultural self-confidence that cannot be ignored (Xiao Junming, 2012).

Through the above research on culture and cultural self-confidence, we can find that cultural self-confidence includes emotional identification and cognitive affirmation of its own cultural subject, whether from the perspective of national development or from the perspective of individual psychology. Therefore, this study synthesizes the previous people's achievements and defines cultural self-confidence as the subject's full recognition and firm belief in its own cultural value under the background of Chinese culture, and includes the positive emotional experience caused by it.

2.2 KPCA Algorithm

Kernel principal component analysis (KPCA) is a nonlinear data processing method. Its core idea is to project the data in the original space into the high-dimensional feature space through nonlinear mapping, and then perform data processing based on principal component analysis (PCA) in the high-dimensional feature space. Its purpose is to trans-form the relevant variables into new variables that are not related to each other through projection data, and extract the main components, but it cannot process nonlinear data [3]. Add kernel function on the basis of principal component analysis, that is, use non-linear function to map raw data to high-dimensional space, and then conduct principal component analysis, as shown in Fig. 1.

When using Naive Bayes algorithm for classification, it is required that attributes are conditionally independent, but this condition cannot be realized in practical applications. Therefore, there are certain restrictions when using Naive Bayes for classification, which also reduces the classification performance. Therefore, in order to meet the independence condition of Naive Bayes, people have proposed various improvement methods, one of

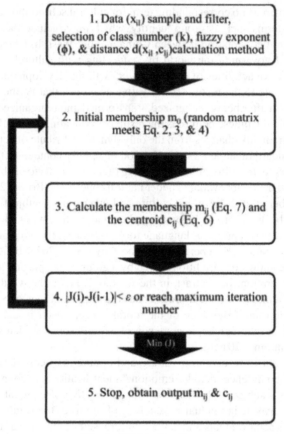

Fig. 1. KPCA algorithm

which is to filter out the relevant attributes in the dataset by using kernel principal component analysis, Make the attributes of the new dataset irrelevant and satisfy the independence condition.

$$\arg \min_{SC} \sum_{i=1}^{k} \sum_{x \in C_i} |X - \mu_i|^2 \tag{1}$$

$$\|y - \theta_i\| = \min(\|y - \theta_i\|) \tag{2}$$

However, since traditional kernel principal component analysis can only be applied to quantitative data, and most of the data are mixed data with multiple attributes, this model uses Pearson correlation coefficient, Minkowski distance and other distance formulas to calculate the distance between quantitative variables, and Kendall coefficient to calculate the distance between qualitative variables. The sum of the two represents the distance between samples, so as to calculate the Gaussian kernel function, Based on the kernel principal component analysis, a new data set is screened, and then naive Bayesian classification is carried out for the new data set.

3 Modeling the Influence of College Students' Cultural Self-confidence Based on KPCA Algorithm

3.1 Cultural Confidence of College Students

The realistic source of cultural self-confidence: "We should strengthen cultural self-confidence, promote the creative transformation and innovative development of the excellent traditional Chinese culture, inherit revolutionary culture, and develop advanced socialist culture". First, the excellent traditional Chinese culture demonstrates the blood line inheritance of the Chinese nation, is the spiritual coordinate for the Chinese people to stand on their own in the world's national forest, and is the historical source of cultural self-confidence. Second, revolutionary culture is the spiritual source of cultural self-confidence [4]. Never forget the person who dug the well when he was drinking water, and never forget the way when he came. The reason why the Red Revolutionary Culture is precious is that it embodies the dauntless spirit of throwing one's head down to the communist ideal and the revolutionary enthusiasm of hard struggle to change the backward face of China. Third, advanced culture is the realistic source of cultural self-confidence. Advanced culture is a culture that meets the requirements of the development of advanced productive forces, reflects the socialist modernization drive, and leads the way forward for socialism.

The basic position of cultural self-confidence: "Cultural self-confidence is a more basic, broader and deeper confidence R.". First, the foundation of cultural self-confidence is reflected in that road self-confidence, theoretical self-confidence and institutional self-confidence need to rely on culture to generate. Cultural self-confidence provides the value soil in the cultural sense for the logical construction of the three self-confidence. Without the nourishment of socialist culture with Chinese characteristics, consensus on the road, theory and system cannot be established uniformly. Secondly, the universality of cultural self-confidence is reflected in its extensibility that the other three self-confidence do not have. Whether from the perspective of historical generation or the universality of space, in the dual concerns of "diachronic" and "synchronic", culture is as if there is nothing, "if there is something, it is not used frequently", which widely exists in people's survival and development. That is why cultural self-confidence can be the internal force of the three self-confidence, Build a broad sense of self-confidence and identity, and build an unbreakable deep value foundation [5]. Third, the profundity of cultural self-confidence is reflected in the profound influence of culture on people. As the ideological road, theory, system and culture in the superstructure, due to their legitimacy and correctness, they can have a profound impact on people's understanding, especially culture. Cultural attributes - or the regularity of culture - directly determine people's way of thinking, and do not shift with people's will, making people unable to do anything beyond their own cultural attributes, so culture has a deeper impact on people.

3.2 Modeling and Analysis of the Influence of Cultural Self-confidence of College Students Based on KPCA Algorithm

In the influence of KPCA algorithm on college students' cultural self-confidence, the data is not monitored, but a new data set is directly obtained by using the improved KPCA method, and then the naive Bayesian model is used to classify it. However, in practical problems, monitoring the data is crucial. The influence of college students' cultural self-confidence is considered [6], The improved local outlier factor algorithm is used to screen the data of non outliers in the training set and the test set respectively. Then, based on the new filtered data set, combined with the improved KPCA method, a cultural confidence impact model is established to classify the new data set and compare the impact of outliers on the accuracy of the test set.

In the process of cultivating college students' cultural self-confidence in the new era, the cultivation subject plays the most important role in educating people, and is the core force to support the realization of cultural self-confidence cultivation. At the current stage, there is no more consistent linkage between the cultivation subjects, which is mainly reflected in the relationship between the ideological and political teachers and other professional teachers, the relationship between the Marxist Institute and the functional departments of the school [7]. The linkage between college counselors and students' parents needs to be further deepened. In order to capture the individual differences of cultural self-confidence perception, two capture forms are proposed: one is systematic difference capture, the other is random difference capture. The system differences are captured using multiple KPCA algorithm models by setting cross variables. In this paper, the form of cross variables is adopted. The cross of gender and cultural self-confidence is used to capture the differences between men and women in their understanding of cultural self-confidence. The capture of random differences is based on the assumption that college students' cultural self-confidence parameters are in different distribution forms in the utility function. KPCA algorithm model is used to capture four distribution forms: uniform distribution, normal distribution, logarithmic normal distribution and Johnson distribution [8]. Figure 2 below shows a comparison chart of the impact of cultural self-confidence.

When modeling, because the lognormal distribution is on the right side of zero, that is, the sign is single, but because college students' cultural self-confidence is reverse to the utility of choice branch, that is, the coefficient corresponding to college students' cultural self-confidence should be negative, so before entering the model to determine parameters, college students' cultural self-confidence should take its opposite number. Similarly, for Johnson distribution, college students' cultural self-confidence should also take the opposite number. In the calculation, the simulation algorithm provided by the multivariate statistical analysis software KPCA algorithm is used to calibrate and solve the model [9].

It indicates the influence of abnormal samples on the accuracy rate of training set and test set respectively. It can be seen that for different data sets, the accuracy rate of training set is higher after the abnormal samples are deleted from the training set. When the test set remains unchanged, the accuracy rate of test set increases after the abnormal samples are deleted from the training set, which indicates that the training effect is better after the abnormal samples are deleted [10]. The abnormal samples of

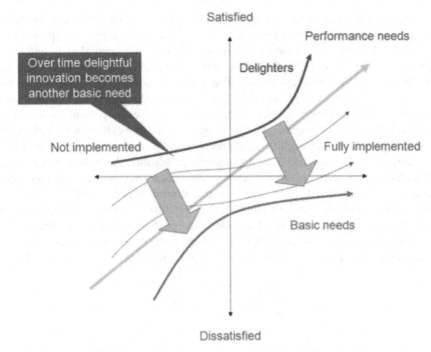

Fig. 2. Analysis Chart of Cultural Confidence Impact

both the training set and the test set are deleted, It is found that the accuracy rate is higher than that of the abnormal samples without deleting the test set, which indicates that it is necessary to monitor the data before using the naive Bayesian algorithm to influence college students' cultural self-confidence, which can make the effect of college students' cultural self-confidence better.

4   Analysis of the Intermediary Effect of College Students' Cultural Self-confidence, Online Prosocial Behavior and Gentleman Personality

Wen Zhonglin et al. Through the above correlation analysis, we can see that there is a statistically significant correlation between cultural self-confidence, online prosocial behavior and gentleman personality. On this basis, this study further tests the intermediary effect between the three variables through stepwise regression.

In order to effectively test the intermediary effect of the personality of the gentleman, this study established three regression models to gradually analyze the intermediary effect between the three variables: to analyze the predictive effect of cultural self-confidence on online prosocial behavior; Analyze the predictive effect of cultural self-confidence on gentleman's personality; This paper analyzes the predictive effect of cultural self-confidence and gentleman personality on online prosocial behavior, focusing on the change of the predictive effect of intermediary variables after controlling the effect of independent variables.

Cultural confidence has a significant positive impact on online prosocial behavior, and the regression coefficient t test of data analysis results is significant ($\beta = 0.203$, $p < 0.001$); From the regression analysis, we can find that cultural self-confidence has a significant positive predictive effect on the personality of the gentleman, and the regression coefficient t-test result is significant ($\beta = = 0.019$, $p < 0.05$). Through the second layer of results, we can find that after controlling the influence of cultural self-confidence on online prosocial behavior, the effect of gentleman personality on online prosocial behavior is still significant, that is, after controlling cultural self-confidence, gentleman personality still significantly affects online prosocial behavior ($\beta = 0.322$, $p < 0.001$). And after the addition of gentleman personality, the influence of cultural self-confidence on online prosocial behavior decreased, and the standard regression coefficient decreased from 0.203 to 0.157, and the influence of cultural self-confidence on online prosocial behavior remained significant ($p < 0.001$). To sum up, the gentleman's personality plays a part of intermediary role in the prediction process of cultural self-confidence on network prosocial behavior. Therefore, the relationship between cultural self-confidence, gentleman's personality and online prosocial behavior is shown in Fig. 3:

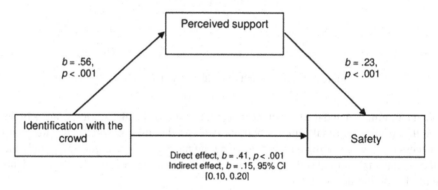

Fig. 3. Mediation effect test results

Next, in order to further analyze the regulatory effect of self-control in the path of cultural confidence on online prosocial behavior, this study took the value of cultural confidence and online prosocial behavior when self-control was positive or negative 1 standard deviation from the average, and carried out a simple slope test. The results are shown in Fig. 4.

It can be seen from Fig. 4 that when the individual's self-control is at a high level, the predictive effect of cultural self-confidence on online prosocial behavior and that of gentleman personality on online prosocial behavior is more significant, that is, the model built in this study has been verified, that is, cultural self-confidence has an impact on online prosocial behavior through the intermediary process of gentleman personality and is regulated by self-control ability.

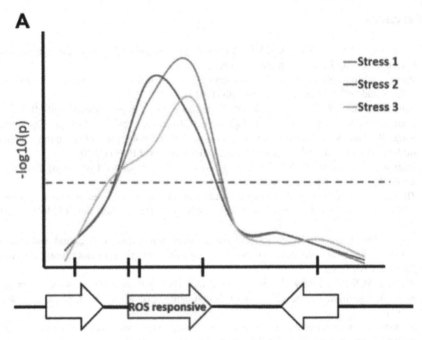

Fig. 4. The regulatory role of self-control in the relationship between cultural self-confidence and online prosocial behavior

5   Conclusion

Cultural self-confidence is a key factor in determining people's tendency to engage in or avoid certain behaviors. The theory of cultural self-efficacy proposes that individuals with a high sense of cultural self-efficacy are more likely to take culturally appropriate behaviors and are less likely to engage in behaviors that are considered "deviant". In this research, I will use Kpca algorithm to analyze the cultural self-confidence of college students. In this study, the first step of the KPCA model is to evaluate the individual's cultural self-confidence by measuring cultural knowledge and language skills, and finally use these data for analysis.

Acknowledgements. University Social Sciences Research Project of Anhui Province in 2020: "A Study on the Core Values of Korea and China Based on Improving CulturalConfidence" (Project Number: SK2020A0435), School level key teaching and research project of Hefei University in 2021: "Research on the integration mode of 'curriculum thinking and politics' of Korean intensive reading course in Applied Universities" (Project Number: 2021hfujyxm34), Anhui Provincial Education and Teaching Reform Key Research Project in 2022: "Construction and Practice of Integration Model of 'Course Thought and Politics' in Intensive Korean Course in Applied Colleges and Universities" (ProjectNumber:2022jyxm1336).

References

1. Shen, X.Q., Sha-Sha, X.U., Xia, Y.F.: Analysis on the influence factors of College Students' Entrepreneurship Based on structural equation model
2. Wang, J.: Micro-blog Content-based analysis and research on the dynamic prediction of college students' thought. J. Tongren Univ. (2017)
3. Sun, F.G., Yue, W.U.: An analysis of the influence of college students' self-efficacy on employment confidence and social adaptability. J. Liaoning Provincial College Commun.
4. Song, B., Qiu, R.: The influence of digital virtual technology on contemporary college students' ideological and political education. IEEE Access PP(99) (2020)
5. Jingxian, X:. Analysis on the Influence Factors of College Students' Consuming Trust under the Background of Mobile E-commerce
6. Zhang, Y.: The influence of ideological and political education on employment quality of college students based on association rule analysis. J. Phys. Conf. Ser. **1744**(4), 042169 (2021)
7. Liu, Y., Zheng, D., Wu, X., et al.: Research on prediction of dam seepage and dual analysis of lag-sensitivity of influencing factors based on MIC optimizing random forest algorithm. KSCE J. Civil Eng., 1–13
8. Wang, L.M.X.P.C.: Fuzzy C-means cluster analysis based on mutative scale chaos optimization algorithm for the grouping of discontinuity sets. Rock Mech. Rock Eng. **46**(1) (2013)
9. Boolani, A.: Influence of grit on physical activity, sitting time and dietary behaviors: a multi-study analysis. Sustainability **15** (2022)
10. Wang, Y., Wang, J., Bunn, D.W.: Design of link prediction algorithm for complex network based on the comprehensive influence of predicting nodes and neighbor nodes (2021)

Research on the Application of Big Data in Smart Teaching

Design and Implementation of College Student Volunteer Service Platform Based on Collaborative Filtering Algorithm

Qingfeng Li[1]([✉]), Chao Zhang[1], Chao Jin[1], Yong Gao[1], Desheng Zhu[1], Li Xia[2], and Yurui Jiang[2]

[1] Shandong Institute of Commerce and Technology, Jinan 250103, Shandong, China
Q2442974184@163.com
[2] Yunnan Medical Health College, Kunming 650000, China

Abstract. In the past decade, voluntary service has mushroomed vigorously. With the promotion of voluntary service and the progress of the Internet, massive voluntary service data have been generated in voluntary activities. How to process and utilize volunteer service data, guide the behavior of volunteer users, and provide valuable reference for participants in volunteer services has become an urgent issue to be resolved. The purpose of the college student volunteer service platform is to strengthen communication between volunteers and service objects to ensure the accuracy of volunteer service. To achieve this goal, collaborative filtering algorithms should be added to the design of the service platform to analyze actual needs. Based on this idea, this paper proposes a collaborative filtering algorithm and designs a volunteer service platform. The volunteer service platform can better solve the three core issues of today's volunteer industry: chaotic activity information, low volunteer service platform efficiency management, and improper activity matching. Compared with existing service platforms, the volunteer service platform designed in this article greatly reduces the time for users to search and find, helps users better participate in volunteer activities, and has certain practical value.

Keywords: Collaborative filtering algorithm · Volunteer college students · The service platform

1 Introduction

In the context of the great development of China's volunteer service, the National Volunteer Service Information System came into being to promote "Internet plus" volunteer service in combination with the characteristics of the information age. The big data of volunteer service is recorded and provided by the National Volunteer Service Information System, which is the only data in the field of volunteer service in the country, and contains great research value. Research big data in the field of volunteering, provide reference for volunteer service managers and participants, promote volunteering to a higher level, and create greater social benefits [1].

Y. Zhang and N. Shah (Eds.): BigIoT-EDU 2023, LNICST 581, pp. 195–206, 2024.
https://doi.org/10.1007/978-3-031-63133-7_19

Establishing collaborative filtering in the field of volunteer services is conducive to the understanding and utilization of data. The volunteer service big data is rich in content and diverse in categories, covering elements such as volunteers, volunteer groups, and volunteer projects. Each element also covers its time, location, and behavioral information, and the relationships between the elements are equally complex. Domain collaborative filtering relies on its semantic integration capabilities and data query capabilities to provide infrastructure support for upper level intelligent applications in the domain [2]. Establishing collaborative filtering for volunteer services can sort out the relationships between volunteer service elements. On the one hand, it can display the correlation between volunteer service elements in the form of a graph, and on the other hand, it can transform the semantic information of volunteer service knowledge into computer services, providing basic data technology support for upper level applications such as retrieval and recommendation.

Utilizing the association relationships contained in collaborative filtering in the field of volunteer services, combined with artificial intelligence technology, to research recommendation algorithms based on collaborative filtering, matching suitable volunteer projects for volunteer users, and providing more personalized services, also has important significance for the development of volunteer services. Currently, recommendation systems are widely used in commercial fields such as e-commerce, video products, news, etc., but they have not been widely used in vertical industries [3]. Using collaborative filtering in vertical industries to research recommendation algorithms not only plays a role in the field of volunteer services, but also provides reference for intelligent applications in other industries.

Early organized students volunteer groups in our country as the social tradition, providing service to specific people mostly superficial, but early service process is difficult, though low, the base of the reason is that certain people but is not fixed, therefore can be divided into various types, and each type of different people on the demand side is different, If the service is provided by subjective judgment of service target needs, the problem cannot be effectively solved in most cases [4]. This phenomenon indicates that the service quality of college students volunteers is low, and the quality problem is reflected in the accuracy of service. In reaction to the phenomenon, the modern field that can make use of advanced technology to develop college students volunteer service platform, using technology to analyze the requirements, but to do this we must reasonable selection algorithm to design platform, collaborative filtering algorithm which got the attention of people, therefore, in order to let the algorithm into the platform design, and play their role, Relevant studies are needed [5].

2 Related Work

2.1 Application Value in the Field of Voluntary Service

Currently, the data in the field of voluntary services are mainly structured data stored in traditional databases. Mining the potential value of these data has important guiding significance for improving the participation of volunteer subjects, promoting the development of voluntary services, and promoting the deepening of volunteer services [6].

The introduction of collaborative filtering technology to the field of volunteer services has more profound application value than traditional database technology:

1) Collaborative filtering presents entities and relationships in the form of graphs. Using collaborative filtering visualization technology, various relationships in the real world can be intuitively and efficiently modeled, consistent with user cognitive habits. Compared to traditional data table formats, it is more able to enable non professional volunteer service participants or managers to understand information. Currently, collaborative filtering visualization technology is increasingly widely used in the vertical field [7]. However, if the data is presented in the form of a traditional database construction network diagram, although it conforms to the entity relationship model of database design, it requires an intermediate transformation process, which incurs certain computational overhead; In addition, when the relationships or attributes of entities need to be extended, there is a cost of re modeling the relational database.
2) Collaborative filtering connects previously unrelated data, making it more advantageous in establishing complex relational networks.

   Potential makes it easier to mine implicit associations. Although structured volunteer service data have clear hierarchical relationships, indirect relationships are difficult to detect, and these relationships have certain potential value. For example, in addition to having direct participation relationships with projects, it is difficult to directly reflect whether volunteers have potential connections with other projects in traditional databases [8]. Using collaborative filtering to establish a relationship network in the volunteer service field can process complex association analysis faster, reducing the query overhead of multiple relationships and multiple hops in traditional databases.
3) Currently, there is no unified knowledge base in the field of voluntary service, and a knowledge map in the field of voluntary service has been established.

   Based on this, developing intelligent applications of volunteer service can help promote the development of volunteer service. Initially, establish a domain map to facilitate the evaluation and expansion of industry experts. Using the semantic association information contained in collaborative filtering, combined with artificial intelligence, to carry out applications such as recommending projects and groups to volunteers, evaluating volunteers participating in projects and groups, knowledge Q&A for volunteer services, and volunteer service retrieval, will provide strong support for volunteer service work in the Internet environment.

   Currently, the research focus in the field of voluntary service is still on management systems and service models [9]. There is little research on data in the current field. There are also studies on volunteer service management platforms in the academic community, but there are few cases of using big data in the field to develop intelligent applications. Therefore, building collaborative filtering in the field of volunteer services and developing its application value is of great significance for the development of volunteer services.

2.2 Construction of Volunteer Service Domain Map

Generally, logically, the knowledge map is divided into two levels: the schema layer and the data layer. The schema layer is above the data layer and is also the core of the knowledge map, involving entity types, relationship types, attribute types, and so on. The data layer stores specific data based on the schema layer. For example, the schema layer of a knowledge map contains the data schema (person, birthplace, region), while the data layer stores real data such as (Yao Ming, birthplace, Shanghai).

Ontology, as a concept that can describe information systems at the semantic and knowledge levels, is widely used to construct a schema layer of knowledge maps. Standard ontology modeling frameworks include RDFS (Resource Description Framework Schema), oWL (Web Ontology Language), and so on [10]. Considering that the hierarchical relationship of volunteer service data sources is relatively clear and it is easy to design top-level concepts, compared to converting source data into RDFS/OWL description language and storing it in a relational database or graph database, drawing on the idea of ontology, the method of manually defining patterns to directly extract knowledge and store it will be faster and more efficient.

The process for building a knowledge map in the field of volunteer service is shown in Fig. 1. First, complete the design of the knowledge map pattern layer: analyze the data characteristics of volunteer service and the subject and object of volunteer service behavior, and conduct entity design according to the "entity attribute attribute value" pattern; After completing the entity design, excavate the relationships between different types of volunteer entities, and complete the relationship design according to "entity relationship entity" [11]. Then, according to the designed structural pattern, use the data processing tool Spark SQL to write scripts, extract corresponding entity relationship knowledge from volunteer service data sources, and fill in the data layer of the vertical domain map. Finally, the knowledge data is stored in a designed database as the basis for knowledge services, which includes the relational database MySQL and the graph database Neo4j.

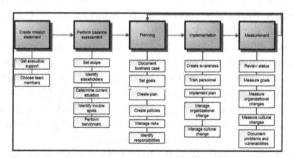

Fig. 1. Construction process of volunteer service domain map

3 Collaborative Filtering Algorithm

3.1 Basic Concept of Collaborative Filtering Algorithm

The rapid development of Internet technology has brought massive amounts of data and information to people. On the one hand, it has made it more difficult for users to search and process information; On the other hand, useful information is diluted by the information ocean, and the gap between users and content producers becomes increasingly apparent. An excellent recommendation system can provide personalized services for users. Collaborative filtering algorithms are the most popular among many information filtering technologies. Collaborative filtering algorithms are divided into user based collaborative filtering algorithm UserCF and item based collaborative filtering algorithm ItemCF. A user based collaborative filtering algorithm uses user historical behavior data to recommend items that other users have similar interests and like [12]. The collaborative filtering algorithm based on items is similar to the collaborative filtering algorithm based on users. It only swaps the roles of goods and users, obtains the connection between items by calculating the ratings of other users on the items, and then uses the similarity between items to recommend similar items to the user. The biggest advantage of collaborative filtering algorithms is that they have no special requirements for recommended objects and can handle unstructured and complex objects. Collaborative filtering algorithms provide personalized recommendations based on user similarity rather than the objective attributes of items [13]. Therefore, it can filter any type of item, such as movies, music, text, and so on. Since the implementation of this volunteer service platform only uses user based collaborative filtering algorithms, we analyze user based collaborative filtering algorithms.

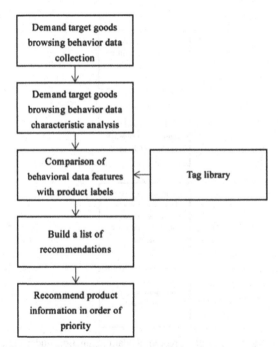

Fig. 2. Topology of "guess what you like" recommendation function under collaborative filtering algorithm

Collaborative filtering algorithm is a typical personalized recommendation algorithm, which can give the possible needs of the target, and can also comprehensively analyze whether other targets have similar needs according to the related needs of the target. Collaborative filtering algorithm with usual used in e-commerce, common in all kinds of electric business platform, the algorithm is implemented by the platform function for "guess you like", "the others like", the two functions will rely on the target platform behavior data analysis of the demand, and then compared with commodity demand, if demand characteristics consistent with the a label of goods, Means the target may need this goods, goods will be included in the list, at the same time match degree on the surface of the product characteristics and the demand is higher, the goods the higher order on the recommended list, on behalf of the recommendation higher priority, such as A demand characteristics, one of all the features of A label with A commodity is the same, there are two features the same as the B goods two labels, Then the recommendation priority of product B will be higher than product A in the recommendation list [14]. Based on this, if A demand characteristics, all and any item in the same label, and will combine the label target characteristics were analyzed, and the demand for other if found existing in the demand of target and label of the same characteristics, will be A demand for target and other related requirements, and to demand A target push other related requirements have ever been browsing, But A needs goods that the target has not browsed. Figure 2 and 3 are the topologies of the recommendation functions of "Guess what you like" and "others like it too" under the collaborative filtering algorithm [1–3].

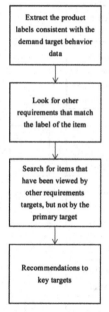

Fig. 3. Topology of "Others also like" recommendation function under collaborative filtering algorithm

College volunteers, from this perspective, if you can provide the services as commodities, demand will be server as a goal, you can in volunteer service platform, collaborative filtering algorithm is used to guarantee college students volunteer service accuracy,

namely according to the students professional ability, set up a number of volunteer organizations, According to different organizational capacity building services and project
label, and then collect the relevant data of different service target groups, characteristics,
extract the data again with service project tag matching, can recommend the service
goal service organizations, service goal to make a choice after the corresponding service
organization to provide services, can also according to other same type service goal ever
make a choice, Provide service items not selected by the service target [15].

It should be noted that although the logic of collaborative filtering algorithm is simple
and easy to understand, a complete algorithm model must be established before it can
be put into use. The algorithm model is called intersection division union (see Formula
(1) for details).

$$J(A, B) = \frac{|A \cap B|}{|A \cup B|} \tag{1}$$

Type J is compatibility, (A, B) is the demand for the target data set of features and
labels, calculated, using jie card similarity coefficient is both matching degree and does
not match the degree, if matching degrees greater than do not match, can recommend,
and vice recommendation is not recommended, and according to the matching degree
exceeds the value does not match the size of the judgment related products recommended
priority.

3.2 Recommended Algorithm Evaluation Indicators

Evaluation indicators are mainly used to evaluate the performance of algorithms. Scoring
prediction requires indicators to evaluate the accuracy of prediction. Top-N recommendation evaluation requires calculating accuracy, recall, and other indicators to evaluate
the performance of algorithms.

Scoring prediction refers to the prediction score given to a project by a user by a
recommendation algorithm. The indicators used to evaluate its accuracy include average
absolute error and root mean square error:

1) The average absolute error (MAE) represents the prediction accuracy of the recommendation. The average absolute error between the algorithm's prediction score and
   the user's actual score. The smaller the value, the more accurate the prediction is, and
   the higher the recommendation quality is, as shown in formula (2):

$$MAE = \sum\nolimits_{i=1}^{N} \frac{|P_i - Q_i|}{N} \tag{2}$$

2) Root mean square error (RMSE) is the arithmetic square root of the expected value
   of the square of the difference between the estimated value of a parameter and the
   true value. It is a more rigorous indicator for punishing user project scoring errors
   with greater effort. The calculation of RMSE is shown in Formula (3):

$$RMSE = \sum\nolimits_{i=1}^{N} \sqrt{\frac{|P_i - Q_i|^2}{N}} \tag{3}$$

The main evaluation indicators for ranking accuracy recommended by Top-N are accuracy rate and recall rate, and the calculation method is as follows:

3) Accuracy indicates the proportion of items that users are interested in and have preferences in the total number of recommended Top N ranking. The higher the value of Precision, the higher the user's satisfaction with the recommendation results. The calculation formula for accuracy is shown in (4):

$$Precision = \frac{\sum_{u \in U} | R(u) \bigcap T(u) |}{\sum_{u \in U} | R(u) |} \tag{4}$$

5) Recall rate indicates how many items that users truly prefer are successfully recommended and displayed by the algorithm. The calculation formula for recall rate is shown in (5):

$$Recall = \frac{\sum_{n \in U} | R(u) \bigcap T(u) |}{\sum_{u \in U} | T(u) |} \tag{5}$$

where R (u) represents the recommended result sequence calculated from the model training set, and T (u) represents the user's true favorite list.

4   College Student Volunteer Platform Design and Practical Application

4.1   Platform Design

Collaborative filtering algorithm is important in the design of college student volunteer platform, but to ensure that the platform can be put into practice, other technologies are needed to build the platform framework. See Fig. 4 for the platform framework built in this paper.

According to Fig. 3, the platform is mainly divided into two levels, the first is the application layer, its application by operation interface, display interface and data source platform, operation application interface is mainly used for target selection service projects, platform display is mainly used for services related information, so the service target is generated under the browse or operation of the behavior of the corresponding data, this data will all be imported into the data source. The data source is like a temporary database with a small repository capacity, but all the databases that enter the data source are directly imported into the analysis layer after preprocessing. Layer, the second is analysis by the database, the algorithm module, the output of three parts, including database are responsible for transmitting data storage application layer, and are classified, after classifying the data according to the classification algorithm module project input, driven collaborative filtering algorithm, through computing the output, the results form for service goals exist which requirements, which service projects are selected in order to schedule, design or adjust the service plan for college student volunteer service organizations? The implementation of each level and related components of this platform is as follows.

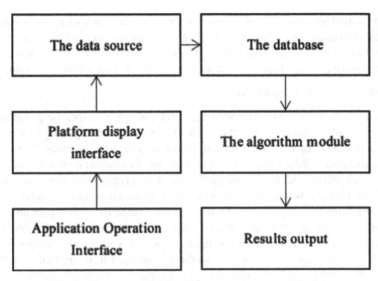

Fig. 4. The framework of college student volunteer platform

(1) Application Layer Implementation.

The first is the application operation interface, the interface mainly uses VB for key design, UI design after completion, and then the use of Java language to develop functional programs, functional programs and corresponding keys together, import into the UI framework.

Secondly, the platform display interface, which is a whole with the application operation interface, will be designed on the basis of the application operation interface. UI technology is mainly used to complete the work in the design, which requires the interface to be concise and logical. After the interface is designed, the jump connection is designed to facilitate the service target operation.

Finally, the data source, which is essentially an information collection function program, is responsible for collecting the behavior data of the service target in the above two interfaces. Therefore, Java language is used to complete the development of the information collection function. In order to ensure the reasonable operation of the information collection function, the functional operation logic design is carried out. Firstly, the data types of service target behavior are manually distinguished, which are divided into browsing and operation. Then, related classified items are commonly found in the functional program, and the representative functional program will collect the data of these two classified items. Second, the information collection delay parameter is set as 1s, which means that the functional program will collect relevant classified data within 1s, ensuring the real-time performance of information collection. Third, for the sake of data quality and the accuracy of the final calculation results, the preprocessing tool is selected, which is now mature and does not need to be developed again. This paper mainly selects the data matching tool, which can check whether the input data is complete according to the standard format. If it is incomplete, it will not be collected, and vice versa. Fourthly, in order to make the data source into all data can be timely analysis layer, in the first set forward logic, namely only forwards data after pretreatment, after setting the data into a time interval, for 5 s, storage time after reaching 5 s forward if meet the logic of data will be forwarded, if the data is still not be within 5 s preprocessing, it forwards the data to adjust to the list of most lower level, wait for the next loop.

(2) Analysis layer implementation

The first is the database. Although the service target is a specific group and the number of people in the group is not large, a large amount of analysis of different types of behavioral data of each person is needed to accurately identify the needs. Therefore, the magnitude of data in the analysis process is large, and the conventional database may not meet the needs of data storage. Aiming at this point, this paper chose the cloud database, the database capacity is infinite, in theory and practice need to limit its capacity for the sake of data security, an entire data storage space is divided into outer space and interior space, and then set up a firewall between the two, the firewall will limit the database capacity, but even if is restricted, In actual applications, you can also temporarily turn off the firewall for capacity expansion, so there is no need to worry that its unlimited capacity advantage cannot be brought into play. In addition, the relevant resources of the cloud database are used to develop the data classification function, which can complete the classification according to the characteristics and sources of data sources.

The second is the algorithm module, which is built according to the model of formula (1) and realizes the model logic with the help of Java language in the process. After testing, the algorithm module can operate normally, indicating that the platform is successfully equipped with collaborative filtering algorithm.

The last is result output, which mainly uses communication technology to connect the output end of the platform with the manual terminal. When the corresponding result is generated after the data is calculated by the algorithm module, the result will be sent to the manual terminal through the communication channel, and the manual can read it directly, and then make judgment and decision.

4.2 Practical Application

A poor rural area in domestic group as an example, the groups involved are 70 years old or older, childless in the home, their basic lose labor ability, usually rely on manual, after a preliminary visit investigation understands, the community of all kinds of demand, but because the old expression ability is limited, and cannot tell oneself all requirements, So volunteers can't provide accurate services under these conditions. On this basis, the elderly in this group are provided with equipment to enter the platform and learn the platform operation under the guidance of special-assigned personnel (considering the particularity of the elderly, the platform operation design adopts one-click design). Then, the behavior data of all the people in this group are collected for one month, and then relevant analysis is conducted to obtain the final result.

The results show that there are two main needs of the elderly in this group. One is that they want someone to help them do and sell handcrafts. The second is to hope that someone can accompany themselves to make up for their inner emotional vacancy. In the face of the two needs, the platform recommends college student volunteer organizations majoring in manual arts and nursing to the relevant groups. After the relevant people choose by themselves or clearly express their needs for help, the organizations provide volunteer services to the corresponding college student volunteer organizations. The service process is about three months.

After three months of service, the needs of this group can be theoretically met to a certain extent. However, in order to verify this point and verify the actual function of this platform, a satisfaction survey is conducted for this group. The survey results are shown in Table 1.

Table 1. Survey Results (10 participants)

Survey questions	Data results
Are you satisfied with the volunteer service process?	Very satisfied (10 people) Satisfied (-) General (-) Not satisfied (-)
Are you satisfied with the results of your volunteer service?	Very satisfied (8 people) Satisfied (2 people) General (-) Not satisfied (-)

According to Table 1, after three months of service, the group all people feel very satisfied, the process of volunteer service on behalf of the group scheduling volunteers accurate, accurate service scheme design, and eight people for volunteer service result was very satisfactory, 2 people are satisfied, so the overall results are in good quality service, the result will be the difference of satisfaction, It may be due to insufficient service level of volunteers or negligence in work, but this does not mean that the service items are not accurate enough. On the contrary, the overall performance of quality results is good, which also indicates that the platform recommendation is accurate and the algorithm application is effective.

5   Conclusion

In conclusion, the collaborative filtering algorithm can improve the accuracy of volunteer service in the college student volunteer platform, and solve the problem that the service cannot be accurately served due to the inability to accurately understand the service target demand. With the help of this algorithm, the effectiveness and effectiveness of college student volunteer service have been improved and protected, which indicates that the algorithm has high application value.

References

1. Gao, C.: Design and Implementation of School-Enterprise Cooperation Information Service Platform Based on Mobile Internet Technology (2022)
2. Zha, Z., Huang, W., Tang, D., et al.: Design and implementation of linkage update management system for geo-information service platform. Copernicus GmbH (2021)
3. Su, X., Cheng, X., Wang, B.: Design and implementation of "multi survey integration" management service platform. J. Phys. Conf. Ser. **1961**(1), 012061 (2021)
4. Wang, H., Shen, Z., Jiang, S., et al.: User-based collaborative filtering algorithm design and implementation. J. Phys. Conf. Ser. **1757**(1), 012168 (6pp) (2021)
5. Ling, Y.: Design and Implementation of the Platform for Multimedia Resource Sharing based on Cloud Technology, vol. 2022(7)
6. Cui, Y., Zhang, L., Hou, Y., et al.: Design of intelligent home pension service platform based on machine learning and wireless sensor network. J. Intell. Fuzzy Syst. Appli Eng. Technol. **2**, 40 (2021)
7. Lee J , Hong J S . Method for providing interior design market platform service using realistic scene image based on virtual space content data and apparatus therefor:, WO2022039567A1[P]. 2022
8. Hu, X.: Improved algorithm of cloud service node path based on cross-border transaction platform under load balancing. Comput. Commun. **177**, 195–206 (2021)
9. Liang, Y., Huang, X., Chen, Z., et al.: Construction method and architecture of integrated energy service ecological platform based on support vector machine (2021)
10. Zhang, F., Yang, L., Liu, Y., et al:. Design and Implementation of Real-Time Localization System (RTLS) based on UWB and TDoA Algorithm (2021)
11. Modares, A., Farimani, N.M., Emroozi, V.B.: A new model to design the suppliers portfolio in newsvendor problem based on product reliability. J. Indus. Manag. Optimiz. **19**(6), 4112–4151 (2023)
12. Domenico, G.D., Panichella, A., Weisman, D., et al.: Large-scale inverse design of a planar on-chip mode sorter. ACS Photonics **9**(2), 378–382 (2022)
13. Wang, J.: The design and development of the internet-based system for testing and analyzing the psychological and physiological responses during creative learning. Front. Psychol. **13**, 886972 (2022)
14. Zhou, H.: Optimization of the Rapid Design System for Arts and Crafts Based on Big Data and 3D Technology. Complexity (2021)
15. Asare, A.L., Beitler, J.R., Cimino, G., et al.: I-SPY COVID adaptive platform trial for COVID-19 acute respiratory failure: rationale, design and operations. BMJ Open **12**(6), 686–689 (2022)

The Evaluation of English Teaching Mode in the Context of Big Data

Lu Li[✉]

Shangluo Vocational and Technical College, Shangluo 726000, China
278899189@qq.com

Abstract. The English curriculum of basic education in China is undergoing major changes. Its guiding principle is to focus on the quality education of students' all-round development. Its core is to emphasize people-oriented, focus on cultivating students' practical ability and innovation spirit, and lay a foundation for lifelong learning and development of learners. The teaching principle emphasizes student centered, developing students' comprehensive language application ability, respecting students' personality and emotion, and actively using learning strategies to complete learning tasks. This puts forward high requirements for the selection and reform of English classroom teaching and English teaching methods. At the same time, higher requirements are put forward for English teaching evaluation. However, there are still many drawbacks in the current evaluation of English teaching. Therefore, we must first understand the connotation, main content and significance of English teaching evaluation. In addition, the current teaching methods are analyzed, compared and evaluated.

Keywords: English teaching · big data · Teaching evaluation

1 Introduction

With the overall promotion of quality education, the reform of educational evaluation and examination system has been widely valued. In June 2001, the State Council issued the Decision on the Reform and Development of Basic Education, and issued a series of documents such as the Outline of Basic Education Curriculum Reform (for trial implementation) and the new curriculum standards for various disciplines. This marks the official launch of a new round of basic education curriculum reform in China [1]. An important goal of this curriculum reform is to change the function of curriculum evaluation that overemphasizes the screening and selection of evaluation, and give play to the function of evaluation to promote student development, improve teachers and improve educational practice. In December 2002, the Ministry of Education issued the Notice of the Ministry of Education on Actively Promoting the Reform of the Evaluation and Examination System in Primary and Secondary Schools, which clearly stipulates how to promote the reform of the evaluation and examination system in primary and secondary schools [2]. This is the first comprehensive guidance document for the reform of evaluation and examination in primary and secondary schools issued by the Ministry of Education since the founding of the People's Republic of China.

Y. Zhang and N. Shah (Eds.): BigIoT-EDU 2023, LNICST 581, pp. 207–217, 2024.
https://doi.org/10.1007/978-3-031-63133-7_20

With the launching of the new curriculum standards in the national experimental teaching, the evaluation of English teaching in basic education in China is also facing significant changes. In order to adapt to the new situation, it is an important step for English curriculum reform in the 21st century to study and reform the evaluation and examination system in a timely manner [3].

English teaching evaluation is an important part of English curriculum. Scientific evaluation system is an important guarantee to achieve the curriculum objectives. It is also an important means to check the organization and implementation of English teaching. English teaching evaluation should effectively monitor the whole teaching process and results according to the objectives and requirements of English curriculum standards. Through evaluation, students can constantly experience progress and success in the learning process of English courses, know themselves, build self-confidence, and promote the overall development of students' comprehensive language use ability; Make the students' quality improve constantly [4]. At the same time, teachers should get feedback from English teaching, reflect on their teaching behavior and make appropriate adjustments, so as to promote teachers to constantly improve their teaching level; To enable the school to timely understand the implementation of the curriculum standards, improve the current situation of English teaching management, and promote the continuous development and innovation of English courses. So as to further improve the effect of English teaching.

2   Related Work

2.1   Meaning of English Teaching Evaluation

Evaluation usually refers to the judgment of the value of things, including the description of the quality and quantity of things and the value judgment made on this basis. It is a kind of value judgment activity and a judgment on the degree to which the object meets the needs of the subject. When evaluation is applied to education, education and teaching evaluation are produced and developed.

Educational evaluation is an activity to judge the extent to which educational activities meet the needs of society and individuals, and a process to judge the actual or potential value of educational activities in order to achieve the value added of education [5].

Education evaluation includes: student evaluation, teacher evaluation, teaching evaluation, curriculum evaluation, school and educational institution evaluation, education purpose evaluation, education system evaluation, education content evaluation, education method evaluation, education management evaluation, etc. The book "English Teaching Method for Junior Middle School in the Context of the New Curriculum" calls it a broad education evaluation [6].

According to the Notice of the Ministry of Education on Actively Promoting the Reform of the Evaluation and Examination System in Primary and Secondary Schools, education evaluation can be divided into three evaluation systems: the evaluation system aimed at promoting students' development; The evaluation system to promote the improvement of teachers' professional ethics and professional level: the evaluation system to improve the quality of school education. As an English teacher, you should evaluate your students' English learning. The book English Teaching Method for Junior Middle School in the Context of the New Curriculum calls the evaluation of students "narrow education evaluation".

The so-called teaching evaluation is a process of systematically collecting information and giving value judgments to teaching activities and teaching achievements in the teaching process according to the requirements of teaching objectives and principles[7].

English teaching evaluation refers to the evaluation in the implementation of English classroom teaching. The author believes that English teaching evaluation refers to the evaluation of students' English learning process, teachers' classroom teaching and schools' organization and implementation of English courses according to English curriculum objectives.

2.2 Main Requirements of Traditional Teaching Evaluation

Traditional education evaluation focuses on the use of effect criteria, that is, the evaluation criteria determined from the perspective of the effect of the evaluation object's completion of various educational tasks, "focusing only on the results, not on the process". When evaluating students, it mainly depends on how much they have mastered book knowledge, while ignoring the inspection of overall quality, that is, it is usually said to only look at scores; The role of traditional education evaluation is to determine the relative position of the evaluation object in the group. Using this standard can make each individual clearly understand his or her advantages and disadvantages in the group, which is conducive to stimulating the competitive consciousness of the evaluation object [8]. However, this standard is a measure of mutual comparison, which is not objective enough to reflect the actual level of the evaluation object. The traditional education evaluation overemphasizes this standard and mainly takes it as the basis for selecting students for higher education. In this way, there will be fierce and endless competition [9].

For the purpose of entering a higher school, multiple grades The education for top students is what people call "exam oriented education" nowadays ", reflects an evaluation view of selection. Under the influence of this evaluation, teachers only pay attention to a few students who have good grades and are expected to enter higher education, while ignoring the possible and due development of most students. The evaluation of development not only pays attention to the improvement of students' intellectual level, but also pays attention to the development of students' psychological level, physical quality and other aspects, so that every student can make progress on the original basis [10]. In a word, selection The evaluation concept of "Li" emphasizes to use a common standard, that is, to ask all students to use a ruler; The evaluation view of development requires students with different standards. Each student can have his own goal and focus on the development of students.

2.3 Big Data Clustering Algorithm

Cluster analysis usually refers to the process of decomposing a dataset with a large number of data objects into many clusters, and in the partitioning process, we need to divide it based on the similarity or some distance between various data objects, classifying the ones with high similarity into the same cluster, and classifying the ones with large differences or low similarity into different clusters. Clustering is an attempt to cluster all records into different clusters without knowing the number of classes in the database [11].

According to different classification standards, clustering analysis can be divided into multiple algorithms. Here, we briefly introduce several common clustering algorithms, including hierarchical clustering, partitioning, density based clustering, and grid based clustering algorithms. Cluster analysis is characterized by its simple calculation, intuitive presentation of results, and ease of understanding. In the field of teaching, cluster analysis can be used to analyze students' learning situation and assess teaching quality [12].

The K-Means algorithm minimizes the sum of squares error of the distance from all samples in the cluster domain to the cluster center through continuous iterations.

Cost function of K-Means algorithm:

$$J(k,\mu) = \sum_{i=1}^{n} \left\| X^{(i)} - \mu_{k^{(i)}} \right\|^2 \tag{1}$$

Assuming a P The vector X of order X is divided into c clustering sets through a clustering algorithm, where the centroid of each set is a P The vector V of order, wherein the set composed of fuzzy classification methods is specified as:

$$\mathfrak{J}_{fc} = \left\{ U \in \mathfrak{R}_{cn} \left| \begin{array}{c} \forall \\ 1 \leq i \leq n \\ i \leq k \leq n \end{array} \right. u_{ik} \in [0, 1], \sum_{i=1}^{c} u_{ik} = 1, 0 < \sum_{i=1}^{n} u_{ik} < n \right\} \tag{2}$$

R is a matrix with c rows and n columns, which has an objective function as shown in the following equation:

$$J(U, V) = \sum_{i=1}^{c} \sum_{k=1}^{n} (u_{ik})^m d_{ik}^2 \tag{3}$$

$$d_{ik}^2 = \|x_k - v_i\|^2 \tag{4}$$

By optimizing the objective function, the FCM algorithm achieves fuzzy classification of object sets through iterative optimization of the objective function.

Based on our understanding of the algorithm, we can draw a flowchart of the K-Means algorithm, as shown in Fig. 1 below:

The biggest advantage of the K-means algorithm is its simplicity and lack of complex operations, which makes this algorithm relatively easy to implement. However, the K-means algorithm has many shortcomings, among which the determination of the K-value and the selection of the starting value restrict the accuracy of the results. It relies too heavily on the initial point, making it susceptible to noise points, which make the cluster center deviate from the true data intensive point and approach the noise point, which leads to deviations in the calculation results[13]. K-means algorithm is an iterative algorithm, which is based on a randomly selected initial point. Through continuous iteration, the cluster center is constantly changed, thereby making the error continuously smaller. However, this clustering algorithm has a relatively slow clustering time, so it is not suitable for large amounts of data.

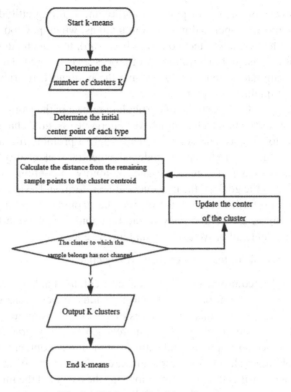

Fig. 1. K-Means algorithm flowchart

The full name of Weka is Waikato Intelligent Analysis Environment [14]. Weka is a relatively popular data mining task platform. Weka collects many algorithms that can be used for data mining, including preprocessing of data objects, classification prediction, clustering analysis, association analysis, and data visualization. These data mining algorithms can be implemented through interfaces.

"Cluster" in Weka's "Explorer" interface provides clustering analysis tools for the experimenter, including algorithms such as K-Means algorithm, K-center point algorithm, and conceptual clustering algorithm. Weka supports files in both CSV and ARFF data formats. The earliest data for data analysis is stored in EXCEL files. First, you need to convert the. Xsl file into a CSV file or ARFF file.

3   New Requirements for Teaching Evaluation in the Context of Big Data

For many years, there have been many problems in the educational evaluation of primary and secondary schools in China, mainly manifested in: overemphasizing the screening and selection function of evaluation, ignoring the function of promoting students' development; The evaluation index is single, basically based on book knowledge, ignoring the comprehensive examination of practical ability and learning attitude; The evaluation methods are mostly paper and pencil examinations, which pay too much attention to quantification: the evaluation technology is backward, too much attention is paid to the evaluation of results, and the evaluation of processes is ignored. The relative backwardness of educational evaluation has become the bottleneck restricting the overall implementation of quality education.

At present, judging from the trend of curriculum reform in the world, the function of evaluation and new evaluation technology have undergone essential changes. Evaluation is no longer just to identify and select students, but to promote the development of students, promote the development of students' potential, personality and creativity, so that every student has self-confidence and the ability to continue to develop [15]. Therefore, it is one of the goals of the new curriculum reform and a significant feature of the new curriculum reform to change the overemphasis on the screening and selection function of evaluation, and to give play to the function of evaluation to promote the development of students, improve teachers and improve teaching.

(1) Multi-level principle of teaching evaluation objective

According to the requirements of the new curriculum standard, we should focus on comprehensive evaluation, pay attention to individual differences, and achieve the diversification of evaluation indicators; That is to say, from paying too much attention to academic achievements to examining comprehensive quality gradually. Academic achievement was once an important indicator of student development, teacher performance and school running level. However, with the development of society, the explosion of knowledge, the intensification of competition, and the advent of the Internet and information age, just mastering knowledge and skills is far from meeting the requirements of society for human development. Therefore, there is a global discussion on "education and people", and the limitations of academic achievement as a single indicator of evaluation are highlighted. While paying attention to academic achievements, people begin to pay attention to other aspects of individual development, such as positive learning attitude, innovative spirit, ability to analyze and solve problems, and correct outlook on life and values. From examining what students have learned, to examining and comprehensively evaluating whether students have learned to learn to learn, learn to survive, learn to cooperate, and learn to behave themselves. Only in this way can we accurately reflect the development level of each individual in different aspects and enable each individual to find their own strengths. Boost your confidence. Modern education places special emphasis on building students' self-confidence, because self-confidence is the foundation of a person's growth.

(2) The principle of diversification of teaching evaluation methods

As for the evaluation method, the new curriculum standard focuses on the gradual shift from overemphasizing quantification to focusing on qualitative analysis and grasp. The worship of science makes people blindly believe that quantification is a synonym of objectivity, science and rigor, so the pursuit of objectivity and quantification has been the development trend of curriculum evaluation in various countries. But today, with the simulation of big data technology and the integration of evaluation content, when describing and evaluating a person's development status in a quantitative way, it shows the characteristics of rigidity, simplicity and superficiality. The liveliness and richness of students' development, their personality characteristics, their efforts and progress are all lost in groups of abstract data. In addition, for education, quantitative evaluation simplifies or only evaluates simple educational phenomena, which in fact often loses the most meaningful and fundamental content in education. Therefore, the content and method of evaluation can be decided by students themselves, not necessarily by teachers. Evaluation in an open, friendly and informal environment is conducive to giving play to students' creativity and practical ability.

(3) Pluralization principle of evaluation subject

In the past, the subject of evaluation mainly refers to school teachers, and students are the evaluated and the object of evaluation. Because students are in a passive position in evaluation, many problems have arisen: evaluation has caused certain pressure on students' psychology, making them fear and even escape from evaluation, thus affecting the normal development of students' psychology. Due to the lack of honest participation of the appraisee in the evaluation, teachers often can not accurately find problems, so that the adjustment, incentive and improvement functions of the evaluation can not be well played. Because of the emphasis on the subject status of the evaluated, the subject evaluation of students is no longer a one-way stimulus response of the evaluator, but an interactive process in which the reason, emotion and behavior of the evaluator and the evaluated are unified.

Based on the obtained data clustering, the indicator system is constructed by combining the standardization of positive and negative indicators, as shown in Fig. 2.

According to the principle of observability, the audition indicators that cannot be obtained from the data are deleted to ensure that the indicator system after preliminary screening can be quantified. The standardized formulas for positive and negative indicators are Eq. (5) and Eq. (6), respectively.

$$p_{ij} = \frac{V_{ij} - \min_{1 \le j \le n}(V_{ij})}{\max_{1 \le j \le n}(V_{ij}) - \min_{1 \le j \le n}(V_j)} \tag{5}$$

$$\hat{p}_{i_i} = \frac{\max_{1 \le j \le n}(V_{ij}) - V_{ij}}{\max_{1 \le j \le n}(V_{ij}) - \min_{1 \le j \le n}(V_{ij})} \tag{6}$$

$\hat{p}_{i_i}$ The higher the value, the better the indicator of business English teaching mode; The smaller the negative indicator index value, the better the indicator of English teaching mode.

The theory of multiple intelligences proposed by Professor Howard Gardner, a psychological development expert at the Harvard Institute of Education in the United States, after years of research, is one of the cornerstones of the fourth generation of educational evaluation theory. Gardner believes that human intelligence is divided into eight aspects: linguistic intelligence, mathematical logic intelligence, spatial intelligence, physical movement intelligence, musical intelligence, interpersonal intelligence, self cognitive intelligence, and natural cognitive intelligence. They coexist in diverse ways and are relatively independent. Due to the impact of the educational environment and the imbalance in the development of one's own abilities, there are significant differences in the

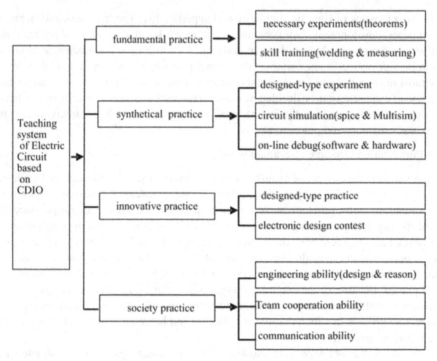

Fig. 2. Evaluation Index System of English Teaching Model

intellectual performance of different individuals. Therefore, in the process of education, it is necessary to emphasize diversified and developmental teaching evaluation, which is also consistent with the perspective of formative evaluation. The purpose of teaching evaluation is to develop students' various intelligences, enable students to be clearly aware of their strengths and weaknesses, and then take targeted measures to develop their potential, so that each student's intelligence can receive the most appropriate development. In the evaluation of English teaching quality in higher vocational colleges, this theory guides teachers to not only focus on evaluating students' intelligence, but also conduct comprehensive and developmental evaluations of students' values, learning methods, emotional attitudes, and other aspects from different levels and perspectives. The widespread application of the theory of multiple intelligences can provide a good reference for the correct and comprehensive evaluation of students' academic achievements, and also contribute to the formation of a correct evaluation view.

4   Evaluation of English Teaching Mode Based on Big Data

The application of big data in English mixed teaching makes the sources of teaching evaluation information more extensive and the feedback of teaching evaluation more timely. In English teaching practice, teachers can use big data technology to collect, accumulate and analyze a large number of students' data at all links and levels, effectively identify teaching problems, find more effective ways and strategies to improve teaching effectiveness, accurately design teaching activities, guide students to optimize and carry out self-directed learning, and achieve the integration of teaching evaluation. Before class, teachers come prepared. They use big data platform to diagnose students and analyze data through testing, questionnaires and other methods, understand students' learning situation and learning behavior characteristics before entering school, find difficulties and weaknesses in their learning and focus on them, develop teaching content that conforms to students' actual conditions, guide them in many aspects and at multiple levels according to their differences, and create high-quality personalized teaching for students, Help students adapt to the mixed teaching mode. In class, teachers set tasks in groups and hierarchies according to students' learning tendencies and problems in learning, set real language learning scenes similar to daily life, and develop evaluation criteria and methods to examine students' ability to solve problems in practical work. The students actively explore the meaning of the teaching theme through the cooperation among the team members, achieve the task, and achieve the organic integration of language, culture and practice. After the task is completed, students will summarize and reflect on it through group mutual evaluation, group member mutual evaluation and self-evaluation according to the evaluation criteria, so as to pave the way for the next study. After class, teachers help students consolidate their knowledge by pushing various exercises and tasks through the big data platform, understand the teaching effect through the data completed by the platform assignments and tasks, and provide personalized online guidance and remedies for students' still weak abilities. The implementation of mixed teaching evaluation should be closely combined with teaching activities and integrated in each link of teaching activities. Teachers should be steady in teaching and not catch up with the progress. They should adjust the teaching content and rhythm dynamically according to the feedback in class and after class to help students effectively improve their English level, as shown in Fig. 3.

The implementation of English mixed teaching evaluation system based on big data requires not only the technical support of data, but also the teachers to keep pace with the times, constantly break the original ideas and innovate, so that the reform can be implemented. The school should also establish an effective support and incentive mechanism to encourage teachers to actively use big data to carry out teaching evaluation. Although the development of computer and communication technology makes it relatively easy to collect data, the vast amount of data comes from a wide range of sources and has different formats. How to screen and summarize complex data forms to form scientific evaluation indicators puts forward requirements for teachers' data analysis ability. Teachers also need to constantly strengthen information learning and practice, improve the ability to integrate information technology and teaching, and make good use of big data scientifically and effectively, so as to effectively play the real effectiveness of big data teaching evaluation system.

For many years, the evaluation of English teaching quality in colleges and universities has been mainly based on summative evaluation, focusing on the results of the final paper and pencil examination. The evaluation of teaching quality focuses more on the students' final examination results, grades A and B, or grades 4 and 6. This evaluation method

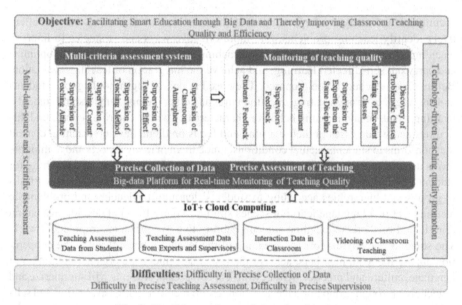

Fig. 3. English teaching mode based on big data

assesses students' ability to take English exams, as well as basic language knowledge such as vocabulary, grammar, sentence patterns, and composition. However, it cannot comprehensively and accurately reflect students' overall language knowledge level and teachers' teaching abilities.

For English teachers, optimizing teaching evaluation methods should be guided by teaching goals and requirements, combined with formative evaluation and summative evaluation, guided by advanced education and teaching, and combined with new teaching models to develop a systematic, scientific, and personalized teaching evaluation index system, which should be applied to the entire process of teaching and student learning. For example, in the past quantitative evaluation system, students' final hundred-point scores were simply divided into small quizzes, mid-term exams, and final exams, each accounting for a ratio of "334", and a simple quantitative score was performed to obtain the final overall evaluation score. At this stage, we can focus on qualitative evaluation, which is also called formative evaluation. We can divide the indicator system of the 100 point system into a "55" proportion, with formative evaluation accounting for half of the proportion, or even higher. Conclusive evaluation can account for the other half, and certain adjustments can be made based on actual teaching conditions. Formative evaluation can be divided into many branches according to actual situations. For example, teachers can assign formative evaluation scores based on: self presentation + team cooperation + classroom participation + platform independent learning + attendance accounting for 20% each. In terms of team presentation, performance can be recorded through situational dialogues, small thematic debates, news reports and comments, and English song PK to determine results. The focus of formative assessment is on personalized learning processes, so teachers can also add activities such as APP punch in memorizing words, brainstorming, and English fun dubbing to help students increase their English learning media and enrich their learning experience.

5 Conclusion

This paper takes the contradiction between traditional English teaching evaluation and mixed teaching in higher vocational colleges as the breakthrough point, integrates big data data mining technology into the traditional evaluation system, adopts a combination of qualitative and quantitative methods, reconstructs a new form of teaching evaluation system, dynamically manages students' learning input, and helps teachers improve teaching and improve teaching quality. In specific implementation, the implementation of the big data based hybrid teaching evaluation of higher vocational English requires the active participation of students, teachers and schools in order to be more effective. The evaluation system needs to be constantly adjusted, further improved and optimized in repeated use to play a more effective role.

Acknowledgements. Department of Education (Humanities and Social Science Project) "Research on Chinese Culture Presentation Mode and Cultural Confidence Improvement based on Higher Vocational Education" (Provincial Department of Education No.: 22JK0063, Provincial Federation of Social Science No.: 2022 HZ1147).

References

1. Ye, B.: Retracted: research on the integration of ESP and big data in modern college English teaching. J. Phys. Conf. Ser. 1852(2), 022046 (7pp) (2021)
2. Zhang, M., Yuan, X.: Application Research of the Current Situation of College English Online Teaching Model in the Big Data Era (2021)
3. Liu, Y., Bai, H.: Teaching research on college English translation in the era of big data. Inter. J. Electr. Eng. Ed, 002072092098431 (2021)
4. Liu, F.: Era of Big Data Is Based on The Study of Physical Education Teaching Mode In MOOC. J. Phys. Conf. Ser. **1744**(3), 032008 (7pp) (2021)
5. Zou, W., Ding, W., Shan, X., et al.: Innovation of College Physical Education Teaching Mode in the Era of Big Data. In: ICIMTECH 2021: The Sixth International Conference on Information Management and Technology (2021)
6. Wu, X.: Research on the reform of ideological and political teaching evaluation method of college english course based on "online and offline" teaching. J. Higher Educ. Res. **3**(1), 87–90 (2022)
7. Wang, H., Du, Y., Tsai, S.B.: Evaluation of the Effectiveness Computer-Assisted Language Teaching by Big Data Analysis. Math. Problems Eng. **2021** (2021)
8. Miao, Y.: Mobile Information System of English Teaching Ability Based on Big Data Fuzzy K-Means Clustering, Hindawi (2021)
9. Zhang, G.: Engineering design and evaluation of the process evaluation method of auto repair professional training in virtual reality environment. Appli. Sci. 12 (2022)
10. Wierzejska, R.: Evaluation of prenatal vitamin-mineral preparations in the context of recommended dietary supplementation. are pregnant women supplied with what they should get?. Roczniki Panstwowego Zakladu Higieny **72**(3), 309–320 (2021)

The Use of Big Data Platform Plays in Building a New Model of English Teaching in Universities

Ning Liu[(⊠)] and Xiaohu Wang

Guangzhou City Construction College, 510925 Guangzhou , China
wyxy@gzccc.edu.cn

Abstract. With the rapid development and application of Big data technology, using Big data platform to build a new model of college English teaching has become a possible direction. This paper mainly expounds the implementation method and effect possibility of this new model from two aspects of building a Big data platform and building a new model of college English teaching. First of all, building a Big data platform is a prerequisite for realizing the new model of college English teaching. The Big data platform needs to include student information, curriculum information, teaching resources, evaluation data and other data, which need to be classified and integrated to facilitate subsequent management and analysis. Secondly, building a new model of college English teaching needs to be supported by the Big data platform and adopt methods based on data analysis and students' personalized learning. This new model can give full play to the advantages of the Big data platform and achieve the goals of standardization of English teaching, sharing of teaching resources, personalized learning and comprehensive evaluation of students. Through this new model, English teaching in universities will be more scientific, advanced, flexible, and able to meet the needs of different student groups, improving the quality and efficiency of English education.

Keywords: big data platform · English teaching in universities · new model

1 Introduction

With the development of globalization and the popularization of information technology, English has become one of the most widely used languages in the world and an important skill that college students must master. The traditional and outdated English education model is difficult to adapt to the rapid changes in students' needs and the development and changes of the information age [1]. Building a new model of college English teaching using the Big data platform will become one of the important development directions in the reform of college English education.

1. Current situation analysis

The current English teaching mainly adopts a traditional teaching model that focuses on building textbooks, teaching by teachers, and evaluating exams. This traditional English education model has many problems, such as insufficient teaching resources, single educational platforms, lack of courses, single evaluation, and so on.

Y. Zhang and N. Shah (Eds.): BigIoT-EDU 2023, LNICST 581, pp. 218–228, 2024.
https://doi.org/10.1007/978-3-031-63133-7_21

2. Necessity of implementing Big data platform

In the era of Big data, Big data technology can help us collect and analyze students' learning data and English education data, so as to help teachers develop more accurate teaching plans, provide students with more appropriate learning content and personalized in-depth teaching services, and improve the effectiveness of English teaching [2].

3. The impact of Big data platform on college English teaching reform.

Using the Big data platform to build a new model of college English teaching has obvious advantages in the following aspects:

(1) The diversity of teaching platforms. English education Big data platform not only involves the construction of online education platform, but also has a special teaching resource center, digital library, intelligent homework management, learning management tools and other platforms. That is, schools, teachers and students can share and obtain various resources here, and freely choose learning methods and models.
(2) Personalized teaching services. Personalized education will become one of the important directions of English education in the future. Through Big data analysis technology, personalized courses will be systematically matched according to students' learning ability, learning habits and foundation, so as to improve the pertinence and effectiveness of the courses and comprehensively improve the quality of education [3].
(3) Information based teaching management. By digitizing and standardizing the information management of teaching, teachers and students can be liberated from the heavy workload of teaching management, truly achieving the integration of education and teaching management systems. It is also more conducive to grasping the changing trends of teaching resources, adjusting teaching strategies and combinations.
(4) Multiple forms of evaluation methods. The English education model of the Big data platform will adopt a variety of evaluation methods, such as learning process data, homework data, examination score data, etc., so that teachers can better evaluate students' learning status and needs, so as to evaluate students' learning achievements more scientifically and impartially [4].

In short, using the Big data platform to build a new model of college English education will not only help improve the quality of education, but also help to provide students with more appropriate learning content and services, and also help to improve the informatization and intelligence level of English teaching, and ultimately realize the reform and progress of English education.

2   Related Work

2.1   The Concept and Characteristics of Big Data

The so-called on computers, the other hardware, with as the main line. Massive data collection, sorting, analysis and feedback, with the required data and information, analyze, process and make information. With the network era, big become a new thinking model

[5]. At, the (as shown in Fig. 1) has of life in China, especially, in the context of environment, the essence of the competition is information competition, enterprises can data statistics between themselves and peers, make comparative analysis, for development planning and optimize competitive strategy is crucial [6].

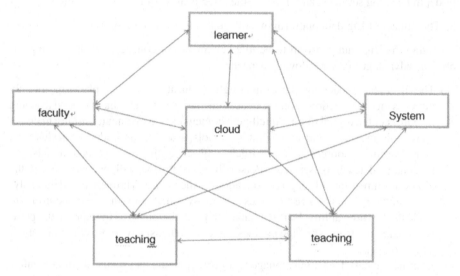

Fig. 1. Struts frame structure

The scale and quantity of various types of data have grown rapidly, and massive amounts of data have permeated. Big data has attracted global attention in a short time, and various related technologies have sprung up and continuously improved and updated [7]. The rise and development has ushered in a transformation of the era, increasingly becoming an factor in competition, becoming the of various, causing major revolutions in government, commerce, culture and education, as well as a major revolution in life, work, and thinking.

Currently, global big data is growing rapidly, and data has become a torrent flowing into various economic fields. In May 2011, and Productive, stating that big data is ubiquitous and exists in every department, every economic system, and every organization and user of digital technology, and contains unlimited business opportunities [8]. The has not given a clear of the concept of big data. Maurl et al. analyzed the four aspects of information, technology, methods, and impact involved in big data, studied relevant papers, and summarized big data as follows: Big data is characterized by high capacity, high speed, and multiple types, and requires specific technologies and analytical methods to transform it into valuable information assets. This summary defines, and summarizes the four characteristics, namely, high capacity, rapidity, diversity, and value [9].

With the continuous development and popularization of big data technology, as the continuous maturity, it has broad prospects and development space in various fields, which can better and faster the significance from collected and integrated data, grasp the rules of things' changes, let the data speak, predict things' changes more accurately, grasp the rules of things' changes, and make decisions more scientifically, Thereby better improving the living and learning environment [10].

2.2 Education Big Data

There definition of the concept of education the academic community. As a part, education big data should also have the characteristics of high capacity, rapidity, and value that big data has, and combine its own uses and constituent elements to form a collection of big data with educational characteristics. In "Developing Education Big Data: Connotations, Values, and Challenges", the connotation of education big data is defined as a collection the educational activities and collected, all of which are used for educational development and can enormous [11]. In "The Core Technology, Application Status, and Development Trends of Education Big Data", education big data is defined as a highly that serves education subjects and processes, and has strong periodicity and great educational value. Hu Bicheng proposed that, while in a broad sense, big human derived [12]. Du Jingmin et al. proposed that education big data refers to a collection of multiple data oriented to the entire education process in time and space.

(1) Composition of education big data. As data is a all education-related data collected the education, and education activities are a special practical activity in human society, with complex and unstable relationship between subject and object, and the education process presents a complex structure (teaching activities and learning activities coexist), according to the main body, the composition four parts: school education management and teaching resource data, and education data [13].

(2) Main functions. Big data technology the collation of massive data, and the mining and analysis of data to obtain the general rules of things' development, so as to make scientific judgments and decisions about the future development of things. Similarly, as a major branch of big data, education mine, and collected during the education process, master the laws of students' learning and educational development, and formulate learning programs that conform to students' habits and strategic policies to promote educational development.

① Develop personalized learning plans. Through the collection of students' learning behaviors, education big data can help them understand their learning habits and interests, master their learning situation in class, and complete homework after class. Through the collected data, personalized learning plans suitable for each student's learning can be developed.

② Improve teachers' work efficiency. In the traditional education process, teachers need to judge students' mastery of the knowledge based on their own "experience" based on long-term homework correction, students' classroom reactions, and exam scores. On the one hand, it is inefficient, and on the other hand, it can involve personal subjectivity [14]. Through the collection of big data on education, through students' reactions in class, the speed and accuracy of completing assignments, and their long-term learning patterns and interests, it is possible to scientifically and accurately understand students' mastery of new knowledge and weak links, thereby providing more targeted guidance and teaching to students.

③ Assist the government. Education Big Data: Through collecting, we can understand the effectiveness of policy implementation. Through analyzing the collected data, we can scientifically predict the development trend and direction of education, adapt measures to local conditions, scientifically formulate and improve education policies, promote more equitable education, optimize the allocation, and make greater progress in education [15]. The education model based on Big data is shown in Fig. 2.

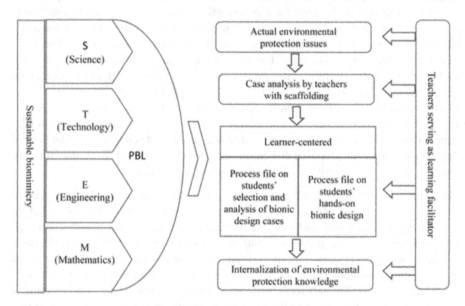

Fig. 2. Big data education model

3   Problems Arising in the Use of Big Data Platform in the Construction of English Teaching in Universities

(1) English translation teaching pays too much attention to scores and ignores

College English translation courses should not knowledge of translation, but also cultivate English and social adaptability, so that they can become a versatile and excellent talents. At present, with the deepening system and economic integration, the training of English applied talents has been paid more and more attention. However, in the traditional English teaching, although some students have very good English grades, but in the actual English communication, the language expression ability is very poor, high scores and low ability is a common phenomenon for the majority of students [15]. Due to the current exam-oriented education system in China, most teachers only pay attention and writing ability, and oral expression in English teaching. Students' ability to use English is not valued, most students are memorized by rote to memorize English words and sentences, but it is not very handy, this is the so-called "can write, can not say". In addition, most teachers lack enough training and guidance for English teaching, which leads to students being not interested in learning this course. Because many teachers lack of understanding of students' listening comprehension ability, using indoctrination teaching methods. In addition, many teachers regard English teaching as a monotonous course. Being bound by books for a long time, students cannot closely integrate English translation with real life, nor can they conduct in-depth investigation of British and American culture with English as the background, which greatly affects the teaching of English translation (as shown in Fig. 3).

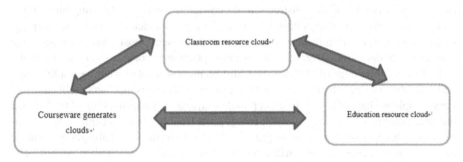

Fig. 3. Interactive platform for educational resources

(2) English teachers lack of teaching level, mechanically teach translation teaching content

In previous English teaching, many teachers neglect English translation and the cultivation of relevant knowledge and skills; in English translation teaching, teachers lack professional English translation skills, while many non-English translation teachers often do not study English theoretical knowledge; they may not know what to say, how to conduct classroom activities, and what teaching skills teachers should master in English translation, which are obtained from scattered daily learning. There is no systematic research, in the quality of English translation, it is necessary to study the content of the textbook. By deepening the knowledge in the translation teaching, the can fully of each unit, so as to gradually improve the students' translation level. From the university English translation teaching, and puts forward some countermeasures. In daily English classes, teachers often explain English translation and other teaching content separately, and cannot combine the improvement of translation skills with the development of other skills, thus affecting the practical application of English translation; the separation of English translation and other English teaching content is very easy. This effective the knowledge contained in English translation, thus affecting the English reading and writing level. Therefore, concept of English translation, and adopt various forms of reform, so that students can get fun and practical meaning in English translation.

(3) Learning attitude and method to increase the difficulties in English translation teaching

English level four, six test is the most important for all college students English test, many people after four, six, feel in all fields of English have a good foundation, but level four and six test focus on listening, reading, say, and do not pay attention to say, translation, so four, six test, and does not well reflect the students 'English level, and the students' translation ability is still a weak link. From the examination situation in recent years, most students English teaching due to the pressure of taking exams and examination education and other reasons, making it difficult for students to express their thoughts in their daily life. In addition, the English translation work is more difficult, and the students' learning enthusiasm is relatively high, they may choose to read the reference questions directly, or through the Internet search. Most students do not and energy in understanding the construction of knowledge, understanding ungrammar and translation; to this, we always have a "careless" mentality, lack of systematic learning, so the English translation level is also very low. At present, most English professional courses in colleges and universities are mainly specialized vocabulary, resulting in the lack of basic knowledge of students. In addition, most students do not have a thorough understanding of English grammar, and the Chinese thinking is mechanical. In addition, some people are lack of a good English foundation, and the understanding of the English sentence pattern is not in place, which brings great trouble to the translation. Some students use Chinese thinking, so in the process of translation, there will often be a "Chinese English" phenomenon, reading will also appear some embarrassing phenomenon. The English translation is stiff by its incomplete content and unfamiliar English language; it to understand its meaning. In the accuracy of English and Chinese translation, it to analyze the causes of problems from multiple angles. English translation should not only master the basic translation knowledge such as English tense and intonation, but also have a solid translation foundation. It should also be modified according to the content of the translation, so that it can simplify and make the expression of English more smoothly. Vocabulary is an important link in English skills and skills. The amount of vocabulary has the effect of translation, but at present, Chinese universities pay less attention to English vocabulary, which. Due to the lack of correct guidance to English vocabulary, the correct transmission of information in translation.

The core service of the platform is mainly to provide users with information retrieval and resource navigation functions, and to present the collected data to users in the most comprehensive way through simple and rapid retrieval. Natural language processing technology is an important technology for human-computer interaction, enabling machines to "understand" human language and make processing. In the platform search function should strengthen the language recognition ability, identify the search and keyword input by users, mine information related to user searches in the platform, and present the most comprehensive information that users need most to users. At the same time, improving the processing ability of natural language is the return rate of game. By analyzing and processing the information input by users, mining relevant information in the database, and memorizing the user's search keywords and search behavior, the platform's indexing ability is improved.

Cua et al. (2001) proposed that projects with higher factor loads. Therefore, we have a factor load higher than 0.5. Next, calculate the extraction (AVE) the following formula:

$$AVE = \sum \lambda^2/n \tag{1}$$

among λ. Represents "standardized factor load", and n represents the projects. The satisfactory convergence effectiveness. Our the AVE of all constructs is above 0.5. Calculate the structural reliability (CR) value using the formula:

$$CR = (\sum \lambda)^2/(\sum \lambda)^2 + \sum \delta 1, \delta = 1 - \lambda^2 \tag{2}$$

4 The Use of Big Data Platform in Building a New Model of English Teaching in Universities

(1) Developing micro-course resources

In traditional English teaching, teaching time, students do not have to conduct practical operation after teaching the knowledge. At the same time, it is difficult to master and consolidate the knowledge without practical operation. Flipped classroom teaching changes the teaching focus from teaching to interactive teaching, analyze and solve problems. The Internet provides rich learning resources for learning. Teachers can compile high-quality teaching materials into micro classes, so that students can use micro classes, in class and after class to consolidate. Applying it to middle school English teaching can make students have an interest sensitivity to language and comprehensive quality. In we through the limitation of time and space, and give students more opportunities for practical practice, so that students can learn relevant knowledge repeatedly in class. Therefore, the use of micro-lessons in English listening teaching is a beneficial exploration. In addition, with the help of micro-courses can also improve students' knowledge and skills of listening, speaking, reading and writing, and constantly improve their English learning ability. When teaching micro-courses, we should pay attention to the personal characteristics of students in order to choose their own choices. This can improve students' autonomy and make them highlight their character academically. At the effectiveness of the micro classroom after implementation, summarize and reflect on it. Based on the above analysis, micro class can be "online and offline", online and offline learning, can obtain dynamic information of students 'learning from big data platform, learning time, login platform, video clicks, playback duration, comments, etc., can be uploaded to the platform to observe students' learning status and analyze students' learning status; teachers can design more targeted teaching content according to different needs.

(2) Introducing a multimedia mechanism

Using multimedia technology, students can easily and intuitively display the vocabulary, grammar and other content and knowledge content in English translation, such as the language structure, so that students can master English vocabulary, grammar and other knowledge while learning. Therefore, in the classroom, we assisted teaching, and constantly innovate in, improve the interest of the classroom. At the same time, English translation should also be closely related to other disciplines, such as geography, history, art appreciation, etc. These are the focus of teaching, which enrich the forms, but also promote. In addition, local films can improve their translation skills, and teachers can show students to understand the dialogue and identify the stylistic differences between Chinese and Western languages.

(3) Optimize the curriculum system

Under the guidance of the new curriculum standard, the universities should constantly optimize and innovate the English translation courses according to their own character-istics, and develop the students' understanding of the English language through a lot of practical practice. At present, many universities have begun offering English translation classes, but the effect is not ideal. Universities to translation, from the arrangement of teaching materials to the implementation of classroom teaching, to cultivate their read-ing ability, improve their understanding, but also to guide them to use English thinking methods, to promote their learning. For students majoring in English, English translation should be taken as a key course to gradually improve their mastery of English knowl-edge. In addition, students should be encouraged to read more English newspapers in their spare time, which can not only cultivate their reading habits, but also help them improve their understanding of English and promote students' all-round development. For non-English students, teachers can also recommend English newspapers, movies to students to cultivate their English ability and increase their vocabulary. In addition, in resources to optimize English courses, so that the role of English translation courses in teaching is more prominent. As shown in Fig. 4.

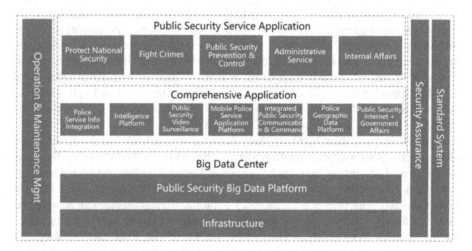

Fig. 4. Framework of Big Data Sharing Platform for College English Teaching

The new model of college English teaching based on Big data focuses on students' personalized learning, takes data analysis technology as the core, makes full use of the advantages of digitalization and informatization, and promotes the development of English education in an efficient and intelligent direction through multi-channel and multi angle education resource network, diverse teaching methods, flexible learning forms and other strategies. Compared with the traditional teaching model, the new college English teaching model based on Big data has the following advantages:

(1) Improve personalized education level

By collecting and processing students' learning data, analyzing their learning abilities, habits, and foundations, systematically matching personalized courses, improving the pertinence and effectiveness of courses, and comprehensively improving the quality of education.

(2) Improving transparency in the education process

Educational data can monitor and track teaching dynamics, provide timely feedback on students' learning situation, better guide teachers' teaching, and improve teaching efficiency. At the same time, educational data can also organize, analyze, and summarize students' learning situations, providing reliable data support for educational evaluation.

(3) Improving the quality and effectiveness of education

The Big data platform can provide teachers with a large number of rich and high-quality educational resources, and can also conduct scientific evaluation and monitoring of teaching achievements, so as to improve the quality and efficiency of education.

(4) Creating online learning opportunities

Online learning platforms can provide students with the freedom of learning time and space, organizing a series of learning materials such as literature, lectures, courses, assignments, etc. online, allowing them to easily and freely learn from home, at work, and even during travel, maximizing the needs of different student groups.

The new model of college English teaching based on Big data is an indispensable part of the digital era, with strong scientific and technological content and application value. However, in the process of implementation, colleges and universities need to cooperate with the active participation and support of all sectors of society to jointly promote the implementation and upgrading of this model.

5 Conclusion

Using the Big data platform to build a new model of college English teaching is an important direction of current education reform and development, with strong application value and scientific and technological content. In this new model, data analysis technology is the most core part. By analyzing and processing students' learning data and English education data, teachers can design more accurate teaching plans and courses, and provide higher quality educational services. By building a Big data platform, students' learning data and English education data can be collected, including students' basic information, curriculum information, teaching resources and evaluation data. These data are an important link in serving the interaction and data sharing between processes, as well as an important source of information for managing issues such as student academic performance and teaching quality. By comprehensively using these data, teachers can conduct comprehensive analysis and evaluation of the curriculum and students' learning situation, provide personalized educational services, customize personalized teaching plans, and improve teaching effectiveness and quality. In general, using the Big data platform to build a new model of college English teaching can make education more intelligent, humanized, adaptive, and more in line with the requirements of modern society and the digital era. At the same time, it can also innovate educational concepts, promote teaching reform, and further improve the quality, coverage, and application level of English education in universities, playing an important role in comprehensively promoting the quality improvement of higher education, especially the construction of educational informatization.

References

1. Jia. X.: Research on the role of big data technology in the reform of English teaching in universities. Wireless Commun. Mobile Comput. (2021)
2. Gan, S.: Evaluation Model of College English Teaching Effect Based on Big Data Platform (2023)
3. Liu, H.: English translation flipped classroom teaching model based on big data. In: CIPAE 2021: 2021 2nd International Conference on Computers, Information Processing and Advanced Education (2021)
4. Gong, X.: Research on discrete dynamic system modeling of vocal performance teaching platform based on big data environment. Discrete Dyn. Nat. Soc. **2022** (2022)
5. Yan, J., Zhou, M., Chen, Y., et al.: Evaluation Model of college english education effect based on big data analysis. J. Inform. Knowl. Manag (2022)
6. Shao, C.: The design of english personalized teaching platform in campus network based on big data. J. Phys. Conf. Ser. JPhCS (2021)
7. Du, Z., Su, J.: Analysis of the practice path of the flipped classroom model assisted by big data in english teaching. Sci. Program. **2021**(Pt.11) (2021)
8. Yahong, L.: A Study on the Practice of Cross-Cultural Education in English Translation Teaching in Colleges and Universities, vol. (4). Clausius Scientific Press (2021)
9. Xing, W., Wang, X.: Understanding students' effective use of data in the age of big data in higher education. Behav. Inform. Technol. **3**, 1–18 (2021)
10. Yang, X.: New Model of Educational Information Service in the Era of Big Data (2021)
11. Zhang, M., Yuan, X.: Application Research of the Current Situation of College English Online Teaching Model in the Big Data Era (2021)
12. Luo, G.: Integration and Optimization of College English Teaching Information Resources in the Context of Big Data. Springer, Cham (2021)
13. Liu, Y., Qi, W.: Application of flipped classroom in the era of big data: what factors influence the effect of teacher-student interaction in oral english teaching. Wireless Commun. Mobile Comput. (2021)
14. Tan, Q., Shao, X.: Construction of college English teaching resource database under the background of big data. J. Phys. Conf. Ser. **1744**(3), 032004 (2021)
15. Zhang, J.: Application of big data collection-analysis-visualization in the teaching process of colleges and universities under the background of the epidemic. J. Phys. Conf. Ser. 2021, 1800(1), 012009 (7pp)

Motivational Design Framework of Online French Interpretation Teaching Model Based on Intelligent Big Data

Shanshan Wang[✉]

Xi'an Fanyi University, Xi'an 710000, Shaanxi, China
27150344@qq.com

Abstract. As the demand for big data computing grows, the processing speed of clusters needs to be rapidly improved. However, the processing performance of the current big data processing framework has gradually been unable to meet this rapidly growing demand. Since the storage architecture of the cluster is distributed storage, the storage of data in the big data processing process becomes one of the factors that affect the processing performance of the cluster. When non-native speakers speak in English, they will show different accents or the characteristics of non-English native accents. Based on this feature, the speaker's accent and its native language can be identified. This paper uses smart big data to design current French online teaching activities It is necessary to carry out motivation design in the network teaching activity design, and put forward the development direction of the framework of how to carry out the motivation design in the network teaching activity design.

Keywords: Intelligent big data · French interpretation · motivation design framework · personalized learning

1 Introduction

Interpretation learning is the most challenging task in foreign language skills learning. There are many emotional factors that affect the success or failure of interpreting learning. Anxiety and motivation are two important factors. Scholars at home and abroad have conducted a lot of researches on foreign language learning anxiety and believe that anxiety may be the biggest emotional disorder in interpreting learning. Studies have also shown that the degree of anxiety is significantly negatively correlated with academic performance [1]. Learning motivation is one of the most active factors in language learning individuals, and it determines the degree of active participation of individual learners in the learning process [2].

The negative effects of the traditional teaching model. In traditional teaching, teachers are at the center of teaching and pay more attention to the teaching and explanation of knowledge. A lot of class time is spent on grammar explanation and content interpretation [3]. In the teaching process, there is less interaction between teachers and students,

© ICST Institute for Computer Sciences, Social Informatics and Telecommunications Engineering 2024
Published by Springer Nature Switzerland AG 2024. All Rights Reserved
Y. Zhang and N. Shah (Eds.): BigIoT-EDU 2023, LNICST 581, pp. 229–237, 2024.
https://doi.org/10.1007/978-3-031-63133-7_22

and students lack opportunities to express their opinions in class. Even in specialized oral classes, students have long been influenced by traditional teaching methods and are not accustomed to actively looking for topics and opportunities to speak, making oral classes often become listening classes [4, 5]. This not only seriously affects teachers, but also affects students. French is one of the important international working languages. Cultivate students with strong reading ability and certain ability of listening, speaking, writing and translating. Therefore, hearing as the most basic foreign language ability has long been everyone's consensus. The current basic teaching requirements and goals are to require students to be able to ask questions and retell the content of the textbook and appropriate listening materials, be able to conduct ordinary daily conversations in French, and be able to make short speeches on familiar topics after preparation, so that they can express their thoughts clearly. The pronunciation and intonation are basically correct [6].

2 Motivation Design Framework Based on Intelligent Big Data

French interpreting dialogue refers to the self-reflective dialogue with the main purpose of community members participating in the dialogue practice activities for information sharing, knowledge construction and meaning negotiation. It is based on the basis of the individual learner's social interaction and meaning negotiation with the community members. Reflecting on your own learning and internalizing the results of group learning into your own learning results. Promoting self-development is a necessary part of the transition from psychological inter-psychological functions to inner-psychological functions. The lack of one of these types of discourse will affect the overall effect of collaborative learning. The key to teaching design is to design a learning environment that supports and promotes these three dialogues [7]. The model is shown in Fig. 1

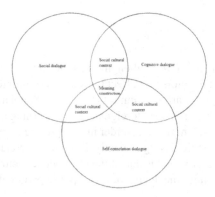

Fig. 1. The dialogue model of the collaborative learning community

This model provides a framework for designing web-based collaborative learning teaching. It shows that the key to dialogue-based collaborative learning teaching design is to promote different types of dialogues to achieve meaning construction and to create a real context for dialogue to make the dialogue contextually authentic. The content of the sexual dialogue is closely related to the learner's own previous experience or experience, so that the learner can have something to express his views and thoughts. It is necessary to design tools that support different dialogues to promote the dialogue between learners and to promote learning. The self-reflective dialogue of the individual's self [8] According to this model, the following is a web-based collaborative learning network course started in this article to explain in detail how to carry out the teaching design based on French interpreting dialogue, based on the big data model algorithm as shown in Fig. 2.

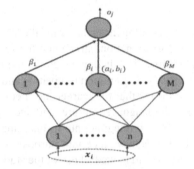

Fig. 2. French interpreting motivation design framework based on big data algorithms

For a above figure, it is supposed that there is an N arbitrary samples, of which N(x, tj) where x = [xi1, xiz, Xi3...xin]$'$ ∈ Rn, ty = $\left[t1, tj2, tj3...tjm\right]'$ ∈ Rm. Foran L SLFN node it can be written as, (1)

$$\sum_{i=1}^{L} \beta_i g(w_i x_i + b_i) = o_j j = 1, 2, ...N \qquad (1)$$

xi, w; and bi put in the equation as, (2)

$$\sum_{i=1}^{L} \beta_i g(w_i x_i + b_i) = t_i j = 1, 2, ...N \qquad (2)$$

This component is able to perform calculations on data and belongs to a distributed computing framework that can perform effective calculations on offline big data. And through this mode of functional programming, so as to achieve more complicated calculations. The distributed computing framework is shown in Fig. 3.

The framework is highly available and fault-tolerant. It is based on block storage and uses streaming data mode for normal access. In general, data nodes have the function of mutual backup. It is the collision and fusion of different voices. More importantly, it has the characteristics of construction to achieve a common understanding and construct shared knowledge and meaning. Dialogue is the process of using language to exchange ideas and construct meaning between the subjects participating in the dialogue. In language learning Only through dialogue can we deepen the understanding of the language

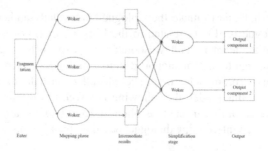

Fig. 3. Distributed framework of French interpreting

content and the construction of meaning instead of using the language as an abstract symbol to learn and use the grade examination, strengthen the foundation, and strengthen the teaching of French interpreting. The theoretical circle divides the motivation of language learning into two categories: assimilation motivation and instrumental motivation [9]. Assimilation motivation means that the learner has a considerable degree of psychological tendency towards the language, culture, and society of the target language nation, and accepts and is willing to integrate into it. Instrumental motivation is to use the second language as a tool to achieve a certain purpose, such as passing an exam. Therefore, in our teaching, we should make full use of the students' motivation to study and pass the grade examination, so that students can strengthen the basic knowledge of writing, which is also conducive to the strengthening of oral teaching. In terms of time, teachers, and context, we must give full attention to French interpreting teaching, create good conditions, arrange enough time, select excellent teachers, and create a favorable context, so that French interpreting teaching can be truly realized.

3   Integrating Motivational Design in the Design of Network French Interpreting Teaching Activities

3.1   The Framework of Teaching Design for French Interpretation Learning Based on Dialogue

Under normal circumstances, students pay more attention to things they have been familiar with. Teachers should use specific, popular and understandable language, as well as examples and concepts related to the students' own experience and values, using analogy methods or through videos wait for image materials to describe and present, to promote unfamiliar things to become familiar, so that students have more opportunities to learn what they believe or familiar with. In French interpreting teaching activities, students are allowed to clarify their learning goals and usefulness. Teachers should work hard to find ways to connect teaching goals to students' interests and motivations in the process of teaching, answering questions, and tutoring. Teachers can publish the learning objectives and effectiveness of this lesson on the Internet, using oral narration, text, or as needed, with a real story video, animation, etc. to express. Organize a big data network chat to discuss a certain issue, and under the guidance of the teacher, enable learners to reach a consensus on the issue in mutual exchanges, so that students can believe that their learning can bring him to his future study, career, and life. Comes with practical meaning to highlight the relevance to oneself, so that learning often has a higher motivation. Use teaching strategies consistent with students' motivational characteristics in teaching activities and use real exercises to make individual and group activities consistent with learning styles [10].

Under normal circumstances, students pay more attention to things they have been familiar with. Teachers should use specific, popular and clear language, as well as examples and concepts related to the students' own experience and values, using analogy methods or through videos wait for image materials to describe and present, to promote unfamiliar things to become familiar, so that students have more opportunities to learn what they believe or familiar with. In the online French interpreting network teaching activities, students are allowed to clarify the learning goals and effectiveness. Teachers should strive to find ways to connect the teaching goals with the students' interests and motivations in the process of teaching, answering questions, and tutoring. Teachers can publish the learning objectives and effectiveness of this lesson on the Internet French interpreter, which can be expressed in oral, text, or as needed with a real situational video or animation with a storyline. Organize a BBS or online French interpreter chat to discuss a certain problem. Under the guidance of the teacher, the learners can reach a consensus on the problem in mutual communication, so that the student can believe that their learning can give him a future study and career., Life brings practical meaning to highlight the relevance to oneself, so that learning often has a higher motivation. Use teaching strategies consistent with students' motivational characteristics in teaching activities and use real exercises to make individual and group activities consistent with learning styles.

3.2 Collaborative Learning and Dialogue Theory Based on French Interpretation

The motivational design model of the French interpreting teaching model puts the main motivational factors into the continuous teaching process sequence to consider and emphasizes its dynamic nature, while the motivational context view emphasizes the design of the learning environment from the perspective of context creation to promote motivational stimulation and maintain. These three motivational design theories have great integration and different design ideas. Their advantages should be comprehensively applied, and related motivational design theories should be applied to specific French interpreting teaching design. The fusion of motivation design theory and the analysis of the relationship between each element are shown in Fig. 4.

Although the independence of the four elements can play a role in the stimulation and maintenance of motivation, they are not only independent of each other. The intelligent big data motivation design framework model tells us such a process: in order to stimulate a person's learning and work motivation, he must first attract his attention and interest in a learning or work task; and then make him understand that completing the task is closely related to him. Relevant; then make him feel that he has the ability to do this well, thereby generating confidence; finally let him experience the sense of accomplishment after completing the study or work task, and feel satisfied [11]. It can be further considered that these four motivation factors not only have such a linear relationship, but they also promote and influence each other.

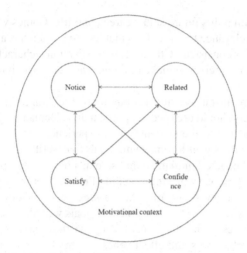

Fig. 4. Design elements of French interpreting motivation design

Students will be more interested and pay attention to things related to them; for learning that has achieved satisfactory results, he may build stronger self-confidence and show stronger motivation in the next study; strong confidence means that Will pay more attention to the problems learned, and the later the satisfaction will be stronger [12]; the acquisition of knowledge and skills related to oneself will have a stronger sense of satisfaction and pay more attention to it. In the design of teaching activities, the strategy adopted by a certain teaching activity promotes one or several elements. Not only does this element directly improve the motivation level of learning, but also can promote other elements to affect the level of motivation. The entire motivational design process is a continuous process, and from the perspective of the larger environment, it is also a process of creating motivational situations.

3.3 Modularization of Design Framework for Network French Interpreting Teaching Motivation Based on Intelligent Big Data

If the student's efforts are consistent with his own expectations, that is, what he experiences is what he hopes to get, then his positive learning motivation will be more maintained. In teaching activities, teachers must consider maintaining a clever balance between inducing and maintaining internal motivation and using external reinforcement. Provide internal reinforcement. At the beginning or expansion stage of teaching activities, through related links, or using virtual reality technology, or preparing multimedia materials to provide a variety of opportunities to apply newly acquired knowledge and skills in simulated situations to promote their psychological Satisfaction [13]. Then give appropriate external rewards, provide feedback and reinforcement that can maintain the expected behavior, such as using praise, positive feedback, symbolic rewards, etc. This is easy to achieve in the network French interpreting education environment. For example, the score recording system is an effective feedback for students. The specific process is shown in Fig. 5.

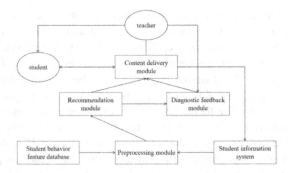

Fig. 5. Motivation design framework for online French interpreting teaching

Provide consistent evaluation standards and fair results presentation methods for the completed tasks to help learners correctly understand the performance of their own efforts. Use the provided online French interpreting teaching and learning service support system, adopt fair examination and scoring methods, and the content of the examination should be authentic and consistent with the learning goals. Create this kind of online classroom environment that encourages students to be psychologically satisfied, and promote greater learning motivation.

3.4   Cultivation of Cross-Cultural Awareness in French Interpretation Teaching

The problem faced by French students is the dual obstacles of language and culture. Familiarity with the native language culture will produce negative cultural transfer in the process of foreign language learning, and then affect foreign language learning [14]. What foreign language teachers should do is to help students reduce the impact of negative cultural transfer as much as possible, and improve students' knowledge of the target language culture while teaching the language. Encourage students to boldly create some relevant communication situations in the classroom, so that students can understand and be familiar with cultural knowledge immersively. Actively add some environment or situations of French communication in daily life, choose to go to places where British and American people often go, and take the initiative to communicate and talk with them.

4   Conclusions

Collaborative French interpreting supported by intelligent big data is a dialogue-based social interaction process. The various communication tools of intelligent big data intermediary provide space for collaborative dialogue and create conditions for surmounting the barriers of time and space. This creates conditions for French interpreting of the language. French interpreting and understanding of the planned language and culture can only be added in communication to achieve a deep understanding and meaning construction of the content of discussion and French interpreting. Therefore, the main task of the teaching design of English-language French interpreting is to design a French interpreter that is conducive to dialogue. Environment creation uses language to perceive language and cultural context to provide resources and tools for dialogue [15].

According to the characteristics of collaborative French interpreting, provide strategies to support and promote the generation and in-depth development of different types of dialogues. From the above design practice, it can be seen that the role of teachers and students in instructional design is positioned. Various dialogue tools are comprehensively considered. The theme process of collaborative dialogue As well as the evaluation of collaborative French interpreting, etc., it can promote the generation and development of dialogue to varying degrees. Improve the quality of dialogue. Cultivate students' language communication skills. However, the text research is preliminary for French interpreters' dialogue process and mode in collaborative French interpreting. In-depth research is needed, especially the factors that affect the quality of dialogue. These studies will provide a theoretical basis for more effective design of a dialogue-based collaborative French interpreting environment.

Acknowledgements. The 2023 Annual Project of the "Tenth Five-Year Plan" of Education Science in Shaanxi Province (SGH23Y2760).

References

1. Dou, R., Li, C., Feng, H.: Planning and construction of smart campus based on "artificial intelligence + big data" technology. Digit. Des. **9**(7), 19–22 (2020)
2. Liu, M.: Framework design of college admissions decision support system based on big data technology. Digit. Des. **7**(22),14–16 (2018)
3. Yu, L.: Research and design of a follow-up intelligent platform based on big data. Electron. Des. Eng. **27**(3), 6–9 (2019)
4. Wang, T., Li, Y., Li, J., et al.: Human-vehicle collaborative perception system based on mobile Internet. Intell. Comput. Appl. **007**(004), 31–33, 36 (2020)
5. None. The National Social Science Fund's major project "building a cloud platform for science and education evaluation and intelligent service research based on big data" held a review meeting. Eval. Manag. **18**(4), 1–3 (2020)
6. Chen, H.: Analysis and design of a data sharing and exchange platform based on campus big data. Value Eng. **38**(18), 34–36 (2019)
7. Zhang, H.: Open University personalized system technology framework based on big data technology. Sci. Technol. Innov. (36), 107–108 (2017)
8. Huang, Y., Mao, L., Zhang, X., et al.: Analysis and process design of online immersive teaching system based on digital twin platform. J. Distance Educ. 39 (1), 12–20 (2021)
9. Yang, J.: Research on intelligent information recommendation based on contextual perception driven by big data. Pop. Sci. Technol. **22**(10), 3–5 (2020)
10. Lu, Y.: The construction of big data corpus under artificial intelligence translation. Gansu Sci. Technol. **35**(17), 5–9 (2019)
11. Zhang, H.: Research on the status quo and countermeasures of English teaching informatization under the background of artificial intelligence + big data–based on a questionnaire survey of English teachers in secondary vocational schools. Engl. Teach. **19**(5), 7–8 (2019)
12. Tian, X., Guo, Z., Du, J., et al.: Research on the construction of big data principles and practice courses for economics and management majors-teaching design based on Python language. Comput. Knowl. Technol. Acad. Ed. **15**(12), 23–25 (2019)

13. Yang, C., Lin, G., Luo, F.: Research and application of log-based machine learning method to achieve rapid fault delimitation. Post Telecommun. Des. Technol. (012), 23–26 (2018)
14. Chang, J., Chen, Y., Xu, X.: Design of intelligent data analysis and recommendation system. Electron. Technol. **46**(9), 44–45 (2017)
15. Zou, J., Sun, Y.: The application of intelligent writing platform based on big data in college English writing teaching——taking Juku Piangai.cn as an example. J. Dalian Univ. **038**(006), 136–140 (2017)

The Construction of the Evaluation System of Physical Education in Colleges and Universities Based on Big Data Analysis

Xiaoyu Shi[1,2], Xinlong Li[3(✉)], Jianxin Zhang[1,2], Chun Jiang[1,2,3,4], and Yajuan Zhang[4]

[1] Physical Culture Institute, Yili Normal University, Yining 835000, Xinjiang, China
[2] Key Laboratory of College Student Physique Monitoring Center, Yili Normal University, Yining, China
[3] Physical Culture Institute, Kashi University, Kashi 844006, Xinjiang, China
xinlongli4561@163.com
[4] Hainan Vocational University of Science and Technology, Haikou 571126, Hainan, China

Abstract. As an important part of our country's higher vocational education, PE must be able to conform to the requirements of the development of the times, highlight its distinctive characteristics of disciplines, and emphasize the training of students' various professional and technical knowledge. While fully developing college students' general health, sports knowledge and skills, and good mental and psychological qualities, and training their sports interests, habits and sports technical capabilities, college students should be instilled with knowledge of occupational fitness and occupational health. According to the types of learning tools they are exploring and researching, they are likely to be required to use these tools in the future. With professional and high-quality comprehensive sports as the core, it organically integrates the teaching of sports knowledge and vocational training, creating a comprehensive sports curriculum with relatively high professional characteristics at the same time. This article discusses the construction of a college PE evaluation system using big data analysis. The problems in college PE evaluation are summarized based on relevant literature, and several related systems are proposed for construction. The current status of PE evaluation in colleges is investigated to provide a basis for the construction of the system. According to the survey results, the theoretical part of PE evaluation content in this city's colleges has a high proportion, at over 45%. The evaluation of sports technology only accounts for about 31%. It can be seen that there are drawbacks in the city's sports evaluation, and the proportion of sports technology evaluation should be increased. This may also be due to the safety of students. Part of it is enlarged, but whether it is possible to account for a higher score for the skills of sports students while ensuring the safety of students.

Keywords: Big Data Analysis · College Sports · Evaluation System · System

Y. Zhang and N. Shah (Eds.): BigIoT-EDU 2023, LNICST 581, pp. 238–245, 2024.
https://doi.org/10.1007/978-3-031-63133-7_23

1 Introduction

How do students develop a healthy body, develop good exercise habits, and love sports [1, 2]. And it is very important to reform the current vocational education evaluation system [3, 4]. Establish a professional sports evaluation system, emphasize the diagnosis and development functions, and reduce the evaluation and selection functions [5, 6], encourage students to have fun in PE, enhance self-confidence, and cultivate a healthy and comprehensive for future professional activities Mental and psychological quality [5, 7].

Regarding the construction of the evaluation system in PE in colleges, some researchers pointed out that the fundamental importance of evaluating sports in the best fitness plan is to allow students to fully understand and participate in the learning process, and to allow students to perform according to their responsibilities and goals set [8]. This can not only train the physical condition of students, but also enable students to easily master sports knowledge, learn sports methods and improve their sports ability [9]. Some researchers pointed out that the current method of evaluating motor learning also broke the traditional cumulative evaluation and gradually transformed it into a diagnostic evaluation [10]. The main advantage is: the ultimate goal of assessment is to encourage students to learn and adjust their teaching progress, rather than just classify students' strengths and weaknesses through test results. This type of evaluation makes the score independent of the review. Emphasize the actual function of assessment, and emphasize the need to make learning objectives concrete and practical. As for the main evaluation agency, it includes a combination of teacher evaluation, self-evaluation and mutual evaluation of students. There are many methods in evaluation, such as evaluation, observation, measurement, inspection, etc. [11].

This study examines the development of a college physical education evaluation system using big data analysis. Through a literature review, the challenges in current physical education evaluation are identified, and several principles for constructing the evaluation system are proposed. Furthermore, a survey is conducted to investigate the current status of college physical education evaluation systems. The results show that theoretical knowledge accounts for over 45% of the physical education evaluation content in colleges in the studied city. These findings provide a foundation for the development of an effective physical education evaluation system.

2 Research on the Evaluation System of PE in Colleges

2.1 Problems in the Evaluation System of PE in Colleges

(1) Evaluation content

In the content of the evaluation, sports performance is particularly emphasized. Therefore, it emphasizes the connection between sports science knowledge and practice, such as participation, physical and mental health indicators, the ability to solve practical problems, good mental quality and sports science mental health are ignored. The overall quality evaluation emphasizes evaluation. The overall trend of the ignorance of personal development and independence.

(2) Evaluation subject

The problem of evaluation is single, like other disciplines, subjective judgments are made from top to bottom. Although self-evaluation is also emphasized in this process, it is usually not taken seriously. Students are in a negative state and are difficult to be evaluated and ignored. The same level of evaluation system and the separation of performance from the bottom to the top are difficult to achieve the teaching effect.

(3) Evaluation results

The current evaluation system only focuses on the final results, neglecting the importance of assessing students' progress at different stages. This results in students participating in physical activities solely for the purpose of passing the exams. Additionally, the absence of intermediate assessments hinders the timely discovery of issues and appropriate supervision.

(4) Evaluation method

The current evaluation method oversimplifies the assessment process by relying solely on quantitative indicators that lack a scientific basis. These indicators are based on traditional performance assessment and lack the necessary quality to produce actual results. Furthermore, the focus on final results instead of procedural level evaluations at different periods and stages leads to students engaging in physical activities only for examinations. Additionally, the lack of intermediate procedural assessments prevents the timely discovery and supervision of problems. Since many indicators such as "attitude" and "habit" cannot be quantified, but there are no corresponding qualitative indicators to correct or supplement, the entire evaluation method lacks innovative ideas, and the entire evaluation process is rigid, closed, and static without flexibility.

2.2 Constructing the Principles of the Evaluation System in College PE

(1) Systematic

Due to the diversity required by sports activities, this feature is also reflected in the setting of evaluation indicators, so it is necessary to comply with the systemic principles: First, the integrity of sports refers to the comprehensive and systematic evaluation of the objects of sports activities. In performance evaluation, all evaluation indicators are included in the content of the evaluation. For example, if student evaluation is limited to the knowledge level of evaluation skills, it is far from enough. Second, its interrelationship refers to the evaluation of PE. When the target is in a large-scale system, pay attention to the relationship between the factors of the target being evaluated and the system factors, as well as the vertical and horizontal relationships; third, the level refers to the development of the target. Different index systems and different types of different evaluation targets. Such as regional differences of students, economic status, etc.

(2) Measurability

It is the knowability of the result. The abstract target description should be turned into a quantifiable indicator unit. This requires that at the beginning of the design of the

PE indicator system, it is necessary to consider that all indicators must have measurable characteristics, that is, through correlation the detection tools and detection methods can get the students' clear indicators to reach the standard value. For example, the score of 100 m can be detected with a stopwatch, and the shooting rate can be observed.

(3) Acceptability

The so-called acceptance principle means that when designing systematic teaching indicators, it is necessary to be based on objective actual conditions, rather than subjective assumptions. In particular, it mainly includes the following aspects: First, the design of indicators must have reliable and sufficient information resources, and these resources must also be considered according to local conditions. Secondly, the index setting must be based on the actual situation and according to the students' physical and mental development rules, so that the test objects can be accepted; due to the particularity of PE assessment, specific issues should be analyzed when formulating specific indicators; fourth, the index should be able to be determined, that is, an index that can reflect the effect of physical education.

3   Investigation on the Status Quo of the Evaluation System in PE in Colleges

3.1   Purpose of the Investigation

The survey of the status quo of the evaluation system in college PE through questionnaires is mainly carried out around two aspects. The first topic is the main content of college PE evaluation, and the second topic is the satisfaction with the evaluation content of the school.

3.2   Questionnaire Survey

(1) Data source

To evaluate the PE evaluation system in colleges, a survey was conducted in various PE colleges with students and teachers as subjects. The survey was conducted in the selected venue of different PE colleges to ensure the accuracy of the survey objects, and a large number of colleges facilitated the distribution and collection of the questionnaire. To ensure the universality of the questionnaire, three randomly selected companies with poor reputation were selected in the city. However, the survey only covered colleges in this city and did not include other regions due to differences in educational syllabus.

(2) Selection of the number of questionnaires

To ensure the effectiveness of the survey, the number of questionnaires must be carefully selected. If the number is too low, the results may not be valid. However, if the number is too high, it may be difficult to carry out the survey. In this survey, the number of questionnaires was determined based on literature materials and the actual situation. 200 questionnaires were distributed to ensure a sufficient sample size while also being feasible for the survey team to manage.

(3) Questionnaire distribution

To improve the validity of the survey, a two-stage process was used for questionnaire distribution and collection. The first stage involved distributing the questionnaires, while the second stage involved collecting them. The collection process was carried out six days after the distribution to provide adequate time for respondents to complete the questionnaire. A total of 200 questionnaires were distributed, and 189 were collected, resulting in a collection rate of 95%.

3.3 Data Processing

(1) To ensure accurate correlation analysis, it is necessary to classify and sort the collected data. This approach can increase the data utilization rate and facilitate cross-data analysis. The completeness and accuracy of the data are the main considerations when sorting the data. Firstly, it is important to ensure data integrity. Sometimes, the sample subjects may complete the questionnaire inappropriately, resulting in data sorting problems. However, as the majority of the data has been retrieved, lost data can be deleted. Secondly, the precision and accuracy of the data are important. During the auditing process, it is necessary to check if the data conflicts with other choices or principles, and selectively remove them if necessary, while retaining as much data as possible.

(2) To analyze the correlation properties of objective phenomena, two main approaches can be used: qualitative analysis and quantitative analysis. Qualitative analysis relies on the researcher's scientific theoretical knowledge and practical experience to accurately judge the presence of correlations between different objective phenomena or the types of factors involved. On the other hand, quantitative analysis involves the use of statistical methods to measure and quantify the correlation between variables. While qualitative analysis may be more subjective, quantitative analysis provides more objective and precise results. This method is relatively subjective. In contrast, quantitative analysis involves using mathematical and statistical methods to measure and quantify the degree of correlation between variables. Among them, the commonly used calculation formula is expressed as:

$$r = \frac{S^{\wedge}2\,xy}{Sx\,Sy} = \frac{\sum(x-\bar{x})(y-\bar{y})/n}{\sqrt{\sum(x-\bar{x})^{\wedge}2/n}\sqrt{\sum(y-\bar{y})^{\wedge}2/n}} \tag{1}$$

$$r = \frac{n\sum xy - \sum x \sum y}{\sqrt{n\sum x^{\wedge}2 - (\sum \bar{x})^{\wedge}2}\sqrt{(n\sum y^{\wedge}2 - (\sum \bar{y})^{\wedge}2)}} \tag{2}$$

4 Result Analysis

4.1 The Main Content of the Evaluation in PE in Colleges

Through a questionnaire survey of the main content of the evaluation of PE in colleges in this city, the results of the survey are shown in Table 1.

Table 1. Main Contents of Test and Evaluation in PE in colleges

	A PE Institute	B PE Institute	C PE Institute
Basic theoretical knowledge of sports	45%	46%	48%
Physical fitness and motor skills	33%	32%	31%
learning attitude	22%	22%	21%

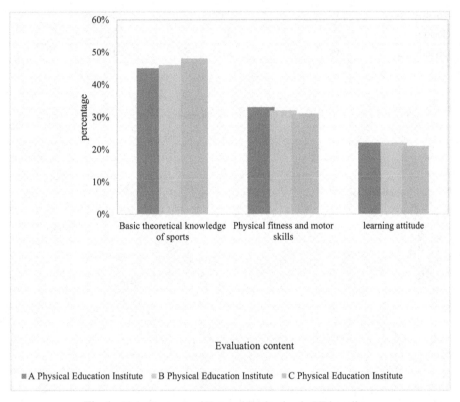

Fig. 1. Main Contents of Test and Evaluation in PE in colleges

It can be seen from Fig. 1 that the theoretical part of the evaluation content of PE in the city's colleges accounts for a relatively high proportion, accounting for more than 45%, while the evaluation of sports technology only accounts for about 31%. It can be seen that the city's sports there are drawbacks in the evaluation, and the proportion of sports technology evaluation should be increased. This may also be due to the safety of the students. The theoretical part has been increased, but whether it is possible to account for the skills of the sports students while ensuring the safety of the students A little higher.

4.2 Satisfaction with the Main Content of the Evaluation

Satisfaction with the main content of the evaluation through the questionnaire survey, the survey results are shown in Table 2:

Table 2. Satisfaction with the main content of the assessment

	A PE Institute	B PE Institute	C PE Institute
Satisfaction	23%	24%	21%
General	33%	35%	34%
Dissatisfied	44%	41%	45%

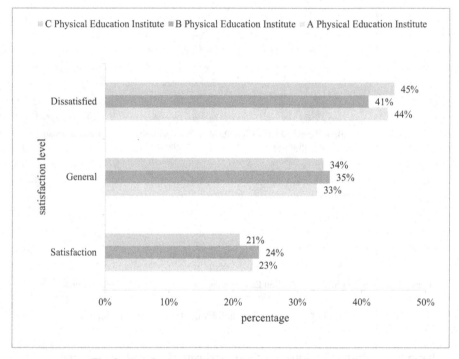

Fig. 2. Satisfaction with the main content of the assessment

Figure 2 clearly indicates that the majority of students are dissatisfied with the current PE evaluation content in their schools, with more than 41% of students expressing their dissatisfaction. This highlights the need for reform in the evaluation system for physical education in colleges.

5   Conclusion

The evaluation indicators, weights and scales, as well as the indicators of student sports learning based on the evaluation content, have a certain degree of objectivity, effectiveness and functionality, reflecting the improvement of the overall level and the continuous improvement of the training of students and teachers. To evaluate students comprehensively, the concept of evaluation should not only focus on their physical and mental health but also on discovering and developing their abilities in many aspects. Sports performance alone cannot be the main method of evaluation.

References

1. Li, B.: Evaluation and improvement of physical education teaching in colleges and universities based on AHP level analysis. Revista de la Facultad de Ingenieria **32**(16), 188–194 (2017)
2. Aleksic-Veljkovic, A., Stojanović, D.: Evaluation of the physical fitness level in physical education female students using "Eurofit-Test". Int. J. Sports Sci. Phys. Educ. **2**(1), 1–15 (2017)
3. Yang, S., Xu, D., Liu, X.: Evaluation of round window stimulation performance in otosclerosis using finite element modeling. Comput. Math. Methods Med. **2016**, 1–10 (2016)
4. Kim, C.Y., Lee, J.S., Kim, H.D.: Comparison of the effect of lateral and backward walking training on walking function in patients with poststroke hemiplegia. Am. J. Phys. Med. Rehabil. **96**(2), 61–67 (2017)
5. Freitas, P., Barela, J.A., Pedo, S.T., et al.: Assessment of digits dexterity and power grip strength in dyslexic children. Braz. J. Phys. Educ. Sport **33**(2), 201–206 (2019). (in Portuguese)
6. Wu, H., Li, F., Cheng, G.: Comprehensive evaluation model of physical education based on grey clustering analysis. Revista de la Facultad de Ingenieria **14**(1), 84–88 (2017)
7. Zhao, Y.: Research on the diversified evaluation index system and evaluation model of physical education teaching in colleges and universities. J. Comput. Theor. Nanosci. **14**(1), 99–103 (2017)
8. Lee, J.C., Kim, S.B., Shin, J.H.: Application of exercise test and prescription in physical education class. Korean J. Sports Sci. **26**(6), 1279–1293 (2017)
9. Zakharova, L.V., Moskovchenko, O.N., Solimene, U., et al.: Organisation of physical education in universities for students with disabilities: modular approach. Educ. Sci. J. **22**(7), 148–175 (2020)
10. Guo, Q., Li, B.: Role of AI physical education based on application of functional sports training. J. Intell. Fuzzy Syst. **2**, 1–9 (2020)
11. Liu, J., Yang, B.: Design of evaluation system of physical education based on machine learning algorithm and SVM. J. Intell. Fuzzy Syst. **1–3**, 1–12 (2020)

The Application of Big Data Analysis Methods in Classical Catalog Studies

Danyang Gong[✉] and Xiaofen Li

Department of Chinese Language and Literature, Northwest Minzu University, Lanzhou 730030, China
kongdy07@163.com

Abstract. In the 21st century, the arrival of the era of big data has brought earth-shaking changes to the development of bibliography, and the needs of users for directory information have also undergone significant changes. How to reasonably and efficiently disclose massive network information resources has become a new mission of bibliography, and bibliography is facing a transformation opportunity. At present, how to develop and meet the information needs of users is the most important task in the field of bibliography research. By comparing the thinking patterns of big data and classical bibliography, this article draws the similarities between big data analysis and classical bibliography analysis. From a methodological perspective, both parties can take the issue as a starting point and form the final result, which is a "concept product data" cycle. Big data analysis can be simplified into three types of data analysis. For classic bibliographic data that needs to be converted, this data conversion can still refer to the big data analysis model, issue oriented, process based data analysis, and mining using classic bibliographic research methods.

Keywords: big data · classical catalog science · thinking mode · data transformation · data analysis process

1 Introduction

As a hot word in today's society, big data can be heard from all walks of life about the changes brought about by the deep integration of big data and a certain industry. So, can we also apply big data analysis to research catalog version science? This article will consider the feasibility of using data analysis for classic catalog research by discovering the similarities between big data analysis and classic catalog research methods under big data thinking [1].

Entering the 21st century, bibliographic research in China continues to advance in depth in the fields of theory and practice. In terms of theoretical research, the introduction of Western catalog theories such as bibliographic information services and bibliographic control has broken the traditional theoretical system of "history, theory, and law". At the same time, with the development of digital technology and network technology, in the era

Y. Zhang and N. Shah (Eds.): BigIoT-EDU 2023, LNICST 581, pp. 246–256, 2024.
https://doi.org/10.1007/978-3-031-63133-7_24

of big data, China's bibliographic theoretical system is facing problems of deconstruction and reconstruction. In practical research, the continuous emergence and widespread use of new technologies have expanded the field of bibliographic work, brought new changes to bibliographic practice, and made the problem of the disconnection between bibliographic work practice and theory even more serious [2]. In recent years, under the general trend of interdisciplinary integration, bibliography disciplines have borrowed theories and methods from similar disciplines such as library science, information science, and archival science, maintaining a certain degree of research vitality, but there have also been phenomena of reduced research results and shrinking discipline status. It can be seen that information science and technology have brought both opportunities and challenges to the development of bibliography. How to seize opportunities and face challenges urgently requires us to objectively and comprehensively examine the development process of bibliography since the 21st century, identify the problems and seek countermeasures [3].

Since the new century, many scholars have mainly adopted the method of qualitative induction when revealing new concepts, new technologies, and new methods based on tracking the research focus of bibliography. Currently, there are no scholars conducting systematic visual analysis of the research hotspots and frontiers in the field of bibliography in China in the new century. Pure qualitative and empirical research is susceptible to the influence of personal subjective experience, making it difficult to objectively and accurately explore the frontier fields and commanding heights of disciplines hidden in the vast amount of information [4]. As an effective knowledge management tool, knowledge atlas can transform massive literature data information in the forefront of catalog science into visual graphics through data mining, information processing, knowledge measurement, and graphics rendering, objectively displaying the hot areas and cutting-edge trends of catalog science that are difficult to obtain based on subjective experience, thereby laying the foundation for future research [5].

With the help of the theory and method of knowledge atlas, this study, based on the reproduction and deep excavation of previous research results, presents the research hotspots and research frontiers of domestic bibliography in the new century, which not only expands the application scope of knowledge atlas, but also enriches the research topics of bibliography, and has important practical value [6]. Moreover, through the analysis of data, the evolution of hot topics and cutting-edge topics in bibliography research is presented, which is also helpful in determining the direction of scientific research topics and scientific management, and in exerting the functions of bibliography and serving the society.

2   Related Work

2.1   Thinking Mode of Big Data

After entering the new century, the development of computer technology and Internet technology has changed the era background of bibliographic work practice, and has also shifted the focus of bibliographic practice research to the disclosure and reporting of network information resources [7]. Zhang Hongyuan (2001) believes that the intellectualization of knowledge organization is a new topic encountered in the practice of bibliographic work and the development of bibliography in modern times. He proposes to deeply study the practice of bibliographic work under computer conditions, clarify the use of computer technology in bibliographic work practice and fully reflect its knowledge organization core: first, strengthen the research of document disclosure methods; Strengthening practical research on bibliographic work; Third, strengthen computer application research in bibliographic work; Fourth, strengthen the research on the combination of traditional bibliographic methods and modern bibliographic methods. Fu Xianhua (2005) pointed out that networking traditional bibliographic information products to adapt them to the needs of the network environment, effectively revealing and deeply developing network information resources, and providing flexible and diverse search methods are important topics in the application research of bibliography in the new era [8]. The author also predicted that future research on bibliography will include specialized bibliography research, online bibliographic control research, bibliographic information research, and bibliographic information industrialization research Breakthroughs have been made in online bibliographic information research. Peng Feizhang et al. (2009), in their monograph "Research on the Theoretical Transformation and Development of Bibliography in the Digital Age", believed that the fundamental issue of contemporary and future bibliography has been a cutting-edge and hot topic in this discipline since the 1990s. The establishment of bibliographic information as the basic point of contemporary bibliography is of great significance to the theoretical breakthrough of bibliography, especially modern bibliography.

In 2013, IBM proposed the 5 V features of big data, namely Volume (huge amount of data), Velocity (high-speed timely and effective analysis), Variety (diversification of types and sources), Value (low value density, high commercial value), and Veracity (the real effectiveness of data). Its strategic significance lies in the real-time interaction and analysis of a large number of large, comprehensive, detailed and timely data, and in applying the analysis results into economic effect [9].

What is the big data mindset? It is to analyze the data and pay attention to the internal correlation, rather than the logical relationship in the traditional thinking mode. This correlation may not be causal, but it is mutually reinforcing. This correlation is the core feature of big data thinking.

The relevance of big data is related to the causality of traditional thinking, but it is not the same. Big data itself produces qualitative change because of its large quantity. Big data is not a single and clear linear causality, but an unspeakable complex correlation. This complex correlation can reveal the connection through quantitative research. The causality of traditional thinking is linear and has a strong logical relationship, which is more suitable to use qualitative analysis to draw relatively fuzzy conclusions [10].

Looking for intrinsic correlations, whether this correlation is reliable requires analysis through a large number of data, multi-level and more comprehensive samples. In the traditional thinking mode, the logical relationship is found through a small number of sample data (which is the larger data) available for analysis reference, and samples with higher fine level. This analysis means that the timeliness and applicability of conclusions are relatively narrow. Compared with the traditional model, it is easier to obtain more comprehensive, more comprehensive, more timely and more representative samples, and the conclusions are more reliable.

2.2   Analysis of Behavior Characteristics of Parameter Directory

The behavior of the parameter directory will be reflected by the specific behavior of the directory system. The biggest difference between the behavior of the big data analysis engine and traditional systems is that every operation on its workflow is executed in a distributed manner in a cluster with data as the center. As shown in Fig. 2, the workflow of Map Reduce can be subdivided into five sub stages (read, map, collect, spill, and merge) in the map stage. Similarly, the reduce stage can be further subdivided into four sub stages (shuffle, sort, reduce, write). Each sub stage sequentially performs some atomic operations of the Map Reduce workflow (such as reading data from a distributed system, serializing map output data, partitioning memory data, sorting output data, merging, and compressing) [11]. If an operation is executed too slowly, it can become a performance bottleneck on the Map Reduce workflow and affect the execution speed of subsequent operations. Therefore, the performance of these operations will ultimately become a key factor restricting the overall performance of the system. If you adjust the values of parameters (such as the number of map tasks, the number of reduce tasks, the threshold size of intermediate result data for merge operations, the size allocation of the task level cache Memory Buffer value, the number of threads used to copy intermediate results, whether the intermediate and final result outputs of the task require compression, and the codec used for output compression), it will have a significant impact on the performance of these operations [12]. Therefore, from theoretical analysis, it can be concluded that the value of directory parameters will significantly affect the performance of various data operations in the system workflow, thereby affecting the overall performance of the big data analysis engine.

Map Reduce Workflow

The focus of this work is to study the search conditions in catalog contacts, where the dimensionless form of the Reynolds equation is

$$\text{key}(P, X, Y; \lambda) = \frac{\partial}{\partial X}(H^3 \frac{\partial P}{\partial X}) + \frac{L^2}{B^2} \frac{\partial C}{\partial Y}(H^3 \frac{\partial P}{\partial Y}) - 6\frac{\partial H}{\partial X} = 0 \qquad (1)$$

X and Y are input and P is output. Each layer of PINN contains several neurons, and the output of each neuron is:

$$z = \phi(\xi) \qquad (2)$$

Here, the sigmoid function is used as an activation function:

$$\phi(\xi) = \frac{1}{1 + e^{-\xi}} \qquad (3)$$

The loss of PINN is evaluated by the difference between Eq. (1) and the Reynolds equation reformulated throughout the catalog area:

$$C(w) = \iint_{D_\omega} (\text{Reg}(\text{N}([X, Y]^T; w); \lambda) - \text{Resy}(P, X, Y; \lambda))dX\,dY \qquad (4)$$

The average execution time of these operations is calculated by dividing the execution time of the sub phase by the number of operations performed in the sub phase. The execution time and the number of executed operations of the sub stages are obtained by tracking the operation of the program using the BTrace tool, and then further counting the data captured by each node BTrace is calculated [13].

Catalog science has become a prominent school since the Qing Dynasty. Wang Mingsheng, the Qing Dynasty, said in the Seventeen History: "The study of catalogue is the first important matter in learning. Only then on, we can enter.", said Zhou Zumo in the preface of the book "Catalogue book can guide scholars to know the path of study". Zhang Xuecheng put forward that "distinguish academic chapters, and examine the source of mirror" made it clear that bibliography is mainly used for the display of literature information and reveal academic information.

What is the mindset of classical bibliography? After academic examination and debate, the source and flow refers to the traceability of bibliographic time and the diversion of bibliographic content, which is the requirement of classification and edition disciplines [14]. It also has the integration of prospecting textual research, collation textual research facts, text, forming a catalogue book with a complete knowledge system, classification and norms.

3 Connecsimilarities of Big Data Analysis with Classical Bibliography

3.1 Big Data Analysis

Big data analysis is a collection of huge data, and the implementation of data integration according to the scenarios required by the users, to form a data chart that can be intuitively expressed and conducive to query.

Big data of the working idea is the most typical of top-down ideas, namely establish the data analysis target——target dimension dismantling——data dimension correlation establish——found problem data and cause of——problem data optimization, this kind of thought line data analysis system or model establishment, so as to ensure the comprehensiveness of data analysis. The bottom-up data analysis idea is mostly used to find out the data problems in the existing data report. The specific idea is——for the purpose of abnormal data discovery.

The workflow of big data analysis is generally analysis design, data collection, data processing, data analysis, data presentation, and report writing [15].

(1) Analysis and design
   Clarify the purpose of data analysis, determine the direction of analysis, and guide the data collection. At the same time, the data analysis ideas can also be sorted out through the purpose orientation, build a process framework, set up the analysis points, and find the internal associations according to the key points.
(2) Data collection
   Data collection is according to determine the previous data analysis framework, collect relevant data, to provide material and basis for data analysis.
(3) Data processing
   Data processing refers to the processing and sorting of the collected data, and the integration into a format suitable for data analysis, to ensure the consistency and

effectiveness of the data. The purpose of data processing is to remove erroneous data from massive, disordered, and apparently unrelated data, and to extract and derive valuable and meaningful data for solving problems. Data processing mainly includes data cleaning, transformation, extraction, merger, calculation, etc.

(4) Data analysis

Data analysis refers to the analysis of the collected data in accordance with the current goal, to obtain useful information and form effective conclusions.

(5) Data presentation

Through analysis, the relationship and rules hidden within the data are mined, and can be intuitively displayed.

(6) Report writing

Data analysis report is actually a summary and presentation of the whole data analysis process. Through the report, the causes, process, results and recommendations of the data analysis are fully presented for the reference of the decision makers.

The performance model of the map phase in MapReduce applications can be expressed using formula (5):

$$ET_{map} = \sum_{i=1}^{4} ETph_i \qquad (5)$$

Wherein ETmap represents the execution time of the map phase, and ETph represents the execution time of the i-th sub phase of the map phase; It can be expressed by formula (6):

$$ETph_i = ETPerWavePh_i \times numTotalWaves \qquad (6)$$

In order to simplify the modeling process, we put the closely related spin and merge sub stages into one model. Therefore, a total of 4 models were generated during the map phase. Taking into account the varying degrees of overlap between the various stages, we calculate the average time of each step and its respective proportional share in that stage. The numTotalWaves parameter is calculated according to formula (7).

$$numTotalWaves = \lceil nummasks/totalSlots \rceil \qquad (7)$$

There are already various algorithms to solve complex optimization problems, such as recursive random search algorithms, pattern search algorithms, and genetic algorithms. Recursive random search algorithm is easy to fall into local optimization; Pattern algorithms typically have a slow rate of progressive convergence. Genetic algorithm is a kind of evolutionary algorithm. The algorithm is inspired by genetic biology, (For example, genetics, mutation, selection, crossover, etc., are widely known because they effectively avoid local optimal performance. The goal of RFHOC is to find configurations that optimize the performance of Hadoop applications from the global configuration parameter space. Due to the existence of many local optimal advantages in the search space for configuration parameters with high-dimensional nonlinear relationships, RFHOC uses GA algorithms and uses the output of the performance prediction model constructed above as fitness values.

Through further research, it is found that among the above research focuses in the field of digital bibliography, the research results on digital resource cataloging are relatively significant, including research on digital resource organization and cataloging, research on digital learning guidance and subject navigation, research on digital bibliographic information and reference services, research on the digital bibliographic information industry, and research on digital intelligent knowledge organization. Moreover, with the development of digital bibliography, in recent years, researchers have begun to focus on building a theoretical system of digital bibliography, exploring how digital bibliography theory can be integrated into the current bibliography education system.

3.2 Analysis of Classical Catalogue

For classical catalogue, liu xiang said: "the article, its will, recorded" and then "don't collect the record" into a book, this shows the classical catalogue program from different, different, correct, class belonging, writing books, the whole process involves classification, version, calibration, textual research and other multidisciplinary, at the same time to study the origin of the disciplines, development, method, experience, and comprehensive summary.

The workflow of classical bibliography can generally be divided into a collection of various——comparison,——modification and non——class secondary attribution of——writing books.

(1) Gather many books

In the process of circulation, ancient Chinese documents and classics rely more on handwritten, and there are often mistakes and omissions, so various versions need to be collected.

(2) Comparison and difference

Due to the different editions, the writing staff are different, and there are mistakes. After collecting multiple versions, it is necessary to compare each versions of ancient books to find the differences. This can remove the wrong version version, show the truth.

(3) Change the right and wrong

In multiple versions, through mutual verification, the correct sentences are corrected, and the original versions of the ancient books are restored to facilitate the subsequent classification. The significance lies in the removal of errors. Through calibration, the classics in the hands of the users are corrected to ensure that the words and sentences of the classics are correct without ambiguity.

(4) Class subownership

After correcting the correct ancient books, they are classified according to the content of the ancient books, and the category and origin and evolution of the ancient books are verified. Ancient books are classified into "classics, history, children and collection".

(5) Write the book record

The book record is an introduction of the ideological content of the book, simple and clear revealing the basic information for readers to understand the book and guide the study. Excellent proofreading version, but also conducive to later generations to learn.

Table 1. Classic philology of big data analysis

Big data analysis	Classical catalogology	similar point
Analysis design	Personal academic requirements	Highly customized, problem-oriented, and clear in purpose
data collection	Gather the people	Collect the basic data
data handling	Examination and approval of the article times, calibration and verification	Processing of the specific data/literature
DA	Class secondary attribution	Classification and analyze in the form that meets the purpose
data presentation The report shows	Write a book	Intuitively show the required results, form the final result report, results show

To sum up, there are similarities between big data analysis and classical bibliography. Work correspondence can be simplified in the following table (Table 1).

From a methodological point of view, both can start with the problem, Form the final result. You can refer to the methodology of big data analysis to form the cycle of "idea——product——data" as shown in the figure below (Fig. 1).

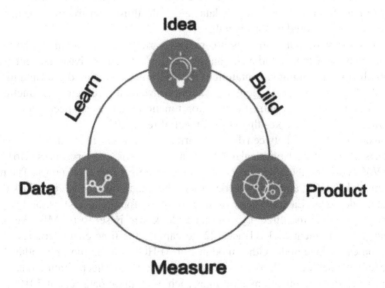

Fig. 1. Big data-based circular pattern

Research on bibliographic recommendation service in the new environment. In the digital environment, with the opening of the network environment and the surge in the number of documents, the main body of compiling recommended bibliographies is no longer limited to celebrities and experts. Organizations such as libraries, readers, and other people from all walks of life have also begun to join the ranks of recommended bibliographies. There are various forms of recommendation, and new media such as Douban, Zhihu, and WeChat official account have become a powerful force for promoting recommendation books. Research has shown that "the compilation method of recommended books in the digital era is more scientific, the scope of recommended books is expanded, the number of recommended subjects is increased, and the functions of recommended books are extended.".

At this stage, there are also some deficiencies in the research on the purpose of recommendation books. For example, there are many problems in the practical operation of personalized recommendation bibliography services. "How to provide accurate personalized services based on users' reading needs and reading records remains to be discussed.". Another example is the lack of research on users' reading needs, access to information, and other aspects of this research only stays at the theoretical stage, lacking specific empirical research. Studying bibliography based on users' reading needs is the development direction of bibliography applications in China.

4 The Application of Big Data Analysis Method in Studying Classical Catalog Science

Big data analysis can be simplified into three types of data analysis: the first is structured data that can be stored and processed in a fixed format; the other is semi-structured data, namely formal structured data without data model; the third is unstructured data, namely data that cannot be stored and analyzed.

In the current digital resources are rich, a variety of traditional literature large database such as "Chinese bidian", "hall collection", "Chinese basic ancient books", these are the maximum implementation of the traditional literature digital and network, reflects the large storage, management, reading convenient level retrieval function, statistical analysis function, contrast calibration function greatly enhanced, etc. Classical bibliography more often takes this as the object of research.

To avoid interference between different virtual machines on the same server, a virtual machine is created on each physical machine. In other words, one server is used to host the master VM node, and the other servers host the remaining nine slave nodes. The master node runs JobTracker and NameNode tasks, and each slave node runs TaskTracker and DataNode tasks. Each VM uses four map slots, four reduce slots, and 300M of memory to initialize the directory. The data block size is set to 64 MB. We use the dynamic test equipment tool BTrace11221 to capture the time characteristics of tasks running on each slave node. Other modules of RFHOC can be run on another VM or on an exclusive device, such as a processing module that collects feature data offline. We ran five Hadoop applications five times each, with input data sets of 50100200500 and 1024 GB respectively. These applications are taken from the HiBench and Puma benchmark sets. They fully cover the characteristics of typical Hadoop applications. For example, WordCount is computationally intensive in the map phase; TeraSort is not only computationally intensive but also memory intensive during the map phase; In the reduce phase, disk operations are intensive. Sort is disk and memory intensive;

Adjlist is computationally intensive in the reduce phase; In addition, Inverted Indeac is computationally and disk intensive.

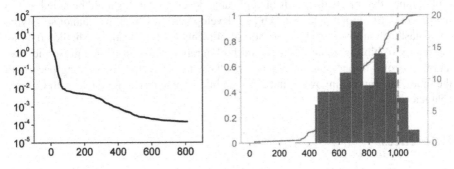

Fig. 2. Prediction error of the model

Figure 2 shows the relative errors of each sub stage of the map phase. As can be seen from the figure, the errors of WordCount and Inverted Indec in the read sub stage are relatively large, with 15.8% and 16% respectively; The model error of Sort in the spmg step is 15.6% higher. This is because the compression ratio has a significant impact on the performance of the read phase, and we only consider three types of training data: gzip, LZO, and zlib. However, these errors are small relative to the performance of CBO. The average error of the prediction model in the map stage is only 9.2%; Compared to the model corresponding to 10 parameters (4.3%), the error rate increased by only 4.9%, approximately 2.1 times that of the latter, while the number of catalog parameters reached 3.4 times.

A basic database can be established using structured text data with relatively fixed poetic formats to collate and analyze phrases and words with phrasing properties, including person names, place names, years, official positions, and interpersonal relationships, to form a directory.

For others, if classical literature is not organized, depicted, or contains errors and omissions, then they are mostly unstructured text. For this part, data conversion is required. After this data conversion, you can still refer to the big data analysis model, conduct data analysis based on the process, and combine classic catalog research methods for mining.

5 Conclusion

In the era of big data, bibliography has undergone changes in its system, theoretical system, education system, and work system. How to reasonably and efficiently collect, organize, disclose, and utilize massive network information resources is the new mission of bibliography. To undertake a new mission, bibliography needs to seek a path of transformation, from the integration of bibliography, abstracts, and indexing to the digitization and networking of bibliographic information work, from the automation of knowledge organization and retrieval to intelligence, and from bibliographic reference to digital reference services. Researchers should also change their minds as soon as possible, establish new concepts of information and networked bibliography, break through the shackles of the old framework, emancipate their minds, and create a new system of bibliography that meets the needs of applicable development. It should be noted that in the process of bibliographic research and development in China, we cannot simply be enthusiastic about the introduction and use of technology. Instead, we should combine the reality of bibliographic research and bibliographic work in China, grasp the laws and trends of bibliographic development, adhere to the attitude of keeping pace with the times, continue to innovate, and form a bibliographic research system with Chinese characteristics.

References

1. Liu, F.: The reform of college physical education teaching methods under the background of big data. J. Phys. Conf. Ser. **1744**(3), 032005 (2021). 7 p.
2. Khan, I., Pintelon, L., Martin, H.: The application of multicriteria decision analysis methods in health care: a literature review (2022)
3. Hua, F., Liu, C.: The application of big data analysis in college English classroom vocabulary memory and learning efficiency teaching (2021)
4. Li, L., Wang, W., Bian, F.: Application of the big data analysis model in higher education talent training quality evaluation. Complexity (2021)
5. Ge, C., et al.: Tectonic discrimination and application based on convolution neural network and incomplete big data. J. Geochem. Explor. J. Assoc. Explor. Geochem. **220**(1) (2021)
6. Riva, C., Mira, I.G.: Global archaeology and microhistorical analysis. Connecting scales in the 1st-milennium B.C. mediterranean. Archaeol. Dialogues **29**(1), 1–14 (2022)
7. Sharma, S., Gadia, S., Tim, U.S.: Subset, subquery and queryable-visualization in parametric big data model. Int. J. Inf. Manag. Data Insights (2021)
8. Abdalla, H.B., Abuhaija, B.: Comprehensive analysis of various big data classification techniques: a challenging overview. J. Inf. Knowl. Manag. **22**(01) (2023)
9. Tanriver-Ayder, E., Faes, C., Casteele, T.V.D., et al.: Comparison of commonly used methods in random effects meta-analysis: application to preclinical data in drug discovery research. BMJ Open Sci. **5**(1), e100074 (2021)
10. Geng, L.: Application status and development suggestions of big data technology in petroleum engineering. Pet. Drill. Tech. **49**(2), 72–78 (2021)
11. Patel, J.C., Parveen, S.: In vitro and in vivo analysis of fentanyl and fentalog metabolites using hyphenated chromatographic techniques: a review. Chem. Res. Toxicol. **35**(1), 30–42 (2022)
12. Green, A.M.: Metadata application profiles in U. S. academic libraries: a document analysis. J. Libr. Metadata **21**(3–4), 105–143 (2022)
13. Kim, H., Matthias, L.: The current state of big data research in tourism: results of a systematic literature analysis. Zeitschrift für Tourismuswissenschaft **13** (2021)
14. Biondini, E., Rhoades, D.A., Gasperini, P.: Application of the EEPAS earthquake forecasting model to Italy. Geophys. J. Int. (2023)
15. Li, Z.: Wisdom media era of big data in the application of the short video from the media. In: MacIntyre, J., Zhao, J., Ma, X. (eds.) SPIOT 2020. AISC, vol. 1282, pp. 283–289. Springer, Cham (2021). https://doi.org/10.1007/978-3-030-62743-0_40

Research on Big Data of Vocational Education Based on Simhash Algorithm

Xuefeng Sun[1(✉)], Jin Xue[1], Jiawei Luo[1], and Limei Song[2]

[1] Dalian University of Science and Technology, Dalian 116052, Liaoning, China
dbisxf@163.com
[2] Shandong Institute of Commerce and Technology, Jinan 250103, Shandong, China

Abstract. The quality assurance of higher vocational education is an important measure to expand the supply of high-quality vocational education and realize the connotative development of higher vocational education. However, the quality assurance of higher vocational education needs to be clarified in theory and mode and optimized and improved in practice in terms of who will guarantee, what to guarantee and how to guarantee. The research on vocational education big data based on simhash algorithm is a research on simulation model. It uses the characteristics of big data to simulate and analyze individual behavior. In this way, it can be used as a tool to analyze and predict social phenomena. It has been widely used in many fields of economics, sociology, psychology and so on. The research on big data of vocational education based on simhash algorithm is very easy to use, because it is just like using Excel or other spreadsheet software.

Keyword: big data · Simhash algorithm · vocational education

1 Introduction

Education is the foundation of a long-term plan. Quality is the measure and lifeline of education. It is an eternal topic to study and promote education to improve quality. Higher vocational education is a new type of education in the process of China's reform and development, which has unique charm and value. In the future, in the new journey of "improving the vocational education and training system, deepening the integration of industry and education, school enterprise cooperation" and "realizing the connotative development of higher education", the realization of high-quality development of higher vocational education will be a key point [1]. At the same time, the country is carrying out in-depth changes in the governance system and governance capacity, and the education sector is also striving to promote the modernization of the governance system and governance capacity. In this context, combining the quality assurance of higher vocational education with the new development of modern governance has important practical significance and theoretical exploration value, It also reflects the development direction that higher vocational education serves the people, the Communist Party of China's governance, the consolidation and development of the socialist system with Chinese characteristics, and the reform and opening up and the socialist modernization drive [2].

Y. Zhang and N. Shah (Eds.): BigIoT-EDU 2023, LNICST 581, pp. 257–267, 2024.
https://doi.org/10.1007/978-3-031-63133-7_25

Driven by the new generation of information technology revolution, especially with the rapid development of new technologies such as the mobile Internet, the Internet of Things, cloud computing, and artificial intelligence, big data, as an emerging thing, is no longer simply "big data" or "large data", but has evolved into a new technology complex that integrates multiple attributes such as technology, tools, capabilities, systems, concepts, methods, and resources. Big data is becoming an effective governance tool and active governance resource, and has played a very important role in the fields of politics, economy, society, transportation, science and technology, medical treatment, culture, education, ecology, and people's livelihood. All sectors of society are aware of the value of big data for social change, and more and more countries and regions are actively taking action to seize the "voice" of data and informatization highlands, and have taken big data as a strategic choice to improve social governance capabilities. At the same time, vocational education, as a type of education that is highly isomorphic to economic and social development, involves multiple entities such as governments, industries, enterprises, universities, intermediaries, and other organizations in the process of running schools. Not only are there significant differences in interest demands, but also network relationships and information flows are extremely complex, which determines the existence of "big data" in the field of vocational education in various forms, types, structures, values, and densities. Of course, it is the existence of diversified big data in vocational education, as well as the increasingly mature intelligent technology of big data, that makes big data technology have unlimited potential in "innovating vocational education decision-making methods, governance models, and other aspects.". This has become a value source for solving governance issues in the current development of vocational education and achieving good governance, naturally providing an opportunity to comprehensively improve the governance ability of vocational education in the era of big data.

The new era has new expectations for the development of vocational education and its governance innovation. "The National Vocational Education Reform and Implementation Plan clearly states that" we should improve the participation of the A forces of the Duobeihua Blade Society in the organization of collaborative education, support and encourage enterprises and social forces to participate in the organization of various types of vocational education. "The pattern of vocational education has basically completed the transformation from being mainly organized by the government to being managed by the government as a whole and running schools in a diversified society." This not only puts forward higher requirements for the new era of education and the acceleration of vocational modern vocational education, "The modernization of vocational education and vocational education is not a breakthrough. In the new era in which the modernization of science and education must be driven by governance capabilities and the information technology revolution in the modern era, big data exists as a means of production. Whether actively adapting or passively following, the field of vocational education will face" opportunities "and" challenges "of big data-driven governance reform." Coexisting conflicts. Because most of the behaviors of various actors are "subject to laws, models, and principles, and are held in the hands of big data", big data also provides vocational education participants with common experience and action logic for multiple collaborative governance, which inevitably leads to the transformation of vocational education governance into a data governance model. The state has issued a series of policies to accelerate the development of modern vocational education, and improving the quality has become the focus of attention. Since 2010, policies such as the outline of the national medium - and long-term education reform and development plan (2010–2020), the decision of the State Council on accelerating the development of modern vocational education, the construction plan of modern vocational education system (2014–2020), and the action plan for the innovative development of Higher Vocational Education (2015–2018) have been issued successively. Improving quality has become the core and key, and is leading higher vocational education into innovative development A new historical stage of comprehensively improving quality. For example, the outline of the national medium and long term education reform and development plan (2010–2020) clearly puts forward "Take improving quality as the core task of educational reform and development [3]. Establish a scientific concept of quality, and take promoting people's all-round development and adapting to social needs as the fundamental standard to measure the quality of education. Establish a concept of educational development with improving quality as the core, pay attention to the development of educational connotation, encourage schools to develop their own characteristics, levels, famous teachers and talents. Establish a management system and working mechanism oriented to improving the quality of education, and Resource allocation and school work focus on strengthening teaching links and improving education quality. We will formulate national standards for education quality and establish a sound education quality assurance system.

2 Related Work

2.1 Higher Vocational Education

The definition of Higher Vocational Education in the dictionary of education is, "Higher Vocational and technical education belongs to the third level of vocational education and technical education. It includes vocational and technical education before employment and relevant continuing education after employment. For example, some teaching plans of American technical colleges and community colleges, some teaching plans of Japanese higher specialized schools and short-term universities and special courses of specialized schools, technical colleges and senior technician classes of universities in France, and early higher industrial schools in China Education provided by specialized schools, junior colleges, and some teaching plans of adult colleges in various countries It mainly cultivates professional auxiliary talents in seven disciplines: liberal arts, science, engineering, agriculture and forestry, medicine, political science and law, and finance and economics [4]." The Encyclopedia of Chinese education defines higher vocational education as "The education of cultivating high-level practical talents belongs to the category of higher education.... The school system for recruiting graduates from secondary vocational and technical schools, ordinary high school graduates and intermediate technical workers with corresponding educational level and practical experience is 2–3 years; a small number of junior middle school graduates are 5 years. The forms of Education are school education and vocational and technical training. This kind of education focuses on the cultivation of students' practical skills, and serves as a foundation for all departments of the national economy The door transports high-level applied talents and high-level skilled workers for the purpose of training [5]."

Originally developed by UNESCO in the 1970s, it was first revised in 1997 and again in 2011. The international standard classification of education defines "Vocational Education" as: "an educational course designed mainly for learners to master the knowledge, skills and abilities required for working in a particular occupation or industry or a certain type of occupation or industry. Such a course may have a work-based component (i.e. Internship). After successfully completing such courses, Can obtain the professional qualification certificate related to the labor market recognized by the relevant national competent authorities and/or the labor market for the purpose of practicing: define "higher education" as: "Higher education is based on secondary education and provides learning activities in the field of specialized educational disciplines [6]. It is highly complex and highly specialized learning. Higher education includes academic education as commonly understood, but it is broader than academic education because it also includes higher vocational or professional education.". According to the new classification, higher education is divided into vocational (Professional) higher education and general (Professional) higher education. Higher education with "professional purpose" and "academic purpose" coexist in higher education at all levels.

2.2 Basic Logic of Vocational Education Data Governance

Generally, big data is considered as "a collection of data that cannot be effectively collected, stored, managed, and processed using conventional technical means and methods within a reasonable period of time due to its large scale.". As a key production factor in the digital economy era, big data has the characteristics of diversity, massiveness, highspeed, and low density. It has generated tremendous value in promoting productivity growth, creating social surplus value, and reshaping the behavior of social entities. It has brought a revolutionary impact on human life, learning, and work, becoming one of the most powerful driving forces in this era, and has permeated the entire education field. At the operational level of social organizations, the importance of the role of big data has been studied from multiple perspectives: As one of the new assets in the current world, big data has changed the form of industry and social organizations, the most significant of which is promoting organizational innovation; Big data can achieve business model innovation through monetization of data assets or digital management transformation, achieve open innovation, and promote the restructuring of internal operational mechanisms and strategic actions of the organization; Big data essentially reflects the digital reconstruction of the real world of human society, becoming the methodological basis for educational governance reform oriented towards a smart society, and reconstructing the educational governance system. Currently, some scholars have studied data governance issues in the field of education, with the aim of providing important information for relevant managers or participants in decision-making to improve the effectiveness of decision-making, mainly through analyzing the legitimacy, logical path, and system construction of data sources and streams in the governance process. The key lies in transforming the support of education governance environment, transforming governance network systems, optimizing governance development patterns, and stimulating institutional and policy innovation. The so-called data governance refers to the collection of activities that effectively exercise rights and control over data asset management, which is a new perspective for the study of social organizations and their governance behavior. The vocational education data governance has become an attempt to transform China's vocational education governance tools because of the integration of the latest technologies and governance concepts such as "Internet plus", big data, and data governance, which provides a new way of thinking and path for restructuring new vocational education governance space and carrying out integration and reorganization. Of course, as a change in governance model, it must comply with the general laws of social evolution, and promoting vocational education data governance should comply with the following basic logic. The vocational education data is shown in Fig. 1 below.

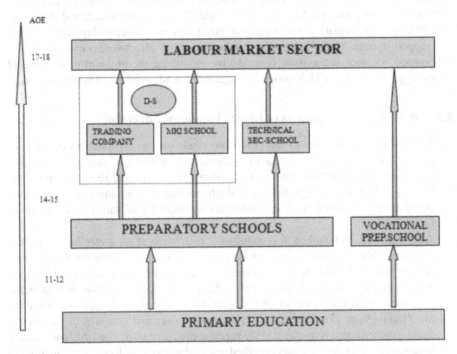

Fig. 1. Vocational Education Data

The research on the relationship between technology and governance has a long history. Herbert Simon, a sociologist and economist known as the "father of artificial intelligence," once believed that "intelligent technology can supplement or extend limited human rationality.". As information and knowledge gradually become the determining variables of economic and social development, the application of technology in various fields of society has become a component of this social transformation, and technological application innovation has provided a replacement tool for social governance. Currently, the accelerated integration of big data technology and various fields of social economy has driven social governance, including vocational education governance, to a new governance paradigm driven by technological innovation and technology. According to the social construction theory of technology, technology itself does not have a unique logic of action independent of human beings. It is not only constrained by human social, economic, and political conditions, but also has two interdependent social attributes, namely, empowerment and supervision. Technology empowerment refers to the fact that technology can bring many real or potential development opportunities to society. In terms of vocational education governance, it can reduce governance costs, improve governance efficiency, facilitate participation in the governance process, enhance social welfare brought about by governance, and promote the development of vocational education. From a technical perspective, the application of big data technology in vocational education revolves around data collection, storage, cleaning, integration, and analysis. Based on continuously innovative technical means, it is embedded in all fields of vocational education, covering all entities, covering all processes, and touching various data analysis tools and data models, providing multiple entities for vocational education to collaborate and update governance methods Providing effective big data technology support in terms of entity behavior prediction, policy effectiveness evaluation, and governance behavior supervision is conducive to solving the problem of insufficient technology application or technology shortage under traditional governance models.

2.3   Talent Training Objectives of Higher Vocational Education

(1) Training objectives refer to the provisions made on the expected results of educational activities, that is, the expected development status of students, according to certain educational purposes and constraints. It is a specific requirement for the training object according to the national educational purpose and the school's own positioning, and it is a specific training requirement for all kinds of talents at all levels.

(2) As the specific standards and requirements of schools at all levels for the people they train, talent training objectives have formed a relatively clear definition in the educational field. This paper adopts the interpretation of "talent training objectives, also known as educational objectives, refer to the specific training requirements of schools at all levels and of all types" in the dictionary of Education Edited by Mr. Gumingyuan [7]. The talent training objectives must conform to the overall development direction specified in the national education policy and the fundamental requirements for talent training specified in the educational objectives. It can provide reference for specific curriculum objectives and teaching objectives.

(3) The talent training objective of higher vocational education plays an important guiding role in the whole modern vocational education system. It is not only the starting point of higher vocational education practice, but also the theoretical standard to test the quality of higher vocational education. "From the perspective of the target orientation subject, the talent training objectives of higher vocational education can be divided into the talent training objectives specified in the policy documents at the national level, the talent training objectives established in the educational practice at the higher vocational college level and the specific talent training objectives at the professional level. This paper studies the talent training objectives established in the educational practice at the level of higher vocational colleges.

2.4 Data Processing

The real data obtained in the real world are generally incomplete and inconsistent "dirty data". Faced with such data, it may not be possible to directly conduct data mining or the results of data mining may not be ideal. In order to improve the efficiency of data mining, a new technology, data preprocessing, has emerged. Data preprocessing technology can greatly improve the quality and efficiency of data mining processes. Its main tasks include: data integration, data cleansing, data transformation, data reduction, and attribute redundancy.

Before carrying out data mining, first of all, make a quality assessment of the dataset and conduct quality analysis on the dataset. The dataset studied in this article mainly has the following problems: data missing, data transformation, attribute redundancy, and so on. By analyzing the quality results of the dataset, we first preprocess the dataset to provide a high-quality dataset for the data mining process, making the analysis results of data mining more accurate.

Real data obtained in the real world often have some missing values. The generation of missing values is mainly divided into mechanical reasons and human reasons. The mechanical reason is a lack of data due to a failure in the collection and storage process or storage of data. Human factors are mainly due to human subjective errors or the concealment of the authenticity of data resulting in data loss. Most of these data are noisy and incomplete, and this data set has a significant impact on the analysis results during the data mining process. Therefore, it is necessary to clean up the noise data and missing values in the data set to improve the accuracy of the analysis process. The main methods for processing missing values include: deleting cases with missing values (simple deletion method and weight method), interpolating missing values with possible values (mean interpolation, using the same kind of mean interpolation, maximum likelihood estimation, multiple interpolation), and so on.

Data transformation is a standardized process that transforms the dataset needed in the process of data mining into a form suitable for data mining, achieving the purpose of being suitable for mining valuable information. Data transformation mainly includes the following methods:; Feature construction, normalization processing, and discretization processing.

The methods for normalizing data mainly include: minimum maximum normalization, z-score normalization, and fractional scaling normalization.

The minimum maximum normalization performs a linear transformation of the original data. Assume that and are the maximum value maxA and the minimum value minA of attribute A. Map the value v of A to the [new_min, new_min] interval. The minimum maximum normalization maintains the relationship between the original data values, but if future input instances fall outside the original data value domain of A, the method will face an "out of bounds" error. In z-score normalization, the value of attribute A is normalized based on the mean and standard deviation of A.

$$M \Sigma E = \frac{1}{mp} \sum\nolimits_{p=1}^{y} \sum\nolimits_{j-1}^{n} (\hat{y}_p - y_p)^2 \tag{1}$$

$$\bar{y}_j = \lfloor \frac{y_i + y_{(i+1)}}{2} \rfloor \tag{2}$$

The value v of A; Is normalized to v'. Where avga and&are the average and standard deviation of attribute A. This method is effective when the actual minimum and maximum values of attribute A are unknown, or when outliers affect the minimum maximum normalization. Decimal scaling normalization is performed by moving the decimal point position of the value of attribute A. The number of decimal places to move depends on the maximum absolute value of A. The value of A, v, is normalized to v'. Where j is the smallest integer such that max $(lv') < 1$:

$$\bar{x} = \lfloor \frac{\sum_{i=1}^{n-1} \mid Y_{(2i-1)} - Y_{(2i+1)} \mid}{n-1} \rfloor \tag{3}$$

$$c_i = m\times \mid y_{(i-1)} - y_{(i+1)} \tag{4}$$

Some data mining algorithms require the data to be in the form of classified attributes when processing data. Generally, it is necessary to discretize the data and convert continuous attributes into classified attributes. After discretizing the data, selecting the best algorithm can produce the best results for the prediction model established by the algorithm.

3 Research on Big Data of Vocational Education Based on Simhash Algorithm

3.1 Introduction to Simhash Algorithm

The traditional hash algorithm maps the input data to a specific length of hash value output through calculation. The greater the difference between the input data, the greater the difference between the mapped signature values. In principle, the traditional hash algorithm is equivalent to the pseudo-random number generation algorithm. For input data with a 1-bit gap, completely different hash values 0 will be output. Therefore, similar documents cannot be detected. The original hash algorithm needs to be improved so that similar documents can output similar hash values [8]. Simhash algorithm is an improved hash algorithm, which can effectively identify whether the input data are similar. Simhash algorithm has two steps:

Step 1: calculate the hash value

First, each document content corresponds to an initial value of O Signature s with length f, an f-dimensional vector V with initial value 0; Secondly, the document content is segmented through the word segmentation library, some modal particles and auxiliary words are filtered out, and the document content is converted into a group of feature words after removing the interference symbols. The weight of the feature words is the number of times the feature words appear in the document; Step 3: map all feature words into signature h with length f using the same hash function, and traverse each bit of H. if the ith bit of H is 1 (I is between 1 and F), add the weight of the feature word to the ith bit of V, otherwise subtract; Finally, traverse v. if the i-th bit of V is greater than 0, the i-th bit of signature s is set to 1, otherwise it is set to 0. The finally generated signature s is the simhash signature corresponding to the document content [9]. The schematic diagram of hash value calculation is shown in Fig. 2.

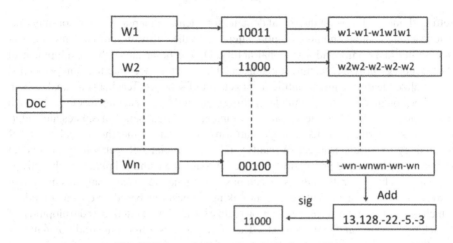

Fig. 2. Schematic diagram of simhash algorithm

Step 2: use Hamming distance 51 to compare and retrieve the simhash signature value.

The Hamming distance of two simhash signature values is easy to calculate, but when the document scale is very large, it is impossible to compare one by one. Google has proposed a solution, which greatly improves the efficiency. The following will give specific examples.

Assuming that f is 64 bits, if it is necessary to find out the simhash signature with Hamming distance less than or equal to 3, it can be seen from the drawer principle that at least one part of the simhash signature divided into four parts is identical. Therefore, the 64 bit simhash signature is divided into four parts, each part is 16 bits, each part is used as a key, and the signature containing a 16 bit key is stored in redis as a value [10]. A signature to be compared is divided into four parts in the same way. Each part is compared with the corresponding key in redis. When the keys in this part are identical, the value corresponding to the key is taken from redis and the Hamming distance is calculated. This method can greatly reduce the calculation of Hamming distance.

3.2   Influence of Simhash Algorithm Based on Big Data on Vocational Education

The arrival of artificial intelligence era has had a profound impact on higher vocational education. On the one hand, facing the great impact of artificial intelligence technology on the job market, higher vocational education has been faced with great challenges. It mainly includes that the school running form of vocational education needs to be transformed, the specialty setting needs to be adjusted and the teaching content needs to be innovated. According to the report released by McKinsey Global Research Institute, about 375million people in the world will face re employment in the future, including 100million in China. In view of this, under the new requirements of the new era, higher vocational education should pay more attention to the needs of students' career transformation, and the form of running schools should be intelligent and open; Specialty setting should be based on the social demand for talents to increase, reduce or integrate; The teaching content should pay more attention to the cultivation of students' innovative ability and compound vocational ability. On the other hand, the development of AI technology provides technical conditions for teachers' accurate teaching, students' personalized learning and scientific management of schools. Teachers can analyze students' personalized needs, formulate teaching plans and share teaching resources through the technical platform; Students can communicate with teachers, classmates and enterprise workers through the technology platform. At the same time, they can also use VR technology to simulate objective reality, and use artificial AR technology to conduct training simulation and production practice; Through the technical platform, the university can conduct overall analysis of campus data, generate visual analysis charts, and provide school managers with decision-making suggestions based on data and models, which makes higher vocational education realize the all-round intelligent development of "teaching, learning and management". Therefore, we must reform the traditional higher vocational education, especially the reform of talent training objectives, face the great impact of new technology, strengthen the modernization and information construction of higher vocational education, improve the quality of talent training, and effectively enhance the vitality of higher vocational education.

4 Conclusion

Higher vocational education is a type of education with distinct cross-border attributes. This paper studies the quality assurance of Higher Vocational Education from the perspective of modern governance, and adds a new "cross-border" on the basis of the original "cross-border", which further increases the difficulty of research. On the one hand, it is the crossover of research scope, involving the relevant theories of modern governance and quality assurance of higher vocational education. It is necessary to use the essence of modern governance to innovate and develop quality assurance of higher vocational education, which is not only the reference and application of theory, but also the crossover and transformation of research. Grasping and developing the essence of theory is a major difficulty. On the other hand, it is the cross-border of research objects, including government departments, higher vocational colleges, industrial enterprises, third parties and other different subjects, especially involving some deep-seated problems such as the transfer of government functions, the separation of management and office scores, and system reform. We should not only avoid walking into the traditional old road, but also avoid the evil road of rote application. The key is to do something and not do something about the practical problems that urgently need to be solved in reality.

References

1. Jiang, W.: Research on education model of "internet great thought and politics" in higher vocational colleges based on big data. In: 2020 International Conference on Information Science and Education (ICISE-IE) (2020)
2. Shi, Y., Xie, J.: A study of personalized training strategies for vocational education based on big data systems. J. Phys. Conf. Ser. **1570**(1), 012027 (2020). 7 p.

3. Mustapha, A., Abubakar, A.K., Ahmed, H.D., Mohammed, A.: Application of big data analytics for improving learning process in technical vocational education and training. In: Misra, S., Muhammad-Bello, B. (eds.) ICTA 2020. CCIS, vol. 1350, pp. 15–25. Springer, Cham (2021). https://doi.org/10.1007/978-3-030-69143-1_2
4. Hu, S., Huang, M.: Design and implementation of vocational education cross border e-commerce comprehensive training system based on big data analysis. J. Phys. Conf. Ser. **1881**(3), 032037 (2021). 7 p.
5. Jiang, X., Pan, Z.: Construction of vocational education information platform under the background of big data (2020)
6. Zong, X., Zhang, C., Wu, D.: Research on data mining of sports wearable intelligent devices based on big data analysis. Discrete Dyn. Nat. Soc. **2022** (2022)
7. Cai, W., Sun, P.: The spatial structure and evolution educational anxiety-research on provincial panel based on big data search. Open J. Soc. Sci. **9**(12), 21 (2021)
8. Cui, L.: Construction of big data technology training environment for vocational education based on edge computing technology. Wirel. Commun. Mob. Comput. **2022**(10), 1–9 (2022)
9. Xiao, Q., Zhong, X., Zhong, C.: Application research of KNN algorithm based on clustering in big data talent demand information classification. Int. J. Pattern Recognit. Artif. Intell. **34**(06) (2020). 1525822X15603149-1987
10. Yang, B.J.: Research on teaching design of the course of fundamentals of college information technology based on big data. Sci-Tech Innov. Prod. (2020)

The Development Trend of Intelligent Law in Colleges and Universities Based on Intelligent Data Collection and Analysis

Xiaolan Guo[1,2(✉)], Wang Yilei[1,2], and Yulin Cao[1,2]

[1] School of Politics and Law, Baotou Teachers' College, Baotou 014030, Inner Mongolia, China
guoxiaolan1978@163.com
[2] Yiyang Medical College, Yiyang 413000, Hunan, China

Abstract. In the 21st century, talent training has become the focus of global attention. As an important part of national education and an important part of the grand project of building a country ruled by law, higher legal education is more and more important in the construction of socialist market economy. In order to make China's higher legal education develop along a healthy track, it is urgent to build a scientific legal education system. The development of legal knowledge in Colleges and universities is a long-term process, which needs to be analyzed from different aspects. The first aspect is the basic research on this topic, including its definition and classification, and its evolution over time. In addition to academic research, other types of research should be carried out: for example, research on the impact of intelligence on legal education; Study how to form intellectuals by studying law; Through the study of history, the study of how intellectuals formed; All these aspects need further study.

Keyword: Law · Intelligent data collection · Intellectualization

1 Introduction

The legal education in Colleges and universities in China is an important part of higher education. It is an educational activity with the content of imparting legal knowledge, training legal thinking and cultivating qualified legal professionals. Influenced by the nature of the legal profession itself, legal education is closely related to many aspects of society, such as politics, economy, culture, science and technology. The level and development trend of legal education will ultimately be the result of comprehensive social factors.

China's higher legal education has been developing for 20 years since its restoration and reconstruction. It has experienced changes from planned economy to socialist market economy. It has moved from the incomplete experimental stage to the basically mature development stage [1]. The management system and school running conditions have been greatly and profoundly improved; The construction of the teaching staff has gradually expanded; The construction of teaching materials has developed from scratch, from the

Y. Zhang and N. Shah (Eds.): BigIoT-EDU 2023, LNICST 581, pp. 268–274, 2024.
https://doi.org/10.1007/978-3-031-63133-7_26

annotation of legal provisions to the formation of a more scientific academic system: the construction of disciplines, especially the construction of key disciplines, has driven the academic research and echelon construction of disciplines and promoted the reform of teaching contents. However, with the further deepening of the national socialist market economy, building a country ruled by law has become the consensus of the whole society. Therefore, the modernization of the rule of law and the reform of education must be compatible with the development of the market economy. The market economy is the economy ruled by law [2]. The law must change from the single dictatorship function in the past to the participation and service function of the market economy. Therefore, we are confident to see another brilliant development opportunity for legal education. At the beginning of the new century, we should plan for future legal education [3]. The Ministry of justice's "Ninth Five Year Plan for the development of legal education and the development plan for 2010" put forward the development target of China's legal education: adjust the educational level and structure, expand the training scale, make the legal education structure more reasonable, significantly improve the quality and efficiency, and minimize the contradiction between the supply and demand of legal personnel in society; To In 2010, a modern legal education system compatible with the socialist market economic system, the national legal system construction and the comprehensive social progress was established, and the legal education management system was legalized and standardized. The training scale and quality of legal personnel basically meet social needs.

2 Related Work

2.1 Overview of Jurisprudence

(1) What is law

Law science is a science that studies law and law, a specific social phenomenon and its development law, and its full name is legal science. In a class society, different classes have different jurisprudence. Therefore, jurisprudence has a strong class nature and reflects the interests and will of a certain class. Historically, the jurisprudence of the slave owner class, the feudal owner class and the bourgeoisie is the jurisprudence of the exploiting class. It is the jurisprudence of different exploiting classes. It serves their respective political and economic systems, especially the formulation and implementation of the laws of their own class. It plays a role of theoretical justification, publicity and education for the legal norms and legal systems of their own class [4].

Marxist jurisprudence was born with the founding of Marxism, is an important part of scientific socialism, is the concentrated embodiment of the proletarian world outlook and interests, and serves the interests of the working class and the broad masses of the people.

(2) The emergence of Jurisprudence

Law is an ancient social science with a long history. Engels has long stated that the emergence of law is based on the emergence of law. When the political, economic and cultural development of society reached a certain stage, there was a social division of labor, especially after the emergence of written law, a professional jurist class was formed. They were specialized in legal research, and thus law came into being. Therefore, law is the premise and foundation of the emergence of law, and law is the inevitable result of the emergence and development of law.

2.2 Modern Legal Education

China is an ancient civilized country with a long history. As the founder of the Chinese legal system, its legal education has a long history. In ancient times, there were governmental or private legal education institutions in all dynasties of China. One of the important contents of the "eight teachings" in Xia, Shang and Zhou Dynasties is the "law" education. Especially since the Qin and Han Dynasties, China has not only created "law science" and "doctor of law", but also set up "law department" specializing in legal posts and official selection examinations.

In modern times, China's legal education was influenced by western legal education. Under the background of "Western learning spreading to the East" and the transformation from a feudal autocratic society to a democratic society ruled by law, China has taken different developed countries as a reference system, introduced and transplanted through various channels, learned from each other, and walked a rough and tortuous road [5]. In the second half of the 19th century, China's legal education was based on the education of British and American universities, and organized the earliest legal disciplines of several modern universities in China, such as the Beijing law school and the Tianjin Chinese western school, which was the first (1895) to set up a university law undergraduate. From the end of the 19th century to the beginning of the 20th century, China's legal education took learning as the fashion, hired foreign teachers, translated foreign textbooks, and adopted various forms of running schools, which were public in various places And private legal education institutions have been established one after another, and a large number of legal talents have been trained. During the period of the national government, China's legal education took the United States as the main object of study, and the modern legal education institutions and legal education system were further developed [6]. Especially since the 14th National Congress of the Communist Party of China, with the establishment and continuous improvement of the socialist market economic system, the proposal and gradual implementation of the strategy of administering the country according to law and rejuvenating the country through science and education, and the reflection and criticism of the educational operation mode and development situation of the previous stage by the educational circles, China's legal education has entered a new period of deepening reform and comprehensive development. The theme of this period is to comprehensively deepen education reform and improve education quality [7]. Around this theme of the times, many new measures have been taken in the legal education circle. The voice of the reform of educational concepts and ideas has become stronger and stronger. Since taking teaching as the center, quality as the life, and cultivating innovative talents as the goal, the high-level education of law has reached a new level; The development of teaching evaluation has further highlighted the central position of teaching and strengthened the quality consciousness.

3   Smart Data Collection Related Technologies

(1) Programmable instrument standard command

Standard commands for programmable instruments (SCPI) is a set of language used to control programmable instruments. It is based on ieee488.2 standard and follows the floating-point operation rules in IEEE754 standard, iso646 information exchange 7-bit coding symbols and other standardized instrument programming languages. SCPI is divided into public command and private command. Public command means that as long as the SCPI type instrument is used, the instrument can be controlled by this command, such as the command "* IDN?" Send it to the corresponding instrument to get the reply from the instrument; The private command is a specific command format formed for the specific functions of the instrument, but its clear logic and simple syntax can enable users to get started quickly and control and develop specific functions according to requirements. As a measurement description language, SCPI is highly sought after by the industry for its simplicity and efficiency [8]. At present, the mainstream measuring instruments in the market use SCPI as the control language, such as oscilloscopes and multimeters of keysight and Tektronix, which use SCPI as the control language. Their measuring instruments can be seen everywhere in the teaching of major universities.

(2) Embedded technology

There are many kinds of instruments in university laboratories. At the same time, due to the need for multiple types of measuring instruments in a single experiment, it is not practical to control a single instrument. The design of the instrument control module needs to support the interaction with multiple instruments, realize the unified management of instruments, and have high expandability. Therefore, embedded technology is essential in the system design process.

(3) USB Technology

The experimental instruments are directly connected with the instrument control module through universal serial bus (USB). USB technology is a kind of interface technology that is applied to connect peripheral devices of computers, and also to connect peripheral interactive devices to computers. It has the characteristics of high transmission efficiency, low power consumption and plug and play. Since its launch, it has been developed to usb4.0, and the high version USB protocol can be downward compatible with the low version protocol to maintain the stability of the technology. The bus structure of USB adopts a layered star topology, as shown in Fig. 1.

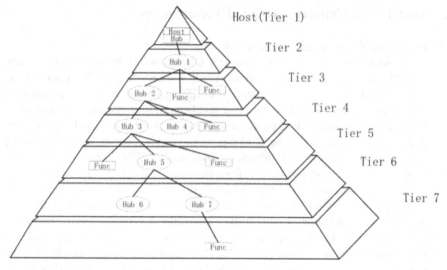

Fig. 1. USB bus structure

4 Research on the Development Trend of the Intellectualization of University Law

At present, the tide of globalization is coming. Whether people realize it or not, this wave has had or will have a profound impact on human society. The so-called globalization refers to the historical process and trend of communication, connection and mutual influence in the global scope. The characteristics of globalization, in terms of form, are that the space-time constraints of human communication have been really broken. Human beings have realized world-wide communication by means of communication and communication provided by modern science and technology; In terms of content, globalization is rich and colorful, involving many fields such as economy, politics, culture and society. Among them, economic globalization is the main line of globalization and also the most basic motivation in the process of globalization [9]. Furthermore, it has an obvious influence on the legal education, which makes the legal education appear the trend of internationalization. The internationalization of legal education is mainly manifested in the activity process or development trend of cross-border, cross-ethnic and cross-cultural multilateral exchange, cooperation and assistance of legal education in the world. This trend follows China's accession to wt O Will be further strengthened. China's entry into WTO is an important step for China to integrate into the mainstream of the world economy, and also another leap for China's legal education to achieve internationalization. It urgently requires legal education to cultivate familiar WT with international consciousness and international vision O The legal personnel of the rules should play an active role in international competition and international affairs [10]. Therefore, legal education should be soberly and profoundly aware of the impact of globalization on legal education, and consciously promote the globalization process of legal education, both in concept and in the goal of talent training and in the teaching process. At present, China's law education has done a lot of work in internationalization. Some key universities have actively exchanged teaching experience and scientific research cooperation with foreign law schools, which has made great contributions to the early integration of China's law education with the international community; However, we must also make it clear that in order to adapt to the international community of the "global village" in the future, law education needs to make greater efforts in curriculum setting and joint education.

The legal cause is supported and constructed by a legal community with the same knowledge structure, common thinking paradigm and common value pursuit. Whether the legal community can be formed and whether it is homogeneous is the decisive factor affecting the rule of law. To some extent, the so-called rule of law is the management and adjustment of social life by legal people who have received strict legal training. The formation of the homogeneous community must start from the time when they receive professional education, which requires legal education to first establish the awareness of cultivating the community from the concept, and run this concept through the whole process of teaching On the one hand, through legal education, we will cultivate the professional lofty sense of future community members, so that students can deeply understand that the legal profession is not only a means of making a living, but also a cause of maintaining social fairness and justice. The legal profession is a noble profession, which requires its members to have the spirit of dedication to the legal ideal. On the other hand, it is their bounden duty to cultivate the historical mission of future community members through legal education and make the rule of law their lifelong pursuit.

5 Conclusion

As a social activity that inherits and creates human legal civilization, legal education is generated and advanced under the resonance of social economy, politics and culture, and is also perfected and developed in the process of influencing society. Therefore, the study of legal education in the 21st century should first focus on the macro level of legal education and social development, and explore the law of legal education development from the interactive relationship between legal education and human development. Secondly, the research on the legal education in the 21st century should also focus on the forward-looking analysis, so that the construction of the legal education model in the 21st century can not only make a strong response to social development, but also enable it to undertake the heavy responsibility of promoting the historical process. Finally, the research of legal education in the 21st century should continue to draw the essence of human legal education thought and education mode from the comparative study of legal education at home and abroad with a broad vision and a tolerant attitude, so as to provide a continuous ideological and empirical power for the shaping of legal education mode in the 21st century. So as to create a legal education model that is not only in line with the world legal education but also has national characteristics.

References

1. He, Z., Zhu, H., Zheng, K.: Research on the trend change of social donation income of colleges and universities in China (2) (2021)

2. Song, J.: The intelligent scientific research management system based on cloud computing. In: Chang, J.W., Yen, N., Hung, J.C. (eds.) FC 2020. LNEE, vol. 747, pp. 2255–2260. Springer, Singapore (2021). https://doi.org/10.1007/978-981-16-0115-6_276

3. Gao, B.: Research and implementation of intelligent evaluation system of teaching quality in universities based on artificial intelligence neural network model. Math. Probl. Eng. **2022** (2022)

4. Shang, H., Hu, C.: Value orientation and development of ideological and political education based on artificial intelligence. J. Phys. Conf. Ser. **1852**(2), 022083 (2021). 6 p.

5. Ouyang, Z.: Research on teaching mode of ecological civilization education based on ideological and political courses in colleges and universities (2021)

6. Lu, L., Zhou, J.: Research on mining of applied mathematics educational resources based on edge computing and data stream classification. Mob. Inf. Syst. **2021**(7), 1–8 (2021)

7. Li, W.: A study on the construction of morality internalization of young teachers in colleges and universities. J. High. Educ. Res. **3**(1), 43–46 (2022)

8. Xia, C.Y., Yuan, Z.H., He, W.Y., et al.: An empirical study on scientific research performance of universities in different regions of China based on PCA and Malmquist index method. Educ. Res. Int. (2021)

9. Chen, L.: Research of the safety path of colleges and universities laboratory basing on the analysis of grey correlation degree. J. Intell. Fuzzy Syst. Appl. Eng. Technol. **40**(4) (2021)

10. Yang, L.H., Liu, B., Liu, J.: Research and development talents training in China universities—based on the consideration of education management cost planning. Sustainability **13** (2021)

Research on Practical Teaching Design of Applied College Mental Health Course in Virtual Simulation Scene

Gou Ying[✉] and Suyun Gan

Yunnan Technology and Business University, Kunming 651701, China
fanny850521@163.com

Abstract. Mental health courses are the main way for universities to carry out mental health education for college students, and also an important means to achieve high-quality talent cultivation. In recent years, due to the frequent occurrence of psychological problems among college students, the state attaches great importance to the effectiveness of college students' mental health courses, and has issued a series of policies and documents to guide the development of college students' mental health courses, in order to improve the effectiveness of college students' mental health education. Based on existing research, there are shortcomings in the traditional teaching mode of mental health courses, and the teaching effect needs to be improved. College students are in a period of rapid physical and mental development, and psychological health education for them is an important task for universities. This study is based on the research of practical teaching design for applied college mental health courses in virtual simulation scenarios. This study aims to explore how to use virtual simulation as a teaching method to improve learning quality. This study uses qualitative methods, namely, case studies and expert interviews, to test the effectiveness of different methods. In addition, there are two parts: theoretical background and practical application.

Keyword: mental health · Virtual simulation · Application oriented universities · Practical teaching

1 Introduction

Mental health education is an important part of ideological and political education. The Party and the state attach great importance to the psychological health and psychological quality training of college students. In 2001, the Opinions of the Ministry of Education on Strengthening the Psychological Health Education of College Students clearly stated the importance of psychological health education for college students, as well as the tasks, contents and methods of education [1]. In 2004, the Opinions on Further Strengthening and Improving the Ideological and Political Education of College Students emphasized the need to carry out in-depth and detailed mental health education [2]. The report of the 19th National Congress of the Communist Party of China clearly stated that we should

Y. Zhang and N. Shah (Eds.): BigIoT-EDU 2023, LNICST 581, pp. 275–285, 2024.
https://doi.org/10.1007/978-3-031-63133-7_27

strengthen the construction of the psychological service system. In the same year, 22 ministries and commissions jointly issued the Guiding Opinions on Strengthening Mental Health Services, which is the first document specially formulated for mental health work at the government level. The importance of mental health work has risen to the national level. Strengthening mental health education for college students is to implement the guidelines and policies of the Party and the country. Under the new historical conditions, college students' mental health education has been further improved and developed, and the rise of positive psychology has injected new vitality and vigor into mental health education [3].

Due to various factors such as the imbalance in the physical and psychological development of college students, the decline in traditional family education concepts and value systems, the increase in learning pressure, and the impact of networked society, interpersonal harassment, depression, and self harm are more prominent among college students, and psychological problems have seriously affected their normal lives. According to a survey conducted in the China National Mental Health Development Report (2019–2020), 18.5% of college students have a tendency to depression, while 4.2% have a high risk of depression; 8.4% have anxiety tendencies, and the mental health status of college students cannot be ignored. Therefore, it is a practical need to improve college students' mental health quality through mental health courses [4]. However, based on the current development of traditional college students' mental health courses, mental health courses are facing many challenges, such as lack of curriculum resources, insufficient teachers, and a single teaching form. It is difficult to mobilize students' learning enthusiasm and interest in curriculum teaching; In the teaching process, teachers often use the role of "leader" to help students acquire mental health knowledge, which makes it difficult for students to exert their subjectivity in the classroom, resulting in a large gap between the expected effect of mental health courses and reality, and it is difficult to improve students' mental health quality [5]. How to implement the mental health curriculum reform, enable students to fully exert classroom active learning, actively participate in curriculum teaching, and promote the improvement of the effectiveness of mental health courses, thereby promoting the improvement of students' mental health quality and application skills is a problem that must be considered in the development of mental health courses in universities.

With the development of modern information technology, it is possible to develop a highly simulated teaching system for real situations. Virtual simulation technology is based on multimedia technology, simulation technology and network communication technology. It uses computer software to build virtual systems to simulate the real world. Based on the virtual simulation technology, the scene and role enhancement experience are preset, and a multi-dimensional and multi-level experimental learning environment is created, which greatly improves students' learning interest and teachers' classroom teaching effect [6].

This research combines the teaching objectives and the characteristics of practical teaching of Consulting Psychology, combines the advantages of virtual simulation experiment technology, applies virtual simulation technology to the practical teaching of consulting psychology, and plans to build a virtual simulation experiment system suitable for the training of mental health workers, so as to achieve the curriculum objectives of making up for the limitations of traditional practical teaching, enriching experimental teaching content, and improving students' practical ability of psychological counseling.

2 Related Work

2.1 Mental Health

The traditional view is that the physiological function and body structure of the human body are in a normal state, and the absence of physical defects and diseases is health. In 1984, the World Health Organization (WHO) proposed that health is not only the absence of disease, but also the best physical, mental and social adaptation. And put forward seven standards of mental health, including good IQ; Be good at coordinating and controlling their emotions; Have good will quality; Harmonious interpersonal relationship; Actively adapt to and transform the objective environment; Personality integrity and health; Psychological age and physiological age adaptation [4]. The Third Mental Health Conference held that mental health is "the ability to develop one's own mind into a perfect state without contradicting others in physical, intellectual and emotional aspects." Ren Jun proposed in his book Le Shang, "No mental illness is not equal to health [7]. Mental health means that people can actively pursue happiness and experience happiness in their daily life, so that their abilities and potential can be fully exerted." Although there is no unified definition at home and abroad, it is indisputable that health should include good conditions at both physical and psychological levels, and only the coordinated development of the two aspects is the real sense of health [8].

"In order to meet the needs of social development and the development of individual mental health, mental health education came into being." Professor She Shuanghao pointed out that, "Mental health education is an educational practice based on the development law of individual physiology and psychology, purposefully and systematically using relevant psychological methods and countermeasures to exert influence on students' psychology, so as to help them form a good psychology and promote their all-round and harmonious development of body and mind." Professor She Shuanghao stressed that mental health education should help the educatees develop their potential and cultivate various excellent psychological qualities Improve psychological quality and prevent and eliminate psychological problems at the same time [9]. Professor Yan Guocai clearly pointed out that mental health education should include both positive and negative aspects. The positive aspect is to "cultivate psychological quality and promote all-round development; the negative aspect is to prevent and treat psychological diseases and achieve mental health." The views of the above two experts are consistent with the educational concept of positive psychology [10].

The curriculum of mental health includes theoretical learning and practical counseling operation training. The content of the curriculum is the systematic learning of theories of various schools of mental health and the simulation or real psychological counseling in counseling experiments. Psychological counseling practice is a necessary link for students to master psychological counseling theory and accumulate counseling experience. The traditional practice teaching method is to use case teaching, observation and demonstration teaching, psychological film appreciation and other teaching methods to carry out experimental training teaching through role playing between students and group simulation counseling.

The traditional teaching mode has the following difficulties: ① Special psychological symptoms are difficult to repeat. The research objects of mental health science include not only the psychology and behavior of normal people, but also the psychological symptoms of some special objects deviating from normal. Psychological activity is a dynamic process, and some special performances are difficult to repeat in the laboratory, such as unreasonable cognition, special emotions and suicide behaviors. ② The principle of confidentiality in psychological counseling is facing difficulties. The Code of Ethics for Clinical and Counseling Psychology of the Chinese Psychological Society clearly states that psychological consultants have the responsibility to protect the privacy of those seeking professional services. In the actual teaching, teachers cannot arrange students to observe the real psychological counseling process, and visitors will not reflect the real problems to the internship counselors. ③ Limitations of teaching methods. Mental health is an applied course with strong operability, and mental health techniques and methods can only be mastered in practice. The traditional counseling psychology skills course mainly adopts case teaching, observation and demonstration teaching, psychological film appreciation and other teaching methods, and exercises students' psychological counseling skills through role playing between students and group simulation consultation [11]. The fatigue effect, negative emotions and negative role play aroused during the experiment may cause harm to students' physical and mental health. ④ The accuracy of the simulation case. Due to the restriction of consulting ethics, students often lack enough real cases to observe and practice. In the process of practical teaching, many occasions are realized by simulating cases or role playing. Role play is a very difficult task. In addition to the above may cause additional harm to the players, the accuracy of role play is also one of the difficulties restricting the practice teaching of psychological counseling [12].

2.2 Virtual Simulation Technology

Virtual simulation is also known as virtual reality technology (VR) or simulation technology, while the two opposing words "virtual" and "reality" can be used together? The creator of the term "virtual" means that the world created through virtual technology is artificial, virtual, and not real; The word "reality" is used to describe the virtual world, although it is artificial and virtual, but for you who enter this virtual world, the feeling is the same as that of the real world and is real. Therefore, it is also called "virtual reality technology".

The so-called virtual simulation technology is a technology that uses computer technology to create objectively existing or non-existent things through computers, making people feel that everything around them is truly existing. It integrates users into a virtual environment through various sensing devices such as digital image processing, computer graphics, multimedia technology, and sensor technology [13]. It is a technology that enables users to interact directly and naturally with the environment. In this artificially created virtual environment, you will feel like real, feel like real, sound like real, look like real, and have an immersive feeling. For example, if you enter a virtual pulp and paper factory, you will see manufacturing instruments running, and the pulp on them is being processed to produce paper [14]. When you approach and observe, you will find that the instrument will continuously change with the distance you approach. You can see the specific process of production and the internal structure of the instrument, deeply understand the processing technology of paper making, and clearly hear the noisy processing noise generated by the operation of the instrument, making you immersive.

(1) The Teaching Purpose of Virtual Simulation Mental Health Education

In the virtual simulation mental health teaching design, teachers actively construct "scenarios" that meet the cognitive level of students, integrate students' original life experiences, cognition, attitudes, emotional experiences, and behavior patterns, and combine them with psychological principles and related theoretical knowledge, core values of sociology, Marxist methodology, and other elements. In the entire process of teaching and learning, students, under the guidance of teachers, deeply integrate, develop, recreate, and obtain new meanings from a series of cognitive and emotional activities, forming new psychological diagrams, further developing students' non-intellectual factors, and further improving their personality. This is the main purpose of the virtual simulation mental health teaching model [15].

(2) Teaching Methods of Virtual Simulation Mental Health Education

In the specific teaching process, the virtual simulation mental health education course uses various technical means to create curriculum models, such as using psychological counseling technology, including situational drama, educational narration, psychological maps, empty chair technology, role playing, and so on. Utilize modern information technology, such as VR, 3D, human-computer games, etc. Through the above technical means, actively explore the immersion path for learners, such as creating scenes through stories to achieve mental immersion, creating scenes through virtual technology to achieve visual immersion, and using various forms of music rendering to achieve auditory immersion.

3 Practical Teaching of Mental Health Courses Based on Virtual Simulation Technology

3.1 Problems in Practical Teaching in Application-Oriented Universities

The application-oriented colleges and universities have developed for more than 30 years, made many reforms and made a lot of progress, but there are still many problems in practical teaching, which can be generally divided into five categories. Here is an overview.

(1) High cost of practical teaching

With the development of science and technology, universities need to purchase a large number of advanced equipment and expensive experimental instruments for better development. In order to complete practical teaching, many equipment and machines need to be operated for a long time, and the operation cost, consumables cost, maintenance cost and repair cost are very high. The expensive running cost has become a big burden for colleges and universities, which is often overwhelmed in colleges and universities with insufficient funds, seriously affecting the quality of practical teaching.

(2) Poor adaptability of practical teaching

Traditional practice teaching is generally divided into practice on campus and practice off campus, with a single model and narrow adaptability. Teachers lack practical experience, and often rely on their own rare experience to analyze and explain cases, unable to guide students. Even in the practice class, due to the limitations of the teaching environment, some simulation operations can not be realized at all. On the contrary, the applied courses are not as smooth as the theoretical courses. The classroom teaching mode is single, which can not widely arouse students' interest [8]. As enterprises have many scruples about customer confidentiality, technology confidentiality and other aspects of off campus practice, students cannot get real practice, which is often a mere formality and fails to achieve the effect of practice.

(3) Practice teaching is difficult to cultivate students' vocational and technical personality

Confucius Saint emphasized teaching students in accordance with their aptitude 2500 years ago. Education is developing, but it still has its drawbacks. With the development of exam oriented education, the relationship between knowledge and ability has not been handled properly, and they have been "getting rich together". Different students use the same mode of education, and their personality is gradually deteriorating. Zhu Xi said in the Commentary on the Analects of Confucius: "Sages teach because of their talents, small success, big success, and no one gives up." The current situation of education is that there are more students and fewer teachers, and teachers are insufficient, which will inevitably lead to the failure to give consideration to the development of all people, and can only be treated the same way, and it is difficult to teach students in accordance with their aptitude [9].

(4) Difficulty in upgrading practical teaching

The traditional practical teaching mode is not strong enough in both software and hardware. It is very difficult to change the mode and upgrade the teaching mode. Among them, software includes limited teaching methods, teachers' level and experience, which often form an inherent model in teaching, with poor innovation. In terms of hardware, investors are often required, which makes some local colleges and universities flinch. It is difficult to purchase appropriate hardware equipment due to insufficient funds, which affects the quality and level of practical teaching, and it is difficult to cultivate students' comprehensive application quality.

3.2 Construction of Situational Teaching Model

Good teaching models and design are important conditions for successful teaching. The Dick Carey teaching model (Fig. 1) has a profound impact on teaching design due to its operational and systematic characteristics. The model is mainly composed of ten parts, including determining goals, teaching analysis, teaching object analysis, teaching strategy development, and summary evaluation.

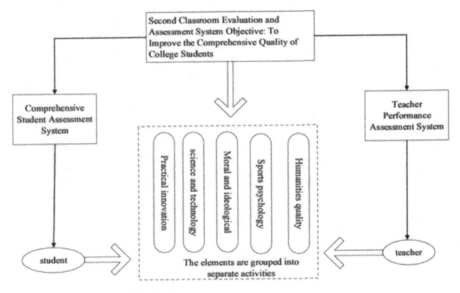

Fig. 1. Construction of situational teaching model

The so-called teaching goal refers to a clear statement of how teaching activities have changed students. All teaching activities are guided by and centered on teaching objectives, which are the ultimate goal of teaching activities and the main basis for objective teaching evaluation. Generally, we will carry out target design in accordance with the "three-dimensional goals" advocated by the country; The so-called teaching object analysis refers to the understanding of the knowledge base and learning situation of learners in teaching, and the selection of appropriate teaching content and learning resources based on their own teaching level and teaching requirements; The analysis of teaching content can be summarized as follows: studying textbooks, grasping textbooks, mining textbooks, and expanding textbooks. Teachers should effectively utilize teaching resources to supplement, improve, and enhance teaching content based on full understanding and familiarity with textbooks. Behavioral performance goals refer to a detailed statement of what students can do after teaching, mainly including three aspects: describing clear behaviors or skills in teaching, describing the conditions required for students to perform tasks, and describing specific criteria used to judge and evaluate students' behavioral performance.

Based on the Dick Carey teaching model, a teaching model combining virtual technology and mental health classes has been studied and designed to create a real teaching situation with the support of VR devices, as shown in Fig. 2.

In creating virtual teaching situations, teachers must first analyze and decompose teaching knowledge points, summarize learning content and teaching methods suitable for combining virtual devices, design and create corresponding teaching situations and tasks for specific teaching content , design teaching strategies, and organize teaching

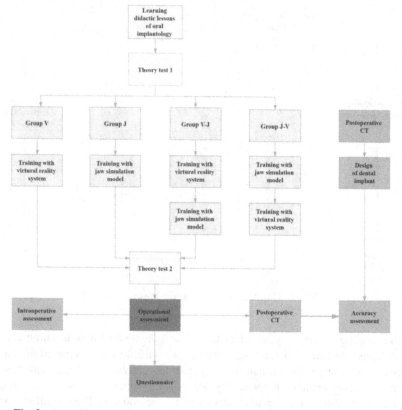

Fig. 2. A teaching model combining virtual technology with classroom teaching

activities. Among them, the commonly used teaching methods are: teaching method, demonstration method, problem situational teaching method, case situational teaching method, etc. According to the characteristics of different content, different teaching methods and strategies should be flexibly applied to give learners sufficient freshness.

4 Practical Teaching of Mental Health Course in Application-Oriented Colleges and Universities Under Virtual Simulation Scenario

The virtual simulation experiment teaching system, which aims at training mental health workers, adopts a mixed teaching mode of "online and offline, virtual reality combination", uses virtual simulation technology, and adopts such experimental teaching methods as scene interaction, scene observation, structured training, and online evaluation to cultivate the psychological consulting ability of students majoring in applied psychology, and uses "simulation experiments" to enable students to better master consulting skills. The overall experimental teaching process is shown in Fig. 3.

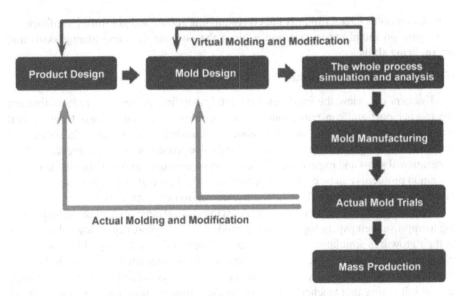

Fig. 3. Flow Chart of Virtual Simulation Practice Teaching

(1) Learning module

The virtual simulation psychological counseling experimental teaching system takes the psychological counseling room of the mental health center of Wenzhou Medical University as the background, minifies the real scene according to a certain proportion, and uses virtual simulation technology to build a psychological counseling environment, which can provide a large number of students with learning scenes at the same time. Psychological evaluation and diagnosis, scale evaluation and screening, and psychological counseling and treatment are the learning module stages. The psychological evaluation and diagnosis module and the scale evaluation and screening module include the basic information of the visitors and the case scale information. Through the intake talks and psychological evaluation of the virtual consultants and virtual visitors, combined with the theoretical knowledge of psychological diagnosis and psychological scale, students can make a preliminary diagnosis and differential diagnosis of the psychological problems in the cases. The module of psychological counseling and treatment includes the basic information of the chief complaint, the overview of counseling technology and the counseling record, and again provides the demographic information of the clients, the introduction and selection of different counseling schools, and the specific situation of the whole counseling process.

(2) Experimental operation module

The training operation and practice is the core module of the virtual simulation experiment system, including the intake talk, psychological diagnosis, differential diagnosis, psychological evaluation, psychological consultation and other stages of psychological consultation. After the first three learning module stages, students can interact with the experimental situation by observing the currently set experimental conditions. Through human-computer interaction, get the corresponding scores and get timely feedback, so as to gain profound experience and achieve the purpose of strengthening skills and internalizing skills.

(3) Feedback and review module

Teachers can view the entire experimental operation process of students through the teacher port and can participate in the entire experimental process to guide and guide students. Effectively mobilize students' learning interest and enthusiasm, and improve their comprehensive ability to find and solve problems. Students' preview effect, experimental steps and experimental results can be evaluated and statistically analyzed. Common problems can be explained according to background inspection, and extended problems can be put forward for interactive discussion with students.

Immersive mental health education serves the general development of students, aiming to improve their psychological quality, guide them to explore psychological problems in their growth in simulated situations, cultivate their ability to solve problems scientifically, establish positive values and thinking orientation, integrate knowledge and action, improve their personality, and achieve comprehensive physical and mental development. It is worth noting that teachers have transformed from the traditional "protagonist" of the classroom to the "organizer" of the classroom, serving as situational participants and team mentors. This puts forward higher requirements for teachers, who not only need to have a solid psychological foundation, but also need to have a process oriented teaching philosophy and scientific methods. Learning in the VR virtual simulation environment increases the interest and creativity of teaching, and also puts forward higher requirements for the support of the campus information environment. VR instructional design requires the joint efforts of VR technicians and mental health teachers. Currently, the research on VR technology mostly stays at the technical level, making the integration of VR technology and mental health education require long-term in-depth exploration.

5   Conclusion

Virtual simulation practice teaching is a new trend in the field of education, which has driven the development of the teaching mode of application-oriented colleges and universities. It is a win-win situation for students and schools. Through virtual simulation practice teaching, students have more and deeper understanding of knowledge theory and practical practice, stimulate students' interest in learning, cultivate students' professional and technical personality, and cultivate more professional technical talents. For schools, through the operation of virtual simulation practice teaching mode, the investment and maintenance costs of equipment and instruments are reduced, and the saved funds can be used in more places that need investment, which improves the competitiveness of colleges and universities.

References

1. Liu, C.: Research on system platform design of applied statistics teaching in colleges and universities. In: Jan, M.A., Khan, F. (eds.) BigIoT-EDU 2021. LNICST, vol 391, pp. 168–174. Springer, Cham (2021). https://doi.org/10.1007/978-3-030-87900-6_20
2. Lv, H., Ling, J., Li, J.: Research on simulation system model of diesel engine applied to virtual calibration development. J. Phys. Conf. Ser. **1982**(1), 012149 (2021). 7 p.
3. Zhou, H., Guan, Y., Huang, L.: Innovative research on practical teaching of ideological and political course in higher vocational colleges of traditional Chinese medicine (1) (2021)
4. Li, D.: Research on teaching design of colleges mathematics micro-course based on the perspective of network teaching platform. J. Phys. Conf. Ser. **1915**(2), 022078 (2021). 7 p.
5. Liu, S.: Practical research on constructing college basketball curriculum with the concept of health first. J. High. Educ. Res. **2**(5) (2021)
6. Alkaabi, M., Mohamed, M., Alshehhi, M., et al.: Design of a microfluidic photocatalytic reactor for removal of volatile organic components: process simulation and techno-economic assessment. ACS Omega **7**(10), 8306–8313 (2022)
7. Hu, N.: Research on the application of VR technology in clothing design teaching. In: ICIMTECH 21: The Sixth International Conference on Information Management and Technology (2021)
8. Cui, H., Yan, Z., Zhang, B., et al.: Research on atmospheric lidar signal simulation based on HITRAN database. Chin. J. Space Sci. **40**(6), 1046–1051 (2022)
9. Ianì, F., Limata, T., Bucciarelli, M., et al.: The implicit effect of action mental simulation on action evaluation. Q. J. Exp. Psychol. **76**(2), 257–270 (2023)
10. Xu, Y., Qin, L., Xu, X.: Research on the method of implementing named data network interconnection based on IP network (2022)
11. Liu, X., Wu, Z.: Research on spatial cognition of engineering management students based on virtual simulation teaching. In: Guo, H., Fang, D., Lu, W., Peng, Y. (eds.) CRIOCM 2021. LNOR, pp. 1454–1464. Springer, Singapore (2022). https://doi.org/10.1007/978-981-19-5256-2_112
12. Deng, Y., Gao, Z., Wang, Z.: Research on teaching method of EDA simulation design based on numerical calculation (2021)
13. Wang, P., Hu, Y., Huo, J.: Practical teaching and research on the design of below-created products in the era of big data (2022)
14. Wang, X.: Analysis of big data survey results and research on system construction of computer specialty system (2022)
15. Carey, T.A., Gullifer, J.: Handbook of Rural, Remote, and very Remote Mental Health (2021)

Teaching Reform of Modern Optimization Algorithm Course Based on MOOC

Shumei Jin[1,2]([✉]), Lijun Huang[1,2], and Xiaojie Jiang[1,2]

[1] Suqian University, Suqian 223699, Jiangsu, China
shirlytang2022@163.com

[2] Yan'an Branch of Shaanxi Roadie and Television University and Television University,
Shaanxi 716000, China

Abstract. The research on teaching reform of modern optimization algorithms based on MOOC is a research carried out by researchers at the University of Tokyo in Japan. The purpose of this study is to determine whether students' learning outcomes and cognition have changed after using MOOC based modern optimization algorithm courses. This is one of the most important aspects of teaching because it determines how students will learn and what they will be able to do with the knowledge gained from this course. This article first analyzes the principles and methods of association rules and collaborative filtering, analyzes and designs the recommendation system in response to actual business scenarios, and proposes a fusion recommendation scheme. Then, through association analysis, it collects and collates relevant data on students' learning conditions in the MOKE system, and merges and integrates the student achievement data to be mined to obtain time series data of students' elective courses and achievements; And use discretization and data sparsization for preprocessing to obtain highly structured data items that can be mined and processed using Veka. The main purpose of this study is to assess whether there are differences between traditional courses taught by professors and courses taught through online platforms, try to find solutions to the current problems of college students' low learning efficiency, lack of initiative, and low knowledge conversion rate, and strive to recommend courses that are more suitable for their learning and conducive to their long-term development and planning.

Keyword: Modern optimization algorithm · MOOC · reform in education

1 Introduction

At present, there are a large number of data that can describe students' learning situation and learning process, such as students' historical scores, accumulated and stored in the educational administration and teaching platform of colleges and universities. However, these data are not really well applied at present, and their processing is still lingering in the primary data entry, backup and statistical query stages, without analyzing and mining the deeper significance hidden in these data. This research attempts to use Data

Y. Zhang and N. Shah (Eds.): BigIoT-EDU 2023, LNICST 581, pp. 286–296, 2024.
https://doi.org/10.1007/978-3-031-63133-7_28

Mining technology to analyze these achievement data from multiple angles and explore them deeply, so as to find potential laws and hidden patterns [1]. Finally, an algorithm and service integrating data collection, data processing, data analysis and course recommendation will be formed to better guide students to choose courses and improve their learning efficiency.

This research will use the data analysis platform of the open source system Weka to analyze the learning data of real students in the online learning platform, select the student data to be tested for data pre-processing, and then conduct an Aprioir based association analysis according to the pre-processing results. By comparing the analysis results of different experimental parameters, we can find the optimal association model. Then the collaborative filtering recommendation is used to generate recommendations for the corresponding students according to the course selection and performance of the adjacent students of the target students, as well as the collection category of the course itself, so as to achieve accurate and effective recommendations [2].

The development of the massive open online course (MOOC) system in recent years has promoted the further improvement of traditional educational resources and early traditional distance education. It not only expands the coverage of education, optimizes students' learning methods, but also further enriches and expands the optimal allocation of educational resources [3]. This will make it easier and more efficient for people in remote areas who are short of educational resources and learning time to access educational resources; At the same time, it also provides a convenient and effective knowledge sharing channel for more people with knowledge and skills. Through the effective integration of education "entrance and exit" resources, it is conducive to upgrading and optimizing the existing social education resource distribution model, expanding knowledge acquisition channels, and meeting the new needs of modern people for knowledge and self-improvement. The construction of the MOOC platform has provided a large number of high-quality teaching resources for higher education teaching activities, profoundly changing the teaching mode of higher education, and posing greater challenges to the traditional higher education classroom. The development of higher education needs to give full play to the advantages of the MOOC platform, reform traditional teaching classrooms, develop personalized education models, mobilize students' learning enthusiasm, improve teaching quality, and cultivate students' autonomous learning ability. Therefore, how to make full use of the shared resources of the MOOC platform, promote the reform of traditional classrooms, learn from each other's strengths, and improve the teaching management level of higher education has become an urgent issue for teaching workers.

The mode of using MOOC platform to carry out online classroom has been relatively mature, and there are more relevant studies at home and abroad. However, online classes have shortcomings such as low completion rates, lack of participation, and little interaction between students. Therefore, scholars have begun to attempt to combine MOOC with actual classroom research. The main teaching applications of MOOC in China include using the MOOC platform as a source of information for students to preview courses, using MOOC as an interactive platform for teachers and students, and studying hybrid teaching models based on MOOC. However, there are relatively few relevant studies that combine MOOC with actual classroom situations to carry out specific course teaching designs.

Aiming at the problems existing in the teaching of traditional modern optimization algorithm courses, this article makes full use of the high-quality resources of famous teachers from famous schools on the MOOC platform, utilizes students' spare time to conduct independent learning, combines case driven teaching and team discussion in the classroom, uses the MOOC platform to conduct homework correction and teaching feedback after class, and designs a scientific and reasonable course evaluation system to overcome the outdated traditional teaching knowledge and slow update speed To improve the teaching effect of modern optimization algorithm courses for students with low learning enthusiasm. Finally, based on the evaluation system, the author analyzed the teaching effect for three years, and the results showed that the new teaching mode based on the MOOC platform can significantly improve the teaching quality of modern optimization algorithm courses.

2   Related Work

2.1   Research on MOOC Initiated Educational Reform

With the continuous development of MOOC, teachers and scholars gradually realized the impact of MOOC on teaching and began to reflect and reform teaching. Li Liping, in the Research on New Perspectives of University Teaching Mode Reform under the Background of "Mourning for Classes", believed that MOOC has impacted the traditional classroom teaching mode, teaching courses, teaching concepts and teacher-student relationship, and has promoted the teaching reform of universities. Universities should take MOOC as an opportunity to carry out teaching reform in terms of innovative teaching methods, building core courses, and teachers' active guidance, so as to further utilize the advantages of MOOC, Strengthen the social service function of universities, so as to improve the quality of education. In MOOC 3.0: Teaching Reform Towards University Noumenon, Zheng Yajun and others viewed MOOC with a rational attitude, abandoned the two attitudes of cold shoulder and "taking", rationally responded to the opportunities and challenges brought by MOOC, reflected on today's university classroom, updated the university teaching concept, and combined large-scale online open courses with traditional classroom, thus promoting the innovation of traditional teaching mode [6]. Professor Zhu Jing analyzed the innovation of MOOC and the opportunities that MOOC brings to local universities in the Analysis of MOOCs' Reference to the Teaching Reform of Local Universities. He believed that MOOC was conducive to the sharing of high-quality resources, eased the shortage of teachers, and provided an opportunity to contact multiculturalism. Therefore, he proposed that local universities in China should learn from the advantages and successes of MOOC. In The Rise of MOOC and the Reform of University Teaching Management, Yu Xiangting pointed out that only by incorporating MOOC into the formal talent training system and teaching management system of universities can MOOC be truly implemented in universities and play its positive role in promoting teaching reform. He believed that MOOC has an important impact on the training program, teaching process and quality management of teaching management. Universities should strengthen professional planning, curriculum construction, teaching organization The exploration of many aspects, such as quality assurance and certification, has constantly promoted the deep integration of information technology and curriculum teaching. In addition, universities should combine the characteristics of the new generation of students with the trend of social development to study, so as to provide high-quality education that conforms to social development and student growth.

2.2 Selection of Clustering Algorithms for Learning Behavior Analysis

(1) Introduction to K-means algorithm

K-means algorithm is a classic and commonly used data mining algorithm. The main idea is to calculate the distance from each point to the cluster center based on the given number of clusters and the initial cluster center, allocate all data points to the nearest cluster center class, recalculate the cluster center in each class, and then calculate the distance from all points to the new center point again and allocate it to the nearest one. Repeat the above steps until the cluster center stabilizes or the iteration number reaches the preset value.

Suppose the data sample is X, where there are n objects $X = \{X1, X2, X3,..., Xn\}$, and each object has m attribute dimensions. To achieve this, first initialize k cluster centers $\{C1, C2, C3,..., Cn\}$, $1 \leq k \leq n$, and then calculate the Euclidean distance from each object to each cluster center, as shown in the following formula:

$$dis(X_i, C_j) = \sqrt{\sum_{t=1}^{m} (X_i - C_{jt})^2} \tag{1}$$

In the above formula, Xi represents the ith object, $1 \leq i \leq n$, Cj represents the jth cluster center, $1 \leq j \leq k$, Xit represents the t-th attribute of the ith object, $1 \leq t \leq m$, and Cjt represents the t-th attribute of the jth cluster center.

At this point, it is necessary to compare the distance between the object and the center point one by one, and divide each object into the class to which the closest center point belongs, to obtain k class clusters $\{K1, K2, K3,..., Kn\}$. Recalculate the coordinates of the class center point. The new center point is determined by all objects in the class, so its value should be the average value of each object in each dimension. The calculation formula is as follows:

$$C_t = \frac{\sum_{Xi \in Sl} X_i}{|S_l|} \tag{2}$$

K-means algorithm is simple and easy to understand, with strong interpretability of results, and small square error of calculated categories. It has good results when data is relatively dense and there are significant differences between categories. It can also maintain high efficiency when processing large data sets. However, its shortcomings are also very obvious. The algorithm is too dependent on initial parameters, and it is difficult to determine appropriate parameters. The algorithm has weak anti-interference ability, and the calculation of center point coordinates will be affected by noise points and isolated points, resulting in deviation in the results. It is possible to overemphasize local optimization while ignoring the overall clustering effect. Moreover, K-means algorithm only performs well in clustering spherical data, and is not effective for non concave data or data with too large scale differences.

(2) Introduction to DBSCAN algorithm

The DBSCAN algorithm uses the degree of tightness between objects as a measure of similarity. Some parameters and basic concepts in the algorithm are as follows:

1) Eps represents the cluster radius
2) MinPts represents the minimum number of objects in a given Eps neighborhood.
3) Core points. The number of objects within the cluster radius is greater than MinPts.
4) Boundary points. It is not a core point in itself, but is located in the neighborhood of a core point
5) Noise points. Points remaining except for core and boundary points.
6) Direct density up to. Point to core points within the core point cluster radius are referred to as direct density reachable.
7) The density can reach. Point to core points that are not within the cluster radius of the core point but are within the cluster radius of points that are directly density reachable by the core point are called density reachable.
8) Density connected. The average density of two points starting from a core point can reach, and the two points are connected in density.

The specific process is as follows: Select any point from the dataset, first determine whether the point is a core point. If so, find a set with the maximum density connected to form a cluster. If the point is not a core point, discard it and search again until the core point is found. Repeat the above steps until all points have been processed to obtain the final clustering result. DBSCAN's clustering method enables it to accurately locate noise points. The idea is to separate high density areas from low density areas, where

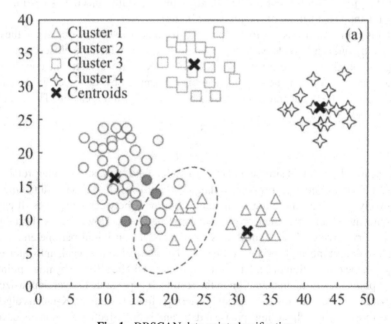

Fig. 1. DBSCAN data point classification

the points are boundary points or noise points. The classification of data points is shown in Fig. 1.

3 MOOC Based Modern Optimization Algorithm Teaching

3.1 MOOC Based Modern Optimization Algorithm Teaching Framework

Modern optimization algorithm courses still generally adopt classroom teaching mode. The course teaching focuses on algorithms, teaching the theoretical basis and application of algorithms respectively. However, this teaching model separates teaching from learning and does not focus on students, so there are many shortcomings:

(1) Learner autonomy is limited. In traditional teaching models, teachers give priority to teaching. Students' autonomy and initiative have not been brought into play and lack the space for independent thinking. Therefore, students can only remember knowledge points to cope with the exam.
(2) Learners are forced to adapt to the curriculum. The traditional teaching mode adopts the form of "flood irrigation". Teachers can only conduct teaching activities at a certain speed. However, students' acceptance abilities vary, which can lead to some students feeling that the course is too simple to listen to, while others feel that the course is too difficult to follow.
(3) The level of teachers determines the curriculum. The traditional teaching mode puts forward high requirements for teachers' teaching ability. The teaching level of a teacher determines the quality of a course. If teachers lack teaching experience and control over the curriculum, it is easy to lead to poor teaching results.
(4) Course updates are slow. With the development of computer science and technology, new optimization algorithms and their improvements emerge endlessly. These latest research findings need to be added to the teaching content of the course, allowing students to closely monitor the development trends in computer science and technology.
(5) This course is difficult to popularize. The establishment of traditional courses requires a large number of teachers with both teaching skills and professional knowledge to conduct theoretical teaching. Modern optimization algorithms are a new field of computer science, which urgently requires a large number of professional teachers to teach. However, the training period for qualified teachers is too long to adapt to the pace of development of science and technology.

The teaching framework based on MOOC is very different from the traditional teaching model. It mainly designs the classroom as a student-centered teaching activity, makes full use of MOOC platform resources, and allows students to choose appropriate video resources to learn knowledge points according to their interests. The interaction between teachers and students in the classroom is mainly used to answer questions about important and difficult points, and consolidate knowledge points in combination with case teaching, And assist students to complete the generation of solutions [8]. The teaching based on MOOC can change the orientation of students from passive learners to active learners, and give full play to their subjective initiative; The orientation of teachers has changed from lecturers to organizers and guides of learning activities. Teachers use the

curriculum resources of MOOC platform to teach students, and are responsible for organizing collaboration and answering questions in the process. Teachers are only required
to have professional knowledge related to modern optimization algorithms. Even teachers who do research on modern optimization algorithms can quickly build a curriculum
construction system, greatly shortening the training cycle of teachers; At the same time,
teachers can also use MOOC resources to quickly update the teaching content, reducing
the difficulty of curriculum promotion [9]. The teaching framework of MOOC based
modern optimization algorithm course is shown in Fig. 2.

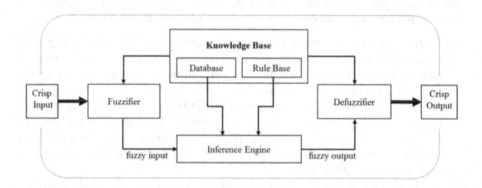

Fig. 2. MOOC based Modern Optimization Algorithm Teaching Framework

3.2 MOOC Based Modern Optimization Algorithm Course Teaching Case Design

The stage of classroom teaching and interaction is mainly conducted in the multimedia
classroom, which is divided into three parts: key and difficult points explanation, question
answering and problem-solving, and case based teaching. Through the teaching and
interaction of the three parts, the knowledge points of the course are connected in series to
guide the students to apply the knowledge learned in the classroom to practical problems
and improve the students' ability to solve practical problems [10].

① Explain the key and difficult points. According to the questions collected on the
   MOOC platform in the pre class preparation stage, analyze the common key and
   difficult points fed back by the students in the course, use the multimedia teaching
   method to string together the knowledge points, and consolidate the students' mastery
   of the key and difficult points. For example, if students have questions about the
   operation mode of the tournament selection operator of genetic algorithm, they can
   use examples to explain the knowledge points in the multimedia courseware.
② Answer questions. For individual students' personality problems fed back on the
   MOOC platform or problems arising from classroom teaching, the teacher adopts
   one-to-one explanation to guide students, and adopts the method of guiding students

to think about and solve problems themselves, which not only improves students' participation and sense of achievement, but also avoids personality problems occupying the common time of all students. For example, the binary encoding and decoding of genetic algorithms can guide students to think about the conversion relationship between binary and decimal systems, and think analogically, so as to understand the encoding and decoding methods of genetic algorithms.

Teaching strategies: ① Make full use of the key and difficult problems fed back by the students to make multimedia courseware, grasp the key points of the course teaching content, and avoid the pursuit of comprehensiveness that leads to the lack of focus; ② Give one-to-one guidance to personality problems, guide students to solve problems independently through their own thinking, analogy, induction and summary; ③ Build simple and understandable cases for teaching, prevent students from being afraid of difficulties, and gradually improve students' ability to solve practical problems; ④ Create a good atmosphere for team discussion and encourage all participants to participate in interaction.

This new MOOC can provide students with a variety of resources and materials, and the teaching content of each related discipline is mainly composed of related videos and corresponding exercises and tests. The relevant videos, materials, and courseware on this website have been strictly selected and processed, which can well ensure the targeted and systematic learning of students. In addition to each class, there is also a very professional after-school testing section. After learning online and passing the test, you can apply for corresponding credits from relevant institutions and departments. Most of these teaching resources come from universities around the world. All students only need to register information on the website, and after logging in, they can enjoy unparalleled free and high-quality teaching resources on campus.

4   Comparison of MOOC Teaching Effects

(1) Appraisal System Settings

The assessment of students in the course mainly involves not only assessing their mastery of knowledge points, but also assessing their comprehensive practical ability, as well as their language expression ability and organizational ability in teaching activities. The comprehensive quality of students is examined from various aspects, and it is also necessary to comprehensively reflect their participation in the course and the completion of course assignments on the online MOOC platform and offline teaching classes. Therefore, it is necessary to build a scientific and reasonable evaluation system. The modern optimization algorithm course evaluation system and its weights designed in this article are shown in Table 1. The evaluation system for students in the modern optimization algorithm course mainly includes three parts: usual scores, course practice, and final exams.

1) Usual performance: Usual performance accounts for 30%, mainly including MOOC online evaluation, classroom performance, and homework assignments. Among them, MOOC online evaluation accounts for 10%, mainly evaluating the scores of students

Table 1. Course assessment system and weight

	Evaluation method	proportion	explain
Peacetime performance	MOOC online evaluation	10%	Evaluate based on MOOC platform mini test
	Classroom performance	10%	Attendance, classroom participation, team discussions
	Homework after class	10%	Completion of homework after class
Course Practice	Achievement of major assignments	20%	Evaluate based on course practical work scores
final exam	Examination results	50%	Evaluate based on written test scores

in the MOOC platform quizzes during the pre class preparation stage, mainly reflecting whether the students' pre class preparation is sufficient; Classroom performance accounts for 10%, mainly evaluating students' attendance, classroom participation, and team discussions, accounting for 3%, 3%, and 4%, respectively; The proportion of homework after class is 10%, mainly evaluating the completion of students' homework after class, and evaluating whether students have fully grasped the teaching content.

2) Course practice: Course practice accounts for 20%, mainly for students to use Matlab tools to program and implement modern optimization algorithms based on their knowledge to solve practical problems given by teachers. This part is an assessment of students' hands-on ability. For example, teachers can require students to use Matlab programming to implement genetic algorithms to solve vehicle routing optimization problems, and visually display the optimization process and results of the problem.

3) Final exam: The exam score accounts for 50%, mainly assessing students' mastery of the theoretical knowledge of modern optimization algorithms. The exam paper should try to achieve comprehensive coverage of knowledge points and reasonable weight distribution. After the completion of the course, the scores will be comprehensively evaluated. Those who score 90 points or above will be considered excellent, and those who score 60 points or above will be considered qualified. The participants evaluate the course using a 100 point system, with a full score of 100 points.

(2) Comparison of assessment results

In order to evaluate the new teaching mode based on the MOOC platform, this article collected and compared the teaching records of the modern optimization algorithm course from 2016 to 2018. Among them, in 2016, students generated teaching data under the traditional teaching mode, in 2017, they first used the new teaching mode based on the MOOC platform to generate teaching data, and in 2018, they generated teaching data to improve the teaching content under the MOOC platform teaching mode based on previous 2017 student feedback.

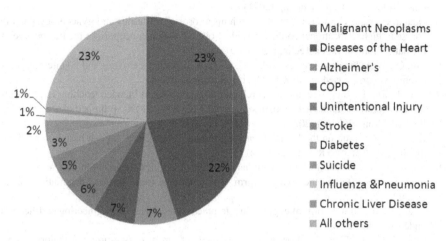

Fig. 3. Student performance and evaluation statistics

As shown in Fig. 3, compared to the traditional teaching mode in 2016, the application of the new teaching mode based on the MOOC platform has led to a significant increase in the excellent rate and qualified rate of students, as well as a significant improvement in the average score of students' evaluation of the course, fully demonstrating that students' love for the course has been improved and the teaching effect has been further improved.

5   Conclusion

According to the characteristics of the modern optimization algorithm course, this paper discusses the operation mode of the new teaching mode based on MOOC platform. This mode can give full play to the advantages of the MOOC platform with many teaching resources, high quality and good interactivity, so that students become the center of teaching. Teachers, as the organizers and questioners of teaching activities, guide students to learn modern optimization algorithms, and improve their enthusiasm for learning, It has achieved good teaching effect. The experience of this model can be extended to other computer courses, which provides a new idea for the teaching reform of computer courses.

References

1. Yang, S.: Teaching reform of database course based on the concept of outcome-based education. J. Contemp. Educ. Res. **2021**(3) (2021)
2. Wang, N., Li, Z., Zhang, B.: Discussion on the teaching model of subject participation based on the map teaching method taking the course reform of geography of international trade (2021)

3. Liu, D.: Research on the reform direction of ideological and political course teaching based on online open courses. Math. Probl. Eng. Theory Meth. Appl. **2021**(Pt.53) (2021)
4. Wei, Q.: Research on the teaching reform of accounting course under the background of innovation and entrepreneurship (2021)
5. Huang, S., Cao, H., Yan, L., et al.: Teaching reform of obstetrics and gynecology nursing course in higher vocational colleges based on obe education concept from the perspective of big data. Biomed. J. Sci. Techn. Res. **37**(2021)
6. Liu, Q., Wan, X.: Practical research on the application characteristics and countermeasures of online course based on MOOC. Open J. Soc. Sci. (2021)
7. Gao, J., Zhi, L., Sun, J., et al.: Research on the application of blended teaching in probability theory and mathematical statistics based on MOOC + SPOC + flipped classroom. Sci. Publish. Group **2021**(6) (2021)
8. Zhao, Y.: Research on the blended teaching model of university english based on artificial intelligence. Tobacco Regul. Sci. (2021)
9. Yu, L., Li, Z.: Discussion on situational teaching of business negotiation course based on practical mode: taking the course reform of international trade business negotiations as an example (2021)
10. Chen, Y.: Teaching reform of engineering graphics course based on engineering certification under big data (2021)
11. Cui, Y., He, F., Feng, X.: Research on teaching reform of design-oriented majors in colleges and universities based on innovation and entrepreneurship education. In: 2020 3rd international seminar on education research and social science (ISERSS 2020) (2021)
12. Tian, D., Wang, T.: Research on teaching reform of operating system course under the mode of school enterprise coordination and education (2021)
13. Shen, H.: On the teaching reform of translation course based on the cultivation of applied talents (2021)
14. Zhang, W., Li, J.: Research on the teaching reform of electronic information specialty based on the concept of cdio engineering education. J. Phys. Conf. Ser. **1744**(4), 042236 (6pp) (2021)
15. Hu, S., Huang, M.: Teaching reform of practical training course for financial management major in higher vocational colleges based on skills. IPEC 2021: 2021 2nd asia-pacific conference on image processing, electronics and computers (2021)

Construction and Application of Medical Laboratory Virtual Simulation Training Teaching Platform Under the Background of Big Data

Chun Xie[✉] and Lirong He

Shangqiu Medical College, Shangqiu 476100, Henan, China
794442734@qq.com

Abstract. The era of big data has quietly arrived, and the education field has already felt the wave of big data. Because the school has a large number of students and can conveniently collect a large amount of data, it has become an existing institution that can make full use of the energy of big data. Virtual simulation has gradually entered the field of medical laboratory education and has incomparable advantages over traditional experimental teaching. Combining with the application status of medical laboratory technology and virtual simulation, this paper discusses the construction and characteristic innovation of virtual simulation training teaching platform, and uses the self-built virtual simulation training teaching platform to practice teaching under the epidemic situation, and achieves satisfactory results. Carrying out virtual simulation experiment teaching can strengthen students' basic experimental skills, stimulate students' thirst for knowledge, cultivate students' creativity and improve students' professional skills, which is of great significance in medical laboratory virtual simulation training teaching.

Keyword: Big data · Medical examination · Virtual simulation · Practical training teaching

1 Introduction

In the era of big data, the importance of virtual simulation in the experimental teaching of medical laboratory specialty has become increasingly prominent [1]. Under the background of modern information education, the traditional offline teaching can no longer adapt to the development trend of medical education [2], and the strategy of combining virtual simulation with other industries by using the Internet platform and creating a new layout has become the main innovation drive of social development [3, 4]. How to use big data to improve students' learning status and learning efficiency is very important for schools, because traditional schools have gradually entered a period when they have to face new competitors in the field of education.

Virtual simulation technology called virtual reality is a computer system that can create a virtual world and apply it to it. By using various interactive devices, the system

Y. Zhang and N. Shah (Eds.): BigIoT-EDU 2023, LNICST 581, pp. 297–305, 2024.
https://doi.org/10.1007/978-3-031-63133-7_29

makes the virtual environment interact with entities, so that operators can have original interactive vision and exchange information automatically [5]. The virtual experiment teaching aims at fulfilling the teaching requirements and contents, and comprehensively applies networked, digital and intelligent technical means such as multimedia, big data, 3D modeling, artificial intelligence, man-machine interaction, sensors, supercomputing, virtual reality, augmented reality and cloud computing to improve the attractiveness and teaching effectiveness of experimental teaching projects [6]. In order to change the existing problems, we established a virtual simulation platform for medical laboratory experiment teaching by using the campus network. The advantages of the network platform, such as abundant resources, rapid update, convenience, economy, no time and space constraints, and no biosafety accidents, have been used in medical laboratory experiment teaching, and achieved good teaching results.

2 Necessity of Constructing Virtual Experimental Teaching Platform

2.1 The Need of Medical Development in the New Era

Medical development has entered the era of big data, and precision medicine has become the development direction of clinical medicine. The original step-by-step experimental teaching system can no longer fully meet the needs of cultivating innovative talents in the era of big data, and needs the assistance and supplement of computer-aided systems and mathematical models to complete some high-end automated, intelligent and high-throughput inspection experiments.

However, in reality, it is difficult for us to repeat the modern high-automated high-throughput testing project with classical methods. Therefore, virtual simulation experiment teaching has become an inevitable supplementary means.

2.2 Internal Drive of Medical Experimental Teaching

The high risk of medical experiments. The safety of students and the environment cannot be guaranteed yet. For example, the experiments of highly pathogenic microorganisms and radioactive and highly toxic substances require very high experimental conditions, which do not provide the conditions for setting up experiments. Even if they are set up, teachers and students will face great risks.

The open virtual experimental teaching system has the characteristics of good interactivity, openness and sharing, which enriches the experimental content, increases students' hands-on opportunities and provides a means for experimental teaching reform. At the same time, the center integrates the original teaching platform resources, breaks the discipline and curriculum restrictions of experimental teaching content, and forms a systematic virtual experimental teaching system based on organs, systems and diseases, which conforms to the law and development trend of medical teaching, and provides the necessary guarantee for the training of high-quality compound and applied medical related talents. Therefore, it is particularly necessary for medical colleges to set about building a medical virtual simulation experimental platform.

2.3 Effective Ways to Improve Teachers' and Students' Information Literacy

Teachers engaged in virtual simulation experiment teaching should not only be familiar with experimental teaching and technology in this field, but also have a high foundation of information quality, be familiar with and accurately according to the requirements of virtual experiment, and constantly update and adjust experimental methods and means, so as to keep the experimental teaching contents and methods scientific and advanced. At the same time, students not only learn the experimental content, but also enhance their ability to acquire knowledge by using network information technology [7, 8]. Therefore, carrying out virtual simulation experiments can speed up the training of young teachers and improve the information literacy of students and teachers in an all-round way.

2.4 Conducive to the Cultivation of Innovative Talents

Talent training needs to be transformed from knowledge teaching to ability teaching, and the virtual simulation experiment platform provides a stage for this training. Through virtual instruments and equipment, experiments can be carried out repeatedly, and experimental operations that are impossible in clinic can be realized, which can not only cultivate students' practical ability, but also train students' clinical diagnostic thinking.

3 Platform Structure Frame

3.1 Build a Pre-experiment Module

The experimental operation software is developed, and some commonly used experiments with large experimental consumables and potential biosafety hazards are constructed into virtual experimental modules. Students can conduct the pre-experiment of each experiment on the Internet, and they need to choose their own equipment, equipment and inspection procedures for the experiment.

The ideal results can appear when all the choices are correct, and the experimental results may be deviated or the next experiment cannot be carried out when the choices are wrong or wrong, thus prompting the students to preview the experimental contents in advance and master the application principles and scope of various experimental equipment, so that the students are familiar with the experimental contents and operation on the virtual experimental platform, which provides more intuitive resources for students to preview the experiment before class and review after class.

Combining the teaching content of the platform with typical cases, the experimental principle, development course, instrument structure, operation steps and clinical significance of the results of the project are comprehensively and systematically answered.

3.2 Structure of Virtual Training Teaching Platform

Database is a tool to organize data according to data structure, and to store and manage it. All databases need to provide API interfaces for creating database tables, adding data, querying data and copying stored data. A database is a structured file used to store specific types of data. A table is composed of columns, in which a series of information is stored. The data in the table is stored in rows; A unique identifier in a table is called a primary key and represents a specific row.

MySQL under Windows is one of the best applications of relational database management system. It manages the data in the library through mathematical concepts and methods such as set algebra. Based on the characteristics of small size, fast query speed, cost and open source, MySQL is chosen as the database solution of this research system.

Using SQL Server database to plan and manage the virtual simulation training teaching platform. Platform management includes user management, curriculum management, resource management and examination management. The user management development software is C/S architecture, and the client and server are set up. The server independently builds the database and the server, and the client realizes the interactive operation of virtual experiment in the three-dimensional virtual scene.

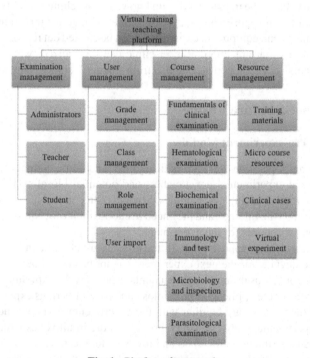

Fig. 1. Platform framework

Including grade management, class management, role management and user import; The curriculum management is divided into six modules according to the medical laboratory courses: clinical laboratory basis, hematology laboratory, biochemical laboratory, immunology and laboratory, microbiology and laboratory, and parasitology laboratory.

The resources of each course are divided into practical training materials, micro-course resources, clinical cases and virtual experiments according to the content.

Resource management is convenient for teachers to add, delete, edit and shield exper-imental contents according to their own teaching ideas. Examination management includes administrators, teachers and students, as shown in Fig. 1.

4   Realization of Virtual Training Teaching Platform

4.1   Scene Building

Unity3D is an integrated development environment, including game engine kernel and graphical development interface, which provides high-quality and efficient development services for developers. Users can see different divided windows when using the Unity3D editor, and they will provide different functions. During the development process, users can drag and drop objects to perform special binding actions between different forms. At the same time, developers can use the programming environment combined with rich API to write scripts and realize customized functions. Unity3D supports the import of external models in various formats, and the commonly supported formats include FBX, OBJ, 3DS, DSE, DXF, etc. therefore, the model required for building this scene should be imported from 3DS Max software [9].

In the real world, objects reflect, diffract and refract light many times, and finally people can see the colorful world. In order to enhance the realism and immersion of laboratory scenes, it is necessary to add illumination. In Unity3D, light sources can be divided into direct illumination and indirect illumination. The final illumination of the laboratory scene is the result of direct illumination and indirect illumination.

When scene illumination is rendered in the scene, it needs a lot of complicated operations, which puts a heavy load on the computer. The lighting effects in the laboratory is invariable. Baking can record the information such as illumination and shadow into the model and generate a new map. When running the system, it is unnecessary to calculate the lighting effects, which saves computer resources and improves the real-time rendering efficiency.

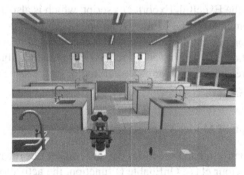

Fig. 2. Scene after baking

The baking process of Unity3D is as follows: firstly, select the imported laboratory model, check the option of Unity3D generating light map UV, then set the models to be baked such as chairs and test bench in the laboratory as static, then set the parameters of baked map size, baking resolution, real-time resolution and indirect intensity, and finally start baking. After baking, the whole scene is shown in Fig. 2.

4.2 Module Design of Interface Display

In the login interface, the Image control is used in the background, and the map is a picture of medical examination, which is consistent with the theme of this system. Text and InputField controls are used for "user name" and "password", Toggle controls are used for "remember password", and Buttton controls are used for "login" and "registration". Note that the user name and password input boxes are regarded as the sub-objects of their respective Text controls, and the Text controls are adjusted, so that the InputField controls will move along with the text controls, which is beneficial to the layout and adjustment of the interface.

The "user name", "password", "mobile phone number" and "mailbox" of the registration interface all use Text and InputField controls. "registration complete" uses the Button control. Text modification and interface layout adjustment are similar to the operation mode of user login interface, so we will not repeat them here.

4.3 Implementation of Data Management Module

The user rights function in the data management module and loading training samples all involve reading the contents of the database, which is completed by the WWW function provided in Unity3DAPI combined with the collaborative process provided by Unity3D script development. After the user obtains the system permission, the user data obtained from the database will be written into the field corresponding to the single instance class DataSingleton of the inherited word SingletonTemplate as the data support of the system; Subsequently, the sample data read according to the user's choice will also be put into the single case class.

The key function in the data management module is to save the training records, which is realized by the ExcelFileExporter.cs script, which is also a single instance that inherits SingletonTemplate. NPOI Library is an open source C# project for reading and writing Microsoft component documents, which can be used to write data into Excel files. The usage method is to refer to NOPI related dynamic link library files (.dll) in the right-click solution resource manager of VisualStudio; At the same time, the script also needs to be referenced.

4.4 Implementation of Model Management Module

The realization of control related functions depends on various rewritable methods provided by MonoBehaviour class. OnEnable () function, the activation of related scripts; In the Start () function, initialize the related parameters; Update () function, to refresh the real-time content; Handling of mouse events in OnMouseDown () function. In addition, it is necessary to pick up objects in the scene in combination with ray detection provided by Unity3D engine.

5 Practice and Effect Analysis

During the epidemic period, practical teaching was carried out through the virtual simulation training teaching platform, and 60 students majoring in medical laboratory technology in medical college were taken as the research objects. After independent practice and practical operation, the final assessment was carried out, which was included in the final total score of clinical immunology laboratory technology, accounting for 12%. Through students' basic theoretical knowledge, clinical skills operation, hands-on practice level, platform experience and satisfaction, teaching effect evaluation, etc., the practical application performance of the virtual simulation training teaching platform is comprehensively evaluated.

An electronic questionnaire was used to investigate, and each ID was limited to one opportunity. Finally, 60 valid questionnaires were collected, with a recovery rate of 100%. In the electronic questionnaire survey of platform experience and satisfaction (0–10 points), ≥ 8 points are satisfactory, 4–7 points are generally satisfactory, and ≤ 3 points are unsatisfactory. The results are shown in Fig. 3.

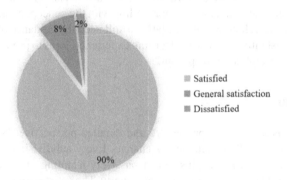

Fig. 3. Investigation on platform experience and satisfaction

Teaching effect evaluation comprehensively analyzes the practical application effect according to basic theoretical knowledge, hands-on practical ability, independent experimental consciousness, clinical thinking, learning interest and operation level, and the results are shown in Fig. 4.

The reliability analysis of the questionnaire shows that the consistency between the questions is ideal and the reliability is good, and the validity analysis shows that the questionnaire data is suitable for factor analysis and the effect is good.

According to the practical requirements of inspection specialty, a virtual simulation training platform is built to carry out social practice activities. In the special period of the epidemic, we actively practiced the reform of experimental teaching mode and explored its application effect. The results show that the virtual simulation training teaching platform can effectively solve practical teaching problems and achieve satisfactory teaching results, inject strong fresh blood into online experimental teaching, realize a

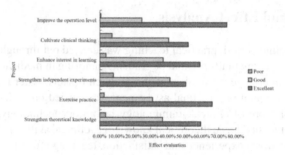

Fig. 4. Comprehensive evaluation of teaching effect

new round of track change and overtaking of teaching forms of disciplines and specialties, and finally enhance the soft power of the college and cultivate innovative and entrepreneurial practical talents in the new era.

Promote the construction of disciplines and specialties. Relying on the teaching mode of virtual simulation and innovation and entrepreneurship, an experimental teaching system with double assessment of theory and practice is constructed, which makes the platform experience and satisfaction more in line with the concept of start-up. However, the operation and development of the platform still need the guidance of double creative thinking, and constantly optimize the learning experience, so as to promote the long-term development of disciplines and specialties.

6 Conclusion

Big data gives us a more comprehensive and detailed perspective. With big data, the nature of education will fundamentally change. Every subdivision of education will face the challenge of big data. Instead of passively adapting, it is better to take the initiative and regard the challenge as an opportunity. The construction of medical virtual simulation training platform can promote both teachers' teaching and students' learning. In the process of using the virtual simulation training teaching platform, teachers should consult the data, observe the students' operation and update the teaching content in time, so as to promote the professional teachers to further strengthen their professional quality and ability. The establishment of clinical practice teaching resource database of medical examination technology provides a basis for the combination of theory and practice teaching, and provides a basis for homogenization teaching in practice bases. To build a quantitative assessment system for interns, so as to solve the problem that the previous single evaluation mode of graduation examination cannot objectively evaluate the internship effect, and to build a quantitative assessment system for interns, so as to improve the quality of internship teaching and evaluate the internship effect.

Acknowledgements. Soft Science Research Program of Henan Province. Project Number: 202400410372.

Project name: Development and Research of Virtual Simulation Practice Teaching Platform for Medical Examination under the Background of Educational Informatization.

References

1. Hao, L,, Han, N., Zhang, J., et al.: A study of application of multimedia virtual simulation teaching method in microbiology experiments. Trans. Comput. Sci. Technol. Chin. English 1, 76–80 (2019)
2. Sun, W., Han, Y., Hu, L., et al.: Application of medical image virtual simulation teaching platform in practice teaching of mudanjiang medical college. Software **040**(005), 98–101 (2019)
3. Farahmand Rad, R., et al.: Randomized controlled trial of simulation vs standard training for teaching medical students high-quality cardiopulmonary resuscitation: the methodological issue. Western J. Emerg. Med. **20**(6), 974–975 (2019)
4. Di, X., Jin, Y.: Evaluation of application effect of integrated simulation training in clinical practice teaching of severe medical science. Chin. High. Med. Educ. **000**(002), 93–94 (2019)
5. Hau, H.M., Weitz, J., Bork, U.: Impact of the COVID-19 pandemic on student and resident teaching and training in surgical oncology. J. Clin. Med. **9**(11), 3431 (2020)
6. He, C., Wang, J., Lou, Z., et al.: Construction and exploration of virtual simulation platform for medical examination technology. China High. Med. Educ. **000**(004), 33–34 (2019)
7. Liu, J., Xu, G., Li. J., et al.: Construction and application of medical laboratory virtual simulation training teaching platform. China Med. Educ. Technol. **033**(001), 83–86 (2019)
8. Zhou, X.: Preliminary study on the construction of virtual simulation experimental teaching platform for medical laboratory. J. Exper. Lab. Med. **037**(003), 534–535, 545 (2019)
9. Xu, M., Min, X., Xiang, J., et al.: Construction of virtual simulation platform for medical laboratory practice and practice of quantitative assessment. Contin. Med. Educ. **34**(02), 38–40 (2020)

Design of Sports Competition Assistant Evaluation System Based on Big Data and Action Recognition Algorithm

Yang Liu[✉] and Fang Lin

Hankou University, Wuhan 430212, Hubei, China
jfliuyang88888@163.com

Abstract. The new method to evaluate the performance of athletes in sports competitions. It can be used as an assistant for coaches, referees and referees to judge the performance of athletes. The main function is to use big data such as video, audio and scores to judge whether each athlete performs well according to his own personal standards. The system is designed for the evaluation of sports competition and can be used to evaluate the quality of athletes and coaches. These data are collected from various sources, including video recordings and images, and then processed by artificial intelligence algorithms. The results obtained from the analysis of these data will help to identify athletes with potential for future success in the selected sports and those who need further development.

Keyword: Sports competition · big data · Action recognition algorithm · Auxiliary review system

1 Introduction

In today's society, with the continuous machine learning, deep learning, there are more and more schemes for people to intelligently process different information in their lives, and intelligent life is gradually favored by more and more people. In ordinary life, sports competitions will make different actions to interact with other people, which is a very intuitive and effective way of communication. Intelligent life requires intelligent devices to recognize and learn actions like humans, so it is particularly important to recognize actions in video sequences [1].

Action recognition is to enable computers or other intelligent devices to distinguish different actions like the human brain, so as to complete some specific work. Because motion recognition has important research significance, many scholars and experts at home and abroad have great interest in this topic, and even many universities have established special research institutes for this topic. This subject is a joint research subject, computer vision, deep learning and artificial intelligence [2]. Motion recognition is not only of great theoretical significance, but also widely used in many fields with the video capture equipment and digital equipment: video surveillance, intelligent security systems, human-computer interaction and motion analysis.

© ICST Institute for Computer Sciences, Social Informatics and Telecommunications Engineering 2024
Published by Springer Nature Switzerland AG 2024. All Rights Reserved
Y. Zhang and N. Shah (Eds.): BigIoT-EDU 2023, LNICST 581, pp. 306–316, 2024.
https://doi.org/10.1007/978-3-031-63133-7_30

In the past decade, many methods, activity recognition have been published. A depth map method based on local feature recognition is proposed. This method explicitly realizes modeling actions by using an extensible graphic model [3]. Compared with the action based, this method has better recognition effect. A global descriptor is proposed, which considers the motion direction. To this end, a 3D grid is the person, and motion recognition is performed using the grid. Hadfield et al. Proposed a new for rgbd video sequences. The descriptor code extracts realize action recognition [4].

AI motion recognition algorithm has a profound impact on sports training, mainly aspects: 1. The data analysis and recognition of the athletes themselves is very important for the sports process. Through the artificial intelligence, we can record, manage and analyze the sports data to determine whether the athletes' pace is balanced Whether the standard can make the data results faster and more reliable. 2. The effect analysis of sports training is particularly important for professional sports players to analyze the error correction after each training. 3. Opponent movement data analysis Through AI movement recognition, we can analyze the video of previous sports competitions, especially the data collection and analysis of competitors' movements, analyze the weak points of competitors through professional technology, complete the countermeasures against the weak points, put forward the correct tactical strategies, find the best response strategies, and improve the probability of winning.

Data analysis and prediction: AI technology can help the sports industry collect, analyze and use a large amount of data. For example, AI technology can analyze players' skills and performance data to predict which players may perform best in the game. This can also be used to analyze the team's strategy, predict the game results, and provide better game broadcast and interpretation. Athlete training and performance: AI technology can help coaches and athletes better analyze and evaluate training plans and performance. For example, AI technology can analyze athletes' movement data to help them optimize training plans and improve performance. Sports equipment and materials: AI technology can help design better sports equipment and materials. For example, AI technology can simulate and test the strength and durability of materials to ensure that they meet the needs and requirements of athletes. Video playback and referee decision-making: AI technology can help the referee make better decisions. For example, AI technology can analyze the video playback in the game to determine whether there are violations. This can help the referee make more accurate decisions and improve the fairness of the game. To sum up, the innovation and of AI the field of sports competition can help the fairness, quality and safety of the competition, and also improve the performance and experience of athletes. Figure 1 the legend of sports movement recognition.

It is the continuous application of these methods that promotes the development of computer vision. Among them, several key applications are advanced human-computer interaction, physical therapy, autonomous psychological development, intelligent environment, video surveillance. Especially in the field of motion analysis, many sports, such as aerobics, need posture and movements. Therefore, can be applied to this field to analyze the performance and training of athletes. At the play an auxiliary role in the scoring of the referee in the competition.

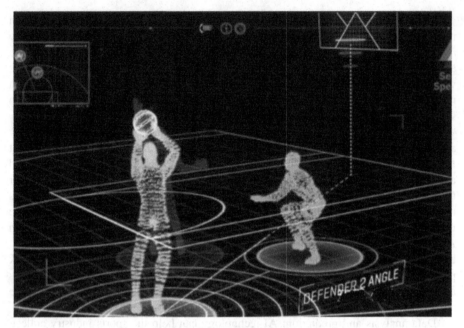

Fig. 1. Legend of sports movement identification

2   Related Work

2.1   Research Status at Home and Abroad

Human motion recognition is an important research direction in the fields of computer vision and pattern recognition. It aims to extract information about human motion from image or video data by analyzing and understanding human posture, actions, and behaviors. At present, significant progress has been made in human motion recognition research.

Firstly, researchers have achieved accurate recognition of human posture and movements through sensor technology and deep learning methods. For example, using an RGB-D camera or inertial measurement unit (IMU) can capture three-dimensional position and motion information of human joints. Meanwhile, methods based on deep learning, such as convolutional neural networks (CNN) and recurrent neural networks (RNN), can effectively extract features of human posture and movements from image or video data.

Secondly, human motion recognition has been widely applied in many fields. In the medical field, it can be used for rehabilitation training and exercise analysis to help restore patient muscle function and evaluate exercise performance. In the field of sports, it can be used for athlete action evaluation and technical improvement. In the field of security, it can be used for behavior recognition and anomaly detection to improve the effectiveness of monitoring systems.

In addition, human motion recognition still faces some challenges and unresolved issues. For example, complex background interference, occlusion, and lighting changes may affect the accuracy of recognition. In addition, the recognition of multi person scenes and fine-grained actions remains challenging.

In summary, research on human motion recognition has made certain progress in both theory and application, but there are still many problems that need to be solved. With the continuous development of technology and in-depth research, it is believed that human motion recognition will be widely applied and breakthroughs in the future.

In China, researchers have actively practiced and studied the application of motion recognition algorithms in sports competitions. They have proposed effective motion recognition algorithms based on technologies such as deep learning and convolutional neural networks, and applied them to multiple sports events such as football, basketball, and swimming. By automatically identifying and analyzing athletes' movements, they provide objective evaluations of their performance [5].

In foreign countries, there is also a large amount of research focusing on the application of motion recognition algorithms in sports competitions. Some studies collect athlete movement data through motion capture systems and sensors, and use machine learning algorithms for analysis and evaluation. Some studies have focused on video based motion recognition and analysis, and have achieved certain results in multiple sports events.

However, current research still faces some challenges. Firstly, for complex motion movements, the accuracy and stability of the algorithm still need to be further improved. Secondly, there are personalized needs and characteristics for action recognition and evaluation of multiple sports projects, requiring customized and optimized algorithm designs for different projects. At the same time, the diversity and variability of motion movements are also a challenge, requiring more flexible and robust algorithms to adapt to various situations. Figure 2 shows the recognition image of key operational actions.

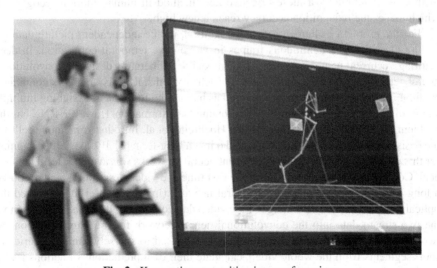

Fig. 2. Key motion recognition image of running

In summary, there has been considerable progress in the research of motion recognition algorithms in sports competition auxiliary evaluation systems both domestically and internationally, but further deepening and improvement are still needed. By continuously improving algorithms and expanding research scope, it is expected to provide more accurate and objective evaluation and analysis tools for sports competitions.

As deep learning networks have made great progress in image detection and recognition, researchers have focused on deep learning networks, and a large number of literatures have proposed the application of CNN (evolutionary neural networks) in pedestrian action recognition. Zhang et al. Selected motion track coding to replace optical flow information, and Kar et al. Proposed an adaptive time pooling method at the CVPR conference [6]. This method will judge the content of video frames, retain informative and discriminative video frames, and remove redundant video frames to ensure the effectiveness of video frames. In 2018, girdhar et al. Introduced a new video representation method, which can obtain the characteristics of local convolution in the temporal and spatial range of video [7]. Tang et al. Constructed a trajectory illusion network, which infers the corresponding optical flow features by establishing the temporal relationship between the spatial appearance features of adjacent frames. After the two branches are fused, the final classification result is obtained. Although these methods can meet the requirements of real-time recognition, the corresponding recognition accuracy has been significantly reduced, so the research of alternative optical flow information still needs a lot of time.

2.2 Research Status of Human Motion Recognition

Compared with traditional recognition methods, the newly introduced deep learning method is undoubtedly a more effective new method in human motion recognition, which makes the recognition accuracy reach a new high.

For the problem of human action recognition, unlike independent picture data for picture classification, continuous frames in video have temporal correlation. In deep learning, recurrent neural network (RNN) model or deliberately designed convolutional neural network is usually used to deal with such problems. RNN is a network containing cyclic information, which can be regarded as having the function of assigning multiple values to the same neural network, thus allowing the information. However, RNN has the problem of gradient disappearance. Sepp Hochreiter et al. Introduced memory cells on the basis of traditional RNN and improved it into a long-term [8]. By specially designing for this problem, the in traditional recurrent neural networks was avoided. Jeff Donahue et al. Combined CNN with LSTM for the first time and video description, and proposed a long-term recursive convolutional neural network (lrcn). Karen et al. Extracted the optical flow image and RGB image of the video data to preserve the data, and then input the two stream data into the convolutional neural network for training. Based on the two stream principle, Limin Wang et al. [9]. Proposed to sparsely sample a series of short segments from the whole video, calculate their own predictions of actions for all segments, and then count the consensus of the segments to obtain a TSN time segment network of prediction results.

2.3 Motion Detection Algorithm

Motion detection algorithm is an algorithm that utilizes computer vision and image processing technology to recognize and track dynamic objects in a scene. It has extensive applications in many fields, such as video surveillance, intelligent transportation systems, motion analysis, etc.

The core task of motion detection algorithms is to extract motion information of dynamic objects from images or video sequences. Common motion detection algorithms include background modeling based methods, optical flow based methods, and object detection based methods.

The method based on background modeling is one of the most common motion detection algorithms. It establishes a background model of the scene, compares the current image with the background model, and detects different pixels, namely dynamic objects [10]. This method is suitable for relatively static scenes, and may pose certain challenges for complex lighting changes, background clutter, and other situations.

Usually, the pixels of a color image are represented as 3 bytes, with each byte corresponding to the brightness of the RGB component. One pixel of the converted gray image is represented as 1 byte. The higher the grayscale value, the brighter the brightness, and the lower the brightness value. The following expressions are typically used to transform relationships:

$$grey(i,j) = 0.11r(i,j) + 0.59g(i,j) + 0.3b(i,j) \tag{1}$$

The color equal. Grayscale processing is to first read the image and copy it into the memory, and then make the value equal to $grey(i,j)$, which completes the original color image into grayscale image.

The optical flow based method is based on the displacement of object pixels in continuous frame images for motion detection. It estimates the motion trajectory of an object by calculating the brightness changes of adjacent pixels in the image. This method is not sensitive to changes in lighting and background clutter, but may have some errors for fast-moving objects.

The method based on object detection is to first detect the object in the image, and then perform motion detection based on the position and motion information of the target object. This method can more accurately locate and track objects, but it has higher computational complexity for complex scenes and large-scale object detection tasks [11]. The general formula for grayscale transformation is shown in (2).

$$s = T(r) \tag{2}$$

The example after contrast stretching is shown in (3).

$$s = T(r) = \frac{1}{1 + \left(\frac{m}{r}\right)^{\bar{E}}} \tag{3}$$

Histogram performs changes on the input to the formula (x.x) to obtain the output gray level s.

$$s = T(r) = \int_0^{-} p_r(w)dw \tag{4}$$

In the formula, and w is the dummy variable of the integration [12].

Moving target detection in image sequence research field. Generally speaking, the target is mainly to identify and analyze the moving target, filter out the information irrelevant to the image, and isolate the moving target from the scene.

3 Feasibility Analysis and Action Expression

According standard of the Internationale de gymnastique: the scoring rules of Competitive Aerobics in the 2017–2020 cycle, it is relatively easy to recognize some simple movements. However, the still faces some difficulties.

1) The complex environment causes the decline of recognition accuracy;
2) Uncertainty caused by the perspective of action shooting;
3) Errors caused by different sizes of human skeleton;
4) Recognition confusion caused by similarity of actions.

Using 3D data can effectively solve the above problems, such as using the insensitivity of bone data to perspective to analyze motion features, and using 3D feature motion similarity.

3D data is not sensitive to the difference of environment (light, perspective, human body) and is suitable for Aerobics action recognition. Therefore, this paper chooses 3D data set to describe Aerobics movements [13]. The specific action representation method is shown in Fig. 3.

The frame difference method is a very common method to detect and extract objects by using the difference of consecutive frame images in the video sequence. Its main principle is to detect objects the two adjacent frames of the video, mainly by extracting moving objects through pixel time-difference and threshold binarization.

Threshold processing has important applications in frame difference methods. Frame difference method is a commonly used motion detection algorithm for detecting moving objects in images or video sequences. In frame difference method, threshold processing is used to distinguish between motion regions and background regions. The frame difference method obtains a differential image by comparing the difference between the current frame and the background frame, where there is a significant difference in the pixel values of the moving object. Then, threshold processing is applied to differential images, marking pixels with differences above the threshold as foreground or moving objects, and pixels below the threshold as background. Due to the fact that the noise generated by images under different lighting conditions may not necessarily be the same, local thresholds can better suppress noise.

The biggest advantage of this method of selecting the difference between two adjacent frames is its simplicity, but the difference image often contains. Collins proposed an improved time difference method. They use the method in VSAM system to replace the traditional method. The mathematical expression formula is as follows:

$$m_t(i,j) = | f_{t \to t}(i,j) - f_t(i,j) | \times | f_t(i,j) - f_{t+l}(i,j) | \tag{5}$$

$$M_t(i,j) = \{ \begin{matrix} 255, m_t(i,j) > T \\ 0 \end{matrix} \tag{6}$$

Where $f_{t\rightarrow t}(i,j)$ is the differential image, $f_t(i,j)$ is the second frame, $f_{t+l}(i,j)$ is the third frame, $M_t(i,j)$ is the changing part of the three frames. After selecting the appropriate threshold T, the foreground and background can be distinguished, and the moving target can be separated. $M_t(i,j)$ is the binary image of the moving target in the middle frame [14].

If the moving speed, and the moving target cannot be segmented [15]. On the contrary, if the moving target speed is too slow and the time between the selected frames is too short, it will cause the target to be over-covered, which will make the detected target appear empty, even if the object is completely overlapped, the moving target cannot be detected at all.

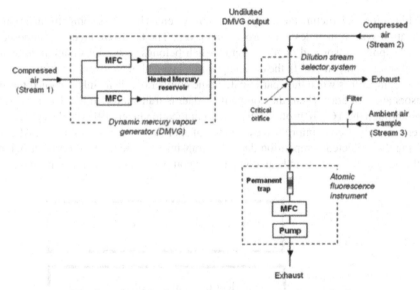

Fig. 3. Schematic diagram of action representation method

Among them, 3D depth action data can be divided into two parts: spatiotemporal feature and trajectory tracking. Spatiotemporal feature representation of actions is mainly used to represent local features of actions, which can process simple actions but not difficult ones [16]. Motion representation based on trajectory tracking can effectively use 3D data to track and recognize more complex movements, but the recognition of Aerobics movements with high difficulty coefficient still needs further research. The use of human 3D skeletal features for action representation has the characteristics of high robustness, fast processing speed and small data volume, so it is widely used in the field of action recognition. It can be mainly divided into spatial description, geometric description and pose description [17]. Spatial description calculates the distance between bones and joints for recognition; The geometric description calculates the relative geometric features of the joint set for recognition; Key pose description selects a specific key pose for pose matching, and then realizes action recognition.

This algorithm has the advantage of fast processing speed and can meet the require-ments of real-time processing. Because it only needs the current single frame image to use it from the to quickly get the moving object in the current frame image. However, this method largely depends on the selected background model image [18]. The premise of the background subtraction method is to have an ideal background model image, and each frame is subtracted from the background model, so that the moving target area and moving target can be accurately obtained.

4 Design of Sports Competition Auxiliary Evaluation System Based on Big Data and Action Recognition Algorithm

See Fig. 4 for the structure auxiliary evaluation system. The sports competition auxiliary evaluation system includes, data processing layer,. The hardware layer is composed of power supply, sensor and depth camera, which belongs to the information collection end of sports competition; In the data acquisition layer, all the movement information of sports competitors when they participate in the competition is mainly obtained through sensors and cameras; Then, the competition data is transmitted to the data processing layer through the TCP/IP protocol in the communication layer [19]. The data processing layer is mainly used to improve the accuracy of sports competition evaluation. After de-noising the collected competition data, it is transmitted. The application layer belongs to the head of the system and can compare the competition data with the database after

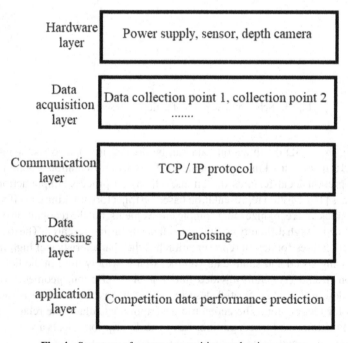

Fig. 4. Structure of sports competition evaluation system

the implementation of the operation. The sports competition performance prediction method is used to achieve the auxiliary evaluation of sports competitions.

The application layer includes main control, database, physical education score module, physical fitness score module, up to standard score module and competition score prediction module.

After the application layer obtains the sports competition data after noise removal, the application layer connects with the database through the main control [20]. Based on the historical score data recorded in the physical education score module, the system score module and the standard score module, the application layer uses the sports competition score prediction method to predict the sports competition scores and complete the auxiliary evaluation of sports competitions.

5 Conclusion

It is simple and convenient to collect only motion video without other external sensors and other devices. For open and close jumps, push ups, squats and other movements, you only need to modify the corresponding parameters to effectively reduce repetitive work and improve efficiency. The data base of visual action detection is to use vision to detect the 3D coordinate information of 25 core key points such as human limbs and hands in real time, which can realize 2D/3D key point data output; Millisecond response, which can quickly and smoothly obtain key points on any device without delay; Easy to integrate customized programs and develop sample source code; Portable 3D manikin display; The solution engine and network layer can receive real-time third-party auxiliary location data; Offline computing, no need to upload to the Internet, to ensure information security. The application of this technology in motion detection and counting has strong flexibility. For the 25 key points of the human body, it outputs information independently, and has strong applicability. The modular configuration can quickly adapt to new actions. At the same time, it also supports negative feedback output to help users adjust the accuracy of actions, without environmental restrictions such as scene, light, etc. High efficiency, strong usability and high stability. It supports identification and counting of rope skipping, sit-ups, push-ups, open and close jumps, squats and other movements. The application field is very wide. For the common fitness app, online sports evaluation system, fitness mirror, etc. on the market, it can respond quickly. If you have more application fields, you can discuss with Jumeng Xiaobian to help the vigorous development of machine vision industriesIn view of the current situation that the scoring rules of aerobics are not detailed and there are many language descriptions, this paper designs. The system uses a large number of standard Aerobics movements to expand the existing comparison database, and carries out Fourier pyramid filtering and fusion of bone features and depth local features, and classifies and recognizes movements according to the fusion results. The system test recognition accuracy.

References

1. Mo, L.V., Wan, L.C.: Design of sports competition aided evaluation system based on big data and motion recognition algorithm. Electron. Des. Eng. (2019)

2. Ma, C., Shou, M.: Sports competition assistant system based on fuzzy big data and health exercise recognition algorithm. Hindawi Limited (2021)
3. Yangzhao. Research on the application of university teaching management evaluation system based on Apriori algorithm. J. Phys. Conf. Ser. **1883**(1), 012033 (6pp) (2021)
4. Xun, G., Lin, S.: Construction of evaluation system of sports talent training scheme based on data mining (2016)
5. Xu, H., Yan, R.: Research on sports action recognition system based on cluster regression and improved ISA deep network. J. Intell. Fuzzy Syst. **39**(4), 5871–5881 (2020)
6. Liu, Y., Wang, L., Tang, Y., et al.: Judgment of athlete action safety in sports competition based on LSTM recurrent neural network algorithm. Math. Probl. Eng **2022** (2022)
7. Wang, L., Sun, J., Li, T.: Intelligent sports feature recognition system based on texture feature extraction and SVM parameter selection. J. Intell. Fuzzy Syst. Appl. Eng. Technol. **2020**(4 Pt.1), 39 (2020)
8. Xia, D., Ma, R., Wu, Y., et al.: Design of military physical fitness evaluation system based on big data clustering algorithm (2022)
9. Wang, L., Qiu, K., Li, W.: Sports action recognition based on gb-bp neural network and big data analysis.[J]. Hindawi (2021)
10. Jing, H., Wen, Y., Si, M., et al.: Research and application of running action sequence recognition algorithms based on Kinect. In: The 3rd asia-europe symposium. ACM (2016)
11. Igor, D., Ficko, M., Balic, J.: 2th A model for prediction and evaluation of production processes based on genetic algorithm (2022)
12. Data processing method of traditional Chinese medicine clinical skill evaluation system based on big data analysis (2016)
13. Jun-Zhen, Y.U., University, X.S.: Design of sports vehicle competition assistant system based on fuzzy logic control. Techn. Autom. Appl. (2019)
14. Ming, D.: Sports quality test recognition system based on fuzzy clustering algorithm. In: Xu, Z., Alrabaee, S., Loyola-González, O., Zhang, X., Cahyani, N.D.W., Ab Rahman, N.H. (eds.) Cyber security intelligence and analytics. CSIA 2022. LNDECT, vol. 123. Springer, Cham (2022). https://doi.org/10.1007/978-3-030-96908-0_47
15. Chu, H., Li, J.: Design of human resources multi-dimensional evaluation system based on big data mining In: Wang, S.H., Zhang, Y.D. (eds) Multimedia technology and enhanced learning. ICMTEL 2022. LNICS, vol. 446. Springer, Cham (2022). https://doi.org/10.1007/978-3-031-18123-8_35
16. Tong-Zhigang. Research on decision support system of sports assistant teaching and training based on association rules and support vector machine. J. Intell. Fuzzy Syst. **2021**(2), 1–12 (2021)
17. Yao, T.K.: A training assistant system based on action recognition. Electron. Design Eng. (2019)
18. Xue-Chao, B.I.: Dance specific action recognition based on spatial skeleton sequence diagram. Inform. Technol. (2019)
19. Li, Z., He, L., Tang, X., et al.: Design and implementation of real assets analysis and evaluation system of power grid based on big data. Electric. Eng. (2019)
20. Mao, Y.: Design of calisthenics choreography and recording system based on action recognition algorithm (2022)

Innovative Research on Piano Education and Teaching Under the Background of Big Data

Xunyun Chang(✉) and Yi Mo

School of Music and Dance, Shaoyang University, Shaoyang 422000, Hunan, China
lqpeng0221@163.com

Abstract. Everyone is discussing big data, which has become a key word in today's world. Borrowing data to record all aspects of human life and reflect it in a specific form has not only changed our way of life, but also has a profound impact on piano education and teaching. The disadvantages of traditional piano education and teaching are becoming more and more obvious. TX. Che advent of the era of big data will provide a good opportunity for innovation in piano education and teaching. The purpose of this article is to conduct research based on the innovation of piano education and teaching under the background of big data. This article first analyzes the internal logic of big data to promote piano education and teaching. Under the guidance of the theory of big data classroom, pay attention to the overall development of students' piano skills, pay attention to the balance and integration, integration and application of piano courses; pay attention to students' learning habits and pay attention to piano education. This article focuses on exploring the teaching methods suitable for popular piano lessons, and summarizes the curriculum reform plans and measures for piano education and teaching under the background of big data. Research shows that the age group and gender ratio of piano students are very different. At the kindergarten level, 68% of girls learn piano, while only 12% of boys learn piano. Only 12% of students practice piano for more than one and a half hours a day. There is not enough time to practice piano after class, and parents have misunderstandings about their children's learning piano. The number of people who choose piano learning in order to cultivate their children's hobbies accounts for 57% of the surveyed population. The traditional teaching model cannot meet the social needs shown, and reforms are urgently needed.

Keywords: Big Data · Piano Education · Teaching Innovation · Innovative Research

1 Introduction

Piano course is a compulsory course for university undergraduates, and it plays an important role in students' study or employment [1, 2]. The author has learned from the teaching work of participating in the reform of applied courses in colleges and universities that the curriculum concepts and ideas of teachers determine their goals [3, 4], the

Y. Zhang and N. Shah (Eds.): BigIoT-EDU 2023, LNICST 581, pp. 317–325, 2024.
https://doi.org/10.1007/978-3-031-63133-7_31

development direction of methods and skills. Traditional piano teaching cannot meet the needs of students for music teaching activities in kindergartens [5, 6]. In response to these problems, the author combined my own teaching experience to conduct a systematic research and analysis, and put forward some methods to promote teaching [7, 8].

Many scholars have conducted research on the innovation of piano education and teaching with the background of big data and have achieved good results. For example, Yazici T conducted research on children's piano education, combining how parents and teachers in small towns can guide children to better learn piano art, and make suggestions to teachers and students [9]. Through research, Deniz put forward some problems in the development of amateur piano education, and thought about them, in order to provide reference for the related personnel of amateur piano education, and provide help for related researchers in this direction in the future [10].

This article starts from the perspective of piano education and uses big data as the background to study how to better promote the training and management of domestic piano education and teaching under the background of big data, how to improve the domestic piano education teaching model, and how to better promote domestic piano education development, provide reference suggestions, and provide practical reference value for the better development of piano education and teaching under the background of big data.

2 Innovative Research on Piano Education and Teaching Under the Background of Big Data

2.1 Role and Approach of Big Data to Piano Education and Teaching

In the context of big data, with the help of the maturity of the network and terminal equipment, piano education presents a variety of new forms. In traditional piano education, the process of error correction when students practice piano often can only be pointed out by the teacher in class. If the students make too many mistakes, it will seriously take up class time and greatly reduce the teaching efficiency. In class, with the help of big data, Teachers can easily find teaching resources (such as score examples, audio), and can visually display the changes in students' performance level over a period of time through the analysis of big data, which has a positive meaning for piano teaching.

In recent years, with the rapid advancement of science and technology, pianos can be connected to the Internet to download content. In a sense, big data piano teaching is an innovation of traditional piano teaching, and has achieved many content that traditional pianos cannot achieve.

2.2 Innovative Strategies for Piano Education and Teaching Under the Background of Big Data

(1) Cultivate the big data thinking concept of piano educators

Big data provides human beings with unprecedented new ways of thinking about the world and new technological means to transform the world. Piano education should track and investigate in depth what changes and effects big data has brought to the growth of students, and establish a big data thinking concept that is synchronized with the changes of the times. One is to establish the concept of system thinking. Big data is not only available now, it takes years to develop. Only through the past and the present can we insight into the laws and innovate methods. Therefore, the construction of "big data" for piano education must establish a comprehensive and systematic thinking and establish a modern information collection system. It is necessary to inherit and carry forward the fine traditions, especially to collect and sort the data entered into the various stages of students' piano learning, and to collect the current data simultaneously.

(2) Enhance the sense of the times and appeal of piano lessons

In the context of the era of big data, piano educators need to give a new sense of the times to the content and teaching methods of piano education theory courses, enhance the appeal and influence of the public, and expand the scope of piano education for students. In the design of piano teaching, it is vital to play the role of big data, effectively combine the teacher's work experience, make full use of the needs of students, focus on optimizing the student's experience, actively introduce popular cases, and conduct targeted classrooms Seminars, especially lectures, social practice, etc. Activities, to solve the problems existing in students' ideological behavior, and use new teaching materials to achieve the goals pursued by ideological and political education. In addition, the use of big data technology to participate in students' classroom management and management, such as student attendance files, classroom answers and other data statistics, will help to fully understand and mobilize students' enthusiasm in classroom learning.

(3) Establish an early warning and evaluation mechanism for students' piano education

In the era of big data, the piano skill level data of students is usually recorded first. Through cloud computing, the advancement of student skills will be converted into long data codes and stored in the cloud. They can use big data processing to analyze and infer learning conditions, draw charts of students' future development trends, and make plans in advance for problems with piano skills or student behavior, such as installing pianos. Piano teachers can understand, analyze and predict in time, which makes piano training management more proactive, which is essential for better work.

2.3   Classification Algorithm in Streaming Data Mining Under Big Data Platform

For a true random variable r with a value range on R, suppose we make n independent observations on the variable r, get n different values of r, and calculate their average value. For the variable r In other words, its Hoeffding constraint is that in the confidence interval, the true value of the variable r is at least, among which,

$$\varepsilon = \sqrt{\frac{R^2 - \ln(1/\delta)}{2n}} \tag{1}$$

In the formula (1), r represents information gain, the value range of R is lb (Classes), and Classes is the number of categories.

Information gain is used to measure the ability of a given attribute to distinguish training examples. The formula is as follows:

$$Entropy(S) = \sum_{i=1}^{c} -p_i \log(p_i) \tag{2}$$

$$Gain(S, A) = Entroy(S) - \sum_{v=Values(A)} \frac{|Sv|}{S} Entropy(Sr) \tag{3}$$

Equation (1) is the calculation formula of information entropy, where Pi is the proportion of samples of different types Ci in the sample set S. Equation (2) is the calculation formula for information gain, where Values (A) is the set of all possible values of attribute A, and Sv is the subset of attribute A with value v in S (Sv = {s ∈ S |A(s) = v).

3 Innovative Research on Piano Education and Teaching Under the Background of Big Data

3.1 Research Methods

(1) Questionnaire survey method

The questionnaire survey method is a commonly used method in empirical investigations. This study uses questionnaires to investigate students to gain insights into the student population's attitude towards piano learning. From the results of the survey, some of the problems can be discovered through the results of the research and survey, and further summarized the innovative countermeasures of piano education and teaching under the background of big data.

(2) Documentary data method

During the research process, I checked articles and books related to piano teaching, music teaching, and the psychological characteristics of students learning piano through manual and Internet, and checked several related literature materials in the past 30 years through CNKI. These have laid a good foundation for text research and writing.

3.2 Collection of Experimental Data

The questionnaires in this article include piano students, piano teachers, training institutions and parents of piano children, etc., to analyze some of the problems in piano education. During the survey, a total of 200 questionnaires were issued and 150 were returned, of which 100 were valid questionnaires. The amateur piano teachers were interviewed, and 50 piano teachers were randomly selected from the training institutions that issued the questionnaire for investigation.

4 Investigation and Analysis of Innovative Research on Piano Education and Teaching Under the Background of Big Data

4.1 Survey of Piano Students' Learning

Through the survey, the distribution of piano students' age groups and male-to-female ratios, as shown in Table 1: 68% of girls in kindergarten learn piano, while only 12% of boys learn piano, and 56% of girls learn piano in junior high school. Boys accounted for 44%. By the time of high school, there were 0 boys and girls studying piano.

Table 1. The age range and male-to-female ratio of piano students

Stage	Grils	Boys
Kindergarten	68%	12%
Primary School	64%	36%
Junior High School	56%	44%
High School	0	0

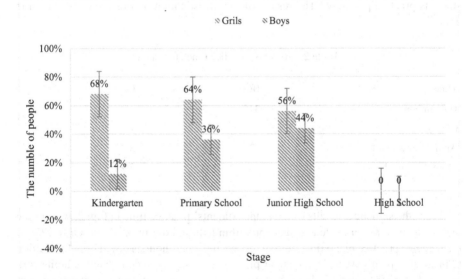

Fig. 1. The age range and male-to-female ratio of piano students

As shown in Fig. 1, it can be seen that, regardless of each stage, the number of girls learning the piano is more than that of boys. In kindergarten, the number of girls learning the piano is far more than that of boys. With the increase of age, the proportion of boys learning piano in elementary and junior high school began to increase relative to that of kindergarten. This is because, through the school's class, discipline and other constraints, boys' attention, intelligence, and finger functions at this stage have begun to develop rapidly, and in recent years, my country has vigorously promoted quality education in order to cultivate children's comprehensive qualities in all aspects. Many parents have rejected the prejudice that boys are not suitable for learning music as a perceptual art. In addition, it can be seen from the data that regardless of men and women, the largest number of piano learners is at the elementary school level. This is also because this stage is the period when children develop the most rapidly, so the number of piano learners is the largest. Since the beginning of junior high school, the number of piano students began to decrease. This is because most students are overwhelmed by the heavy cultural courses and the pressure of entering a higher school. Therefore, the number of piano students is very small.

4.2 Insufficient Time for Students to Practice Piano After Class

As we all know, piano is a technical subject that requires a lot of practice. The time for piano practice in school is arranged by the teacher, but the vacation time is determined by yourself. The course in the introductory period is relatively simple, and the time for practice is relatively small. It can be completed in about half an hour. When the basic courses are completed, students will enter a relatively complicated learning phase, and the time for practicing piano will increase to about one hour. How much time do piano students practice privately? The results of the investigation on this issue are shown in Table 2:

Table 2. Students' practice time after class

Time	Boys	Girls
Half an hour	34%	49%
One hour	49%	12%
An hour and a half	12%	34%
More than two hours	5%	5%

From the statistical results of the piano students' practice time in Fig. 2, we can see that most students' practice time is kept within half an hour to one hour. Only 12% of the students practice piano time more than one and a half hours a day. These In addition to practicing piano every day, amateur piano students have to complete the homework assigned by the teacher at school. Some students even go to cultural cram school after school every day. The heavy learning tasks make them have no more time to practice piano. And the piano children who can practice piano for one and a half hours to two hours or more are all over 12 years old. It can be seen from this that among these children who learn piano in their spare time, apart from the increased difficulty in playing the music There are many children who like to learn piano very much, and some even want to study piano in the future. Therefore, in piano education, the professional level of piano teachers and the scientific nature of teaching methods are very important.

Table 3. Parents' Purpose for Children's Piano Learning

Purpose	girls	boys
Develop skills	29%	50%
Cultivate interest	53%	20%
Occupation	2%	10%
Parents love	12%	14%
Conformity	4%	6%

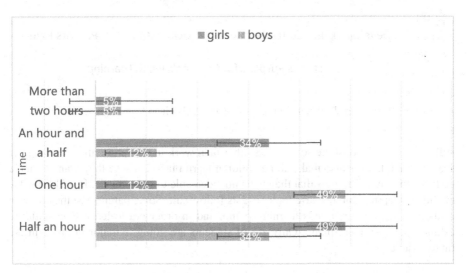

Fig. 2. Students' practice time after class

4.3   Purpose of Parents for Their Children to Learn Piano

Every child comes to this world, and the first teacher who begins to learn to contact and understand the world is the parent. Parents are the most important guardians and companions of the child in life and learning. Therefore, the parents' ideas and ideas are right. The influence of children plays a very important role. In the context of the new era, what is the parent's attitude towards children's piano learning?

It can be seen from Fig. 3 that the number of people who choose piano learning in order to cultivate their children's hobbies accounted for 53% of the surveyed people. Nearly half of the data show that most parents hope their children can learn in addition to cultural lessons. Influenced by some musical literacy. In addition, one skill accounted for 29%. Many parents said that because they were restricted by the economic and social conditions at the time when they were young, they could not accept the influence of music literacy other than cultural courses. After going to work in society, they discovered that apart from their own work, they did not have any talents to show in the face of cultural activities organized by the company or society. Therefore, they hope that their children

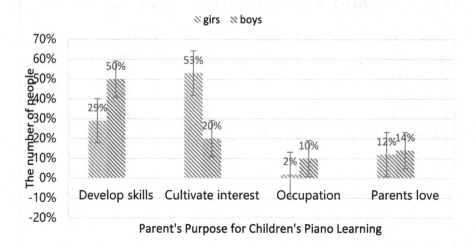

Fig. 3. Parents' Purpose for Children's Piano Learning

will be able to demonstrate some skills other than work in the future after entering the society. Such factors also make some children learn piano because they want to make up for their parents' regrets that they have not been able to learn music. In addition, 4% of children learn piano because their parents follow suit. Some parents see the children of their colleagues or friends learning piano, and in order not to leave their children behind, they also learn piano. Only 2% of students are going to major in piano in the future (Table 3).

5   Conclusions

This article analyzes and explores the current situation of piano education through the investigation of amateur piano education and professional college piano education. Amateur piano education conducts investigation and analysis in the form of questionnaires from social piano training institutions, piano children and parents of piano learners. For the analysis of piano professional schools, Changzhi College and Changzhi Art School are used as examples to conduct research and analysis.And put forward some constructive comments.

As a part of national education, piano education is gradually accepted, valued and recognized by students and parents in flexible and diverse forms. Although there are deficiencies and unsatisfactory aspects in the development process, the development of everything is not Perfect to perfect such a process, and the development of piano education in our country will inevitably go through such a development process.

This article's investigation and analysis of the development of piano education in the context of big data will provide academia with a specific material to continue to explore how to better improve this piano education method, hoping to arouse peers' thinking and find one Practical and feasible solutions for the development of piano education provide mobile theoretical data references for piano education and teaching research under the background of big data.

References

1. Wang, J.: Innovative research on the teaching mode of piano group lessons under the background of big data. J. Phys: Conf. Ser. **1744**(3), 032031 (2021)
2. Tan, Q., Shao, X.: RETRACTED: construction of college english teaching resource database under the background of big data. J. Phys. Conf. Ser. **1744**(3), 032004 (2021). https://doi.org/10.1088/1742-6596/1744/3/032004
3. Li, M.: Smart home education and teaching effect of multimedia network teaching platform in piano music education. Int. J. Smart Home **10**(11), 119–132 (2016)
4. Yucetoker, I.: The visual memory-based memorization techniques in piano education. Eurasian J. Educ. Res. **2016**(65), 111–128 (2016)
5. Chen, Y.: The problems of professional piano education in China: description and summary. Философия и культура **9**, 46–57 (2020)
6. Mukhamedova, F.: Formation, development of piano performance and education of Uzbekistan. Eurasian Music Sci. J. **1**(1), 7 (2019)
7. Pala, F.K., Türker, P.M.: Developing a haptic glove for basic piano education. World J. Educ. Technol. Curr. Issues **11**(1), 38–47 (2019). https://doi.org/10.18844/wjet.v11i1.4008
8. Zhang, X.: Teaching method and innovation of piano teaching method constructed in virtual environment in comprehensive university. IPPTA: Quar. J. Indian Pulp Paper Techn. Assoc. **30**(7), 816–822 (2018)
9. Yazici, T.: A study of developing attitude scale for piano teaching. Educ. Res. Rev. **11**(7), 358–370 (2016)
10. Deniz, B.C.E.K.C.: Students and instructors opinions about piano instruction*. Educ. Res. Rev. **11**(10), 966–974 (2016)

Dynamic Early Warning System of Ideology Education Based on Psychological Big Data Analysis

Wenxin Jiang[✉] and Ren Yuankun

Beijing Institute of Technology, Zhuhai 519088, Guangdong, China
hyei001@163.com

Abstract. The ideological and political education dynamic early warning system based on psychological Big data analysis is an education system that uses Big data technology to analyze students' psychological state and timely warn potential risks. This system can identify students' psychological biases and personalized needs, predict potential problems, and provide timely intervention and support through the acquisition and analysis of students' psychological, emotional, and behavioral data.

This system can obtain a large amount of student emotional and behavioral data through various data collection devices, such as psychological assessment questionnaires, mobile device sensors, and student learning records. Then, using machine learning, artificial intelligence and other technologies, analyze and process these data to obtain information about students' emotional states, psychological biases, and behavioral characteristics.

In terms of early warning, the system can detect abnormal situations in students' emotions, psychology, and learning status based on the changing trends of student data, and timely provide early warning and intervention. For example, when a student's academic performance decreases or their absenteeism rate increases, the system will automatically issue warning signals to notify teachers and parents to pay timely attention to the student's academic status. In addition, the system can also provide targeted mental health courses, psychological counseling and other support services to improve students' psychological and learning outcomes.

In a word, the dynamic early warning system of ideological and political education based on psychological Big data analysis is an educational technology worth studying and investing. It can help schools and teachers better understand students' psychological and emotional needs, timely warn and intervene in possible problems, and thus achieve more personalized, intelligent, and scientific education and teaching.

Keyword: Psychological big data; Ideology education; early warning system

© ICST Institute for Computer Sciences, Social Informatics and Telecommunications Engineering 2024
Published by Springer Nature Switzerland AG 2024. All Rights Reserved
Y. Zhang and N. Shah (Eds.): BigIoT-EDU 2023, LNICST 581, pp. 326–333, 2024.
https://doi.org/10.1007/978-3-031-63133-7_32

1 Introduction

In today's world, the influence and application of information technology and artificial intelligence technology in various fields are becoming increasingly widespread. In the field of education, these technologies are also driving the reform of educational teaching methods. Unlike traditional and primitive teaching methods, the introduction and application of advanced educational technology can greatly promote the depth and breadth of teaching, while also meeting the needs of students of different levels and needs [1]. In response to such challenges, intelligent education based on artificial intelligence technology has gradually become a research and application hotspot, including adaptive education systems, personalized education, educational assistance robots, and so on.

An important application in the field of intelligent education is ideological and political education. Ideological and political education is an excellent tradition and important science of the Chinese nation [1]. The application of the ideological and political education dynamic early warning system based on psychological Big data analysis can better help us understand students' psychological and ideological conditions, and timely predict and intervene potential problems. This not only helps to promote the inheritance and development of Core Socialist Values, but also helps to improve the positive mood and cohesion of social groups. Therefore, the significance and value of studying and applying this system are very important and significant.

However, so far, most ideological and political education has adopted traditional teaching models and educational methods. In this situation, students' comprehension, memory, emotional attitudes, behavioral habits, and other issues cannot be comprehensively monitored and resolved [2]. At this time, as a new technology, the application of psychological Big data in ideological and political education will be very important. Psychological Big data is a technology based on Big data, machine learning and artificial intelligence, which can be used to collect and analyze all relevant factors to predict and intervene potential psychological deviation or risk. Therefore, the dynamic early warning system of ideological and political education based on psychological Big data analysis can better help schools and education departments understand students' psychological state, and timely predict and reduce the risk of coping with problems.

In short, intelligent education technology is one of the inevitable trends in education reform, and is an important learning tool and means to assist students in meeting their personalized needs and characteristics. In this context, the ideological and political education dynamic early warning system based on psychological Big data analysis has almost become an inevitable research direction in the advocacy and application of the education industry [3]. This paper will deeply discuss the significance, application, technical difficulties and prospects of the ideological and political education dynamic early warning system based on psychological Big data analysis. At the same time, this opportunity calls on the academic community and practitioners to pay more attention to the integration of education and technological innovation, and truly transform these technologies and applications into practical contributions that can promote China's education reform.

2 Ideology Education Based on Psychological Big Data Analysis of College Students

2.1 Analysis on the Sources of Mental Health Data of College Students

The sources of college students' psychological Health data can be divided into the following aspects:

Psychological assessment: Psychological assessment is a scientific method that can obtain specific quantitative data by testing the psychological personality and behavior of college students [4]. These data can include multiple aspects such as emotions, emotions, personality, cognition, etc., and play an important role in studying the mental health of college students. Student questionnaire survey: Student questionnaire survey is one of the common methods to obtain college students' psychological Health data [5]. By conducting quantitative surveys on college students, a large amount of data and information related to mental health can be obtained, including data on various aspects of students' emotions, learning, and social habits. Mobile smart device data: With the continuous development of technology and the increasing sensitivity of humans to data information, many college students have also started using smart mobile devices to record their own life situations. For example, devices such as smartwatches, trace sensors, and electrocardiographs have the characteristics of miniaturization, diversity, and portability. These devices record personal psychological and even physiological data, which can help researchers obtain more detailed data that is helpful for research. Student learning records: there is a lot of information about students' psychological Health data data in the student's learning records. The learning status, homework completion level, and absenteeism rate of students can all reflect their psychological states such as stress level, interests, hobbies, and emotional fluctuations [6]. Therefore, by analyzing students' learning records, it is possible to better explore data information on college students' mental health. Personal social platform data: college students use various social platforms for communication and interaction, which often involve some psychological Health data. For example, personal blogs, Weibo, WeChat, and other places can provide data and information about students' emotional and mental health by posting questions and answers, expressing likes and dislikes, and making aggressive remarks. There are many factors forming psychological problems, and the data of mental health need to be analyzed from many aspects. The mental health data obtained from different angles reflect different mental states.

There are many subjects that need feedback on mental health in colleges and universities, such as students, teachers, managers, families and so on. With the introduction of educational reform measures in colleges and universities, every college teacher's responsibility of educating people begins to shift from typical technical teaching to the combination of morality and technical education.. Feedback is helpful for students to clearly understand their own problems, and at the same time, teachers, managers and parents can help students to improve. The relationship between students and the environment is also subtle. If students get along with the environment harmoniously, then their psychology will be healthier, on the contrary, psychological problems will appear

[7]. The environment not only affects students' mental health, but also affects the collection and feedback of psychological data. When the environment around students is concerned about students' mental health, it will be easier to collect health data.

2.2 Construction of Dynamic Early Warning for Ideological and Political Education

Ideological and political education is an excellent tradition and important science of the Chinese nation. In the new era, the importance of ideological and political education has become even more prominent in promoting comprehensive strict governance of the Party and cultivating the responsibility for national rejuvenation. However, in reality, there still exist issues of unclear direction and insufficient means in ideological governance and educational practice. In order to better fulfill educational responsibilities and timely, comprehensive, and targeted grasp of students' mentality, behavior, and other aspects, some universities have established dynamic warning systems for ideological and political education [8]. The implementation process mainly includes the following steps:

1. Data collection
   The system uses various methods such as psychological assessment questionnaires, mobile device sensors, and student learning records to obtain student psychological, emotional, and behavioral data as input. These data cover students' learning situation, negative emotions, behavioral habits, social relationships, and other aspects, providing an important data foundation for subsequent analysis and prediction.
2. Data preprocessing
   Due to the diverse sources and forms of data, as well as differences in quality, various data preprocessing and standardization are required. For example, through Data cleansing and sorting, duplicate, missing or abnormal data can be removed, and data from different sources can be improved and integrated. By normalizing and standardizing data, unify the proportions and measurement standards of data for different indicators for later analysis and prediction.
3. Data analysis
   Data analysis is the core part of the system. Analyze and extract features from student data through various technological means such as machine learning, data mining, and deep learning. In the later stage of data analysis, the system will establish a dataset suitable for students' mental health characteristics to make decisions and handle adverse mental health events. At the same time as data analysis, the early warning system will conduct scientific quantification and refined analysis of student situations, obtaining accurate student evaluation data and visualized online control interfaces.
4. Early warning and intervention
   Based on data analysis results and model reasoning, the system can generate prediction results and risk assessment reports. By sending corresponding notifications in real-time to relevant educators and students based on factors such as warning levels and importance, accurately guiding student behavior, adjusting educational methods, and achieving the goal of effectively controlling and reducing risks.

To sum up, the dynamic early warning system of ideological and political education is an innovative system that relies on advanced technologies such as Big data, machine learning and artificial intelligence to monitor, analyze and intervene students' psychological and emotional conditions [9]. The construction of this system requires scientific data collection and processing, data analysis model construction, algorithm optimization.

3   Design of Dynamic Early Warning System for Ideology Education in Colleges and Universities

3.1   Preparation for Dynamic Early Warning

The impact will be greater. It is necessary to mobilize all the forces that can be mobilized to complete this task as much as possible. Colleges and universities have a large number of personnel and some are complicated, but colleges and universities are relatively simple and more maneuverable in mobilizing personnel. Colleges and universities are mainly divided into administrative management, professional departments, student management departments, ideology education full-time departments, logistics departments and security departments. They are not subordinate to each other, but cooperate with each other. If they can be effectively coordinated and used, they will become crisis warning One of the organization members.

In order to better implement and implement the crisis early warning strategy of ideology education, all personnel involved in crisis early warning must have very high professional skills and coping ability, and these personnel in macro planning. Especially in the aspects of ideological guidance, mental health guidance, guidance of vocational education, answers to employment puzzles and coping ability of crisis management, to ensure that problems can be easily handled at any time and in any state. Effectively improve their sensitivity and adaptability to crisis, so as to timely and accurately judge and discover the potential problems, learning and environment, the preparation of Ideology education also needs to be changed from time to time and carried out in stages. For senior students, we should focus on the prevention of emotional education and growth education. The Colleges and universities should build various career and employment platforms for students, strengthen employment guidance for students, establish correct career direction, attitude and location, help students correctly deal with setbacks in life, face up to reality, find reasons, find gaps, actively solve problems, maintain a positive and optimistic attitude towards life, turn setbacks into motivation and reduce employment pressure, Learn psychological adjustment, and truly realize that you can choose a job, get employment, understand entrepreneurship and have a good job. The composition of system functional modules is shown in Fig. 1.

3.2   Establishment of Dynamic Early Warning Mechanism

The formulation of its early warning mechanism can not be simply copied. It must be targeted to the various characteristics and possible different crisis situations of Colleges and universities, which is both professional and humanized. There are various search methods for aircraft early warning information, which can not only learn from

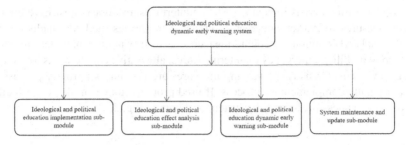

Fig. 1. Composition diagram of system functional modules

the existing experience of foreign countries in early warning information, but also with the help of many proven and effective experience and professional tools in China. The multi-dimensional application-oriented. The Gradient descent can start quickly, but its convergence cannot be guaranteed, so a reasonable termination condition needs to be set. The usual practice is to stop the iteration when a certain number of iterations have been reached or the change rate of the Loss function has become very small.

$$f(\omega) = \min_{\omega} \frac{\lambda}{2} \|\omega\|^2 + \frac{1}{m} \sum \iota(\omega, (x, y)) \tag{1}$$

$(\omega, (x, y))$ in formula (1) is as shown in formula (2).

$$\iota(\omega, (x, y)) = \max\{0, 1 - y < \omega, x \gg \omega\} \tag{2}$$

When using the random Gradient descent, the training data need to be processed to avoid gradient explosion and disappearance. The usual method is to normalize or standardize the data. $O\left(\frac{n}{\lambda_\varepsilon}\right)$, where n line is the sum of dimensions in the constraint space of ω and x. In order to solve the dual problem of nonlinear correspondence, the following mapping transformation is carried out as shown in formula (3).

$$\sum a_i y_i x_i \rightarrow \omega \tag{3}$$

And $i \neq 0$ is an integer.

Establish a basic understanding of college students in order to compare and predict the severity of the crisis and the possibility of intervention. Explore students' potential needs and psychological confusion through different ways, and strive to find problems as early as possible to provide information for crisis prevention and control. Simple information can be completed in the first stage. For some potential information and crises that are not easy to be found, it is necessary to establish indicators and make quantitative analysis, so as to dig out various potential incentives and risk factors more accurately and deeply. In addition to the early warning index system, we also need to have a response system to deal with sudden early warning. Therefore, the information tracking and monitoring system is carried out as an auxiliary measure of the early warning system, specifically for students with special individual situations and sharp problems. After the establishment of crisis early warning indicators, we need to establish the corresponding countermeasure database for various crisis indicators. The countermeasure library must have effective countermeasures for various degrees of crisis, with various methods, including both conventional and common use countermeasures, as well as intelligent countermeasures, with strong mobility, emergency countermeasures, alternative countermeasures, etc. for emergency needs. Crisis early warning measures are not only an orderly process, but also a mutually complementary process. If used properly, they can play a good effect. The overall business process of the system is shown in Fig. 2.

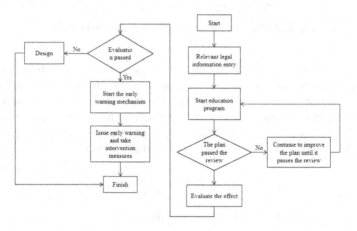

Fig. 2. The overall business process of the system

4 Conclusions

With the rapid development of Big data and artificial intelligence technology, the dynamic early warning system of ideological and political education based on psychological Big data analysis has gradually come into people's sight. This system takes college students as the target, takes psychological Big data as the basis, uses machine learning and artificial intelligence and other technical means to comprehensively grasp, analyze, predict and intervene the psychological situation of students, so as to help students carry out ideological and political education more effectively. The system adopts various data collection methods, including psychological assessment, student questionnaire survey, mobile intelligent device data, student learning records, etc., which provide an important foundation for subsequent data analysis. On the basis of data collection and preprocessing, the system relies on technical means such as machine learning and artificial intelligence to conduct comprehensive analysis and feature extraction, generate prediction results and risk assessment reports, and provide necessary warning information and intervention suggestions for educators and students. In short, in the context of rapid social development, the ideological and political education dynamic early warning system based on psychological Big data analysis can provide students with accurate, personalized and scientific psychological health education services, and better promote the reform and development of China's ideological and political education.

References

1. Adjerid, I., Kelley, K.: Big data in psychology: a framework for research advancement. Am. Psychol. **73**(7), 899 (2018)
2. Harlow, L.L., Oswald, F.L.: Big data in psychology: introduction to the special issue. Psychol. Methods **21**(4), 447–457 (2016)
3. Obschonka, M., Lee, N., Rodríguez-Pose, A., Eichstaedt, J.C., Ebert, T.: Big data methods, social media, and the psychology of entrepreneurial regions: capturing cross-county personality traits and their impact on entrepreneurship in the USA. Small Bus. Econ. **55**(3), 567–588 (2019). https://doi.org/10.1007/s11187-019-00204-2
4. Giusino, D., Fraboni, F., De Angelis, M., Pietrantoni, L.: Commentary: principles, approaches and challenges of applying big data in safety psychology research. Front. Psychol. **10**(2801), 1–3 (2019)
5. Vincze, L., MacIntyre, P.: Accent stigmatization as a moderator of the relationship between perceived L2 proficiency and L2 use anxiety. Appl. Linguistics Rev. **8**(1), 61–78 (2017)
6. Brammer, L., et al.: Organizational and political issues in counseling psychology. Couns. Psychol. **16**(3) (2016)
7. Matthew, H.: Ruling Minds: Psychology in the British Empire. In: Erik, L. (ed.), p. 1 (2016)
8. Collins, T.P., Crawford, J.T., Brandt, M.J.: No evidence for ideological asymmetry in dissonance avoidance. Soc. Psychol. **48**(3), 123–134 (2017)
9. John, W.L., Eric, D.S., Lucy, W.G., et al.: Core personality traits of managers. J. Manag. Psychol. **31**(2), 434–450 (2016)

Research on the Design of College Student Education Management System in the Era of Big Data

Xiangzhou Liu[1,2](✉) and Liu Lu[1,2]

[1] Yunnan College of Business Management, Yunnan 650106, China
liuxiangzh365@aliyun.com
[2] College of Ethnic Culture, Yunnan Minzu University, Kunming 650504, China

Abstract. Based on the Big data era, combined with the current situation and needs of college students' education management, this paper designs and researches a college students' education management system based on Big data analysis. The system is mainly divided into modules such as student management, teaching management, resource management, statistical analysis, etc. In the system design process, technologies such as data mining, machine learning, artificial intelligence, etc. are mainly used. By continuously adjusting system parameters and optimizing algorithms, the goal of quickly and accurately extracting information from massive data and evaluating student performance is achieved. After design and implementation, the application effect of this system is significant. The analysis of Big data not only makes the management of the teaching system more scientific and effective, but also greatly improves the teaching quality and students' learning achievements. Based on the learning plan and feedback mechanism in the system, students' learning motivation has been greatly improved, targeted solutions have been provided to students' learning problems, while also reducing teachers' teaching pressure, enabling interactive learning to be achieved. In the system, it is also possible to analyze students' learning situation, identify their problems and difficulties, and recommend targeted learning resources, providing convenience and effectiveness for learning. The system can also quantitatively evaluate students' performance and provide suggestions for deficiencies in the teaching process, providing precise teaching management and service support for universities. The design and implementation of college students' education management system based on Big data analysis has important practical application value for promoting the improvement of quality and effect, optimizing the teaching system and training objectives.

Keywords: big data · College students · Education management system

1 Introduction

In the current rapidly developing era of informatization and digitization, the education field is also facing unprecedented opportunities and challenges. On the one hand, the continuous innovation and application of educational technology have led to an explosive

Y. Zhang and N. Shah (Eds.): BigIoT-EDU 2023, LNICST 581, pp. 334–344, 2024.
https://doi.org/10.1007/978-3-031-63133-7_33

growth of education related data, which contains a large amount of valuable information. On the other hand, the singularity and limitations of traditional education models also provide space and necessity for the improvement and optimization of education.

In this context, Big data analysis technology, as a new technology that is very suitable for education management and evaluation, has attracted more and more attention and application [1]. Education Big data analysis refers to a series of processes to collect, process, analyze, diagnose and improve the information involved in the education process based on Big data technologies and algorithms. In addition to the characteristics of "large-scale", "high dimension" and "complexity", education Big data analysis also needs to have important attributes such as "accuracy", "real-time" and "quantification".

Therefore, in the era of Big data, the application of educational Big data analysis can become a new trend and path of educational reform and development. Education Big data analysis can help educational institutions improve teaching quality and effect, promote education fairness and optimize resource allocation, and provide reference and guidance for education development and improvement.

On the one hand, education Big data analysis can help educational institutions fully understand students' learning conditions and characteristics, develop personalized teaching plans and goals, improve students' learning motivation and enthusiasm, and further improve students' learning achievements and academic levels through the collection and integration of students' information, as well as in-depth analysis and mining of these information.

On the other hand, education Big data analysis can provide comprehensive education resources and services, optimize the allocation of education resources, and supplement and optimize the talent training structure through the collection and analysis of information on school organizational structure, teaching staff, teaching facilities and other aspects. At the same time, long-term tracking and evaluation of students' growth and development after graduation, as well as providing targeted suggestions and guidance, can help students better adapt to society and achieve personal development and career planning faster.

However, the application of educational Big data analysis also faces many challenges and difficulties. For example, issues such as data acquisition and processing, data reliability, and privacy protection. In addition, education Big data analysis also requires targeted modeling and algorithm optimization in combination with practical teaching experience and specialized domain knowledge [2]. Only by overcoming these problems and challenges can we make better use of education Big data and promote education reform and development.

Therefore, this paper aims to explore the application of education Big data analysis in the era of Big data, and deeply explore the advantages, challenges and opportunities of education Big data analysis. At the same time, through the analysis and research of the article, we try to dig out the key technologies and methods in system design, model development and data statistical analysis in education Big data analysis, and make full use of the advantages of Big data technology to better improve.

2   Related Work

2.1 "Big Data" in University Education Management

The effectiveness and accuracy of college student education management must be based on the comprehensive grasp, effective analysis and accurate judgment of students, and the production of massive structured and unstructured data, this has become a reality And these data are updated rapidly, large in scale and in different forms, which has exceeded the connotation of traditional data [3]. Because of its value density, authenticity and complexity, new value and significance emerge, which is also increasingly concerned by university education managers.

"Big data" of college students mainly refers to various information data sets generated on campus during the process from student admission to employment and leaving school. The main sources include: admission source information, freshman enrollment registration form, first classroom transcript, second classroom transcript, campus one card use information (library borrowing, consumption and other information), mental health information, employment information and special research data on a certain topic are shown in Fig. 1. Over the years, the data in these fields have lasted a long time and a large number, which is a perfect ideal database [4]. However, at present, each stage of College Students' development belongs to different college education management departments, such as the Academic Affairs Office for course learning and the group for campus cultural life Party committee and belong to the student work department, which has not received enough attention and has been deeply excavated and analyzed.

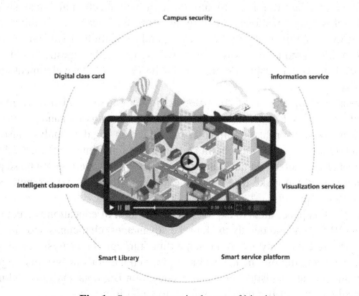

Fig. 1. Smart campus in the era of big data

In fact, looking at the current situation of student education management in Colleges and universities, it is common that the data on each line is too repetitive, scattered and broken, and has not realized systematization and modularization. In addition, it has not been well excavated and used for a long time. If we can adopt appropriate methods to collect all kinds College Students' education and management, and explore appropriate data mining methods and analysis tools, we will be able to better summarize and interpret the current social mentality.

The current university data management has begun the evolution of the source, application value and connotation and goal of education big data and digital campus construction. To understand the challenges faced by digital campus construction, and how to seize this opportunity and do a good job in digital campus construction, and the key technology realization required for the development of university smart campus has been deeply studied.

2.2 Research Status of "Big Data" Application in Colleges and Universities at Home and Abroad

For example, by analyzing a large amount of information related to students, the State University of the United States can even predict how many of the new undergraduate students of the university can achieve academic success, and the accuracy of the prediction is as high as 96%; In addition, the interactive behavior and emotional status among students are studied by collecting the data of students' social networking sites [5, 6].

As an important position for national teaching, scientific research and personnel training of higher education, Chinese universities produce a large amount of data in normal operation, including various scientific data sets and relevant information in scientific research, The research on "big data" came into being and is a powerful supporting tool in the fields of management and public administration. Some domestic scholars discuss issues such as population and health, education and economy through the quantitative analysis of the student status card data of college students in modern Chinese universities, and some scholars discuss the urban-rural differences of higher education inequality and gender inequality through CGSS;

At present, domestic scholars' investigations on the situation of college students mainly focus on the interpretation and suggestions of social structure and national policies at the macro level, and pay less attention to the solution and response to specific business problems at the operational level. Although a number of universities.

(1) The campus data is diversified and multi-dimensional, and there are information islands between multiple systems. Although the data has been saved, it has not yet been highly integrated. Some clustering algorithms, association analysis and other traditional data mining technologies cannot process the semi-structured and unstructured data in the existing university data.

(2) In addition to the "island" of system data, there is also the "island" of university data, that is, only the data of students during the period of university can be analyzed, and can not be associated with the data of pre-enrollment and graduation employment, ignoring the more comprehensive and meaningful whole process information of students.

(3) It is difficult to fully share between different systems, the construction and operation of shared databases are difficult, and authoritative data is lacking.

(4) Most of the existing campus data analysis systems passively provide analysis results, and can not achieve dynamic monitoring. Most of them are active queries with users.

3 Analysis of College Student Education Management System in the Era of Big Data

3.1 Analysis of Problems in College Student Management System

Although schools try their best to provide a better environment for students to become adults, there are still many problems that can not be noticed but can not be taken lightly in management.

(1) Student work is a mere formality, not really implemented. In many universities, the management of most departments is related to students. The closest contact with students is Committee of the Youth League Committee of the student work office. These departments will formulate rules and regulations on student management and carry out various activities from the perspective of schools or departments. However, in the actual implementation, many activities are carried out in form, in order to carry out, and some are just going through the motions. Under various pressures, students have to sign up for these activities, which not only does not receive good results, but wastes people and money, ignoring the most urgent needs in the depths of students' thoughts [7, 8].

(2) Many systems are too rigid and lack of humanization. In order to better manage and carry out teaching work, the school has formulated many rules and regulations according to the situation of the school, such as student status management measures, student reward and punishment measures, leave system and so on. These systems management of students, but in the implementation process, many students lack "humanization", let alone personalized care, do not regard students as an ideological subject, and many rules and regulations ignore students' rights and interests, resulting in many students' resistance to this rigid system.

(3) Lack of "normal" and "intervention" management for some students. Many of the daily management of students by head teachers and counselors is to educate and guide students after problems occur, and there is a lack of effective intervention in advance. Moreover, teachers usually give more care to the students at both ends of the class. Excellent students and backward students are easier to attract the attention and attention of teachers, and there is little care assigned to secondary students. Although they are adults, many students leave their parents and familiar environment for a long time for the first time, lack of social experience and mature cognition, and it is normal to have all kinds of problems. Counselors and head teachers need to deal with many people and many complicated affairs. It is almost difficult to really rely on manpower.

(4) The Faculty of student management is still relatively weak. The people who directly face students are mainly deputy secretaries of colleges and departments, counselors and head teachers. Their work includes students' study style construction, performance management, financial assistance for students with difficulties, mental health education, award and excellence, dormitory management, leave management,

employment management and many other complicated affairs. Counselors and head teachers often complete the tasks uploaded and assigned, only pursue the solution of problems, and it is difficult to provide constructive guidance to students. This is mainly attributed to two aspects: first, the teacher-student ratio of the school is not enough, and one person needs to face too many students. Secondly, many head teachers and counselors are not from professional backgrounds. Some teachers know the professional knowledge of students, but they have no research on students' mental health; Although other teachers are graduates majoring in psychological education, they do not understand the students' major, so it is difficult to give comprehensive guidance to students [9, 10].

It can be seen that urgently needs new technologies and new ways to improve efficiency. Big data technology obtains valuable information by analyzing massive data. Many things that rely on human or subjective experience judgment can be handed over to the machine for scientific analysis.

3.2 Design Path of College Student Education Management System in the Era of Big Data

Modern Internet technology has added many ways of information dissemination and expression to the student group, such as QQ, wechat, forums, blogs, etc., and has also increased the demand for students' self-control. Many college students suddenly switch from the "arranged" in high school to the university time that needs "independent decision", and have a strong sense of maladjustment to the changes of the outside world. In case of emergencies, there is little effective help around them, coupled with poor adaptability, they will have feelings of inferiority and anxiety, which is difficult for the teachers around them to detect. At this time, it is very important for schools to rely on technical means for thousands of pre-school, homework and classroom attendance; Analyze the retrieval data of the school library and push interested books and related elective courses for students; Recommend relevant recruitment positions for students through the analysis of students' keywords on the recruitment website; By extracting students' QQ, wechat and other data, we can get students' Ideological and emotional dynamics, and identify students with psychological abnormalities to facilitate early intervention. Reflect students' learning dynamics with objective data, create suitable education programs for students, and promote humanized and personalized service of school management.

The intelligence of data acquisition and foreign friends, interests and hobbies, family and social relations, etc. the data is huge and wide. From this information, we can identify which may infringe on students' personal privacy, which information can be mined and studied, and which data analysis results can be disclosed and published to what extent. Only on the basis of not infringing on students' personal privacy and not being abused, this kind of data mining and analysis behavior can help students grow into talents and be more meaningful.

3.3 Design of University Student Education Management System Based on Big Data

The design of the software architecture in the system is mainly to design the software architecture. The current software development will use a relatively mature architecture to build the software system. The most used is the three-tier architecture design, which divides the business part and data part of the system into modules, The three-layer architecture of the system is shown in Fig. 2.

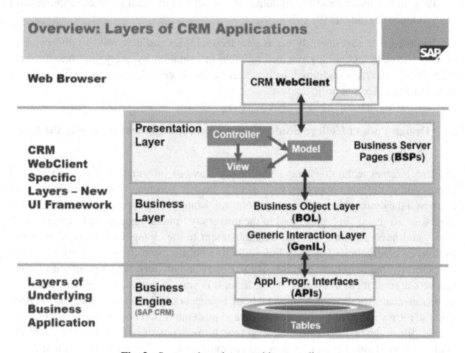

Fig. 2. System three-layer architecture diagram

According to the demand analysis, the student management system is divided into the functions of the whole system at the levels of students, teachers, courses, student grades and basic data. The most basic addition and deletion functions are considered in the design process of the module functions of teachers, students and courses. Batches are added in consideration of the maturity of future applications in practice. Refer to mature system design ideas for other basic modules, users and data modules. Divided according to the actual needs of Zhangjiakou Vocational and Technical College, and the system structure diagram is drawn as shown in Fig. 3.

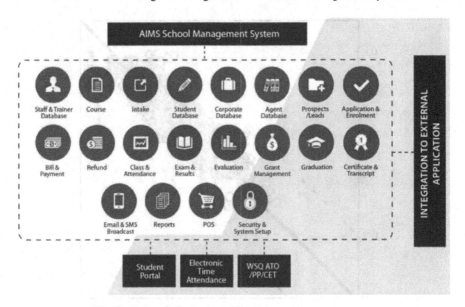

Fig. 3. Framework diagram of student management system

4   Experimental Results and Analysis

In order to verify the effectiveness of the university student education management system in the era of big data, we conducted a series of experiments. The following is a detailed introduction to the experimental process and analysis. We chose a university as the experimental object to collect students' personal information, course selection data, course evaluation data, and other aspects of information. Then, we preprocess, integrate, filter, and clean these data, and store them in the database. Next, we use machine learning and data mining algorithms to analyze and mine these data. We first analyze students' course selection data to understand their interests and characteristics, in order to provide personalized learning suggestions and plans for students. At the same time, we also analyze the course evaluation data to identify shortcomings and provide suggestions for improving the teaching process.

In the analysis process, we also utilized artificial intelligence technology to predict and analyze students' growth and development, thereby helping them better plan their future development direction and career planning.

Finally, we also use an interactive control panel to visualize the experimental results, facilitating real-time monitoring and control by administrators and teachers, ensuring the transparency and scientificity of the education management system. The simulation results are shown in Fig. 4.

Our experimental results indicate that the university student education management system based on big data analysis can significantly improve the quality of education and student learning outcomes in practice, and has significant application value. Firstly, education big data analysis can help teachers better grasp students' learning patterns and characteristics through the analysis of information such as course selection and

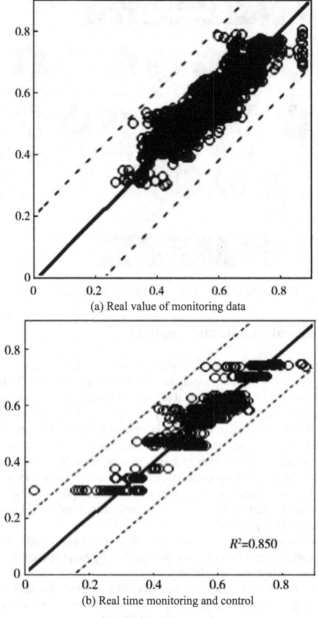

(a) Real value of monitoring data

(b) Real time monitoring and control

$R^2=0.850$

Fig. 4. Simulation result

course evaluation data, provide scientific teaching suggestions and strategies for teachers, strengthen personalized education for students, and better meet their needs and expectations. Secondly, education big data analysis can also help students plan their future careers and development directions. By analyzing and predicting students' growth trajectory, it helps them better understand their own characteristics and advantages, and find their own development direction and goals. In addition, education big data analysis can also help educational institutions optimize resource allocation and management. By analyzing and evaluating teaching facilities, teaching staff, curriculum design, and other aspects, we aim to promote the optimization and efficient utilization of educational resources.

In summary, our experimental results indicate that the university student education management system based on big data analysis has broad practical application value and promotion prospects. However, there are still many challenges and difficulties in application. We need to continuously research and improve the theory and practice of education big data analysis in order to better respond to the needs of education reform and modernization, and achieve the goals of education modernization and universal quality education.Education Big data analysis technology is a product of the information and digital era, which has a broad application prospect and huge development potential. This paper explores the application of education Big data analysis, deeply discusses the advantages.

5 Conclusion

Education Big data analysis technology is a product of the information and digital era, which has a broad application prospect and huge development potential. This paper explores the application of education Big data analysis, deeply discusses the advantages, challenges and opportunities of education Big data analysis, and introduces the key technologies and methods of education Big data analysis system design, model development and data statistical analysis. It provides a feasible technical means for the education and management of college students. Schools collect, store, and analyze data and information related to students, comprehensively understand their interests, psychology, life, and other situations, analyze the development trends of students' learning and emotions, and enable students' work to truly emerge from experience and subjective judgments. They rely on data from macro to micro perspectives to develop personalized education plans for individual students.

Preliminary research has shown that the application of modern education big data analysis technology can have significant driving effects on personalized training, teaching strategies, teaching management, and other aspects. It can carry out research on key issues such as students' personalized learning, educational investment, and educational equity from the depth dimension of the whole teaching process, students' behavior, and layer upon layer organization, so as to provide support for Educational assessment and promote the fair and balanced development of education.

Of course, the application of educational Big data analysis technology also faces many challenges and difficulties, such as privacy protection, data security, data acquisition and processing, and the shortage of professionals and resources. Therefore, we must continue to explore and adopt practical technology management models, strengthen cooperation between school education management departments and relevant research institutions, integrate school development and research capabilities, promote the combination of digitalization and informatization with education and teaching, and achieve optimization and innovation of education processes.

Based on the above, although the educational Big data analysis technology still faces many challenges and limitations, we believe that this technology can provide new development ideas and innovative models for educational research, constantly explore and expand the boundaries of educational technology, and further improve the efficiency, satisfaction and fairness of education.

Finally, we hope that our research can be promoted in the field of education, promote the efficient development of education, and achieve personal growth and social progress.

References

1. Wang J . An Intelligence Probe of College Student Management in the Big Data Era (2021)
2. Chen, T.: Research on the dilemma and breakthrough path of ideological and political education in colleges and universities in the era of big data. J. High. Educ. Res. 3(2), 203–206 (2022)
3. Li, F., Gao, W.: Research on the design of intelligent energy efficiency management system for ships based on computer big data platform. J. Phys. Conf. Ser. 1744(2), 022026 (2021)
4. Khammatova, R.S., et al.: Specific features of value orientations among the student youth in the context of digital transformation of the education system. World J. Educ. Technol. Curr. Issues 13(2), 297–306 (2021). https://doi.org/10.18844/wjet.v13i2.5714
5. Pan, K.: Exploration and innovative research on the training of party branch secretaries of students in colleges and universities in the new era. Chinese Studies 11(02), 90–96 (2022). https://doi.org/10.4236/chnstd.2022.112008
6. Bian, F., Wang, X.: The effect of big-data on the management of higher education in China and its countermeasures. Int. J. Electr. Eng. Educ.Electr. Eng. Educ. 60, 2986–2994 (2021)
7. Liang, B., Yang, Z.: Exploration and application of college students€ management model during the epidemic based on big data technology. Math. Probl. Eng.Probl. Eng. 2022, 1–9 (2022)
8. Krause, A.J., Moore, S.Y.: Creating an online peer-to-peer mentoring program: promoting student relationships, engagement, and satisfaction during the era of COVID-19. Coll. Teach. 4, 1–13 (2021)
9. Wang, P., Hu, Y., Huo, J.: Practical teaching and research on the design of below-created products in the era of big data. In: Hung, J.C., Chang, J.W., Pei, Y., Wu, W.C. (eds.) Innovative Computing. LNEE, vol. 791, pp. 1015–1021. Springer, Singapore (2022). https://doi.org/10.1007/978-981-16-4258-6_124
10. Hu, B.Z.: Research on the security of accounting information system in the big data era. Acad. J. Comput. Inf. Sci. 4(4), 60–63 (2021)

The Design of Student Comprehensive Education Evaluation System in the Background of Big Data

Xianli Zeng[1(✉)], Cheng Maomao[2,3], Wuyi Zhao[1], and Lin Gang[1]

[1] Student Affairs Office, Guilin University of Electronic Technology, Guilin 541004, Guangxi, China
`{zxl1982,zhaowuyi}@guet.edu.cn`
[2] Faculty of Education, Northeast Normal University, Changchun 130024, Jilin, China
[3] Guilin University of Electronic Technology, Guilin 541004, Guangxi, China

Abstract. The transformation of the education evaluation system is the core content of solving the problems of teaching management, and the process management and process evaluation based on big data are the core methods to solve the problem of talent training. Therefore, it is necessary to systematically analyze the learning evaluation, put forward the evaluation index system of college learning based on educational big data, and reconstruct the educational evaluation system. The purpose of this paper is to study the reform of students' comprehensive education evaluation. First, it conducts research on the current situation of colleges and universities, and collects relevant information on the comprehensive quality evaluation of students in the International Education College; secondly, it analyzes the strategies to challenge the reform of student evaluation. The actual data related to the student evaluation are extracted; finally, the construction of indicators and the establishment and application of the model for the comprehensive evaluation of students are carried out. The experiment shows that the model in this paper can deeply reflect the comprehensive quality level of college students.

Keywords: Big Data Background · Comprehensive Education · Student Education · Evaluation Reform

1 Introduction

In order to change the current problem that the quality of teaching is difficult to supervise, it is necessary to implement comprehensive education evaluation for students; at the same time, the national policy also proposes to improve the quality of training by strengthening the supervision and evaluation of the teaching process. The proliferation of educational process data caused by the informatization of content also provides a data basis for comprehensive education-oriented learning evaluation [1]. Based on this, college education evaluation based on educational big data is an important content to solve the teaching problems in my country. How to establish a college evaluation system based on educational big data has become one of the important contents of educational big data [2].

Y. Zhang and N. Shah (Eds.): BigIoT-EDU 2023, LNICST 581, pp. 345–352, 2024.
https://doi.org/10.1007/978-3-031-63133-7_34

With the sharp increase of students' process data, learning evaluation has turned to be carried out on the basis of educational big data. This evaluation runs through students' comprehensive learning, and no longer takes a quantitative evaluation of students as the evaluation result of students [3]. Cahyadi examined the quality of ERT using a meta-analysis (CCA) approach involving 2,957 primary school students from 22 universities in 10 provinces in Indonesia. The results seem to indicate that affordability and flexibility are two sub-criteria for the student experience in Indonesian universities [4]. Satoshi demonstrates the use of instructional analytics by teachers to achieve student goals by assessing student achievement for student reflection, student remediation, and teacher curriculum evaluation. The learning management system includes resource analysis tools to assist the analysis process. Learning analytics tools provide direct and indirect information to many stakeholders in advising, student reflection, student learning, and course evaluation [5]. Therefore, it is necessary to systematically analyze the overall evaluation of college students' education, put forward a comprehensive index system of student education evaluation based on educational big data, and reconstruct the education evaluation system [6].

This paper collects various data of education and teaching (including the results of various examinations in the region, research on education and teaching, multi-channel questionnaire surveys, and feedback from teaching departments at all levels, etc.), and uses statistics, information technology and other means to collect data. The collected data are analyzed and mined to find meaningful information for promoting the improvement of teaching quality, collect and organize this information, form corresponding analysis reports and countermeasures, and feed back the research results to the school to improve school management and promote higher education. Improve teaching quality.

2   Research on the Reform of Students' Comprehensive Education Evaluation Under the Background of Big Data

2.1   Strategies for Students to Evaluate the Challenges of Change in the Era of Big Data

(1) Analysis of the connotation of rational big data concept
    A rational big data view, in addition to recognizing that the characteristics are consistent with the principles of student evaluation, recognizing the role and value of big data in the reform of student evaluation, and recognizing the many challenges faced by student evaluation, also means Comprehensive, in-depth and objective knowledge and understanding of educational big data [7].
(2) The development of educational big data technology requires multi-party cooperation
    The technical system of educational big data has the characteristics of complexity, innovation and high investment, and its development requires the full cooperation of the government, various schools and enterprises [8]. The government needs to provide policy guidance, funding, supervision and coordination in the development. Specifically, it includes promoting the open sharing of educational data and providing a broad space for the development of educational big data technology; standardizing

educational data formats and proposing requirements for educational big data storage technology; providing financial support to provide material for the development of educational big data technology Foundation; supervise the big data application process and standardize the application behavior of educational big data technology [9].

(3) Improve teachers' data analysis ability through special training

Teachers have received professional education and special training, have certain evaluation knowledge and evaluation skills, and are an important subject in the implementation of student evaluation. In view of the lack of knowledge, skills and practical experience related to data-based student evaluation among teachers, it is necessary to establish a supporting teacher training system to improve teachers' awareness and ability to use educational big data to carry out student evaluation [10].

2.2 Reform of the Comprehensive Education Evaluation Framework for Students

Compared with traditional student evaluation, this paper solves the problems of lack of consideration of individual factors of students, neglect of feedback of student evaluation, and timeliness of evaluation. A comprehensive education evaluation framework for students is proposed. According to the principle of combining subjective and objective factors in student evaluation, the comprehensive evaluation model of students is divided into two parts: soft evaluation and hard evaluation [11]. Among them, the rigid evaluation uses classroom tests as the carrier to evaluate students' knowledge mastery. The soft evaluation is to analyze the information hidden in students' learning behavior, such as students' hobbies, learning attitudes, learning attitudes, etc., and then evaluate these hidden information [12, 13]. Due to the flexibility of the source of indicators for subjective factor evaluation (the evaluation of subjective factors is called soft evaluation), the evaluation model constructed for subjective factors usually has certain flexibility and scalability [14, 15]. As for the evaluation of the course test, because the relevant information records of the test are real and objective, the test and related information are regarded as a rigid evaluation result of the student evaluation. The student evaluation framework is shown in Fig. 1.

2.3 Fuzzy Comprehensive Evaluation

There are two types of mathematical models for fuzzy comprehensive evaluation: single-level model and multi-level model. According to different assessment items, different models can be used for assessment [16, 17].

Evaluation indicators are all indicators of the evaluation object. These metrics include evaluating the characteristics or properties of an object, also known as parametric metrics or quality metrics. We can calculate evaluation items as indicator data or these features.

According to the maximum membership degree method of fuzzy global evaluation, the maximum value of sample quality is determined as the final evaluation level. This evaluation method is not only influenced by the opinions of many evaluators and various evaluation factors, but also scientific, and there is a confusion problem in the evaluation process [18].

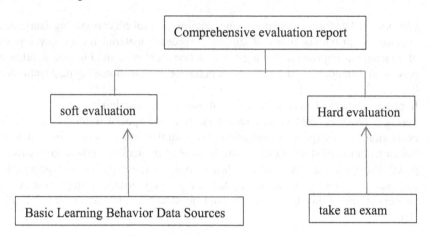

Fig. 1. Student evaluation framework

3 Systematic Summary of Student Comprehensive Education Evaluation Reform Under the Background of Big Data

3.1 Overall Architecture

The survey of students' comprehensive education evaluation system shows that teachers, counselors, students and administrators are the largest user groups of the current college student evaluation system, and the largest number of users are students.

Each module is described below:

System login module: The function of this function module is to authenticate and identify the identity of the login user.

Query service module: This function module provides students with query functions, including grades or related information.

Evaluation Management Module: The main function of this module is to manage students' comprehensive evaluation scores.

Teacher performance management module: This functional module provides teachers with evaluation services, such as grade setting, course information addition, and so on.

Counselor management module: This functional module provides counselors with management functions such as sorting of students' grades and entering comprehensive information.

System management module: This function module mainly provides management functions for system administrators, such as adding, deleting, editing users, importing and exporting log information, etc.

3.2 Comprehensive Evaluation Management Module

The original intention of the system is to manage the students' summary evaluation results, therefore, the summary evaluation results are the core information of the comprehensive evaluation system.

The comprehensive evaluation module is the most important module in the whole system module. According to user requirements, the comprehensive evaluation module performs relevant calculations according to the established fuzzy comprehensive evaluation model, and at the same time refers to the basic scores given by the system and the attachment scores of each part for detailed calculation and evaluation.

3.3 Fuzzy Comprehensive Evaluation Steps

(1) Create a comment set
   The comment set is: V = (v1, v2,..., vm), where vi (i = 1, 2,..., m) represents comments at all levels. Comment sets have different meanings according to different evaluation objects. For the evaluation of the comprehensive quality of college students, the comment set is a collection of comprehensive quality grades.
(2) Establish an indicator set
   The index set is a collection of various evaluation indexes.
(3) Establish a single-factor evaluation matrix
   When the comment set V and the index set U are determined, we can establish a fuzzy mapping from U to F(V):

$$f : U \rightarrow F(V), \forall u_i \in U \tag{1}$$

$$u_i \rightarrow f(u_i) = \frac{r_{il}}{v_1} + \frac{r_{i2}}{v_2} + \ldots + \frac{r_{im}}{v_{m0 \le r_{ij} \le 1, 1 \le i \le n, 1 \le j \le m}} \tag{2}$$

The fuzzy matrix R can be obtained from f, so (U, V, R) constitutes a comprehensive evaluation model.

4 An Empirical Study on the System Model of Students' Comprehensive Education Evaluation Reform Under the Background of Big Data

4.1 Indicator Weight Distribution

This chapter is used to further verify and discuss the model for evaluating the comprehensive quality of students in a certain university. The empirical analysis work is set to be carried out in a small area, and 30 students in a certain class are selected to evaluate the comprehensive quality. In the actual situation, the questionnaires were made for each of the first-level indicators and distributed in a targeted manner. Considering the subsequent calculation work, the final number of valid questionnaires for each student was set to 20.

According to the construction of the index set, a weight evaluation table is made, and the weight evaluation work is carried out by the student management experts. The obtained weight distribution of each index and the calculation results of its specific weight score are shown in Table 1.

Table 1. Weight distribution table of students' comprehensive evaluation indicators

Target layer	First-level indicator	Secondary indicators
Comprehensive evaluation of students	Cultural knowledge quality 0.35	Course Study 0.7
		Various grade exams and competitions 0.3
	Ideological and moral quality 0.30	Daily Code of Conduct 0.6
		Collective Ideas 0.4
	Independent living ability 0.20	Ability to communicate with people smoothly 0.7
		Protect your own security ability 0.3
	Innovative practice quality 0.15	Social practice performance 0.5
		Scientific and technological innovation achievements 0.5

4.2 Analysis of Evaluation Results

In the actual operation process of applying the fuzzy comprehensive evaluation method based on AHP to evaluate the comprehensive education of students in the School of International Education, in addition to the comment results, which can clearly indicate the comprehensive quality level of each student, the overall score ranking of the comprehensive evaluation can be used for the evaluation of colleges and departments. In addition to the implementation of excellent work, the comprehensive evaluation matrix obtained in the calculation process is also an important part of the evaluation results of empirical analysis. The comprehensive evaluation matrix obtained in the process of calculating the comprehensive education of each student can reflect the level of each quality of the student. On the basis of analysis and comparison, a more comprehensive quality evaluation can be given to the student, and its shortcomings For the student management workers of colleges and departments, they can carry out the training of students' comprehensive education in a more targeted manner (Fig. 2).

The empirical results of the comprehensive student education evaluation system can deeply reflect the comprehensive quality level of college students, accurately evaluate the development trend of students' morality, intelligence, physical fitness, etc., correctly guide the development of students, provide effective reports, and provide simple and effective reports to colleges. The assessment and evaluation of students play a positive role in promoting the improvement of students' management level.

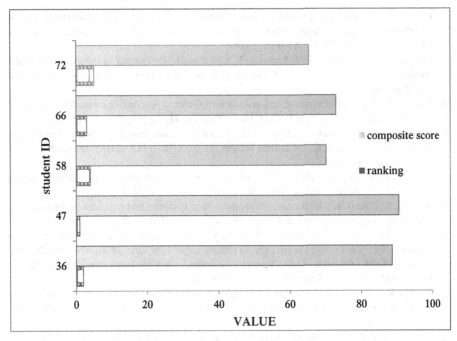

Fig. 2. Students' overall quality ranking

5   Conclusions

With the continuous development of quality education, the requirements of schools for students' education have also changed. Education should start from the perspective of students, take students as the main body, treat students equally and comprehensively, and promote all-round development. This paper uses the basic process of analytic hierarchy process to design the comprehensive education evaluation system for students, and at the same time provides a reasonable and feasible index system for the comprehensive evaluation, establishes a systematic evaluation model and implements it. Under the premise of fully examining the limited amount of information that can be used for learning effect evaluation during students' learning process, this study proposes the research content of using fuzzy comprehensive evaluation to establish a comprehensive evaluation model of learning effect, and verifies the book through actual research and expert interviews significance of research.

References

1. Souza, A., Filho, M.R., Soares, C.: Production and evaluation of an educational process for human-computer interaction (HCI) courses. IEEE Trans. Educ. **64**(2), 172–179 (2020)
2. Couto, J.G., McFadden, S., Bezzina, P., McClure, P., Hughes, C.: An evaluation of the educational requirements to practise radiography in the European Union. Radiography **24**(1), 64–71 (2018)

3. Ceyhan, D., Akdik, C., Kirzioglu, Z.: An educational programme designed for the evaluation of effectiveness of two tooth brushing techniques in preschool children. Eur. J. Paediatr. Dent.Paediatr. Dent. **19**(3), 181–186 (2018)

4. Cahyadi, A., Hendryadi, S.W., Mufidah, V.N., Achmadi: Emergency remote teaching evaluation of the higher education in Indonesia. Heliyon **7**(8), e07788 (2021). https://doi.org/10.1016/j.heliyon.2021.e07788

5. Satoshi, N., Yuya: The impact of self-assessment of learning evaluation on student's approach in junior high school science. Japan J. Educ. Technol. **42**(Suppl.), 033–036 (2018)

6. Rodrigues, M.W., Isotani, S., Zárate, L.E.: Educational data mining: a review of evaluation process in the e-learning. Telematics Inform. **35**(6), 1701–1717 (2018). https://doi.org/10.1016/j.tele.2018.04.015

7. Pkgr, A., Jcmrc, A., Jldmr, B., et al.: A systematic evaluation of advance care planning patient educational resources. Geriatr. Nurs.. Nurs. **40**(1), 174–180 (2019)

8. Atsuko, S., Takao, K.: Evaluation of program-based educational practices in international education cooperation. Japan. J. Disabil. Sci. **42**(1), 217–226 (2018)

9. Noh, Y., Lee, S.Y.: An evaluation of the library's educational value based on the perception of public library users and librarians in Korea. Electron. Libr.Libr. **38**(4), 677–694 (2020)

10. Scharrer, M.H., Peterson, M.J.: Teaching decisional capacity evaluation. Am. J. Geriatr. PsychiatryGeriatr. Psychiatry **26**(3), S115–S116 (2018)

11. Sebillo, M., Vitiello, G., Di Gregorio, M.: Maps4Learning: enacting geo-education to enhance student achievement. IEEE Access **8**, 87633–87646 (2020). https://doi.org/10.1109/ACCESS.2020.2993507

12. Mesg, A., Hmdb, C., Js, D.: Standardized testing in nursing education: preparing students for NCLEX-RN and practice. J. Prof. Nurs.Nurs. **35**(6), 440–446 (2019)

13. Ellaway, R.H., Topps, D., Pusic, M.: Data, big and small: emerging challenges to medical education scholarship. Acad. Med. **94**(1), 31–36 (2019)

14. Rezaee, Z., Wang, J., Cooper, B., et al.: Relevance of big data to forensic accounting practice and education. Manag. Audit. J.. Audit. J. **34**(3), 268–288 (2019)

15. Inquimbert, C., Tramini, P., Romieu, O., et al.: Pedagogical evaluation of digital technology to enhance dental student learning. Eur. J. Dentist. **13**(1), 053–057 (2019)

16. Vengrin, C., Westfall-Rudd, D., Archibald, T., Rudd, R., Singh, K.: Factors affecting evaluation culture within a non-formal educational organization. Eval. Program Plan. **69**, 75–81 (2018). https://doi.org/10.1016/j.evalprogplan.2018.04.012

17. Nikolic, S., Suesse, T., Jovanovic, K., et al.: Laboratory learning objectives measurement: relationships between student evaluation scores and perceived learning. IEEE Trans. Educ. **64**(99), 1–9 (2020)

18. Allison, C., Patrick, L., Steeves, E.A., et al.: P155 process evaluation of a sustainable food systems course for first-year college students. J. Nutr. Educ. Behav.Nutr. Educ. Behav. **52**(7), S89–S90 (2020)

Research on Teaching Design of Smart Classroom for Tourism Management in Colleges and Universities in 5G Era

Guo Weimin[(⊠)] and Chen Jin

Jiangxi University of Applied Science, Nanchang 330100, Jiangxi, China
gweim@163.com

Abstract. Tourism is one of the most important economic sectors in the world. It has great potential to generate income for many countries and also contributes to the development of many other economic sectors. With the rapid development of domestic social economy, the living standard of the people has been significantly improved, and higher requirements have been set for daily life and entertainment. These changes have brought huge development prospects and development space for the tourism industry. Tourism plays an important role in promoting cultural diversity, promoting peace and security, improving health care standards and supporting local economy. In this era of technological progress, tourism management has become more challenging due to the increasing number and types of tourists visiting different destinations around the world. In the 5G era, college students are accustomed to learning and communicating with modern information methods. Therefore, it is imperative to reform the traditional teaching mode. Based on this, this paper deeply analyzes the high-quality teaching design of building smart classroom for tourism management majors in colleges and universities under the background of 5G era.

Keywords: Major in tourism management · Smart classroom · 5G · instructional design

1 Introduction

China officially entered the mobile internet era in 2010. With the rapid development of modern information technology, the 5G era has quietly arrived. Compared with 4G mobile communication technology, 5G communication technology has a faster transmission speed [1]. As the core group growing up in the 5G era, college students have already adapted to the development environment of the Internet era and are accustomed to acquiring knowledge with modern information equipment, which also urges the traditional teaching model to make corresponding adjustments and optimization. In the context of the 5G era, domestic colleges and universities should take this as a breakthrough to organically integrate the modern teaching mode with the traditional teaching mode, and jointly build a complete teaching system for tourism management specialty, and create an efficient smart classroom [2].

Y. Zhang and N. Shah (Eds.): BigIoT-EDU 2023, LNICST 581, pp. 353–360, 2024.
https://doi.org/10.1007/978-3-031-63133-7_35

The proposal of educational modernization strategy has created conditions for intelligent teaching and also promoted the development of intelligent teaching. The Education Reform and Development Planning Program issued by the Ministry of Education pointed out that: "By 2020, all parts of the country need basic construction - a comprehensive education information system covering all kinds of campuses in both urban and rural areas of the province, from the most basic campus network coverage to the popularization of education information technology, to promote the scientific and technological development of school teaching methods, teaching methods and teaching models, to effectively apply various high-quality online education resources and advanced education technologies, to improve the school operation mechanism and management form, and to integrate existing teaching Educate teaching resources and strive to build the campus into an intelligent, efficient and technologically advanced digital education base [3]. Governments at all levels should overcome all difficulties, fully cover the campus with high-speed network, vigorously promote the construction of terminal technology and equipment, and promote the digitalization and scientific and technological development of the campus. "Premier Li Keqiang put forward the concept of smart education for the first time in the 2015 government work report, which inspired the learning enthusiasm of all Chinese people in the Internet era It is pointed out that we should strive to promote the application of AI technology in the whole process of school teaching management and digital construction, vigorously cultivate intelligent talents, promote the reform of teaching methods, construct a new education system, and improve the refinement level of education services [4]. In April 2018, the Ministry of Education issued the "Education Informatization 2.0 Action Plan", which clearly pointed out that "based on the new generation of information technology such as artificial intelligence, the Internet of Things, big data and so on, relying on a variety of advanced AI technology equipment and mobile 5G network, accelerate the implementation of smart education science research and smart campus demonstration construction", and deeply integrate AI technology into the whole process of smart education, It provides new ideas and methods for the construction of smart classroom and the development of smart teaching in schools, and creates favorable conditions for China to comprehensively strengthen the promotion of AI technology in the field of education [5]. In February 2019, China Education Modernization 2035 proposed to accelerate the development of intelligent education in the information age, gradually establish intelligent campus, and create a good learning environment for students.

2   Related Work

2.1   Research on the Connotation of Intelligent Teaching Design

The progress of science and technology has brought the continuous enrichment of wisdom teaching, and different perspectives have added different connotations. This study studies the connotation of intelligent instructional design from the perspective of theory, technology and teacher development.

Understand wisdom teaching from a theoretical perspective. Intelligent teaching is an important new teaching method nowadays. Scholars have scientifically analyzed the connotation of intelligent teaching from a theoretical perspective. Huang Mei identified the key elements of intelligent teaching and believed that the key of intelligent teaching is classroom teaching, which means that teachers should teach according to scientific educational laws in teaching, fully display their teaching wisdom and teaching tact in the teaching process, and further improve their teaching level in teaching practice [6]. Wu Yuqi believes that intelligent teaching is a comprehensive ability of teachers to create a free and harmonious learning atmosphere by creating teaching situations conducive to learning based on their understanding of teaching laws and phenomena. It is emphasized that we should attach importance to the four corresponding relationships between teachers and students, curriculum and teaching, students and disciplines, and process and results [7]. This study believes that intelligent teaching is the teaching to promote the generation of students' wisdom. Based on the teaching wisdom of teachers, artificial intelligence technology is effectively applied to intelligent teaching design, implementation means and multiple evaluation process to achieve efficient classroom teaching.

Understand intelligent teaching from the technical level. With the rise of cloud computing, Internet of Things, 5G and other new generation of information technology, intelligent teaching has been given new features and has become an important new teaching method nowadays. Scholars in the field of educational technology have analyzed the connotation of intelligent teaching from the perspective of informatization.

Yang Xianmin and others put forward that smart teaching is in the smart teaching environment. Through the integration of information technology and its depth, teachers comprehensively adopt various advanced AI technologies and massive teaching resources to carry out teaching activities, and promote the generation and sustainable development of students' wisdom. Pang Jingwen and others believe that intelligent teaching aims at cultivating intelligent students, uses advanced teaching methods with the help of information technology to teach, give full play to students' enthusiasm for learning and stimulate students' active learning. The main purpose of intelligent teaching is to promote students' personalized learning, master scientific learning methods, strengthen students' learning ability, and enable students to learn independently. Dai Hongbin put forward that the key of intelligent teaching is to cultivate students' intelligence and strong practical ability, effectively use artificial intelligence and other educational technologies, create an intelligent learning environment, and create favorable conditions for the teaching of students with teachers' minds. Tang Yewei proposed that intelligent teaching is to change teachers' teaching concepts, improve teaching methods and means, skillfully use various information technologies in classroom teaching to display knowledge and solve problems, build the classroom into an intelligent, personalized and contextualized learning environment, let students learn happily and efficiently, and promote the cultivation of students' intelligent ability.

2.2 New Requirements for Intelligent Teaching

Use the new generation of information technology such as artificial intelligence, Internet of Things, big data and mobile internet to serve intelligent teaching and promote the intelligent transformation of teaching design and learning methods. The use of artificial intelligence technology has also brought new changes to the teaching mode. A series of new intelligent teaching modes, such as micro-class teaching, Muke teaching, flipped classroom teaching, and double-teacher classroom teaching, have been born, which has changed our traditional classroom teaching mode that focuses on naval warfare. The leading role of teachers is to guide students to work hard to solve practical problems. Students actively participate in and actively study to make teaching more vivid and efficient, form an effective teaching idea and approach to solve practical problems, and cultivate and develop students' ability of intelligent learning.

(1) The transformation of teachers' functions. The functions of teachers should also be changed, from the traditional single preacher to the compound intelligent teacher, becoming the leader of students' life, the guardian of life, the collaborator of learning, the teacher and the friend, playing the role of superman every day. The teaching method of teachers should be changed from traditional theoretical explanation to leading students to learn independently, cultivating students' ability and enlightening students' wisdom.

(2) Improvement of teaching objectives. Teaching objectives are the soul of the whole teaching process and the primary task of each class. The new curriculum reform has once again determined three aspects of teaching objectives, namely, knowledge learning and ability training, mastering the learning process and learning methods, and cultivating emotional attitudes and correct values.

(3) The transformation of teaching mode. Smart classroom is not only a simple model for teachers to teach students to learn, but also a process for teachers and students to learn and grow together. It is a new teaching attitude centered on students' learning. Teachers are like directors. In the process of smart classroom, teachers should be the planners and leaders of the whole teaching activity, leading the healthy development of the whole class, as shown in Fig. 1.

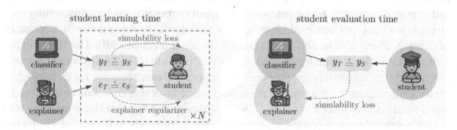

Fig. 1. Smart classroom teaching mode

3 The Role and Significance of Smart Classroom in Colleges and Universities in the 5G Era

Smart classroom is built on the support of modern information technology and Internet technology. It is used in the implementation of pre-class teaching design, in-class teaching design and after-class teaching design. The Internet teaching platform can achieve more scientific, more efficient and more intelligent teaching links. It is a new teaching model with advanced concepts and significant effects.

(1) Promote teachers to change traditional teaching concepts

At present, most college students are post-95 and post-00. They grow up in the Internet environment and are used to accepting new things. The arrival of the 5G era has triggered the revolution of the mobile internet era, and also led to the earth-shaking transformation of the internet environment, making college students have a deeper understanding of things and knowledge. In general, the mobile internet has not only changed the way of thinking of college students, but also changed their learning habits and attitudes [8]. Therefore, teachers should take the reform of teaching mode as a breakthrough, introduce the modern education concept, change from traditional teaching as the main body of classroom teaching to the main participant of classroom teaching, improve their professional quality, update their knowledge reserves and knowledge structure, and adjust their own status, change the traditional teaching mode and teaching methods.

(2) Challenges for all educators in the 5G era

The emergence of Internet technology has changed the traditional way of life, work and learning of the public, and has brought important assistance and challenges to the reform of teaching mode in colleges and universities. From the macro level, the 5G era has completely broken the space and time constraints, and students can use online devices to carry out autonomous learning and online learning anytime and anywhere; From the micro level, the development of education informatization has promoted the curriculum teaching content and teaching methods, student assessment methods and teaching evaluation methods to become more objective and more data-based. With the continuous progress and development of modern information technology, China has completely entered the 5G era. The learning environment of college students has already broken through the limitations and constraints of traditional classroom teaching. Teachers should properly optimize and adjust the teaching mode and teaching methods, which is also an important link to promote their own teaching level.

(3) 5G era brings good ideas for classroom design

At present, smart phones have become the "standard configuration" of college students, and mobile Internet devices such as tablets and laptops are almost all available. Mobile Internet has already become one of the important ways for college students to acquire knowledge, and mobile devices have become one of the necessary items in students' life. Mobile phones have always been a double-edged sword in the eyes of educators. While bringing convenience to students in acquiring knowledge, they have also seriously affected classroom discipline. However, it is undeniable that after the popularization of mobile internet, smart phones have become more efficient and convenient in acquiring knowledge and information. Through mobile Internet devices such as mobile phones, learning materials can be searched anytime and anywhere, or software learning can be carried out through the Internet teaching platform [9]. Therefore, while facing the challenges brought by mobile Internet devices such as mobile phones to the traditional classroom, it also brings new ideas and new perspectives to the reform of teaching models for college teachers. Now, in the 5G era, the functions of mobile phones are more perfect, the Internet coverage is more extensive, and the connection methods are more convenient. The teaching resources in the Internet are also broader and more diversified, bringing good learning resources to students. In this context, how to make mobile phones become an important help to build smart classrooms is an urgent problem for all college teachers.

4 Teaching Design of Smart Class for Tourism Management Specialty in 5G Era

The teaching design of smart classroom is the sum of teaching arrangement and design carried out by teachers to achieve teaching objectives. The core content of smart classroom teaching activity design for tourism management majors in colleges and universities is mainly divided into three parts: before class, during class and after class.

4.1 Before Class - Establish a Smart Classroom Teaching Platform

Before class, the teaching resource sharing platform is built through the Blue Ink Cloud classroom APP, which can be built according to the teaching class. The teaching platform is a booster for the reform of smart teaching methods in the 5G era, and a guarantee for the input and output of teaching resources for teachers and students. After the platform is built, the teacher can design the pre-class materials and push them to the mobile platform through the device. The students can preview the materials before class through the platform. The preview materials include guide cards, text materials, courseware PT, videos, micro-classes, relevant lectures and related expansion materials of this knowledge point. On the platform, students can ask questions about the teacher's preview materials, express their opinions, express their opinions, share their experiences, and also send the knowledge points that are difficult to understand or need to be explained to the teacher in the form of messages [10]. The teacher adjusts the teaching content and activities according to the students' feedback and messages, and aims to improve the learning effectiveness of the offline classroom, as shown in Fig. 2. Classroom teaching design is to better complete the teaching content and achieve good education and learning results. In the past classroom, teachers mainly designed classroom teaching according to the curriculum syllabus, teaching objectives and teaching content of each class, while smart classroom can comprehensively sort out and analyze the teaching content, design and optimize teaching activities according to the students' pre-class preview, cognition of knowledge points and interaction between students, so as to better achieve the teaching objectives.

4.2 In Class - Set up Two-Way Interactive Teaching Links

In the offline classroom of smart classroom, in addition to teaching classroom knowledge, teachers should also strengthen teacher-student interaction, so that students can also have a voice in the classroom and improve their sense of participation. The key of smart classroom in colleges and universities is to realize real-time and dynamic two-way interaction between off-class and on-class. In the teaching process of smart classroom, the teacher's teaching design should reflect the students' main learning position, and the teacher should play the role of guide and promoter. Therefore, the smart classroom should be designed with news broadcast, new lesson explanation, task assignment, summary and other links.

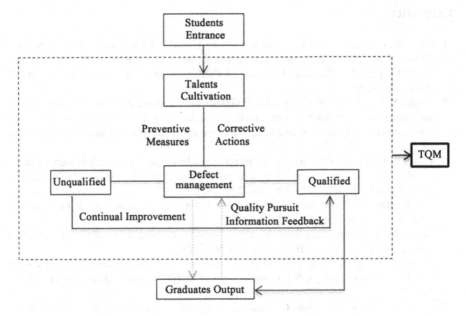

Fig. 2. Smart classroom teaching platform structure

4.3   After Class - Platform Discussion and Sharing of Homework Results

After-class teachers can release, collect and correct students' after-class assignments through the learning platform of Smart Classroom, and students can submit the assignments assigned by teachers on the platform after completing them within the specified time. Teachers can check and check students' homework in real time on the platform, and give individual answers to different students' personalized questions. Common questions of most students can be uniformly answered on the intelligent platform. On the one hand, teachers can timely understand the students' mastery of knowledge; On the other hand, students can quickly receive teachers' feedback on homework and make timely corrections to achieve real-time online communication and interaction with teachers after class.

5   Conclusion

In a word, the background of 5G era is very compatible with the smart classroom of tourism management specialty in colleges and universities, and there are many interconnections between them. Teachers of management major in colleges and universities can carry out smart classroom teaching design by building a perfect teaching platform in the pre-class preparation process, building a high-quality teaching system for teacher-student interaction in the classroom teaching process, and laying a solid and solid foundation for the comprehensive quality development and core nutrition development of tourism management major students in colleges and universities.

References

1. Shen, D.: Exploration of smart classroom teaching mode of basic courses of visual communication design major in colleges and universities based on MOOC + Flipped classroom. In: ICIMTECH 21: The Sixth International Conference on Information Management and Technology (2021)
2. Zhong, Y., Liu, X.: Design and research of virtual reality teaching assistant system for colleges and universities experimental course under the background of wisdom education. In: 2021 International Conference on Intelligent Transportation, Big Data & Smart City (ICITBS) (2021)
3. Guan, Y.: RETRACTED: research on the reform of ideological and political theory courses in colleges and universities in the big data era. J. Phys. Conf. Ser. **1852**(2), 022061 (2021). https://doi.org/10.1088/1742-6596/1852/2/022061
4. Wei, B.: Research on the mixed teaching model in colleges and universities in the context of "Internet+." Asian Agric. Res. **12**, 71–74 (2021)
5. Lu, Y.: Research and analysis on the improvement of teaching ability of young teachers in colleges and universities. J. High. Educ. Res **2**(6) (2021)
6. Wang, Y., Zhang, N.: The optimization of classroom teaching in colleges and universities based on network topology. Sci. Program. **2021**, 1–12 (2021). https://doi.org/10.1155/2021/1271438
7. Göbel, K., Neuber, K., Lion, C., Cukierman, U.: Self-efficacy in online teaching during the immediate transition from conventional to online teaching in German and Argentinian Universities—The relevance of institutional support and individual characteristics. Educ. Sci. **13**(1), 76 (2023). https://doi.org/10.3390/educsci13010076
8. Cheng, Q., Li, B., Zhou, Y.: Research on evaluation system of classroom teaching quality in colleges and universities based on 5G environment. In: Proceedings of the 2021 1st International Conference on Control and Intelligent Robotics, pp.74–85 (2021)
9. Qi, L.: Research on hybrid teaching pattern design in applied colleges and universities under the background of big data. In: Jan, M.A., Khan, F. (eds.) Application of Big Data, Blockchain, and Internet of Things for Education Informatization: First EAI International Conference, BigIoT-EDU 2021, Virtual Event, August 1–3, 2021, Proceedings, Part II, pp. 278–284. Springer International Publishing, Cham (2021). https://doi.org/10.1007/978-3-030-87903-7_35
10. Liu, J.W., Dong, L.N.: Construction of online distance three dimensional teaching platform for industrial design major in colleges and universities. In: Fu, W., Liu, S., Dai, J. (eds.) E-Learning, e-Education, and Online Training. LNICSSITE, vol. 390, pp. 75–89. Springer, Cham (2021). https://doi.org/10.1007/978-3-030-84386-1_7

Evaluation Model and Algorithm of Physical Education Teaching

Lei Li[1](✉) and Liu Suiying[2]

[1] Nanchang University College of Science and Technology, Nanchang 330001, Jiangxi, China
lileibazx1983@163.com

[2] Foreign Languages Schoolichuan University Jinjiang Collegeeishan, Sichuan 620800, China

Abstract. This article proposes an evaluation model and algorithm based on data mining and machine learning for physical education teaching evaluation, based on the needs of educational evaluation. In this study, we quantified the key factors and elements in the physical education teaching process by developing relevant indicators and standards, and transformed them into a form that can be used for data analysis and processing for evaluation and analysis. The system consists of four steps. The first step is to plan and evaluate. In this step, we should plan our activities based on the goals of each lesson or unit. We can also use some simple tools, such as scales, checklists, etc., to facilitate the preparation of the evaluation. The evaluation teaching model of physical education teaching refers to the process in which teachers evaluate and provide feedback on students' performance in physical education teaching. This process helps teachers improve their skills and physical education knowledge. The feedback provided by the teacher should be positive so that students can learn from it. This also helps to improve their performance in sports.

Keyword: Physical education · Teaching evaluation · Evaluation model

1 Introduction

Physical education is an important component of the school education system and is crucial for students' physical health and quality development. At the same time, the quality and effectiveness of physical education teaching are increasingly valued by educators and managers for the comprehensive development and improvement of students' overall quality [1]. Therefore, the evaluation of physical education teaching has become one of the important issues that urgently need to be solved in the current field of physical education. In recent years, with the continuous development and application of information technology and Big data technology, Big data analysis technology has been applied to education evaluation in the field of sports, and its application scope and application effect have also been expanding and improving. Through the application of Big data analysis technology, we can have a deeper understanding of students' physical education learning, physical fitness evaluation, sports training effect and other information, and provide

Y. Zhang and N. Shah (Eds.): BigIoT-EDU 2023, LNICST 581, pp. 361–372, 2024.
https://doi.org/10.1007/978-3-031-63133-7_36

more scientific decision support for educators and managers [2]. The quality of under-graduate teaching in some schools has begun to decline, and there is a trend towards a decline in teaching quality in some schools [3]. There is a potential danger of a decline in teaching quality in some schools. Especially in July 1999, China's national economic and social development plan made significant strategic adjustments - expanding enroll-ment in universities. That is to say, an additional 300000 people will be recruited on top of the original 1.3 million. This evaluation method is the most widely used and easily quantifiable method, but it also has its own drawbacks. For example, physical education teaching supervisors use measurement data for integration and provide a total score for evaluation.

At present, there are four serious investment deficiencies in universities, namely, a serious shortage of education funds, a serious lack of energy investment by leaders at all levels in teaching, a considerable number of teachers' energy investment in teaching, and a portion of students' energy investment in learning.. Physical education is particularly prominent [4, 5]. Firstly, after the expansion of enrollment in universities, the investment and utilization of sports teaching venues and equipment have seriously lagged behind. Secondly, with the progress of social civilization, the demand for sports among students is also rapidly increasing. Therefore, this paper aims to study the evaluation model of physical education and the evaluation algorithm based on Big data analysis to improve the efficiency and scientificity of physical education evaluation.

In this study, we will focus on the construction of sports teaching evaluation model and algorithm design based on Big data analysis, and provide more complete, com-prehensive, accurate and scientific methods and means for sports education evaluation based on data mining, machine learning and other technologies. Education evaluation is a complex process that involves multiple factors and indicators. Although traditional qualitative analysis and fuzzy evaluation methods have played a certain role, this method has the drawbacks of lacking scientificity and operability, making it difficult to provide accurate digital support for the development and evaluation of physical education. There-fore, this paper uses the evaluation model and algorithm based on Big data analysis to quantify the evaluation indicators of physical education, and uses the real-time collected data such as sports data and anthropometric technology to mine the elements such as people, teaching, facilities, etc. from large-scale physical education data through data processing and analysis methods. This can help us analyze the current situation of phys-ical education more accurately, identify influencing factors, and propose improvement suggestions and measures accurately and targeted, providing real-time and effective data information support for education managers and decision-makers, and promoting the development and progress of physical education. At the same time, this article will also introduce the design and implementation of a physical education data management and analysis system, presenting data analysis results through visualization, improving the readability and operability of data, and facilitating decision-making and management by relevant managers and educators.

To sum up, this paper will focus on the evaluation methods and data processing technology of physical education based on Big data analysis, so as to improve the efficiency and scientificity of evaluation, provide more reliable and scientific evaluation methods for education management departments and educators, and promote the overall development and progress of physical education.

2 Related Work

2.1 Teaching Evaluation

University: It is the abbreviation of colleges and universities that implement higher education and is established through the national approval process.

evaluating teachers' teaching work and making value judgments on teaching and learning, guided by teaching objectives. "Mass" is a word that belongs to the category of philosophy. In physics, it means the measurement of the physical quantity of an object; In the field of value, it means the quality of the product; In the field of sociology, quality is dynamic, is shown in Fig. 1 below.

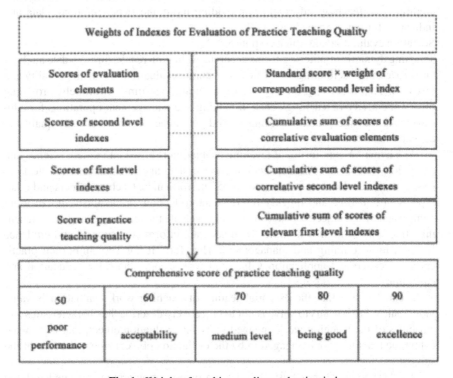

Fig. 1. Weight of teaching quality evaluation index

Dynamic monitoring of teaching evaluation is a teaching evaluation method based on real-time data collection and analysis, which analyzes and evaluates the teaching process and effectiveness in a real-time, fast, and accurate manner. It uses modern technology means such as sensor technology, network technology, Big data analysis, etc. to realize information collection and processing in the teaching process, form quantitative indicators and standards, and achieve real-time and accurate teaching evaluation. It mainly has the following characteristics:

1. Large data volume, easy to quickly collect and analyze
   The dynamic monitoring and evaluation adopts a real-time data collection method, so the data volume is larger and more comprehensive, and there is no need for manual collection and organization. This allows for the rapid collection of various data in the teaching process, including difficult to quantify characteristic indicators such as student participation, attention, and focus. The analysis of these data is of great help in improving the quality and effectiveness of teaching.
2. Wide monitoring range, capable of collecting various information and data
   The education dynamic monitoring and evaluation system can monitor various situations in the teaching classroom, and can instantly collect various information data, such as dynamic learning process, learning effectiveness, learning behavior, etc., analyzing from multiple dimensions, reflecting the comprehensiveness, objectivity, and credibility of teaching information, providing more and richer reference data and indicators for teaching evaluation.
3. Scientific evaluation and quick response
   Teaching dynamic monitoring forms accurate evaluation results through data analysis and processing, facilitating scientific and accurate evaluation of teaching quality and progress. This evaluation method is fast, accurate, real-time, and timely, providing timely and effective teaching decision-making and management operations for educators and managers, and providing a solid guarantee for improving the quality of education and teaching.

   The dynamic monitoring of teaching evaluation is based on modern science and technology, which uses sensor technology, Big data and other means to reflect the progress of the education process, students' performance, teaching effects and other aspects in real time and quickly realize data collection and analysis. It can more comprehensively, objectively and accurately evaluate the teaching process and teaching effects, so as to provide timely and accurate information support and guidance for education, training and management. Therefore, it has very important practical significance and application value, and will become the future education and education.

   It can be seen that the essential feature of teaching work evaluation is value judgment. What it wants to solve is not to objectively describe the characteristics and attributes of the teaching work engaged in by the evaluation object, that is, to what extent the teaching work Engaged in by the evaluation object meets the needs of the subject.

   The key points of the physical education investigation are: on the one hand, the pass rate of the students' physical health standard issued in 2002 and implemented in 2003; On the other hand, it investigates the mass sports activities and competitive sports activities of the school [6]. Investigation contents: statistical table of physical health standard test conducted on students in recent three years (system data query shall be provided); Relevant systems of school physical education [7]; Relevant materials of the school's sports meetings over the years; Students' participation in various sports competitions and awards, participation in various sports meetings and awards; Students' morning exercises and related materials, etc.

2.2 Basic Theories and Skills of College Students' Physical Education

With the comprehensive implementation of quality education and the improvement of social civilization, the sports awareness of modern college students has also been strengthened. They should not only master the basic sports technology and basic skills, but also master certain basic sports theories, and have a strong ability to apply basic theories, sports aesthetics, health education and other knowledge systems. They can arm their minds with these basic sports knowledge.

Basic skills refer to students' basic practical ability, self-study ability, adaptability, communication ability, innovation consciousness, etc. During the investigation, it is necessary to understand the overall design of the school for students' knowledge structure and ability improvement, as well as its teaching plan, training plan and syllabus of main courses [8]. At the same time, it is necessary to understand the elective courses of the school and the cultural, scientific and technological atmosphere of the school. In physical education and elective, volleyball, football, track and field, Wushu, gymnastics and other contents. At the same time, they also enrich the sports skills of table tennis, badminton, tennis, roller skating, traditional national sports, swimming, bodybuilding, sports dance and so on. This can not only train high-quality sports professionals for the country. Therefore, college students have a solid grasp of the basic sports theory and basic skills, which has laid a foundation for students to further study sports and develop lifelong sports awareness.

2.3 Teaching Analysis of Particle Swarm Algorithm Evaluation

Particle Swarm Optimization (PSO) is an intelligent algorithm based on swarm optimization. Its main idea comes from simulating the behavior of a group, treating each member of the group as a particle. During the search process, particles will continuously adjust their search positions based on their own search experience and the mutual influence of the optimal information within the group, achieving the global optimal search effect. Therefore, particle swarm optimization is widely used in multi-objective optimization, parameter optimization, and other problems.

In teaching evaluation, the core issue is how to use multiple emotional and scenario data for analysis and optimization. The learning habits, subject characteristics, and subject emotional characteristics of students belong to multi-dimensional and highly nonlinear data, and traditional evaluation methods are difficult to obtain high-precision evaluation indicators. Therefore, applying particle swarm optimization algorithm to teaching evaluation analysis can design different objective functions and evaluation functions based on different evaluation indicators, and obtain comprehensive and accurate analysis and evaluation results for learning transactions. In the following example, we will design a teaching evaluation model based on historical student data and particle swarm optimization algorithm.where $X_i = (x_{i1}, x_{i2}, ..., x_{in})$ is the current position of particle i, $V_i = (v_{i1}, v_{i2}, ..., v_{in})$ is the current flight speed of particle i, $P_i = (p_{i1}, p_{i2}, ..., p_{in})$ is the best position that particle i has experienced:

If $f(x)$ is the minimum objective function, the current best position of particle i is determined by Eq. (1):

$$\mathbf{P}_i(t+1) = \begin{cases} \mathbf{P}_i(t) & f(\mathbf{X}_i(t+1)) \geq f(\mathbf{P}_i(t)) \\ \mathbf{X}_i(t+1)f(\mathbf{X}_i(t+1)) < f(\mathbf{P}_i(t)) \end{cases} \tag{1}$$

The number of particles in the initialization population is N, assuming that the best position experienced by all particles in the population is $P_g(t)$, which is called the global best position, then:

$$\begin{aligned} P_s(t) &\in \{P_g(t), P_l(t), \ldots\ldots P_s(t)\} | f(P_s(t)) \\ &= \min\{f(P_s(t)), fP_l(t), \ldots . f(P_s(t))\} \end{aligned} \tag{2}$$

The evolution process of basic particle swarm optimization algorithm can be described as follows:

$$v_q(t+1) = v_q(t) + c_1 r_{ij}(t)\big(p_q(t) - x_q(t)\big) + c_2 r_{1j}(t\big(p_{q'}(t) - x_q(t)\big) \tag{3}$$

$$x_y(t+1) = x_y(t) + v_y(t+1) \tag{4}$$

Analysis is crucial for evaluating disciplinary accuracy. We can use the mean and standard deviation of historical grades as parameters of the objective function to ensure that the evaluation results match the distribution of student grades.that is:

$$v_\theta(t+1) = v_\theta(t) + c_1 r_{1j}(t)(p_\theta(t) - x_\theta(t)) \tag{5}$$

We can design adaptive group search strategies based on students' personalized evaluation results. If the speed evolution equation only includes the physical education teaching evaluation model, that is:

$$v_\theta(t+1) = v_\theta(t) + c_z r_{2j}(t)\big(p_{gj}(t) - x_\theta(t)\big) \tag{6}$$

Integrate them into an objective function and use particle swarm optimization as the optimizer to optimize historical data to obtain more accurate and reliable prediction results.

Specifically, the average and standard deviation of the distribution of historical grades are used as optimization parameters for the objective function, and the weight coefficients of the objective function are modified using students' personalized evaluation results. Historical data from different semester grades are used as reference data in group search. During the optimization process, by continuously adjusting parameters and search strategies, the particle swarm optimization algorithm can balance multiple objectives, quickly find the global optimal solution, and obtain the most accurate and meaningful evaluation results.

Of course, due to the inherent uncertainty and randomness of particle swarm optimization algorithms, optimization parameters and strategy adjustments need to be made according to specific application scenarios. Meanwhile, if more complex evaluation factors and scenarios are involved, the accuracy and relevance of teaching evaluation can be improved by introducing more information and scene features.

In summary, the teaching evaluation analysis method based on particle swarm optimization algorithm can effectively solve the problems of incomplete, inaccurate, and non real-time evaluation indicators in traditional evaluation methods. It quickly analyzes teaching data and provides accurate and practical evaluation results through efficient optimization algorithms and appropriate evaluation models. This method can not only be applied to subject performance evaluation, but also to multi-disciplinary student behavior analysis, subject selection direction prediction, and other aspects, and has good prospects for promotion and application.

3 Current Situation of Physical Education Teaching Evaluation

The application of particle swarm optimization algorithm in the field of physical education teaching has gradually received attention and research. In the field of physical education, teaching evaluation is a very important part. It can help teachers better understand students' physical fitness and training status, timely correct their own shortcomings in teaching, and provide important data support and basis for the evaluation and management of physical education teaching quality in schools. The application of particle swarm optimization algorithm can improve the efficiency and scientificity of physical education teaching evaluation, and help to improve the quality and effectiveness of physical education.

At present, domestic and foreign scholars have conducted research on particle swarm optimization algorithm in teaching evaluation in the field of physical education, with specific application scenarios including:

1. Optimization of athlete training evaluation model: Based on data indicators such as training performance and physical fitness, design and optimize particle swarm optimization algorithm evaluation models at different training stages to provide scientific evaluation of training effectiveness.
2. Personalized and precise evaluation during training: Develop personalized evaluation indicators for different athletes' physical fitness, training time, and habits, optimize evaluation models, and improve training effectiveness.
3. Comprehensive consideration of evaluation indicators: In training evaluation and talent selection, different objective functions and evaluation functions are designed based on different evaluation indicators, integrating multiple indicators to improve the comprehensiveness and accuracy of the evaluation, and comprehensively evaluate the comprehensive competitive ability of athletes.
4. Focus on key training stages: By systematically collecting and analyzing training data, integrating evaluation models, and taking into account the training quality of specific stages, scientific evaluations are made for better training results.

In summary, the application of particle swarm optimization algorithm in the field of physical education has become one of the research hotspots. The application of this algorithm can provide scientific, efficient, and comprehensive effective means for physical education workers, helping to improve the management level and teaching quality of physical education. Only by constantly seeking the best solution through practice and exploration, and promoting its application, can we better promote precision and scientificity in the future field of physical education evaluation.

The optimization of physical education teaching quality is a nonlinear constrained combinatorial optimization problem, which can generally be expressed as follows:

$$\min_{x \in x} f(x) = \begin{cases} g_i(x) \leq 0, i = 1, 2, \ldots, m \\ h_j(x) = 0, j = 1, 2, \ldots, r \end{cases} \tag{7}$$

Including:

$$x = \left(x_1, x_2, \ldots, x_n \right)^\tau \in R^* \tag{8}$$

That is, a function of x. It is an objective function of the deviation rate of reaching the standard obtained in order to optimize the allocation of teaching resources per student of n items. The optimization problem is the solution when the objective function $f(x)$ takes the minimum value. X is a decision variable of the distribution proportion of the total budget in n teaching indicators, $g_i(x)$ is the inequality constraint, m is the number of inequality constraints, $h_i(x)$ is the equality constraint, The value of x is limited by constraints.

The optimization of physical education teaching evaluation is an optimization in approximate quantity, which allows constraint deviation within a certain range, and can be processed by transforming the equality constraint into an inequality within a certain range of deviation:

$|h_j(x)| - \varepsilon_j \leq 0$, where s is the constraint offset of the jth equation constraint.

$$\min f(x) = g_k'(x) \leq 0, i = 1, 2, \ldots, 2r + m \tag{9}$$

Specific countermeasures are as follows:

First, the indicators of the evaluation scheme are further classified and refined. How to strengthen the classified guidance, make the colleges and universities better develop their individuality and characteristics, how to simplify the evaluation methods and methods, which will not only facilitate the schools but also save costs.

Second, the evaluation plan focuses on strengthening the guidance of rectification. After all, the time for the expert group to enter the university is limited. In addition to investigating the hardware construction of the University, a small number of lectures and visits, most of the objects investigated are the paper documents and documents of the University, which is the only possibility for the university to improve in a short period of time. Teachers and administrative staff work overtime to catch up with materials[9]; Teachers invest a lot of energy to supplement materials; If there are more than ten or even twenty experiments that have not been carried out, they should be done quickly. However, it is not enough to find out the gap through evaluation and pay attention to rectification and guidance, which seriously affects the normal teaching order.

Third, the evaluation method should not be too single. The current undergraduate teaching evaluation in China mainly refers to Taylor's behavior goal model, Bloom's educational goal classification theory, and the goal centered evaluation model. The starting point and ultimate goal of the evaluation all point to the predetermined teaching goals [10]. According to the situation that the regional differences in Colleges and universities in China cause great differences in students' sources, climate, economic conditions, etc., according to scriffin's goal dissociation model, we should strengthen the evaluation of the unexpected effects of educational activities, so as to make the teaching evaluation more objective.

3.1 Teaching Quality Monitoring

Furthermore, through the establishment of the evaluation system combining internal and external, macro and micro, a quality assurance and monitoring system of higher education with Chinese characteristics has been gradually formed.

The internal teaching quality monitoring system of the evaluated School: target determination, establishment of quality standards for each main teaching link, information collection (including statistics and measurement), evaluation, information feedback, regulation and other links, forming a closed loop. Through the evaluation of teaching work, the school's teaching infrastructure, teaching reform and teaching management have been raised to a new level.

Quality Control. The school's basic teaching documents and basic working systems are sound. These documents and systems reflect modern educational ideas, actively use modern management technologies, and earnestly implement them. Each school has formulated the quality standards and operation systems for various teaching links of physical education, such as theoretical teaching, practical teaching, sports training, extracurricular guidance, examination and assessment, college students' physical health standard test, etc. Some of the evaluated schools have established a scientific, reasonable and easy to operate evaluation index system for physical education. The evaluation work is carried out in a purposeful, targeted, planned and step-by-step manner, with implementation methods and corresponding reward and punishment systems. 91.9% of the PE teachers who have evaluated the school think that the PE quality monitoring system is scientific, perfect and effective.

3.2 Evaluation Teaching Model

At present, there are many methods and algorithms used to solve combinatorial optimization problems. The particle swarm optimization algorithm with linearly decreasing inertia factor are used to find the optimal solution, and they are compared [19].

The main content of the optimization in higher education is to optimize the allocation of funds and resources on the basis of various teaching indicators, and to seek a better resource allocation scheme, so as to realize the scope of the limited education funds budget, ensure the excellent teaching evaluation, make more students accept higher education.

According to the constraint formula in the actual situation:

$$\lim_{k \to \infty} \| \Delta e_{k+1}(t) \|_\lambda \leq \left(\frac{m_1 m_5}{b - \lambda} \frac{1}{1 - \breve{\rho}} + \frac{p}{b} \right) cd \tag{10}$$

The evaluation teaching process of physical education teaching is shown in Fig. 2.

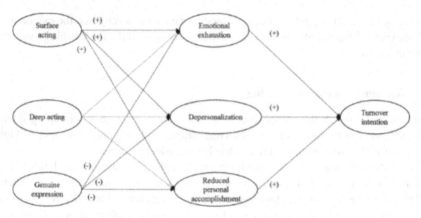

Fig. 2. Physical education teaching evaluation process

4   Simulation Analysis

In order to better illustrate the application of particle swarm optimization algorithm in physical education teaching evaluation, we can conduct simulation experiments based on the historical grades of a certain course and other student data to explore the effectiveness of this evaluation method. Assuming we want to evaluate the historical performance data of physical education teaching and use particle swarm optimization algorithm for evaluation and prediction. Firstly, we need to collect historical student performance data for this course. Assuming our data contains grade data for 8 semesters, each semester contains grade data for 100 students, totaling 800 pieces of data. Next, we will use particle swarm optimization algorithm for evaluation and prediction. We design an objective function based on multiple factors such as the average score and standard deviation of history students' grades, personalized evaluation results such as students' gender, age, family background, and trends in academic performance across different semesters. We will use historical performance data as training data, use particle swarm optimization algorithm to optimize the objective function, calculate the optimal evaluation indicators, and verify and analyze them through test data. In this experiment, we can use the performance data of the first 6 semesters as training data, and the performance data of the last 2 semesters as test data to verify the effectiveness and accuracy of the evaluation model. The simulation results are shown in Fig. 3.

Through the particle swarm optimization algorithm evaluation model, we can calculate the weight of each evaluation indicator and apply it to test data for performance prediction and evaluation. Ultimately, we can obtain predicted grades as a criterion for evaluating the effectiveness of physical education teaching and students' learning outcomes in the subject. After conducting the experiment and obtaining the predicted results, we need to analyze the experimental results. Firstly, we can compare the error between predicted grades and actual grades to evaluate the effectiveness of particle swarm optimization algorithm in physical education teaching evaluation. If the error is small and the predicted results are highly correlated with the actual results, it indicates that this method

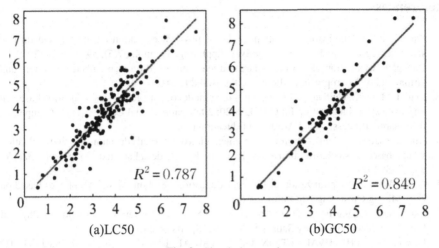

Fig. 3. Simulation result

has excellent feasibility and application value. Furthermore, while analyzing and predicting performance, we can analyze and reflect on the weights of evaluation indicators and parameters in the optimization algorithm, thereby further improving the accuracy and efficiency of the algorithm. In summary, particle swarm optimization algorithm can accurately evaluate the effectiveness of physical education teaching and student learning outcomes, and provide effective decision-making and guidance suggestions for educators and managers in physical education teaching. At the same time, we still need to continuously explore and improve this method, and expand its application prospects in the field of education.

5 Conclusion

The application results and effects of particle swarm optimization algorithm in physical education evaluation: improve the accuracy and reliability of subject performance evaluation, and provide feasible and accurate evaluation references for teachers and students. A personalized and precise evaluation model can evaluate based on the characteristics and needs of different students, making the evaluation results more reasonable and scientific. Integrating multiple indicators to improve the comprehensiveness and accuracy of evaluation indicators can help provide more specific and valuable advice and guidance for teaching staff. The particle swarm optimization evaluation model can improve the efficiency and effectiveness of teaching evaluation, provide decision-making support and basis for school teaching management, and promote the steady improvement of education and teaching quality. The application of particle swarm optimization algorithm in educational evaluation is gradually recognized and applied. Although further exploration and improvement of algorithms and evaluation models are needed in practical applications, it undoubtedly makes positive contributions to the scientific development and progress in the field of education.

References

1. Wang, Y.: The automatic evaluation model of physical education teaching based on two screening algorithms. J. Intell. Fuzzy Syst. Appl. Eng. Technol. **37**(5), 5945–5953 (2019)
2. Cheng, J.: Evaluation of physical education teaching based on web embedded system and virtual reality. Microprocess. Microsyst. **83**, 103980 (2021)
3. Liao, L., Liu, X.: Cultivation of social teaching model of college physical education based on improved apriori algorithm. In: CIPAE 2020: 2020 International Conference on Computers, Information Processing and Advanced Education (2020)
4. Xu, H., Zhang, X.: Construction and implementation of physical education teaching evaluation system based on stochastic simulation algorithm. Revista de la Facultad de Ingenieria **32**(15), 632–636 (2017)
5. Li, R., Wang, Y.: Optimization of Physical Education Teaching Mode in Colleges based on Data Mining Clustering Algorithm (2016)
6. Zhou, S.W., Guang-Feng, W.U.: Contentment Evaluation System Construction of Physical Education Teaching Quality Satisfaction. Hubei Sports Science (2017)
7. Firdaus, K.: THE EVALUATION OF PHYSICAL EDUCATION ASSESSMENT TO ENHANCE TEACHING PROGRAM IN SCHOOLS (2016)
8. Gu, J.: Taking Interest as the Guide to Realize the Effective Teaching of Physical Education in Primary Schools **2022**(4), 4 (2022)
9. Lang, A.: Evaluation Algorithm of English Audiovisual Teaching Effect Based on Deep Learning. Math. Probl. Eng. **2022**, 7687008 (2022)
10. Igor, D., Ficko, M., Balic, J.: 2th A model for prediction and evaluation of production processes based on genetic algorithm (2022)

Research on the Development Trend of Intelligent Law in Colleges and Universities Based on Intelligent Data Collection and Analysis

Xiaolan Guo[1](✉), Min Liu[2], and Liu Pei[3]

[1] School of Politics and Law, Baotou Teachers' College, Baotou 014030, Inner Mongolia, China
guoxiaolan1978@163.com
[2] Shangqiu Normal University, Shangqiu 476000, Henan, China
[3] Shandong Institute of Commerce and Technology, Jinan 250103, Shandong, China

Abstract. AI generated data is the generated result of AI's independent or as an auxiliary tool after perceptual analysis. In two cases of copyright disputes over AI generated data in China, the people's court decided to analyze the reasons why AI generated data belong to works and not belong to works; At the same time, there are unresolved issues in the case. The protection of AI generated data through copyright is both reasonable and insufficient. In the 21st century, talent training has become the focus of global attention. As an important part of national education and an important part of the grand project of building a country ruled by law, higher legal education is more and more important in the construction of socialist market economy. In order to make China's higher legal education develop along a healthy track, it is urgent to build a scientific legal education system. The development of legal knowledge in Colleges and universities is a long-term process, which needs to be analyzed from different aspects. The first aspect is the basic research on this topic, including its definition and classification, and its evolution over time. In addition to academic research, other types of research should be carried out: for example, research on the impact of intelligence on legal education; Study how to form intellectuals by studying law; Through the study of history, the study of how intellectuals formed; All these aspects need further study.

Keyword: Law · Intelligent data collection · Intellectualization

1 Introduction

The legal education in Colleges and universities in China is an important part of higher education. It is an educational activity with the content of imparting legal knowledge, training legal thinking and cultivating qualified legal professionals. Influenced by the nature of the legal profession itself, legal education is closely related to many aspects of society, such as politics, economy, culture, science and technology. The level and development trend of legal education will ultimately be the result of comprehensive social factors.

© ICST Institute for Computer Sciences, Social Informatics and Telecommunications Engineering 2024
Published by Springer Nature Switzerland AG 2024. All Rights Reserved
Y. Zhang and N. Shah (Eds.): BigIoT-EDU 2023, LNICST 581, pp. 373–383, 2024.
https://doi.org/10.1007/978-3-031-63133-7_37

University legal education is an important part of higher education. It is an educational activity with the content of imparting legal knowledge, training legal thinking and training qualified legal professionals. Influenced by the nature of the legal profession itself, legal education is closely related to many aspects of society, such as politics, economy, culture, science and technology. The level and development trend of legal education will ultimately be the result of comprehensive social factors. In 2007, the British court accepted a case of suspected infringement of the copyright of computer-generated images displayed to players when the game was running. However, with the increasing popularity of AI applications in modern society, more and more disputes involving AI generated data are bound to occur. It is an inevitable fact to protect AI generated data. In 2008, there have been cases in China where the defense is based on the fact that the infringing object is generated by artificial intelligence. However, limited to the social cognition at that time, the people's court has not made too much explanation in the judgment on whether the defense is tenable or not. In recent years, lawsuits involving data generated by artificial intelligence have emerged one after another, and there are also some top companies in the industry such as Baidu and Tencent. As Yelin said, law should conform to the purpose of society, and it is a collection of the realization of social purpose through the enforcement of state power. The number and influence of cases related to data generated by AI have changed from the past. Minor disputes can cause waves of public opinion. In such an environment, it is imperative for the law to respond to the protection of data generated by AI, otherwise it will inevitably result. At the same time, the data generated by AI seems to be generated by AI itself. Most of the time, it appears to be cheap and simple. In fact, the process of AI research and development, training, testing, promotion and other processes condense a lot of money and labor. It is not a matter of one day, but a process of accumulation from small steps to thousands of miles. Therefore, the resulting AI generated data has protection value.

Although there are still many questions about the protection of AI generated data, the academic debate has not yet reached a widely recognized answer. However, the relevant disputes in reality can't wait for the academic community to sort out, think and debate. The contradiction between the urgency of reality and the lag of current laws makes the protection and discussion of AI generated data extremely necessary. China's higher legal education has been developing for 20 years since its restoration and reconstruction. It has experienced changes from planned economy to socialist market economy. It has moved from the incomplete experimental stage to the basically mature development stage [1]. The management system and school running conditions have been greatly and profoundly improved; The construction of the teaching staff has gradually expanded; The construction of teaching materials has developed from scratch, from the annotation of legal provisions to the formation of a more scientific academic system: the construction of disciplines, especially the construction of key disciplines, has driven the academic research and echelon construction of disciplines and promoted the reform of teaching contents. However, with the further deepening of the national socialist market economy, building a country ruled by law has become the consensus of the whole society. Therefore, the modernization of the rule of law and the reform of education must be compatible with the development of the market economy. The market economy is the economy ruled by law [2]. The law must change from the single dictatorship function in the past to the participation and service function of the market economy. Therefore, we are confident to see another brilliant development opportunity for legal education. At the beginning of the new century, we should plan for future legal education [3]. The Ministry of justice's "Ninth Five Year Plan for the development of legal education and the development plan for 2010" put forward the development target of China's legal education: adjust the educational level and structure, expand the training scale, make the legal education structure more reasonable, significantly improve the quality and efficiency, and minimize the contradiction between the supply and demand of legal personnel in society; To In 2010, a modern legal education system compatible with the socialist market economic system, the national legal system construction and the comprehensive social progress was established, and the legal education management system was legalized and standardized. The training scale and quality of legal personnel basically meet social needs.

2 Related Work

2.1 Overview of Jurisprudence

(1) What is law

Law science is a science that studies law and law, a specific social phenomenon and its development law, and its full name is legal science. In a class society, different classes have different jurisprudence. Therefore, jurisprudence has a strong class nature and reflects the interests and will of a certain class. Historically, the jurisprudence of the slave owner class, the feudal owner class and the bourgeoisie is the jurisprudence of the exploiting class. It is the jurisprudence of different exploiting classes. It serves their respective political and economic systems, especially the formulation and implementation of the laws of their own class. It plays a role of theoretical justification, publicity and education for the legal norms and legal systems of their own class [4].

Marxist jurisprudence was born with the founding of Marxism, is an important part of scientific socialism, is the concentrated embodiment of the proletarian world outlook and interests, and serves the interests of the working class and the broad masses of the people.

(2) The emergence of Jurisprudence

Law is an ancient social science with a long history. Engels has long stated that the emergence of law is based on the emergence of law. When the political, economic and cultural development of society reached a certain stage, there was a social division of labor, especially after the emergence of written law, a professional jurist class was formed. They were specialized in legal research, and thus law came into being. Therefore, law is the premise and foundation of the emergence of law, and law is the inevitable result of the emergence and development of law.

The emergence of AI generated data has gradually led the academic research to focus on this field. For the legal protection of AI generated data, the academic research and discussion mainly focused on the field of copyright protection, and some scholars have jumped out of the framework of copyright protection and studied it from other perspectives. Some scholars believe that the research context of legal protection of AI generated data is divided into two stages: the first stage mainly discusses whether AI data constitutes a work under the background of strong AI technology and the corresponding right protection mode selection, specifically including special work system protection mode, general work system protection mode, neighboring right protection mode, special copyright system protection mode There are six modes of civil law fruits protection and anti-unfair competition law protection. In the second stage of the research on data copyright generated by AI, the academic community began to question the phenomenon of legal research based on strong AI or even super AI as the technical background, and believed that the research on legal issues assumed by advanced technology is of no practical significance, and the legal research of AI should return to rationality. Although AI generated data is dependent on emerging technologies, it can not break through the background of the era and is limited by current technologies. On this premise, the research on the legal protection of AI generated data should start with the existing system, and it is not advisable to focus too much on the special protection of AI generated data. For example, the "network law" was also considered to be special at the beginning of its birth, but ultimately based on the existing law, established a law for its characteristics to protect it and achieved considerable results. The representative scholars of this view include Liu Yanhong, Li Chen, Wang Qian, etc. The protection mode of unfair competition is a bottom-up protection mode. When the above mode cannot be remedied, it can be adopted if it involves the damage of competitive interests; The other methods of protection are reasonable, but there are still some things worth considering.

At the same time, it is precisely because of the existence of the above objective factors that it is impossible for the academic community to form a general theory on relevant issues. Scholars have gone to different branches since defining what AI is. The choice of protection mode is only compatible with the data generated by self-defined AI. Therefore, it seems that the academic community is full of arguments about AI generated data, but in fact, the AI generated data studied by various scholars are not the same thing, and the result is only endless disputes.

2.2 Modern Legal Education

China is an ancient civilized country with a long history. As the founder of the Chinese legal system, its legal education has a long history. In ancient times, there were governmental or private legal education institutions in all dynasties of China. One of the important contents of the "eight teachings" in Xia, Shang and Zhou Dynasties is the "law" education. Especially since the Qin and Han Dynasties, China has not only created "law science" and "doctor of law", but also set up "law department" specializing in legal posts and official selection examinations.

In modern times, China's legal education was influenced by western legal education. Under the background of "Western learning spreading to the East" and the transformation from a feudal autocratic society to a democratic society ruled by law, China has taken different developed countries as a reference system, introduced and transplanted through various channels, learned from each other, and walked a rough and tortuous road [5]. In the second half of the 19th century, China's legal education was based on the education of British and American universities, and organized the earliest legal disciplines of several modern universities in China, such as the Beijing law school and the Tianjin Chinese western school, which was the first (1895) to set up a university law undergraduate. From the end of the 19th century to the beginning of the 20th century, China's legal education took learning as the fashion, hired foreign teachers, translated foreign textbooks, and adopted various forms of running schools, which were public in various places And private legal education institutions have been established one after another, and a large number of legal talents have been trained. During the period of the national government, China's legal education took the United States as the main object of study, and the modern legal education institutions and legal education system were further developed [6]. Especially since the 14th National Congress of the Communist Party of China, with the establishment and continuous improvement of the socialist market economic system, the proposal and gradual implementation of the strategy of administering the country according to law and rejuvenating the country through science and education, and the reflection and criticism of the educational operation mode and development situation of the previous stage by the educational circles, China's legal education has entered a new period of deepening reform and comprehensive development. The theme of this period is to comprehensively deepen education reform and improve education quality [7]. Around this theme of the times, many new measures have been taken in the legal education circle. The voice of the reform of educational concepts and ideas has become stronger and stronger. Since taking teaching as the center, quality as the life, and cultivating innovative talents as the goal, the high-level education of law has reached a new level; The development of teaching evaluation has further highlighted the central position of teaching and strengthened the quality consciousness.

AI generated data is the non-material form of data that records various information including knowledge generated by computer through AI technology. Its characteristics are: (1) immaterial. This is the characteristic that the generated data is different from the "thing" in the traditional civil law. It is a kind of data form and record of information, which can be expressed as symbols, codes, words, graphics, etc., but it does not belong to the physical world, but belongs to the abstract category of thinking and cognition. (2) Content carrier complexity. For information and knowledge, data is a carrier and a record of knowledge and information. But at the same time, data itself is also a kind of content, which can directly become the object of protection. Especially when the form used to record information is text, graphics and other forms that can be directly recognized and understood by human beings, data is the information itself. (3) Reproducible transmissibility or reproducible transmissibility. Data belongs to immaterial information records and can be reproduced on different other carriers, including tangible carriers such as paper and intangible carriers such as network. Once the data itself is determined, it is only the same object in terms of "quality" and will not become multiple due to reproduction. However, data can be continuously reproduced and spread due to the replication of its carrier. Therefore, its replicable transmissibility does not mean that it is copied into many different "qualities", but that its carrier is replicable, so that it can be reproduced and has transmissibility, which is the characteristic of "things" that are not real rights. (4) The intelligence of the generation process. Intellectual property, the object of intellectual property protection, has the first three characteristics of generating data, but in the process of generating data, it belongs to the "intellectual achievements" generated by human mind, not the "intelligent achievements" of machines or computer programs.

In the process of AI generating data, the perception and analysis of the "fed" basic data is essential, which is the embodiment of intelligent behavior in AI generation. Without computers or computer software for perception and analysis, artificial intelligence does not have the ability to face different scenes and make different behaviors, and its generated results are just mechanical products, which have nothing to do with artificial intelligence. Because the generated data comes from the intelligent generation process of artificial intelligence, it has "intelligence", but not "intelligence", let alone the "rationality", "sensibility" and "spirituality" derived from ideology and ethics in human generation.

3 Intelligent Law in Universities Based on Intelligent Data Collection and Analysis

3.1 Dilemmas and Reasons for Legal Protection of AI Generated Data in China

For the data generated by artificial intelligence completely automatically or with little human intervention, the consensus reached by all circles is that it has property value and should be provided with legal protection. However, in the path of protection, the understanding is extremely inconsistent, and even there are opposing views, showing the dilemma of poor protection.

(1) Insufficient understanding and research on data generated by AI

In the existing discussions, AI generated data is limited to a small part of the extension that is objectively original, and then entangled in the theory and legislation of whether human authors can be broken through by AI, while little attention is paid to other data that are not original but still have personality or property value in the generated data. In fact, compared with the existing works in objective form, the data generated by AI may or may not be original, but they are all agglomerated with relevant labor and have property value; If personal information is involved, the generated data also carries personality value; If it involves national and social interests, it also concerns the values of national sovereignty, national security and social public interests. If we do not jump out of the category of "works" and "authors" and look at it at a higher level, the legal protection of the generated data will be extremely narrow and biased. At the same time, affected by the research and development of AI itself, the academic community has not reached an agreement on the understanding of AI, and there have been differences in the understanding of AI concepts. The subject of the subsequent debate also does not belong to the same thing. The academic debate is like talking to itself, and the views are reasonable, but it is difficult to convince the other party.

(2) The legislative protection of data property is too late

If personal information is involved in the data generated by AI, it is required to comply with the legal provisions of personal information; This article focuses on data that has nothing to do with personal information, has property value, and is intended to spread and use to play a role. The result data generated by artificial intelligence, whether automatically or as a tool combined with people, can be objectively divided into two categories: original and non-inventive. As for the original data, from the perspective of two precedents, it can be seen from the analysis and interpretation that there is no real "automatic generation" at present, but it can be ultimately attributed to human creative behavior, so it can be included in the copyright category of AI developers or users for protection. For data without originality, such as the analysis report in the film case, we should face up to its property value and include it in the category of data property, and establish its new property object status. As for how to protect the property, whether to grant absolute rights or usufruct rights, China's current legislation is too backward. Article 127 of the Civil Code refers to the name of data and network virtual property, but there is no doubt about whether to protect it and how to protect it. Instead, it links to other legal provisions and expresses its respect for its provisions. "In this regard, the academic, legislative and judicial circles still need to be discussed in depth and detail.

(3) The value orientation of the development of AI industry and the purpose of the legal protection of generated data need to be consistent with the legal protection of AI generated data, which involves the conflict and balance between the interests of industrial development and personal interests. Therefore, the purpose of generating data legal protection should be to promote the balance between the two, rather than sacrificing one party to the other. In addition to social and personal economic benefits, the value orientation of the development of artificial intelligence industry should also consider social responsibility and social benefits, as well as fair order and good customs conducive to human society. From the perspective of the rights and interests of private entities, the generated data should be protected to ensure that the investors and labor parties obtain the due returns and benefits; From the perspective of industrial development, data has become a market factor and is the foundation of the artificial intelligence industry. Therefore, in order to make more data freely available to the public to promote industrial development, the protection of private rights and interests in the generated data should be limited. At present, there is no balance between data freedom and rights protection.

3.2 Smart Data Collection Related Technologies

(1) Programmable instrument standard command

Standard commands for programmable instruments (SCPI) is a set of language used to control programmable instruments. It is based on ieee488.2 standard and follows the floating-point operation rules in IEEE754 standard, iso646 information exchange 7-bit coding symbols and other standardized instrument programming languages. SCPI is divided into public command and private command. Public command means that as long as the SCPI type instrument is used, the instrument can be controlled by this command, such as the command "* IDN?" Send it to the corresponding instrument to get the reply from the instrument; The private command is a specific command format formed for the specific functions of the instrument, but its clear logic and simple syntax can enable users to get started quickly and control and develop specific functions according to requirements. As a measurement description language, SCPI is highly sought after by the industry for its simplicity and efficiency [8]. At present, the mainstream measuring instruments in the market use SCPI as the control language, such as oscilloscopes and multimeters of keysight and Tektronix, which use SCPI as the control language. Their measuring instruments can be seen everywhere in the teaching of major universities.

(2) Embedded technology

There are many kinds of instruments in university laboratories. At the same time, due to the need for multiple types of measuring instruments in a single experiment, it is not practical to control a single instrument. The design of the instrument control module needs to support the interaction with multiple instruments, realize the unified management of instruments, and have high expandability. Therefore, embedded technology is essential in the system design process.

(3) USB Technology

The experimental instruments are directly connected with the instrument control module through universal serial bus (USB). USB technology is a kind of interface technology that is applied to connect peripheral devices of computers, and also to connect peripheral interactive devices to computers. It has the characteristics of high transmission efficiency, low power consumption and plug and play. Since its launch, it has been developed to usb4.0, and the high version USB protocol can be downward compatible with the low version protocol to maintain the stability of the technology. The bus structure of USB adopts a layered star topology, as shown in Fig. 1.

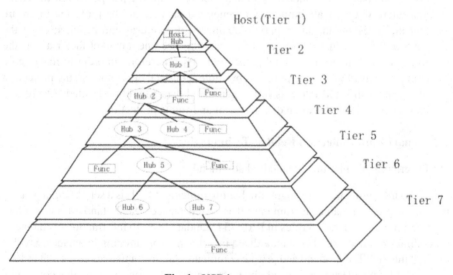

Fig. 1. USB bus structure

4 Research on the Development Trend of the Intellectualization of University Law

At present, the tide of globalization is coming. Whether people realize it or not, this wave has had or will have a profound impact on human society. The so-called globalization refers to the historical process and trend of communication, connection and mutual influence in the global scope. The characteristics of globalization, in terms of form, are that the space-time constraints of human communication have been really broken. Human beings have realized world-wide communication by means of communication and communication provided by modern science and technology; In terms of content, globalization is rich and colorful, involving many fields such as economy, politics, culture and society. Among them, economic globalization is the main line of globalization and also the most basic motivation in the process of globalization [9]. Furthermore, it has an obvious influence on the legal education, which makes the legal education appear the trend of internationalization. The internationalization of legal education is mainly manifested in the activity process or development trend of cross-border, cross-ethnic and cross-cultural multilateral exchange, cooperation and assistance of legal education in the world. This trend follows China's accession to wt O Will be further strengthened. China's entry into WTO is an important step for China to integrate into the mainstream of the world economy, and also another leap for China's legal education to achieve internationalization. It urgently requires legal education to cultivate familiar WT with international consciousness and international vision O The legal personnel of the rules should play an active role in international competition and international affairs [10]. Therefore, legal education should be soberly and profoundly aware of the impact of globalization on legal education, and consciously promote the globalization process of legal education, both in concept and in the goal of talent training and in the teaching process. At present, China's law education has done a lot of work in internationalization. Some key universities have actively exchanged teaching experience and scientific research cooperation with foreign law schools, which has made great contributions to the early integration of China's law education with the international community; However, we must also make it clear that in order to adapt to the international community of the "global village" in the future, law education needs to make greater efforts in curriculum setting and joint education.

The legal cause is supported and constructed by a legal community with the same knowledge structure, common thinking paradigm and common value pursuit. Whether the legal community can be formed and whether it is homogeneous is the decisive factor affecting the rule of law. To some extent, the so-called rule of law is the management and adjustment of social life by legal people who have received strict legal training. The formation of the homogeneous community must start from the time when they receive professional education, which requires legal education to first establish the awareness of cultivating the community from the concept, and run this concept through the whole process of teaching On the one hand, through legal education, we will cultivate the professional lofty sense of future community members, so that students can deeply understand that the legal profession is not only a means of making a living, but also a cause of maintaining social fairness and justice. The legal profession is a noble profession, which requires its members to have the spirit of dedication to the legal ideal. On the other hand, it is their bounden duty to cultivate the historical mission of future community members through legal education and make the rule of law their lifelong pursuit.

When AI is used as an auxiliary tool to generate data, it is no different from general computer software. At this time, AI can be seen as a tool manipulated by human beings in essence. The user shall be regarded as the right subject of all results obtained by using the artificial intelligence. At this time, the original judgment of AI generated data should adopt the judgment standard in the traditional copyright law.

(1) Not original: general data property protection

Data generated by artificial intelligence without originality is still data in nature and has certain value, which can be protected by the provisions of general data property rights. AI users use AI as a tool to generate and create the data, which should be regarded as being done by AI users, and the data property right subject is AI users.

However, in view of the lack of legislative protection of data property in China, the adoption of data property protection mode to protect it is bound to fall into a dilemma due to the defects of the data property protection mode itself. China needs to accelerate and improve the construction of the data property protection model, and make more detailed provisions on the exercise and protection of its rights, so that things that apply to the data property protection model can be correctly protected.

(2) Originality: protection of human works

When human beings use AI as an auxiliary tool, AI is equivalent to the pen in the hand of a writer and the brush in the hand of a painter. Create original AI generated data. The creative subject is naturally AI users. At this time, AI generated data is the expression of AI users' thoughts. According to the general constitutive requirements of the work, in the case that other conditions are met, the creative subject is human, and the AI generated data is original and has met the constitutive requirements of the work. The AI generated data belongs to the object protected by the copyright law, and the relevant provisions of the copyright law apply. From the overall perspective of this generation process, in addition to the auxiliary tool of new technology AI, there is no difference from the birth process of ordinary works, and the general provisions of the copyright law can be directly applied.

5   Conclusion

As a social activity that inherits and creates human legal civilization, legal education is generated and advanced under the resonance of social economy, politics and culture, and is also perfected and developed in the process of influencing society. Therefore, the study of legal education in the 21st century should first focus on the macro level of legal education and social development, and explore the law of legal education development from the interactive relationship between legal education and human development. Secondly, the research on the legal education in the 21st century should also focus on the forward-looking analysis, so that the construction of the legal education model in the 21st century can not only make a strong response to social development, but also enable it to undertake the heavy responsibility of promoting the historical process. Finally, the research of legal education in the 21st century should continue to draw the essence of human legal education thought and education mode from the comparative study of legal education at home and abroad with a broad vision and a tolerant attitude, so as to provide a continuous ideological and empirical power for the shaping of legal education mode in the 21st century. So as to create a legal education model that is not only in line with the world legal education but also has national characteristics.

References

1. He, Z., Zhu, H., Zheng, K.: Research on the trend change of social donation income of colleges and universities in China (2) (2021)
2. Song, J.: The intelligent scientific research management system based on cloud computing. In: Chang, JW., Yen, N., Hung, J.C. (eds.) FC 2020. LNEE, vol. 747, pp. 2255–2260. Springer, Singapore (2021). https://doi.org/10.1007/978-981-16-0115-6_276
3. Gao, B.: Research and implementation of intelligent evaluation system of teaching quality in universities based on artificial intelligence neural network model. Math. Probl. Eng. 2022 (2022)
4. Shang, H., Hu, C.: Value orientation and development of ideological and political education based on artificial intelligence. J. Phys. Conf. Ser. **1852**(2), 022083 (2021). 6 p.
5. Ouyang, Z.: Research on teaching mode of ecological civilization education based on ideological and political courses in colleges and universities (2021)
6. Lu, L., Zhou, J.: Research on mining of applied mathematics educational resources based on edge computing and data stream classification. Mob. Inf. Syst. **2021**(7), 1–8 (2021)
7. Li, W.: A Study on the construction of morality internalization of young teachers in colleges and universities. J. High. Educ. Res. **3**(1), 43–46 (2022)
8. Xia, C.Y., Yuan, Z.H., He, W.Y., et al.: An empirical study on scientific research performance of universities in different regions of China based on PCA and Malmquist index method[. Educ. Res. Int. (2021)
9. Chen, L.: Research of the safety path of colleges and universities laboratory basing on the analysis of grey correlation degree. J. Intell. Fuzzy Syst. Appl. Eng. Technol. **40**(4) (2021)
10. Yang, L.H., Liu, B., Liu, J.: Research and development talents training in china universities—based on the consideration of education management cost planning. Sustainability 13 (2021)

Research on the Design of Ideological and Political Module in the Internet-Based Higher Mathematics Learning Platform

Yan Liu[✉] and Guan Fengting

Shandong Xiehe University, Jinan 250109, Shandong, China
Ly1234561129@126.com

Abstract. At present, the traditional teaching mode is still used in the classroom teaching of colleges and universities in China. In today's society, where information technology and discipline integration are gradually studied in depth, the teaching needs of colleges and universities are obviously not satisfied by traditional teaching. This requires the design of a more interactive e-learning platform that is no longer limited by traditional education time and region. Through the elaboration of the theory of learning platform, this paper studies the current development stage of learning platform, and points out the significance of this research at the current stage. The research on the design of the ideological and political module in the network-based higher mathematics learning platform is a research carried out by myself. I have been trying to find out whether it has any ideological or political content to ensure that it will not offend anyone. The main purpose of this study is to understand how much ideological and political content there is in the Internet-based higher mathematics learning platform provided by our university, and their impact on students' performance.

Keyword: Learning platform · internet · Advanced mathematics · Ideological and political module

1 Introduction

The increasing investment in information technology in higher education is inseparable from the rapid development of information technology. In some relevant national documents, it is clearly pointed out that "the construction of educational information infrastructure needs to be accelerated, and we must attach great importance to the revolutionary impact of information technology in the process of educational development." "Gradually strengthen the pace of promoting the modernization of teaching contents, methods and means, develop the management mode and operation mode, make rational use of advanced science and technology and rich high-quality resources, integrate existing resources, and build a practical, efficient and advanced platform for digital education infrastructure[1]." "Excellent educational resources should be fully developed

Y. Zhang and N. Shah (Eds.): BigIoT-EDU 2023, LNICST 581, pp. 384–394, 2024.
https://doi.org/10.1007/978-3-031-63133-7_38

and applied." "To improve the level of students' using science and technology to analyze and deal with problems, we need to encourage students to use information means to study independently and actively."

Under the concept of information technology and balanced development of the Ministry of education, colleges and universities have basically entered the information age, and the application of information technology has also rapidly entered the classroom of colleges and universities. Great changes have also taken place in students' learning methods and teachers' teaching methods. At present, almost all learning platforms are designed for universities or adults, rarely for college students, and it is more difficult to find those for college students.

With the transformation of teaching methods and infrastructure, the learning thinking mode of college students has also undergone great changes. The traditional teaching methods and learning methods can not meet the learning requirements of college students, and obviously they are increasingly unable to adapt to the college stage [2]. Therefore, real-time or non real-time communication across time and space is necessary between teachers and students. Students not only hope to communicate with teachers in school, but also hope to fully communicate with teachers in other places, such as at home. Students hope to make their own learning plan at home, arrange their own learning content and time, and be able to raise their own questions at any time and get timely answers. Teachers also want to know about students' learning at home and help students answer their questions in time.

Higher mathematics teaching should organically combine knowledge teaching, ability training and value shaping, excavate ideological and political elements in the curriculum, deepen ideological and political education in teaching, and achieve all-round education. Therefore, the teaching objectives of this course are divided into three levels. 1. Knowledge objectives: master the basic theoretical knowledge of mathematics (mathematical concepts, theorems), basic skills and mathematical thinking methods. 2. Competence objective: to cultivate students' ability to solve practical application problems with mathematical thinking and innovation. 3. Moral education objectives: through the penetration of mathematical culture, mathematical thinking and mathematical spirit, improve mathematical literacy, cultivate students' positive and down-to-earth style, and enhance students' cultural self-confidence and patriotism. Teachers should give full play to their subjective initiative, with the help of domestic and foreign mathematical culture, mathematical knowledge, and teaching content containing ideological and political thoughts in mathematical methods, while improving the interest and practicality of mathematics, so that the teaching and educating function can be fully penetrated in the classroom, and cultivate students' rigorous academic, pioneering and innovative, adhere to the truth, meticulous scientific spirit, and enhance students' patriotic enthusiasm, sense of social responsibility, and national self-confidence [3]. Humanistic spirit. We can start from the following aspects: 1 Mining ideological and political education elements from the theorem, definition and method of teaching content; 2. From the origin and development of the curriculum content, use the content in the history of mathematics to realize the integration of ideological and political education; 3. Carry out dialectical materialism education for students in combination with the characteristics of the curriculum; 4.

Conduct ideological and political education from students' daily behavior; 5. Teachers should be strict with themselves and play an exemplary role.

Due to the abstract and complex teaching content of higher mathematics and the difficulty of students' learning, it is difficult to improve students' learning interest in the process of classroom teaching, which leads to too depressing classroom learning atmosphere and low students' activity and learning enthusiasm. Integrating mathematicians' historical stories, mathematical culture, philosophical thoughts, literary and artistic knowledge, traditional culture of China and the world, and social hot issues into teaching can not only carry out ideological and political education for students, but also stimulate students' interest in learning, so as to improve the teaching quality of higher mathematics and cultivate college students of a new era with all-round development of morality, intelligence, physique, beauty and labor.

This paper studies the design of the ideological and political module in the Internet-based higher mathematics learning platform. The main audience is science and engineering students in Colleges and universities. During the University, due to the difficulty of higher mathematics courses and the high degree of logical abstraction, many students feel difficult to move forward [4]. Therefore, this topic takes higher mathematics courses as a breakthrough and relies on the data generated by learning activities to provide a more scientific and efficient new learning mode for the majority of students.

2   Related Work

2.1   Research on Learning Platform Theory

Transmitting information from the teacher to the student is the most basic requirement of online learning. If it can be effectively combined, it can achieve significant results, and can transmit diversified information, such as graphics, text, audio, video, etc. The learning platform is simply a learning system, which takes the curriculum standard as the criterion and the network resources as the cornerstone, systematically and pertinently integrates the key and difficult knowledge in the discipline, and provides a variety of learning resources, related learning content and knowledge to help learners deepen and widely learn the relevant knowledge they need to learn [5]. Learning platform is an independent research-based learning system based on Web, which can integrate learning related application tools. When students encounter problems, they can choose the direction of the problem in the platform, collect relevant information, and combine their learned knowledge to solve this problem through exploration and cooperation.

The scientific and reasonable processing and storage of teaching resources and learning resources is the advantage of the learning platform. Learners can carry out exploratory autonomous learning without teachers' guidance. Students can learn and communicate with each other on the learning platform. Through the learning platform, students' learning space is expanded, students' awareness of autonomy is virtually enhanced, and students' dominant position in inquiry learning is emphasized [6]. At the same time, students' information literacy is also enhanced. With the network learning platform as the background, many changes have taken place in education and teaching, including space, time, way, content and so on.

(1) Space expansion. The concept of classroom has been different from the traditional meaning in the network learning environment It is an open virtual space, information space and cyberspace where learners are located.

(2) Time expansion. In the context of online learning platform, learning breaks the time limit of traditional classroom learning. Learners can arrange their own learning time and question answering time according to their own needs.

(3) Expansion of educational objects. In addition to providing teaching guidance and teaching resources for students in school, the learning platform can also provide the same function for people in the whole society and become an open platform.

(4) Expansion of teaching content. Traditional book knowledge is obviously not enough. The platform extends the information space in the whole Internet to the teaching content, which makes learning more autonomous and teaching content more preventive. The learning platform framework is shown in Fig. 1 below.

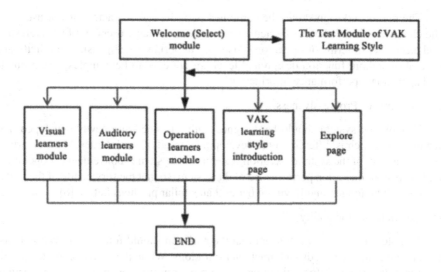

Fig. 1. Learning platform framework

The online learning platform is no longer dominated by teachers in traditional teaching, but pays more attention to the cultivation of students' innovative ability and students' personalized learning experience. It emphasizes the communication, discussion, cooperation and exploration between students and resources, students and students, teachers and students [7].

2.2 Development Principles of Learning Platform

(1) Principle of multiplicity of learning mode

The object of the learning platform is learners, and the function of the platform is to serve the object. In the process of platform development, we should take into account the design requirements of personalized learning mode, discussion mode and cooperation mode, so as to better show its adaptability and flexibility.

(2) Principle of rationality of resource occupation

The learning platform is limited by various aspects, such as network, terminal equipment, user economic affordability, etc., so we should consider reducing the cost of users when using resources, reflecting the ease of access to resources in the design, not increasing the economic burden of learners, and achieving the unification of offline and online use of resources.

(3) Friendly and simple interface design principle

The platform design should be combined with the age characteristics of users and the characteristics of devices. When designing the interface, users can feel interesting and attractive. In terms of operation, it is more important to emphasize simplicity and ease of operation, function design and level are not easy to be complex, and accurate and appropriate performance information.

(4) Principle of Progressiveness

Usually, the system should be designed with advanced and newly developed new technology, which is different in the development trend of the Internet. Make an article on the stability of the system operation, whether the system is convenient for operation, and the overall operation performance of the system, so that the service life of the whole system will be longer, and it will be better than similar products before [8].

(5) Principle of practicality

"People oriented" is the concept that the platform should follow to fully meet customers' personalized needs and practical aspirations. While the system completes various functions such as information release, sharing, transmission, processing, collection, etc., it should take into account whether users are convenient and fast when using [9]. The main business of the function is to be satisfied by the application system. At the same time, it is also necessary to make the network platform using streaming media technology reflect social significance in practice.

2.3 Platform Design Objectives

Centered on the construction of ideological and political modules of higher mathematics courses, the network teaching platform integrating the production, release and maintenance of ideological and political modules of higher mathematics courses is a relatively mature network teaching application system [10]. The design of the network teaching platform must be guided by modern educational ideas and teaching concepts, provide teachers with more practical courseware development tools and teaching methods, and provide students with an interactive network learning application system. An excellent network teaching platform should have the characteristics of convenient use, complete functions, friendly interface, strong compatibility, easy maintenance, and better adaptability to auxiliary teaching [11]. The following basic objectives must be achieved by an excellent online teaching platform:

(1) Good commonality between ideological and political modules of higher mathematics courses in various disciplines An excellent network teaching platform must be a universal system for the network teaching of ideological and political modules of higher mathematics courses in various disciplines, so as to facilitate the unified management of network teaching in colleges and universities.
(2) The design of an excellent network teaching platform that is open and easy to expand must have an open architecture, which can not only provide open space for users, but also reserve space for system expansion and technology upgrading.
(3) An excellent network teaching platform that is easy to operate must be easy for users to use and operate.

Platform technology solutions
Technical framework
In order to make the system achieve the above design goals and ensure the usability, simple operation, scalability and stability of the platform, the current mainstream technology design route is adopted. The platform interface uses PHP technology and HTML language for development. WEB services are implemented through Apache, and the database management system uses MySQL relational database development environment [12].

(1) The hardware environment configuration is no less than Pentium 2.4G processor, 320G hard disk, and 1G memory.
(2) The operating system of the software environment is Linux, the browser is IE8, Chrome and Firefox are recommended, and Apache and MySQL databases are installed.
(3) The development tool uses Eclipse to design PHP code, and the database management system uses MySQL database. During the development process, Photoshop CS, Flash MX, etc. are used as development aids, and Apache is used to configure platform services. As shown in Fig. 3, the configuration platform development part of the code (Fig. 2).

The ideological and political elements that can be integrated into the teaching can be summarized as follows: 1. Through the history of Chinese mathematics and the stories of ancient and modern mathematicians, students' sense of national pride and mission can be stimulated and patriotism can be strengthened. 2. Ignite students' enthusiasm for knowledge and cultivate their feelings of family and country with the spirit of mathematicians. 3. Infiltrate the achievements of China's contemporary construction into the classroom and enhance students' national self-confidence and pride. 4. Carry out materialistic dialectics education in combination with teaching content, such as dialectical thinking from quantitative change to qualitative change, from limited to infinite, from

```
 1  index.php: 系统的入口
 2  <?php
 3      define('ENVIRONMENT', 'development');
 4  if (defined('ENVIRONMENT'))
 5  {
 6      switch (ENVIRONMENT)
 7      {
 8          case 'development':
 9              error_reporting(E_ALL);
10          break;
11          case 'testing':
12          case 'production':
13              error_reporting(0);
14          break;
15          default:
16              exit('The application environment is not set correctly.');
17      }
18  }
19      $system_path = 'system';
20      $application_folder = 'application';
21      if (defined('STDIN'))   {
22          chdir(dirname(__FILE__));}
23      if (realpath($system_path) !== FALSE) {
24          $system_path = realpath($system_path).'/';
25      }
```

Fig. 2. Some key codes

special to general, and cultivate students' philosophical dialectics. 5. Rely on the connotation and extension of mathematical knowledge to elaborate the philosophy of life and cultivate students' moral sentiment. 6. Combine the teaching content, tell the beauty of mathematics, improve aesthetic quality and stimulate creativity. 7. Connect mathematical knowledge and methods with beautiful poems, enlighten students' wisdom, improve cultural accomplishment, and feel humanistic feelings. 8. Improve students' hands-on ability and cooperation awareness through extracurricular group activities such as mathematical modeling and mathematical experiments [13].

3   The Design of Ideological and Political Module in the Internet-Based Higher Mathematics Learning Platform

3.1   Functional Requirements of Learning Platform

There is an important recommendation function in the homepage of the mobile teaching aid system for ideological and political courses in colleges and universities. The setting of recommendation function can provide good guidance and assistance for students' study after class, reflecting the guiding significance of ideological and political courses. Therefore, the recommendation function in the homepage module is the focus of this article. The implementation of the recommendation function uses some recommendation algorithms, the most important of which is the implementation of personalized data recommendation [14]. We initialize the data through the previous recommendation list, add the new recommended teacher recommendation, and call the personalized recommendation items calculated by the algorithm. Finally, we use the hash data table to save the recommendation items and transfer them to the client direction.

(1) Personal center module

The users of the personal center function module are teachers and students. Teachers need to be able to use the personal center function to manage teachers' basic information, receive system notifications, and manage the created teaching resources. Students need to be able to manage their basic information through the personal center and receive system notifications.

(2) Homework practice module

In the process of teaching, most teachers face the main problem of subject knowledge detection. The function of providing teachers with the ability to detect knowledge points needs to be considered in the development of the platform, and the test paper is one of the carriers. With its help, teachers can detect the situation that students master knowledge points. In the traditional teaching mode, teachers print and distribute it to students, which virtually adds a lot of work. This module should have the following functions: the test paper is mainly composed of test paper template, discipline, study section, knowledge points, question type and other elements [15]. The teacher user can define the learning segment, discipline, knowledge points, select the question type, set the corresponding score according to the judgment question, fill in the blank question, multiple-choice question, solution question and other methods, and select a test paper template, and can modify, add, download, save and other operations for the questions in the corresponding question type.

(3) Autonomous learning module

Autonomous learning module is designed for student users. Teachers can publish some classroom materials in this module, such as PPT, lesson plans, knowledge points, teaching videos, audio, etc., to help those students who are not strong in school to continue to consolidate their knowledge points at home. If some students say that they have mastered the knowledge points well and want to expand some knowledge points, they can go to this module to find some expanded knowledge points published by teachers to help students expand their knowledge [16].

(4) Question answering module

The function of the question answering function module is to answer the questions raised by students online. Student users raise questions through this module. Teachers can answer online instantly through this module, and teachers can also answer by leaving messages. After the teacher answers the question, he can also notify the students to remind them to check it.

3.2 System Use Case Analysis

The teaching method of Ideological and political course in Colleges and universities is the general name of the teaching and learning methods or means adopted by teachers and students in order to complete the teaching purpose of Ideological and political course in Colleges and universities and realize the teaching task of Ideological and political course in Colleges and universities [17]. The teaching methods of Ideological and political courses in Colleges and Universities under this definition have the following characteristics: first, the teaching methods of Ideological and political courses in Colleges and universities emphasize the unity of knowledge and practice, which is determined by the characteristics of Ideological and political courses in Colleges and universities. Secondly, the ultimate goal pursued by the teaching method of Ideological and political courses in Colleges and universities is that the educatees become the builders and successors of the socialist cause of moral, intellectual and physical development, and provide qualified talents for the socialist modernization construction. Thirdly, the teaching methods of Ideological and political courses in Colleges and universities, including both teachers' teaching methods and students' learning methods under the guidance of teachers, are an effective combination of teaching methods and learning methods [18]. At the same time, this definition also shows that the teaching method of Ideological and political courses in Colleges and universities is the main form of connecting the teaching and learning of Ideological and political courses in Colleges and universities, and it is the most obvious factor reflecting the relationship between teaching and learning of Ideological and political courses in Colleges and universities.

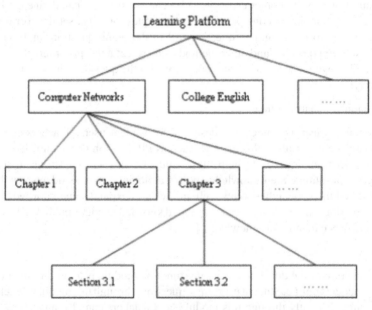

Fig. 3. System use case

According to the main requirements of the system function module, combined with the analysis of the system use cases, the functions used by users are described. By registering teachers and students to become registered users, browse, view and other operations. The teacher releases the homework exercises that need to be completed in the homework exercise module. When students enter the homework exercises, they download and print them to complete the homework exercises. Students receive the homework that needs to be written through the assignment module, and complete the paper homework at home. In the online question module, students ask questions to teachers. After entering the question answering module, teachers receive questions to answer questions, and feed back the answers to student users [19, 20]. In the personal center, teachers and student users can set information and other settings respectively. See Fig. 3 for the use case.

4 Conclusion

As an important part of the mobile teaching aid system of ideological and political courses in higher mathematics, its setting is to better reflect the need of ideological and political courses to cultivate college students' ideological and moral ability and better improve their comprehensive ability. In the recommendation module, the first is the windowed recommendation page, followed by personalized recommended video courses, famous teachers' lectures, hyperlinks, reference materials, current affairs and politics, hot spots interpretation, and current comments and short comments. At the bottom is the teacher's recommendation, which fully reflects the new mobile teaching idea of students' autonomous learning, supplemented by teachers' opinions. This paper mainly focuses on the network learning platform developed for college students. At present, most of the platforms are mainly developed for college students. The development of this platform fills this part of the gap. The platform takes full account of the characteristics of the student group, carefully analyzes the user's design needs for the platform, and helps students not only limited to the learning materials in textbooks, but also effectively assists teachers in the online Q & a part for off campus tutoring and teaching. At the same time, considering that students spend most of their extra-curricular time copying homework topics, so they have less extra-curricular time to play with their partners, the development of the platform helps the homework topics to the homework assignment module, which better solves students' extra-curricular time.

Acknowledgements. Shandong Education Science "13th five year plan" 2020 project: Practical Research on Integrating Ideological and political education into higher mathematics teaching, project number: 2020ZC427 .

References

1. Peng, X., Liu, W.: Exploration of Integrating Ideological and Political Education into the Classroom Teaching of Higher Mathematics (2021)
2. Li, J.: The Analysis on the Way of Integrating the Ideological and Political Education into the Teaching Mode of Higher Mathematics Courses (2020)

3. Wang, H., University S.T.: Exploration of ideological and political practice of "higher mathematics foundation" course in distance education. J. Shanxi Radio TV Univ. (2019)
4. Wang, D.: Design of online test module in the curriculum development learning platform. J. Guizhou Educ. Univ. (2016)
5. Fangguo W. Design of teaching model of ideological and political education network course based on educational cloud platform. In: 2020 5th International Conference on Smart Grid and Electrical Automation (ICSGEA) (2020)
6. Wang, T.: Mathematical analysis of the functions of dao's following nature in the ideological and political education. 美中外语:英文版 **17**(12), 11 (2019)
7. Liu, Z.: Discussion on the ideological and political practice of computer graphic design from the visual image design of "Three Cows Spirit" **2022**(5), 4 (2022)
8. White, E.E.: Game-based learning in Design and Technology: an evaluation of a multi-media environment (2022)
9. Nguyen, M.H., Sun, L., Grinsztajn, N., et al.: Meta-learning from Learning Curves Challenge: Lessons learned from the First Round and Design of the Second Round (2022)
10. He, H.: Design and Application of Pre-school Music Teaching System in Moodle Platform (2022)
11. Chen, T.: Research on the dilemma and breakthrough path of ideological and political education in colleges and universities in the era of big data. J. High. Educ. Res. **3**(2), 203–206 (2022)
12. Liu, S., Yan, P.: Research on the necessity and practical path of ideological and political reform of higher mathematics curriculum. In: 2020 3rd International Conference on Humanities Education and Social Sciences (ICHESS 2020) (2020)
13. Tian, Y.: Research and design of political and ideological learning platform based on wechat mini-apps. Digital Technol. Appl. (2018)
14. Yang, N., Ding, Y., Du, Y.: Design and application of MOOCs system in the course of Ideological and political education on the Android platform. Autom. Instrum. (2016)
15. Zhang, H., Tang, Q., University, Z., et al.: Design and implementation of optimal content push system in self-service network learning platform. Mod. Electron. Tech. (2017)
16. Zheng, J., Jianhong, G.E.: Analysis and design of learning platform based on Internet mobile terminal. Mod. Electron. Tech. (2017)
17. Duan, L.B.: The design of ideological and political classroom teaching resource sharing system based on streaming media technology. In: 2020 IEEE International Conference on Industrial Application of Artificial Intelligence (IAAI). IEEE (2020)
18. Jia-Wei, X.U., Zhao, L.X.: Research on the design of incentive mechanism in web-based autonomous learning platform. J. South. Vocat. Educ. (2016)
19. Duan, L.Y.: On the teaching design practice of ideological and political teaching based on big data of cloud teaching. J. Yan'an Vocat. Tech. Coll. (2018)
20. Wei, Z., He, J.: Effective approaches to ideological and political education of higher mathematics curriculum in applied technology universities. Sci. Educ. Art. Collects (2019)

Design of University Public Curriculum Education System Platform Based on AHP Algorithm

Pei Liu[1]([✉]), Lei Li[2], and Lin Lin[3]

[1] Shandong Institute of Commerce and Technology, Jinan 250103, Shandong, China
liupei1980@163.com
[2] Nanchang University College of Science and Technology, Jiang-Xi, Nanchang 330001, China
[3] Harbin Normal University, Harbin 150000, China

Abstract. This paper briefly expounds the requirements of university public curriculum education system platform design under the background of intelligent classroom, From the physical, logical architecture, platform access design and system evaluation design, The design of the university public curriculum education system platform based on the AHP algorithm is analyzed in detail, Aimed to provide a reference for relevant researchers, Then the design effect of the public curriculum education system is analyzed, Find the problem in the layer-by-layer comparison, To realize the further optimization and adjustment of the platform design, Give full play to its practical role in improving the teaching level of public curriculum in colleges and universities.

Keyword: University · public curriculum · education system platform · AHP algorithm

1 Introduction

Public curriculum as a basic curriculum for college overall education effect has crucial influence, in the era of modern information technology upgrading, universities began to actively promote public curriculum reform, there are many universities set up the public curriculum education system, but from the reality, its practical application stage still faces some obstacles, based on this, it is necessary through the application of AHP algorithm on its implementation effect, and take corresponding adjustment measures based on the evaluation results.

1. Requirements of Public Curriculum Education System

Public curriculum in colleges and universities for all college students, good public curriculum education system platform can effectively meet the wisdom campus under the background of the current era of public curriculum reform and innovation, based on the AHP algorithm of university public curriculum education system platform design should meet the needs of intelligent classroom, management and information sharing.

Y. Zhang and N. Shah (Eds.): BigIoT-EDU 2023, LNICST 581, pp. 395–405, 2024.
https://doi.org/10.1007/978-3-031-63133-7_39

1.1 Intelligent Classroom

From the present, although the vast majority of universities in China has introduced a large number of multimedia teaching equipment, but the form of communication is relatively single, intelligent classroom requires public curriculum teaching in colleges and universities should fully apply the Internet of things and cloud technology, etc., for the efficient application of public curriculum education system platform to provide the necessary technical support. The platform should be able to comprehensively analyze and process all kinds of information generated in the public curriculum teaching activities, and completely record the information and data fed back by teachers and students, so as to realize the comprehensive evaluation of the classroom implementation effect.

1.2 Intelligent Management

University public curriculum education system platform design should be able to meet the actual needs of intelligent management, from the perspective of the current actual situation, most of the university management system need to operate on the basis of the PC end, the application stage is facing great limitations, and is difficult for mutual communication between teachers and students and managers to create good conditions, greatly affect the smooth and effectiveness of communication. Although many universities have begun to actively carry out the research and development of relevant platforms, its operation is relatively complex, and it involves a large maintenance cost investment, so the overall feasibility is poor [1].

1.3 Intelligent Information Sharing

For public curriculum education in colleges and universities, itself is a relatively complex systematic engineering, combined with the current era background, if you want to further improve education results, universities and teachers should not be limited in the classroom teaching, but need through the construction of the public curriculum education system platform, let students to real-time dynamic access to the required curriculum information and learning resources, in order to enhance the humanized level of college course education service, better meet the needs of students' public course learning [2].

2 Design Practice Analysis of University Public Curriculum Education System Platform Based on AHP Algorithm

2.1 Physical and Logical Architecture

2.1.1 Physical Architecture

The university public curriculum education system designed in this paper mainly includes three parts: intelligent terminal, database and information interaction system, which can be effectively connected on the basis of the Internet and the mobile Internet. Among them, the intelligent terminals can independently choose the PC, tablet computer or mobile phone according to the actual situation of the students, and connect to the mobile Internet, and then log in to the public course education platform can be relatively connected to the teaching system, and then complete the learning of the public courses. Cloud server terminal can be through the application of mobile network for the data information storage and transmission, and it can play the role of a transfer station, as a server placed in the campus, convenient public course teachers and students to access the information interaction system, for all kinds of important course data or school information management and read [3].

2.1.2 Logical Architecture

The system is mainly divided into three layers of logic architecture, among which the first layer is the representation layer, which can provide the users with the corresponding interface based on the client side, and the users can use this interface to smoothly enter the system for internal operation [4]. The second layer is the business logic layer, which is mainly composed of the cloud platform of the public course education system and the campus system server. Users involve the application of the system server logic layer in the process of calling the course materials and course information. The third layer is the data access layer, which plays a fundamental role in the public curriculum education system in colleges and universities [5]. The database involves two parts: intermediate data and permanent data, which can effectively extract and store the teaching task data in the application process. The system logic architecture is shown in Fig. 1.

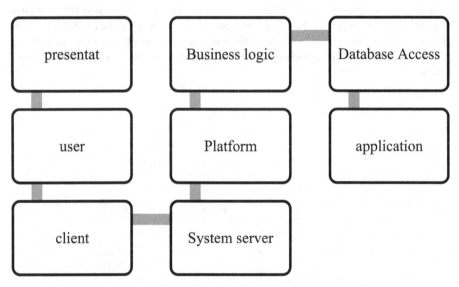

Fig. 1. System logic architecture

2.2 Platform Access Design

The public course education system platform of the university adopts HTTP protocol to access it. Users can register their account through the login system platform, add the server address, and fill in the third URL address [6]. Token information is an important part of the security of the platform, at the same time, it can also realize the user authentication, system after Token information configuration, maintenance personnel will be based on the actual request, according to the relevant requirements and specific steps of the platform configuration server, configuration parameters are shown in Table 1.

Table 1. Query results of system

1. Configuration parameter	2. Configuration description
3. Times	4. Time, date
5. NJCP	6. Random parameter
7. EKSTAN	8. Random characters
9. Signature	10. Encryption authentication

2.3   System Evaluation and Design

2.3.1   Model Construction

This paper mainly uses the AHP hierarchical analysis method to analyze the various elements in the operation of the system platform, and sort them on the basis of clarifying their respective importance, and then judge the application effectiveness of different schemes according to the relevant basis [7]. The framework of AHP is shown in Fig. 2 below.

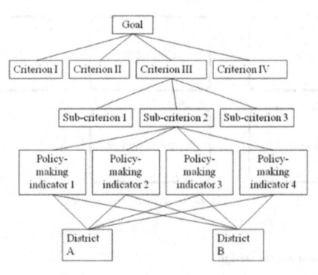

Fig. 2. AHP analytic hierarchy process

First, the planning decision target U is set, including the importance weight and various types of influencing factors, and the two respectively use wiAnd uiTo represent, the formula is as follows:

$$U = u_1w_1 + u_2w_2+, \cdots, +u_nw_n \tag{1}$$

In the above expression, u1w1, u2w2as well as unwnIs the influencing factors and the importance of the actual weight, in view of the research objectives, when in the influence of different factors, the research is affected by the degree of the target will present a certain difference, so relevant personnel need to make reasonable comparative analysis, through the final comparison results, can get the matrix is as follows:

$$A = \begin{bmatrix} w_1w_1 & w_1w_2 & \cdots & w_1w_n \\ w_2w_1 & w_2w_2 & \cdots & w_2w_n \\ \cdots & \cdots & & \cdots \\ w_nw_1 & w_nw_2 & \cdots & w_nw_n \end{bmatrix} \tag{2}$$

In this matrix, the letters represent differences in the degree of influence.

If the A in this matrix is regarded as a judgment matrix, so that it can effectively meet the consistency test conditions, then the eigenvalue problem is expressed as follows:

$$Aw = \lambda w \tag{3}$$

The w in this formula refers to the weight values of the influencing factor, but it represents the actual distribution of the weight values. λ

The computational solution yields that:

$$w = \{w_1, w_2, \cdots, w_n\} \tag{4}$$

Based on the university public curriculum education system platform, the following operations should be followed in the process of evaluating the quality of teachers in the platform:

First of all, the corresponding evaluation factors and specific grades should be made clear, and then the actual state of it when being under the action of different factors should be described, expressed as follows:

$$V = \{v_1, v_2, \cdots, v_n\} \tag{5}$$

Changes in the state of the various factors represented by V in this expression.

Secondly, the evaluation matrix should be constructed, and the weight value should be clarified on this basis. Specifically, pretreatment measures should be taken for a single factor to complete the construction of the single factor evaluation set [8]. The m factor evaluation should be adopted to realize the construction of the total evaluation matrix, as follows:

$$R = \left(r_{ij}\right)_{m \times n} = \begin{bmatrix} r_{11} & r_{12} & \cdots & r_{1m} \\ r_{21} & r_{22} & \cdots & r_{2m} \\ \cdots & \cdots & & \cdots \\ r_{m1} & r_{m2} & \cdots & r_{nm} \end{bmatrix} \tag{6}$$

Generally speaking, after expanding the normalization process for the total evaluation matrix, the total evaluation matrix should meet the corresponding constraints, as follows:

$$\sum_i r_{ij} = 1 \tag{7}$$

Finally, under the AHP level analysis method, the teaching situation reflected in the teaching platform of the public curriculum should be divided at different levels according to the actual situation of colleges and universities and the setting principles of the evaluation index system.

This paper adopts six evaluation factors, such as teaching content and teaching attitude, which can be expressed as follows:

$$U = \{u_1, u_2, u_3, u_4, u_5, u_6\} \tag{8}$$

For different evaluation factors, the evaluation factors are also different in terms of type. The above 6 set of evaluation factors can be expressed by the following formula:

$$\begin{cases} u_1 = \{u_{11}, u_{12}, u_{13}, u_{14}, u_{15}, u_{16}\} \\ u_2 = \{u_{21}, u_{22}, u_{23}\} \\ u_3 = \{u_{31}, u_{32}, u_{33}\} \\ u_4 = \{u_{41}, u_{42}\} \\ u_5 = \{u_{51}, u_{52}, u_{53}\} \\ u_6 = \{u_{61}, u_{62}, u_{63}\} \end{cases} \tag{9}$$

The collection is mainly described in various types of evaluation indicators, which can be divided into v_1, v_2, v_3, v_4 Four evaluation levels.

In the application stage, it is necessary to table the different grades through the application of different values, and use the percentage to represent each evaluation index, and use the hierarchical analysis method to determine its weight [9].

2.3.2 Determine the Weights

For the AHP evaluation system, the weight is a relative numerical existence. If we want to further improve and optimize the platform design scheme of the university public curriculum education system platform, it is necessary to ensure that the weight allocation should be set scientifically and accurately. In order to minimize the problems such as insufficient information, unscientific evaluation indicators and weight imbalance, this paper mainly builds on the first-level indicators at three levels, and finally clearly uses each detailed index to form the corresponding weight. This study was conducted in a combination of expert consultation and online questionnaire. In the process of calculating the total evaluation score, it is necessary to establish the n n judgment matrix from the three dimensions of the public curriculum education system platform and students and teachers [10]. It represents the importance of the elements obtained by comparing each element, and then the maximum feature root needs to be calculated. The formula is as follows:

$$\Upsilon_{max} = \frac{1}{n} \sum_{k=1}^{n} \frac{(A_w)_k}{w_k} \tag{10}$$

The relative weights of different refinement indicators are calculated, and the ranking work is completed according to their importance.

2.3.3 Analysis of Rating Elements

Through the above analysis, it can be determined that the evaluation indicators for the university public curriculum education system platform mainly include four parts: functional organization, technical support, course display and mobile learning, as shown in Fig. 3 below.

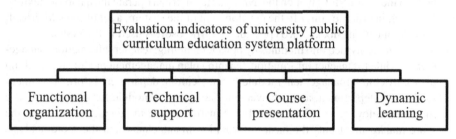

Fig. 3. Evaluation indicators of university public curriculum education system platform

The functional organization index involves the teaching interaction function, which specifically refers to the design and organization form of the platform in the communication area, q & A area and discussion area; the design content of the homework, examination and stage test in the evaluation function; the teaching form and the rationality of the task setting used in the teaching activities; and the related functions of the student activities involve the learning analysis, student participation and the convenience of online interaction [11].

The technical support index mainly includes the server performance elements, which focuses on the smooth implementation of the online teaching; the network performance focuses on the network bandwidth load presented by the real-time online public course; the performance elements of the system are composed of the fluency of video playback and the actual quality of the video media; in the feedback mechanism, which includes the technical services involved in the whole process of the university public course implementation and help instructions [12].

In the course display index, this evaluation element is mainly designed to analyze whether the introduction content can reflect the advantages and the comprehensiveness of the introduction; the learning objective elements are specific to the specific learning objective information that students can obtain in the platform; the learning resource element refers to the configuration and display of examination papers, homework, video and courseware in the public curriculum education system platform.

The evaluation elements in the mobile learning index include the basic support obtained by the platform design and construction, and judge whether the platform can meet the actual needs of mobile learning in terms of stability and convenience.

3 Design of Public Curriculum Education System Platform

The overall functional modules of the system are as follows:

1. The system divides modules by function, uses B-S structure, uses. Net platform, SQLSERVER database, and IIS server (supporting asp. Net) as development tools.
2. Use three layers of architecture: data access layer, business facade layer and presentation layer.
3. The data access layer (DataAccess) is responsible for the processing of the database. It only adds, deletes and modifies the data in the database [13]. Generally, it is directly built on the ADO.NET layer on the. NET platform. It can operate the database flexibly. However, in order to simplify the development of the system, a set of tools Microsoft Data Application Block (DAB) provided by Microsoft is used in the system.
4. The system is divided into modules by object, including: teacher information management module for teacher information, teaching plan management module for teaching plan, curriculum management module for curriculum, department information query module for department, and achievement management module for grades [14]. The functions below are used as a function function in the module. Among them, the score management puts the basic information management and the score analysis and adjustment together, and at the same time, the individual student's score query is included in it, which shows the difference between the module divided by object and the module divided by function.
5. The advantages of module division by object over module division by function are that the idea is clearer, consistent with the user interface design idea, convenient for thinking and future function expansion, better realize low coupling and high cohesion, and convenient for maintenance and modification.
6. There is no control coupling between the function functions, and the independence is good. There is public environment coupling [15]. The emphasis is on the processing of the database, and the requirements for database processing technology are high.
7. With the help of the UIA (Unified Identity Authentication Subsystem) of Mycollege. Net, the user authentication and permission allocation are completed.
8. The system data update function in the function description can be implemented in three ways (refer to the access policy of public data resources in MyCollege.Net):

Synchronous access strategy: the system does not set up a special database to save the required public data resources. Whenever the system needs to use public data resources (students, department information), it will obtain data through the Web Service in the network call. (The CResource subsystem stores the latest data under the MyClege. Net system) [16]. The advantage is that the system can obtain the latest data, but the disadvantage is that it requires high performance and reliability of the network.

Asynchronous access strategy: set the basic information storage of students and departments locally, and access it directly from the local database when needed. The advantages are simple implementation and short response time [17]; The disadvantage is that the administrator can only update the local database with the basic information of the main system on a regular basis, so the information stored in the local database may not be instant information.

Caching strategy: The basic information storage of students and colleges and departments is also set locally. When information is needed, the system first views to retrieve data from the local database. If it hits, it will call directly. If it misses, it will obtain the latest data through WebService. At the same time, it will take a certain caching strategy to cache the obtained data into the local database to support the high-speed access to the data later. The advantage is that the response time and data immediacy are relatively compromised, while the disadvantage is that the implementation is more complex [18]. The system development framework is shown in Fig. 4 below.

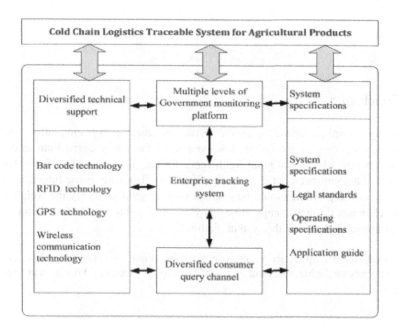

Fig. 4. System development framework

Next, we will use Django's low code to improve these two pieces of content. First of all, we should use the database to manage the network equipment, so that the data is centralized and unified. From Django's MTV mode, we know that Django has a corresponding data layer to handle the interaction with the database. It has a complete, easy-to-use and powerful ORM system, which can convert the operation of the database into the operation of Python objects [19]. Through Django's ORM function, we first create a table structure and define a Model object. The code is shown in Fig. 5 below:

These three field types represent fields of integer type, corresponding to the int type in the database [20]. The value range of IntergerField is - 2147483648 to 2147483647. BigIntegerField uses more bits to store numbers, so its upper limit is 9223372036854775807. As a beginner, you can generally choose IntergerField, unless you consider switching to BigIntegerField in some extreme cases.

```
import numpy as np

data = np.array([[1,2,7,7],[1/2.0,1,6,8],[1/7.0, 1/6.0, 1,3],[1/7.0,1/8.0,1/3
eigenvalues , vector = np.linalg.eig(data)
eigenvalue_max = max(list(eigenvalues))
index_max = list(eigenvalues).index(eigenvalue_max)
weights = vector[:, index_max]
weights = np.real(weights)
weights = weights/np.sum(weights)
print(weights)

>>array([0.51247524, 0.35654443, 0.08503711, 0.04594321])
```

Fig. 5. Critical code

4   Conclusion

To sum up, the unified university public curriculum education system platform can create good conditions for the online development of the public curriculum in colleges and universities, which is of great significance for the cultivation of students' learning interest and the improvement of learning efficiency. Therefore, in the future, the application of AHP algorithm should be continuously adopted to clarify the weight of the system elements through comparative analysis, so as to lay a solid foundation for the optimization and design of the system platform.

Acknowledgements. Specialized Project in the construction of Double high-level colleges. No.C103. Study on the Measures and Effects of Morality and Technical Education in Vocational Colleges.

References

1. Yang, W.: Curriculum Design and Practice Exploration of "Business English Listening and Speaking" in the applied university international trade major based on the intelligent teaching platform. —— takes "Rain Classroom" as an example. Sino-foreign Exch. **28**(5), 28–29 (2021)
2. Lei, H.: Quality evaluation of ideological and political courses based on fuzzy mathematics. Microcomput. Appl. **38**(6), 69–71,78 (2022)
3. Bin, H., Kunyu, D., Yong, H.:—— takes the course of "Computer System Structure" as an example. Educ. Teach. Forum (20), 108–111 (2022)
4. Xianbin, W., Jiansheng, W.: Build a diversified university curriculum teaching quality evaluation system. China Inf. Technol. Educ. (6), 100–102 (2021)
5. Liu, Q., Huang, D.: Modeling of supply chain vendor selecting system based on AHP-BP algorithm and its application. J. East China Uni. Sci. Technol. (Natural Science Edition) **33**(1), 108–114 (2007)
6. Zhen-Fa, Q.I., Cheng, J.M., Fu-Yuan, X.U.: Improved AHP algorithm based on system structure decomposition. J. Univ. Shanghai Sci. Technol. (2002)

7. Shi, Y., Shan, D., University P.: Research on monitoring public opinio system based on hadoop. Electron. Test (2015)
8. Jia, C.: The construction of TRIZ Teaching Curriculum System Based on the Cultivation of College Students' Innovative Ability——A Case Study on the Innovation Teaching of Automobile Specialty (2018)
9. Wang, S., Song, M.: Research on fuzzy evaluation of teaching practice based on AHP—an example of evaluating curriculum design performance in computer major. In: International Conference on System Modeling and Optimization. 0
10. Song, S.: Computer science and technology undergraduate curriculum system construction and analysis. In: The Third International Conference on Education Management Science and Engineering.Department of Information Engineering, Jilin Business and Technology College, Changchun, P.R.China, pp. 130062 (2010)
11. Guo, S., Chen, Y., Zheng, C., et al.: Mixture-modelling-based Bayesian MH-RM algorithm for the multidimensional 4PLM. Br. J. Math. Stat. Psychol. **76**(3), 585–604 (2023)
12. Poulton, G., Guo, Y., Valencia, P., et al.: Designing Enzymes in a Multi-Agent System based on a Genetic Algorithm (2004)
13. Jinxiu, Y.U.: Research on the evaluation of teaching quality of curriculum of public art education in colleges and universities based on AHP fuzzy comprehensive evaluation method. J. High. Educ. (2019)
14. Jiang-Yong, G.: Feasibility analysis of the comprehensive evaluation system of PE course in Universities in Jiangsu based on AHP. J. Hubei Financ. Econ. Coll. (2011)
15. Gao, T.T., Cheng, Y.: Study of second-hand carsnew rate based on AHP algorithm. J. Tianjin Univ. Technol. Educ. (2012)
16. Fei, L., Yong, Q., Li, X., et al.: The research of new university public P.E.curriculum platform based on modularized teaching. J. Jilin Inst. Phys. Educ. (2011)
17. Chen, X.M., Tang, X.Y.: Implementation of AHP algorithm in teaching quality evaluation system based on data mining. Comput. Modernization (2012)
18. Gong, J.Y.: Feasibility analysis of fuzzy comprehensive evaluation based on AHP evaluation system of college PECours. J. Taizhou Polytech. Coll. (2011)
19. Zhong, Z.Q.: Multimedia courseware quality evaluation and algorithm realization research based on AHP. J. Anshan Normal Univ. (2008)
20. Ying, Z.: Research on the knowledge service evaluation system in university library based on neural network. Inf. Stud. Theor. Appl. (2013)

The Specific Construction Path of Vocational Education Group Based on Big Datag

Chao Zhang[1](✉), Jing Tian[1], Desheng Zhu[1], Runling Wang[1], Aiguo Gong[1], Zhenhua Cheng[2], and Jilin Xu[1]

[1] Shandong Institute of Commerce and Technology, Jinan 250103, Shandong, China
Chaochao20041984@163.com
[2] Sports Department, Modern College of Northwest University, Xi'an 710130, Shaanxi, China

Abstract. With the advent of the era of big data, it has brought great help to the reform of vocational education groups. Vocational education is an important aspect of the education system, preparing individuals for specific occupations. With the emergence of big data, vocational education groups can now use data analysis to create a specific construction path that meets the needs of the job market. The construction path includes identifying the skills and abilities required for a particular occupation, and developing training plans to equip learners with these skills. Big data provides in-depth understanding of industry trends, job requirements, and labor skill gaps. This information helps vocational education groups design courses that meet the needs of employers and provide learners with relevant skills. In addition, big data enables educators to track learners' progress and adjust their teaching methods accordingly. The specific construction path of vocational education groups based on big data ensures that learners have relevant skills that match the needs of the industry. The vocational education group combines its own development to develop teaching facilities related to big data. For example, big data information exchange platforms and data centers have promoted the further development of vocational education groups. This approach improves employability, reduces the skill gap in the workforce, and ultimately contributes to economic growth. In summary, using big data in vocational education is crucial for cultivating a skilled workforce that can meet the needs of the industry. This article analyzes the basic connotation of vocational education group education, discusses the challenges faced by vocational education clusters and construction strategies for reference.

Keywords: big data · vocational education group · construction path

1 Introduction

Vocational Education Group is a school running consortium formed by vocational colleges, industry enterprises, and other organizations to achieve resource sharing, complementary advantages, and cooperative development; It is an important mode for China to accelerate the reform of vocational education mechanism and promote the opening and

Y. Zhang and N. Shah (Eds.): BigIoT-EDU 2023, LNICST 581, pp. 406–417, 2024.
https://doi.org/10.1007/978-3-031-63133-7_40

sharing of high-quality resources; It is an effective platform carrier for deepening the integration of industry and education, school-enterprise cooperation, and collaborative education; It is an important starting point for coordinating the promotion of vocational education and the comprehensive development of economic society. In recent years, the collectivization of vocational education in China has achieved rapid development in various regions [1]. However, the development mode of vocational education groups is mostly loose, and their organizational structure, institutional mechanisms, connotation construction, and service capabilities significantly restrict the collectivization of vocational education and economic and social development. To solve these constraints, it is urgent to explore and establish a new model of vocational education groups.

Vocational education groups differ from social groups with typical attributes of the third sector in terms of their constituent elements, which include both educational, economic, and social sectors [2]. In terms of organizational classification, it mainly belongs to the category of organizations in the third sector: affiliated organizations and non-governmental organizations, while the category of registered organizations is rare, and currently the legal definition is relatively vague. In his "Reflections on the Basic Issues of Vocational Education Groups", Ma Chengrong believed that vocational education groups can be classified as non-profit organizations in social organizations (including government organizations, for-profit organizations, and non-profit organizations) and belong to a part of the "third sector" (the collection of non-profit organizations is referred to as the third sector in academia) [3]. Because the organizational characteristics of the vocational education group and the third sector summarized by the American scholar Salamon are highly consistent: (1) Organizational. (2) It is civil and independent from the government in terms of system. (3) Non profit organizations may earn profits, but profits must serve the basic mission of the organization and cannot be distributed to owners and managers. (4) Autonomy. (5) Volunteerism.

The research group on "Theoretical Research and Practical Exploration of Collective Schooling in Vocational Education" believes that, as a school consortium with a quasi public nature and the introduction of market mechanisms, vocational education groups have the following characteristics: vocational education groups do not have legal personality, but they are a joint school consortium composed of several entities with independent legal personality [4]; The organizational structure of vocational education groups is diversified, multiform, and multi-level; Vocational education groups are mainly connected by assets, contracts, as well as mixed forms of asset custody operations and long-term preferential contracts; There is sharing and consistency of interests within vocational education groups, but externally it must prevent the commercialization of education.

The discussion on the role and advantages of vocational education groups involves many researchers, for example, some researchers have used economic theories to analyze. Xie Yuan used the Maxi Silverstone curve in economics to illustrate that vocational education obtains economies of scale through the expansion of a certain scale. Deng Liming pointed out in more detail that after the formation of the vocational education group, it is necessary to carry out internal restructuring and streamline redundant cross department and cross level operational links to generate large-scale efficiency. Jiang Wei not only cited the definition of economies of scale in material production in this regard, but also cited five other economic theoretical analyses [5]. It includes six aspects: "system optimization theory", "order theory", "scope economy theory", "speed economy theory", and "network economy theory". Based on this, it is believed that the collectivization development of higher vocational education as an effective expansion path and institutional innovation has both advantages and limitations.

As a consortium composed of vocational colleges, enterprises, industries, and other organizations, vocational education groups are an important operating mode of vocational education in China. At the same time, it is also an important carrier of industry-education integration, school-enterprise cooperation, and collaborative education [6]. In the context of the continuous development of big data, the development scale of vocational education groups is becoming larger and larger, but there are many problems in the development process of vocational education groups. Therefore, vocational education organizations should pay attention to it.

2   Related Work

2.1   Big Data

In recent years, the term "big data" has repeatedly appeared in our vision; At the same time, its related theories and technologies are also widely used in various fields. The emergence of "big data" can be traced back to the Hadoop project in 2005, achieving efficient web search; Until 2008, the World Organization Computer Community Alliance published a white paper titled "Big Data Computing: Creating Revolutionary Breakthroughs in the Business, Scientific, and Social Fields", which truly had a vague concept of "big data". In 2009, the establishment and implementation of a biometric database in India, Data.gov in the United States, and a network of European research institutions further enhanced the effectiveness of using data for tracking and forecasting. In 2010, Kenneth Kukol proposed in his special report "Data, Everywhere Data" that the world has a huge amount of data with rapid growth, and the term "big data" was coined. In 2011, IBM's Watson supercomputer defeated two competitors in a quiz competition; McKinsey released "Big Data: The Next New Field of Innovation, Competition, and Productivity", proposing the arrival of the big data era; In December of the same year, China's Ministry of Industry and Information Technology proposed an innovative project for big data processing technology in the 12th Five Year Plan for the Internet of Things. In 2012, "Big Data, Big Impact" was released at the World Economic Forum in Davos, Switzerland; The United States released the "Big Data Research and Development Initiative", and the first big data processing company, Splink, went public [7]. The United Nations released a white paper on big data governance, and Alibaba established a "Chief Data Officer"; It marks the official entry of the world into the era of big data. In 2014, there were no special reports on "big data" in many parts of the world. From 2015 to now, various countries are still making future plans around "big data".

"Big data" refers to data information that cannot be manipulated using normal means and tools within a limited period of time, which is due to its characteristics. The data capacity of big data is quite large, which cannot be compared with conventional quantities; The second is that it contains a wide variety of data, not a simple set of data; Third, the speed of receiving new data is extremely fast; The fourth is the variability of data, which may change all the time; The fifth is the complexity of data structures, which requires simultaneous processing of structured, unstructured, and intermediate data [8]. Because of these characteristics, "big data" is also used as a new technology and model for the analysis, acquisition, and prediction of data information and information assets, achieving the optimization and value of data information collections.

Due to the emergence of "big data", traditional data models have been broken, and big data thinking has emerged as the times require. Big data thinking refers to not thinking and solving problems in a conventional logical way. The traditional problem-solving thinking is to first find the cause, then find out the relevant factors from the source for analysis, and finally verify the results again [9]; Big data thinking is to provide solutions directly to problems using big data methods, as shown in Fig. 1. It has the following characteristics: first, there can be no causal relationship between things; The second is that the concepts of part and whole are equivalent; Accepting erroneous data information; Fourth, big data thinking focuses on efficiency.

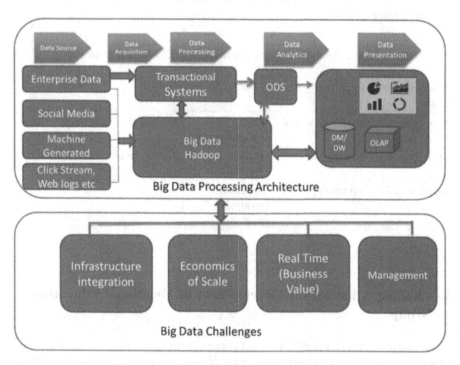

Fig. 1. Big data mode

2.2 Basic Connotation of Vocational Education Group

Vocational education group as an important part of the whole education system, its system structure mainly includes level, form, stage, type and distribution, etc., in the hierarchy, vocational education group system mainly for different levels of object training,

training object will involve certain technical workers and have preliminary technical talents, farmers or other industries. At the same time, the trained talents trained will also involve front-line talents such as production, service and technology. In addition, senior management personnel with high technology skills will also be responsible for the training [10]. In terms of schooling, vocational education group is not limited to secondary vocational workers, but also to bachelor's degree, graduate degree and higher level talents. In terms of type structure, the society directly determines the vocational education group teaching type, and vocational education group in the teaching stage, also includes primary and secondary schools, family and social intention of career as the direction of education and employment direction, and social development needs fit each other, to have from education industry personnel training employment, in some form, vocational education group college can not limit vocational school education, including social personnel with no academic qualifications [11]. In terms of distribution, within the range of vocational education with better economic development, the larger the range of vocational education groups is. Table 1 is the component composition of the vocational education group system.

Table 1. The element composition of the vocational education group system

administrative levels	form	stage	type	distribution
Primary level	vocational school	Career enlightenment	Medical class	Urban distribution
Medium level	education	Career preparation	Traffic class	Urban and rural distribution
Higher level	job training	Vocational continuing education	......	

3 Challenges Facing the Development of Vocational Education Group

In the construction process of vocational education group, there are many factors that limit the construction and development pace of vocational education group. There are mainly two external and internal factors that restrict the development of vocational education group. Its main problems have the following two aspects: first, the external influence factors, mainly reflected in the policy, the government of vocational education group lack of corresponding incentive policy, the government and vocational education group lack of integration, in terms of resources, the number of supply, and supply channels have certain constraint, the way of communication obstacles, then lead to vocational education group in the work departments and industry communication lack of effectiveness [12]. In the supervision of the vocational education group, there is a lack of fair and equal communication subjects. In the daily operation of the upper and lower working departments, the lack of effective solutions and the defects of laws and regulations cause the failure of the vocational education group, and the failure to coordinate the communities of interests. In addition, the operation guarantee mechanism of vocational education group is not perfect, which leads to the failure of each community of interest to meet the corresponding demands, and then reduces the enthusiasm of other interest communities to participate, resulting to the daily management work becoming a formality, and each management positions of vocational education group are empty and lack of practical activities [13]. The internal management level and quality of the vocational education group is also different, which leads to the poor economic benefits generated after the deep cooperation, the horizontal work is too loose, the depth cooperation cannot reach the ideal state, and ultimately the vocational education group cannot play the maximum effectiveness [14].

The reform of China's economic system is crucial for the intervention of vocational education. At least two aspects of the occurrence of vocational education groups have been directly affected by economic changes:

The establishment of the socialist market economic system provides two methodologies for the design of vocational education running models: industrial intensification and resource market allocation. In the era of planned economy, at that time, most enterprises had their own technical schools, industry bureaus had their own technical secondary schools, a few had bureau run technical schools, and there were multiple vocational high schools in prefecture-level cities. In the era of planned economy, vocational schools had no relationship with the market, and school running activities were basically not affected by the market [15]. The whereabouts of graduates were uniformly distributed and managed by the government, and schools did not have to worry about the source of education funds, It is not necessary to consider whether talent cultivation meets social needs. In general, almost all activities of the school are arranged by the government. Although the school has no survival risk in an environment and conditions without awareness of hardship, its development is inevitably greatly limited, lacking vitality, and inefficient. For example, at that time, technical schools were usually very small in scale, with some even recruiting only a few dozen people a year. However, due to the systematic and departmental nature of running schools, regardless of quality and efficiency, all vocational schools lived "calmly" as planned. After the establishment of the socialist market economy system, vocational colleges saw the progressiveness of resource market allocation and industrial intensive development from the restructuring, reorganization and merger of enterprises, and felt the ideological revolution brought by "improving economic efficiency". The cross sectoral and cross regional form of vocational education groups is precisely the social allocation of resources in the economic field, while the form of professional ties in vocational education groups is also modeled after the highly industrialized and intensive industrial structure of enterprises. It can be said that the transformation of China's economy is an incubator of vocational education groups, and the reform of the economic system has become the initiator of educational system reform.

The deepening of economic system reform has directly stripped enterprises of their social functions. In the era of planned economy, both the state and enterprises provide socialized services, while enterprises also engage in "small and comprehensive" activities, establishing social service institutions such as schools and hospitals. With the improvement of China's market economic system and the establishment of modern enterprise systems, this way of running society by enterprises is considered to run counter to the principles of market economy. In particular, some vocational colleges affiliated to joint-stock enterprises do not receive funding for non operating assets even if they remain in the enterprise. Therefore, a large number of vocational colleges and universities in industries and enterprises have left the system and entered society, waiting for the local government to take over and merge with other schools; Some colleges and universities with complex circumstances and difficult for the government to take over have to be classified under the name of the Industry Bureau, which does not include funding in its own budget. Therefore, schools are almost in a state of self seeking and self-development. Due to the fact that enterprises no longer provide substantive support to vocational schools, the schools are facing a series of difficult problems such as difficulty in assigning graduates (which was then assignment), difficulty in arranging teaching content, and difficulty in formulating student training goals. Under pressure, a group of vocational schools have gathered resources and strength through mergers and restructuring, and established various flexible and effective cooperative relationships with enterprises to unblock students' employment channels, ensuring the survival and development capabilities of vocational schools. This has formed the first wave of vocational education collectivization in running schools that we discussed at the beginning.

The ideological enlightenment and rigid adjustment of the market economy have enabled some vocational colleges that have begun to awaken to become self developing individuals, considering the issue of survival and development. It is at this time that vocational colleges begin to have the idea of breaking the institutional constraints and resource shackles of the original planned economy, and forming an optimal allocation and utilization of resources. This should be the group consciousness that occurs in vocational education groups.

4 Construction Strategy of Vocational Education Group

4.1 Innovate the Management Mechanism and Build a Group Community of Shared Interests

Vocational education group should innovate the management mechanism and further optimize and improve the existing management mechanism. The main solution should start from the following points: First, the decision-making mechanism is mainly formulated by the vocational group committee and other councils and the joint meeting, which is the highest position at the management level of the vocational education group, and is mainly responsible for the decision-making power of major issues within the group. Second, the funding guarantee mechanism for various activities is mainly based on the funds donated by government grants, social personages and industry associations. Third, the adjustment mechanism of the management members of the vocational education group is mainly to adjust the members of the vocational education group who cannot perform their duties, and to solicit the high-quality units with the intention of cooperation. Fourth, the benefit-sharing mechanism is mainly to build and improve the community of interests generated in the process of building vocational education groups, so as to promote the members of the community of interests to share the fruits of development, and then achieve a win-win situation. Fifth, the achievement reward mechanism, which is mainly to strongly support the scientific research projects in the vocational education group that help to improve the economic benefits, and appropriately encourages the scientific research projects that have made achievements. Sixth, the appraisal reward mechanism, it is mainly in the process of vocational colleges construction, in the government, colleges, groups and social enterprises at different levels and different levels to set up the assessment mechanism, and make scientific and reasonable reform plan, at the same time, set the reward corresponding reward mechanism, and then further promote the development of vocational education group construction pace.

4.2 Build the Information Platform of Vocational Education Group

In the context of big data, vocational education groups should build relevant information platforms, because vocational education groups, as a fully developing enterprise, should make greater financial support for building information exchange platforms and encourage relevant members to participate in the construction. First of all, build information exchange platform should design employment information sharing function, design employment information sharing function should actively seek social enterprises and graduating students for effective docking, then vocational education group should set up graduate employment exchange, with vocational education group as the carrier, recruitment and employment information sharing mechanism, social enterprises provide professional counterpart jobs, released through the employment information exchange platform. In this way, graduates and social enterprise talents can exchange and share employment information and enrollment information. In addition, building an employment information sharing platform can not only meet the employment needs of social enterprises, but also meet the needs of students to choose their favorite enterprises, students and social enterprises for two-way choice, and then achieve the win-win goal of schools, students and social enterprises.

At the same time, the vocational education group should be aimed at information exchange platform construction, should start from the grassroots construction, and then effectively solve the relevant personnel needs began to start, vocational education group in the process of construction, should be actively looking for interest community and people interested in construction involved, in turn, to realize talent docking, internship training docking, technical service docking and technical training resource sharing. In addition, the vocational education group will be the successful construction of the information exchange platform, but also to arrange special maintenance personnel, help to continuously improve the information exchange platform, avoid failure problems, and make full use of big data information technology, constantly expand the information exchange channels, and then fully realize the information exchange and sharing mode.

4.3 Build an Apprenticeship Education System

Vocational education groups should build an apprenticeship education system, which is an effective way to promote China's modern education strategy. The apprenticeship education system has a positive impact on cultivating students familiar with the job process, professional technical ability and innovative technical ability. Along with the opinion of apprenticeship pilot work issued by the education department, vocational education groups should follow the educational idea of "recruitment is recruitment, entry into school, school and enterprise joint training", realize the new mode of double subject and work practice, and then cultivate high-quality talent team for the society. Take China Modern Animal Husbandry Vocational Education Group as an example. At the present stage, the vocational education group mainly includes vocational colleges, social enterprises and industries, including 114 units, among which 23 are apprenticeship pilot units. China modern animal husbandry vocational education group as a consortium of vocational colleges, its member unit details are mainly shown in Table 2, and each member unit can effectively assist vocational education group to achieve economic benefits and common development, promote better apprenticeship education work, vocational education group to create greater value, Table 2 for China's modern animal husbandry vocational education group member distribution.

Table 2. Distribution of members of China Modern Animal Husbandry Vocational Education Group

area	Secondary vocational colleges	higher vocational school	university	enterprise	trade
Eastern China	1	14	1	42	
South China	1	5		1	
central China		4		2	
North China	2	3		9	2
Northwest Terr	1	6		5	
southwest	2	3		3	
Northeast China		5		2	
subtotal	7	40	1	64	2

4.4 Attach Importance to Cultural Adhesion

As an important carrier, the vocational education group should give full play to its own influence, deepen the high-quality culture within the group, take the high-quality cultural factors as its influence, and then improve the quality level of talent training. It can mainly show the excellent cultural achievements within the group, carry out high-quality cultural experience activities and advanced work deeds, maximize the high-quality cultural achievements, strengthen the influence of the vocational education group through the excellent cultural experience activities, and attach importance to the cultural cohesion effect. The relevant members are encouraged to use the professional website and media resource platform within the group to vigorously publicize the high-quality cultural achievements, enhance the communication and interaction among the members of the vocational education group, promote the vocational education group and vocational colleges to form a unified value concept, and play a cohesive role in the high-quality culture. Members through high quality cultural exchange, can further understanding of professional group cultural factors, at the same time, also can carry out cultural competition or advanced deeds learning activities, and then play a role of cultural adhesion, promote the development of vocational education group concept can be recognized within the group, and then form an effective leading role.

4.5 Establish a Cooperation Framework of "Government, Banking, Enterprises and Universities"

To build a perfect cooperation framework of "government, bank, enterprise and school", mainly with schools, the government and industrial enterprises as the main line to carry out cooperation. First of all, to the school as the main line should establish technical personnel training service framework, and in accordance with the requirements of the national technical personnel training standards, build scientific and reasonable vocational education personnel training service framework, develop perfect strategic goals, and then build the related professional service measures, to realize vocational education resource sharing as the core, to technical talents one-stop training for the school main line, and then to provide one-stop education for vocational group enterprise technical support.

Secondly, the government establishes the guiding framework of combining government and industry teaching, and constructs a perfect government guidance framework according to the requirements of China's education department. Take the general Office of the Government, the Provincial Education Department and the human resources security department as the basis of building the government guidance framework to promote the further development of the vocational education group.

Finally, the industry as the main line to build social enterprise industry for worker education development service guidance framework, and according to the requirements of science and technology innovation and development, in order to improve our science and technology innovation ability, cultivate high technology ability of professional team, to social enterprise industry development requirements for the framework, to meet the demand of social enterprise industry of choose and employ persons, build perfect social enterprise industry service for the worker education development guidance framework.

Conclusion: to sum up, under the background of big data, our country vocational education group development has a positive influence, at the present stage, vocational education group should constantly improve its management mechanism, and build information communication platform, help social enterprises and graduates information sharing, build the apprenticeship education system, build "bank enterprises" cooperation framework, etc., and then improve the quality level of vocational education group construction, promote the sustainable development of vocational education group.

5 Conclusion

The vocational colleges within the group actively meet the development needs of local industries, and carry out in-depth school-enterprise cooperation in accordance with the requirements of "professional and industrial, curriculum matching positions, teaching and production matching". By establishing professional training bases, "double quali-fied" teacher training bases, and industry-university-research cooperation experimental bases in enterprises; Through activities such as order training, modern apprenticeship training, and student internship and practical training, we will fully leverage the func-tions and irreplaceable role of enterprises in vocational education, implement school-enterprise cooperation in educating people, and jointly improve the quality of skilled talent cultivation. In addition, we have innovated the school-running mode of colleges and universities, and carried out a pilot school-running mode of "building vocational colleges in parks and specialties in the industrial chain" in accordance with the path of integrated development of "colleges and parks", giving full play to the advantages of close vocational education groups in integrating resources, promoting school-enterprise cooperation, deepening the integration of industry and education, and jointly building and sharing.

References

1. Zhang, Y., Yao, W.: Research on the construction of mental health education system for higher vocational students based on computer software analysis. Springer, Cham (2021).https://doi.org/10.1007/978-3-030-87903-7_78
2. Yin, J., Wang, J., Jiang, J., et al.: Research on the construction and application of breast cancer-specific database system based on full data lifecycle. Front. Public Health **9**, 712827 (2021)
3. Jin, H.: Research on the path of mathematics discipline construction based on demand ori-entation: a case study of Tianjin agricultural university. Asian Agric. Res. **12**(5), 63–64 (2021)
4. Tian, G., Han, P.: Research on the application of offshore smart oilfield construction based on computer big data and internet of things technology. J. Phys. Conf. Ser. **1992**(3), 032002 (2021). IOP Publishing
5. Tang, Z., Liu, P.H., Peng, S.Y., et al.: Research on the construction of theory and practice integration professional classroom based on information technology. In: Proceedings of the 6th International Conference on Information and Education Innovations, pp. 1–5. (2021)
6. Li, B.: The construction path of innovation and entrepreneurship education in secondary vocational schools from the perspective of maker era. Int. J. New Dev. Educ. **3,** 50–54 (2021)
7. Zhang, P.: On the construction of higher vocational teachers' ethnics in education poverty alleviation. J. Higher Educ. Res. **2**(2) (2021)
8. Qin, G.U.A.N., Xinfu, Y.A.O., Qingping, L.I., Jinhai, L.I., Yao, H.U., Zhang, B.: Construction of the forecast system of classified severe convection weather in qinghai province based on ingredients-based method. Meteorol. Environ. Res. **13**(5), 47–55 (2022)
9. Zhang, X., Shen, J., Wu, P., et al.: Research on the application of big data mining in the construction of smart campus. Open Access Libr. J. **8**(11), 1–10 (2021)
10. Zuo, Z., Billings, T., Walker, M., Petkov, P.M., Fordyce, P.M., Stormo, G.D.: On the dependent recognition of some long zinc finger proteins. Nucleic Acids Res. **51**(11), 5364–5376 (2023)

11. Xiao, C., Zhang, H., Chang, Y., et al.: In situ construction of black titanium oxide with a multilevel structure on a titanium alloy for photothermal antibacterial therapy. ACS Biomater. Sci. Eng.Biomater. Sci. Eng. **8**(6), 2419–2427 (2022)

12. Kons, R.L., et al: Relationships of field-normalized and non-normalized scientometrics with the physical education web-qualis grades. Rev. Bras. Cineantropometria Desempenho Humano **25**, e89743 (2023)

13. Pröbster, M., Marsden, N.: The social perception of autonomous delivery vehicles based on the stereotype content model. Sustainability **15**(6), 5194 (2023)

14. Raventós, B., Pistillo, A., Reyes, C., Fernández-Bertolín, S., et al.: Impact of the COVID-19 pandemic on diagnoses of common mental health disorders in adults in Catalonia, Spain: a population-based cohort study. BMJ Open **12**(4), e057866 (2022)

15. Liu, F.: Research on the Paths of School-enterprise Culture Integration in Higher Vocational Colleges from the Perspective of Integration of Industry and Education (4), 4 (2022)

Author Index

Y. Zhang and N. Shah (Eds.): BigIoT-EDU 2023, LNICST 581, pp. 419–420, 2024.
https://doi.org/10.1007/978-3-031-63133-7

Printed in the United States
by Baker & Taylor Publisher Services